Critical Theory, Marxism and Modernity

Parallax 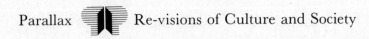 Re-visions of Culture and Society

STEPHEN G. NICHOLS, GERALD PRINCE, AND WENDY STEINER
SERIES EDITORS

Critical Theory, Marxism, and Modernity

DOUGLAS KELLNER

The Johns Hopkins University Press

Baltimore

For five terrific friends: Bob Antonio,
Steve Best, Steve Bronner, Judy Burton
and Gloria Gannaway

Copyright © Douglas Kellner 1989

First published 1989 by
The Johns Hopkins University Press
701 West 40th Street
Baltimore, Maryland 21211

Library of Congress Cataloging-in-Publication Data
Kellner, Douglas, 1943–
Critical theory, Marxism, and modernity / Douglas Kellner.
p.   cm.—(Parallax : re-visions of culture and society)
Bibliography: p.
Includes index.
ISBN 0-8018-3913-3.—ISBN 0-8018-3914-9 (pbk.)
1. Critical theory.   I. Title.   II. Series: Parallax (Baltimore, Md.)
HM24.K445   1989   89–32113
301′.01–dc20   CIP

Printed in Great Britain

Contents

Preface and Acknowledgments

During the 1960s, many among my generation of New Left radicals in the United States and Europe turned for theoretical and political guidance to the works of Max Horkheimer, Herbert Marcuse, T. W. Adorno, Erich Fromm, Leo Lowenthal, Frederick Pollock, Jürgen Habermas and their colleagues. Their neo-Marxist 'Critical Theory' helped illuminate those oppressive social conditions and problems which we were experiencing, and provided compelling reasons for our rejection of capitalist society and our demands for radical social change. Consequently, Critical Theory helped radicalize a generation of intellectuals and activists.

During the 1970s, the major works of the so-called Frankfurt School were translated, and Critical Theory has become part of the theoretical and political debates of the past two decades. In this book, I shall attempt to document the relevance of Critical Theory to some of the central issues of radical social theory and politics from the 1930s to the present, and will indicate why I believe that a reconstructed Critical Theory can continue to be significant in the future.

I began writing this book in the early 1980s, during a period of conservative reaction in the United States and elsewhere. Intense study of Critical Theory helped preserve a stance of radical opposition during this era, and provided weapons for a critique of the conservative hegemony. As we move into the 1990s and toward a new century, Critical Theory might help to produce theoretical and political perspectives which could be part of a Left Turn that could reanimate the political hopes of the 1960s, while helping to overcome and reverse the losses and regression of the 1980s. Such a hope motivated this undertaking.

Over the years, my knowledge of Critical Theory has benefited from conversations with and the writings of Herbert Marcuse, Jürgen Habermas, Leo Lowenthal, Albrecht Wellmer, Martin Jay, Stanley Aronowitz, Fredric Jameson, Thomas McCarthy, Helmut Dubiel, Alfons Sollner, Wolfgang

Bonss, Axel Honneth, Hauke Brunkhorst, Michael Ryan, Osvaldo Guariglia and many other individuals from all over the world whom I have met or with whom I have corresponded.

Many people have read and commented on chapters of this book over the years. They include Kevin Anderson, Mark Ritter, Rick Roderick, Clay Steinman and Anthony Giddens, who made some extremely useful proposals which have been incorporated in the final version. But I would like to dedicate the book to five terrific friends who read and commented on every chapter, and discussed every aspect of the book with me: Bob Antonio, Steve Best, Steve Bronner, Judy Burton, and Gloria Gannaway. It has certainly benefited from their criticisms and our discussions, and I am extremely grateful to them for friendship and support during a difficult political epoch.

Bibliographical Abbreviations

A   Frederick Pollock, *The Economic and Social Consequences of Automation* (Oxford: Basil Blackwell, 1957)

AP   T. W. Adorno et al., *The Authoritarian Personality* (New York: Norton, 1950)

B   Franz Neumann, *Behemoth* (New York: Oxford University Press, 1944)

CoP   Erich Fromm, *The Crisis of Psychoanalysis* (New York: Fawcett, 1970)

CT   Max Horkheimer, *Critical Theory* (New York: Seabury, 1972)

D&D   Max Horkheimer, *Dawn and Decline. Notes 1926–1931 and 1950–1969* (New York: Seabury, 1978)

DoE   Max Horkheimer and T. W. Adorno, *Dialectic of Enlightenment* (New York: Herder and Herder, 1972)

EoR   Max Horkheimer, *Eclipse of Reason* (New York: Oxford University Press, 1947; republished Seabury, 1974)

FS   Rolf Wiggershaus, *Die Frankfurter Schule* (Munich: Hanser, 1986)

FSR   Andrew Arato and Eike Gebhardt, eds, *The Frankfurt School Reader* (New York: Continuum, 1982)

LC   Jürgen Habermas, *Legitimation Crisis* (Boston: Beacon Press, 1975)

LPCS   Leo Lowenthal, *Literature, Popular Culture, and Society* (Englewood Cliffs, N.J.: Prentice-Hall, 1961)

MM   T. W. Adorno, *Minima Moralia* (London: New Left Books, 1974)

N   Herbert Marcuse, *Negations* (Boston: Beacon Press, 1968)

ODM   Herbert Marcuse, *One-Dimensional Man* (Boston: Beacon Press, 1964)

P   T. W. Adorno, *Prisms* (London: Neville Spearman, 1967)

SS   Erich Fromm, *The Sane Society* (New York: Holt Rinehart Winston, 1955)

Refugees are the keenest dialecticians. They are refugees as a result of changes, and their sole object of study is change. They are able to deduce the greatest events from the smallest sampling – that is, if they have intelligence.

Bertolt Brecht

Something of the freedom and spontaneity of the future appears in the organization and community of those in struggle, despite all the discipline grounded in the need for success.

Max Horkheimer

Pessimism all along the line. Absolutely. Mistrust in the fate of literature, mistrust in the fate of freedom, mistrust in the fate of European humanity, but three times mistrust in all reconciliation: between classes, between nations, between individuals. And unlimited trust only in I. G. Farben and the peaceful perfection of the air force.

Walter Benjamin

. . . while the notion of society may not be deduced from any individual facts, nor on the other hand be apprehended as an individual fact itself, there is nonetheless no social fact which is not determined by society as a whole. Society appears as a whole behind each concrete social situation.

T. W. Adorno

. . . thought in contradiction must become more negative and more utopian in opposition to the status quo.

Herbert Marcuse

1

Theory, Politics and History

Critical Theory was a product of the Institute for Social Research, which was the first Marxist-oriented research institute in Germany. The group is sometimes referred to as the 'Frankfurt School', but this term is misleading, because much of the group's most important work was done in exile in the United States.[1] Further, the members of the Institute rarely shared a readily identifiable collective position, and the differences between them often overshadowed the similarities. Yet the project of developing a Critical Theory of society is one of the most enduring contributions of the Institute for Social Research, and it is this project which will be the central focus of this book.

Critical Theory is informed by multidisciplinary research, combined with the attempt to construct a systematic, comprehensive social theory that can confront the key social and political problems of the day. The work of the Critical Theorists provides criticisms and alternatives to traditional, or mainstream, social theory, philosophy and science, together with a critique of a full range of ideologies from mass culture to religion. At least some versions of Critical Theory are motivated by an interest in relating theory to politics and an interest in the emancipation of those who are oppressed and dominated. Critical Theory is thus informed by a critique of domination and a theory of liberation.

In this book I shall indicate how Critical Theory responded to a series of socio-historical transformations generated by key developments associated with the dynamics of capitalism and what has become known as 'modernity' – those projects of rationalization, secularization and modernization generated, above all, by industrial capitalism and its fateful history.[2] My thesis is that Critical Theory began as a primarily Marxian critique of capitalist modernity, and then progressively moved away from orthodox Marxian positions in response to the vicissitudes of twentieth-century history. From this perspective, I interpret Critical Theory as a series of responses to succeeding crises of·capitalism and Marxism and throughout this book I will reflect on the continued relevance or obsolescence of Marxism and Critical Theory as the trajectory of modernity encounters new socio-historical conditions and the postmodern critique. This study will therefore engage the current debate as to whether modernity has reached its end-point and whether it has been replaced by an epoch of 'postmodernity'.

I shall accordingly provide both a historical introduction to the Critical Theory of the Institute for Social Research and contributions to it in confronting contemporary problems and concerns. I believe that this procedure is fully consistent with the spirit and intentions of Critical Theory, which endeavored to provide a socially and politically relevant theory of history and the contemporary epoch. At its best, Critical Theory has been updated and revised periodically in the light of new social conditions, problems, research and intellectual insights. If Critical Theory is to remain on the cutting edge of social theory, then it must be subject to the sort of critique which it applies to traditional theories and must move beyond previous inadequate or obsolete positions. Similarly, it must promote the development of new theories to account for the newly emerging social conditions and changes within contemporary neo-capitalist and state socialist societies. This means that some of the 'classical' positions held by earlier generations of Critical Theorists must be modified or surrendered in the light of socio-historical transformations and theoretical developments which have called into question some of its past positions.

Consequently, in this study I examine, probe and develop Critical Theory in relation to what I consider to be the central theoretical and political problems for social theory and radical politics from the 1930s to the present. In so doing, I attempt to indicate the important contributions and frequent limitations of the now 'classical' positions developed by its major theorists. This is not just another book on Critical Theory therefore; it is also an attempt to *do* Critical Theory. Critical Theory is not presented here as a museum of artifacts, texts and arguments from a bygone age to be solely contemplated with delight or nostalgia. In contrast to authors of most previous books on Critical Theory, I shall present the tradition as providing methods and a set of positions that are of relevance and importance for contemporary social theory and politics. My aims are therefore both pedagogical and political: I shall indicate what I consider to be its major contributions, and shall intervene in some of the central debates concerning the status, key issues and politics of Critical Theory today. Consequently, I intend my studies to be of use to both specialists and more advanced students of Critical Theory, as well as to those who are seeking a first introduction.

1.1 Critical Theory and Modernity

Critical Theory has become a major force in the debates about the nature, trajectory and impact of what has become known as modernity. Following the leads of Marx, Nietzsche and Max Weber, Critical Theory has been deeply concerned with the fate of modernity, and has offered systematic and comprehensive theories of the trajectory of modernity, combined with critical diagnoses of some of the latter's limitations, pathologies and destructive effects – while providing defenses of some of its progressive elements. From the time of Hegel to the present, modernity has been conceived most broadly as the 'new age' which emerged from feudalism and the Renaissance.[3] The discovery of the Americas, the Renaissance and the Reformation, and the beginning of capitalism are often taken as marking the origins of modernity. It was thus characterized as a new era of history, interpreted as a process of increasing secularization and innovation which posed the 'new age', 'modern times', against tradition and a static past. Modernity was thus associated with innovation, change, novelty and critical opposition to tradition and dogmatism.

Marx and Engels in *The Communist Manifesto* interpret the rise of industrial capitalism and the bourgeoisie as a revolutionary force that dramatically swept away the remnants of the old feudal society: 'The bourgeoisie cannot exist without constantly revolutionizing the instruments of production, and thereby the relations of production, and with them the whole relations of society.'[4] They described the dramatic revolutionizing of production, transportation, communication and all of social life by the bourgeoisie and concluded: 'All fixed, fast-frozen relations, with their train of ancient and venerable prejudices and opinions, are swept away, all newly-formed ones become antiquated before they can ossify. All that is solid melts into the air, all that is holy is profaned, and man is at last compelled to face with sober senses, his real conditions of life, and his relations with his kind' (ibid.).

This process, however, is both 'progressive' – creating new needs, connections, possibilities and so forth – and destructive – creating commercial crises, the alienation of the working class, impoverishment and proletarianization of the 'lower strata of the middle class' and the peasantry leading to class war (pp. 478ff.). The first generation of Critical Theorists followed Marx in seeing modernity as the result of capitalist industrialization, and followed classical Marxism in seeing political economy and economic development as the foundation, or base, of the historical trajectory of modernity. Yet, from the beginning they also appropriated Max Weber's analysis of modernity as a process of secularization and rationalization giving rise to new modes of thought such as rationalism, liberalism and positivism and new institutions such as bureaucracy and the bureaucratic state. More recently, Habermas has taken up Weber's interpretation of modernity as a process of differentiation of functional systems such as the economy and the state and the differentiation of cultural spheres such as religion, philosophy and art (which were more unified in pre-modern times). Thus, we shall see that eventually Critical Theory provides its own original and specific theory and critique of modernity.

In recent years there has been intense focus on various dimensions of modernity, including debates over modernization produced by the dynamics of industry, science and technology; modernism as a set of cultural tendencies hostile to industrial modernization (or complicit with it, as more recent interpretations have argued); and the current debate concerning whether modernity has come to an end, and whether this should be viewed as a positive, negative or ambivalent development.[5] Critical Theory has been in an especially favorable position to address these issues, for it was conceived in the 1930s as a historical theory of the modern age which provides critical accounts of the trajectory of capitalist modernity and the transitions to a new stage of capitalist development (see Chapters 2 and 3). Then, in the 1940s, it attempted to characterize modernity in terms of a 'dialectic of enlightenment' which would explain in new ways the origins of what Adorno and Horkheimer saw as the crisis of Western civilization, or modernity, in the era of World War II and the death camps (see Chapter 4).

From the beginning, Critical Theory has been a dialectical theory which – at its best – attempted to sort out the matrix of progressive and regressive, oppressive and emancipatory, forces bound up with the history of modernity. Thus, while some theories of modernization present modernity as a purely positive force bound up with progress in science, industry and technology, others see it as a wholly negative force bound up with dehumanization, destruction of the environment, technology out of control and totalitarian political development. Although Critical Theorists have maintained sharply critical perspectives toward modernity, they have – following Marx – also attempted to appraise its positive contributions – though on the issue of the dialectics of modernity, we shall eventually see important differences emerge between the critiques of Adorno, Horkheimer and (sometimes) Marcuse and its qualified defense by Habermas.

Critical Theory also provides a useful perspective on modernity because it is a comprehensive, totalizing, social theory which includes analyses of the interrelationships among economic, political, social and cultural spheres. Thus, while some discussions of modernization remain in rather narrow economic or political spheres, and some discussions of cultural modernism are hermetically sealed in literary or cultural debates, Critical Theory addresses the full range of issues raised by the impact of modernity on the spheres of economic, political, social and cultural life. Consequently it provides one of the most comprehensive vantage points from which to address a broad spectrum of issues involved in the current debates over the fate of modernity.

Finally, Critical Theory provides excellent access to modernity because it has incorporated the positions of some of the major theorists and critics of modernity in its work. From the beginning, Critical Theory has been closely connected with Marxism; and in the 1930s it began engaging the positions of Nietzsche, Freud, Weber, Heidegger, Lukács and others who have carried out both rationalist and irrationalist critiques of modernity. Eventually, Critical Theorists incorporated many positions from these thinkers, and thus were able to provide much more complex, multidimensional and stimulating perspectives on modernity than those who took a more one-sided approach.

In the following chapters I shall point to the ways in which Critical Theory during the 1930s followed Marx in seeing modernity primarily as a product of industrial capitalism, and interpret the trajectory of modernity in terms of theories of the vicissitudes of capitalist development. Yet some of the major contributions of Critical Theory involve a systematic, sustained attempt to revise, update and develop the Marxian critique of political economy into a critical social theory that greatly expands the scope, comprehensiveness and in some cases the depth of the Marxian critique of capitalism (though we shall also see some of the ways in which classical Marxism is superior to Critical Theory). In this book, I shall argue that Critical Theory articulates the transition from the stage of market, entrepreneurial capitalism (best described by Karl Marx) to the stage of organized, or state, capitalism. I shall argue that Critical Theory provides one of the most comprehensive accounts of the rise of the new stage of capitalism characterized by new concentrations of wealth and power (described by Rudolf Hilferding as 'finance capital', or 'organized capitalism'), and by new relationships between the economy and state (defined as 'state capitalism' by both some Critical Theorists and other Marxists).[6] This new economic-political configuration of capitalism also produced new forms of imperialism, consumer and mass culture, science and technology, and experience and everyday life, the nature and impact of which have been major topics of Critical Theory from the 1930s to the present.

Accordingly, the Critical Theorists' analyses of the new relationships between the economy and the state in the totalitarian and democratic forms of state capitalism required updating and developing the Marxian theory. Their analyses included new theories of consumerism and the development of the consumer society, of the culture industries, of the incorporation of science and technology into relations of production and new forms of social control, of changing patterns of socialization, personality development and values, and of the decline of the individual. I shall claim that these theories provide some of the best theoretical and critical analyses of the socio-economic and cultural conditions which prevailed during the period in which the theory was produced.

Yet I shall also argue that changes in the social conditions and techno-cultural infrastructure of capitalist societies from the 1960s to the present put in question aspects of Critical Theory's previous accounts of the economy, state, culture, media and everyday life, and therefore that Critical Theory now requires development, revision and updating. In criticizing and reconstructing 'classical' positions, I believe one to be following the actual practice of Critical Theory, for in my view, one of its enduring contributions is its appropriation of the Hegelian-Marxian dialectical heritage which sees socially critical categories and analysis to be fundamentally historical and in need of development and revision as historical conditions change.[7] The very spirit of Critical Theory precludes orthodoxy; thus interpretations must be resisted which transform it into yet another orthodoxy which provides a refuge for true believers against the disappointments of the utopian hopes of the 1960s and the vicissitudes of social development in the 1970s and 1980s.

This book differs from previous studies in focusing primarily on those elements of Critical Theory that are of primary importance for critical social theory and radical politics today. Thus the focus will be neither intellectual history (as in Martin Jay's and Rolf Wiggershaus's books) nor a systematic explication of the ideas of the various Critical Theorists (as in David Held's book and other introductions to Critical Theory).[8] Nor is it my intention to denounce Critical Theory from a supposedly superior point of view – as Phil Slater, Zoltan Tar and most Marxist-Leninist critics frequently do from Marxian positions or as George Friedman and a variety of German critics do from conservative or neo-conservative standpoints. Further, I will not focus primarily on the normative foundation of Critical Theory or its philosophical components, as some recent commentators have done.[9] Instead, I will set out the fundamental ideas and arguments on topics of central importance to radical social theory today, trace the impact of Critical Theory on contemporary social theory and politics and offer criticisms of the classic version of Critical Theory, as well as some new perspectives and topics.

In opposition to those interpretations which present Critical Theory as a form of idealist social theory inimical to Marxism, I shall attempt to depict both its kinship with the Marxian theory and the ways in which it differs. I will show that Critical Theory has had an extremely complex relation to classical Marxism, which is in part responsible for the variety of conflicting tendencies and positions within it today. From an external vantage point, the theoretical and political positions of the Institute for Social Research can be distinguished in terms of four periods of development: (1) the rather orthodox Marxian historical and theoretical studies carried out from 1923 through the late 1920s, when Carl Grunberg was director (Chapter 1); (2) the work produced from the early 1930s through the 1940s, when Max Horkheimer was director and when the Institute, from 1933 on, was in exile from fascist Germany in the United States (Chapters 1-4); (3) the period from the Institute's return to Frankfurt in 1950 until the death of Horkheimer and Adorno (Chapters 4-8); and (4) the 1970s and 1980s work of Jürgen Habermas, his colleagues and students, who form the second and third generations of Critical Theorists – including those of us who attempt to carry on the tradition today in various environments and situations (Chapter 7 and 8).[10]

One can draw various distinctions concerning developments within this periodization, and in this book I shall be concerned to indicate the differences within and between the various phases of Critical Theory.[11] Yet, while there is no unitary Critical Theory, I will suggest that there are features which define it in terms of method, presuppositions and positions. From the beginning to the present, Critical Theory has refused to situate itself within an arbitrary or conventional academic division of labor. It thus traverses and undermines *boundaries* between competing disciplines, and stresses *interconnections* between philosophy, economics and politics, and culture and society. Critical Theory is distinguished from traditional, mainstream social theory through its multidisciplinary perspectives and its attempts to develop a dialectical and materialist social theory. This project requires a collective, supradisciplinary synthesis of philosophy, the sciences and politics, in which critical social theory is produced by groups of theorists and scientists from various disciplines working together to produce a Critical Theory of the present age aimed at radical socio-political transformation.

Note that I said 'supradisciplinary' and not 'interdisciplinary'. The Critical Theory project initially involved groups of individuals from various disciplines working together collectively to develop theories of such topics as the family and authority, the transition from market entrepreneurial capitalism to state capitalism, and fascism, rather than just bringing together individuals from separate disciplines to chat or assigning different specialists different topics for research and inquiry. As Leo Lowenthal put it in a 1986 interview, the term 'interdisciplinary work' simply 'means nothing more than to leave the disciplines as they are while developing certain techniques which foster a kind of acquaintance between them without forcing them to give up their self-sufficiency or individual claims'.[12] The Institute for Social Research, on the contrary, criticized the validity claims of the separate disciplines, and attempted to create a new kind of supradisciplinary social theory.

Throughout this book, I will show how Critical Theory challenges traditional academic boundaries between one sphere of social reality and another. Dividing social life into specialized spheres of inquiry reproduces the division of labor typical of contemporary modern societies, while intensifying tendencies toward increased professionalization, specialization and fragmentation. It also mystifies social reality, excludes significant factors from discussion and abstracts from social conflicts, problems and complexities, thus occluding fundamental connections within social life while excluding significant factors from analysis.

The Critical Theorists, however, attacked the *abstraction* involved in drawing boundaries between various disciplines. Generally speaking, within traditional academic disciplines, someone analyzing politics or culture, say, in a specialized 'professional', disciplinary manner would abstract from economics in dealing with issues within their specialized discipline. For Critical Theory, on the contrary, economics plays a constitutive role in all social processes, so that it would be impossible to discuss politics concretely without discussing economics, just as one cannot adequately discuss economics without considering the role of politics and culture in constituting the economy. Critical Theory is thus, among other things, a critique of the boundaries between disciplines and a theory of the mediations which connect and integrate various modes and dimensions of social reality into a social system or society.

In particular, Critical Theory subverted the established boundary between philosophy and social theory, and strove – not always successfully – to overcome the division between theory and politics. It presented itself both as a social theory of the contemporary epoch which constantly attempted to conceptualize and criticize new social conditions and as a historical theory which, following Hegel and Marx, demarcated the *borderlines* between various stages of history. Thus, while I use the term 'boundaries' as a synchronic concept to describe certain conceptual divisions within a given domain of social reality at a specific point in time, I use the term 'borderlines' as a diachronic concept to trace historical stages of development from one era to the next.[13] Critical Theory is thus both a *social* theory which aims to describe and criticize the current form of social organization and a *historical* theory concerned with socio-historical change and development. As a historical theory, Critical Theory attempts to conceptualize borderlines between previous and present phases of socio-economic development by conceptualizing new socio-historical conditions which require revision of previous radical theory and politics. Or it criticizes widely held claims concerning, for example, the alleged transition from modernity to postmodernity by denying such a socio-historical rupture or break.[14]

Critical Theory is thus intrinsically historical, and maintains that to properly describe and comprehend a given phenomenon, one must contextualize it within its historical world. Accordingly, let us begin by situating what would eventually emerge as Critical Theory in its historical, political and intellectual context, and examine the ways in which the Critical Theorists responded in the 1920s and early 1930s to what has become known as the 'crisis of Marxism'. These historicizing and contextualizing remarks are themselves in the spirit of Critical Theory, which maintained that one must contextualize and historicize problems and ideas to see how society and history enter into theories and debates.

1.2 Critical Theory and the Crisis of Marxism

Critical Theory claims that the socio-historical context is crucial in determining which questions a theory poses, how it formulates and answers them, and what the limitations, grounds and insights of a theory are. What experiences, then, were crucial for those young intellectuals who were later to produce Critical Theory?

It was primarily the experiences of World War I, the Russian revolution of 1917, the German revolution of 1918 and a strong belief in the bankruptcy of bourgeois capitalist society which erupted into war and revolution that led many young intellectuals and activists to embrace Marxism.[15] Marxism had previously served as the official doctrine of the working-class movement, and was not fashionable in bourgeois social and cultural circles. Many young members of the middle and upper classes were driven to pacifism and Marxism by their experiences in World War I, however. Biographical material shows that Horkheimer, Marcuse, Pollock, Fromm, Lowenthal and others were opposed from the beginning to Germany's war policy, and were deeply alienated from bourgeois society by the senseless slaughter and destruction produced by the war. They were all drawn to Marxian ideas, which explained the war in terms of the dynamics of capitalism and imperialism and produced a thoroughgoing critique of capitalist society, as well as an alternative to it.[16]

Many of the young Germans who would later join the Institute for Social Research were also attracted to the Russian revolution, and saw socialism as an appealing, viable alternative to bourgeois capitalist society. Marcuse, Horkheimer, Pollock and others enthusiastically embraced, and in some cases participated in, the abortive German revolution of 1918, and generally sympathized with the more radical attempts to overthrow the existing bourgeois order.[17] Marcuse was a member of a soldiers' council in Berlin entrusted with protecting the Social Democratic government against a Rightist coup; while Horkheimer and Pollock experienced the upheavals in

Munich, where workers, soldiers and students tried unsuccessfully to establish a socialist republic.

The Social Democrats soon suppressed the more Leftist groups, and the young radicals who would later constitute the core of the Institute returned to university life. They were all now keenly interested in the Marxian theory, and combined their academic courses with a study of Marxism. At the time Georg Lukács and Karl Korsch were producing exciting new interpretations of Marxism, which deeply influenced the genesis of Critical Theory.[18] Both Lukács in *History and Class Consciousness* and Korsch in *Marxism and Philosophy* broke with official Communist and Social Democratic interpretations of Marxism as a theory of 'scientific socialism', and stressed its philosophical and Hegelian components. The early 1920s was a time of intellectual ferment and radicalization in Weimar Germany, with intense struggles between the Left, Right and Centre. It was a time of rapid cultural change, breaking down old values and searching for new – promoted by discussion of Freud, Expressionism, Hegel, Marx, Heidegger, phenomenology, and what became known later as existentialism – as in the 1960s in the United States and elsewhere. The young radicals who would later join the Frankfurt Institute for Social Research were deeply influenced by these currents, and were especially drawn to Hegel's dialectical method and its appropriation and development by Marx. They followed Lukács and Korsch in appreciating the Hegelian roots of Marxism, and they utilized the dialectical categories of totality, mediation, the relative autonomy of the superstructures, and reciprocal interaction between base and superstructure as fundamental elements of their theory and method.

Hegelian categories of rupture, historical development and contradiction seemed to be embodied in their experiences of contemporary history, and the use of these categories by revolutionary Marxists such as Luxemburg, Lenin, Korsch, and Lukács helped attract them to the most radical forms of Marxism. Yet by 1923, the German and European revolutions had failed, which Korsch attributed in part to an inadequate grasp within socialist theory and practice of the subjective conditions of revolution. Lukács and Korsch stressed the need both to free individuals from bourgeois capitalist indoctrination and to produce a revolutionary consciousness that would confront an oppressive production process and society. They therefore saw the importance of culture and philosophy for revolutionary theory and politics. In addition, Lukács made important contributions to Marxian social theory, expanding Marx's critique of capitalism to many current social phenomena, while developing the concept of 'reification' – the process through which human beings are turned into things, and thing-like, objectified relationships and ideas come to dominate human life – as an important component of the critique of capitalism.

Korsch stressed the need to apply the historical materialist method consistently to all social and intellectual phenomena, including Marxism itself.[19] In effect, he was calling for a more self-reflexive, critical version of Marxism, a project taken up later by Critical Theory. In addition to the political and economic struggle that had previously been the center of Marxian politics, Korsch stressed the importance of 'intellectual action' and 'ideological critique' as fundamental components of revolutionary struggle.

Lukács and Korsch were reacting against what they saw as the theoretical and political deficiencies within the orthodox Social Democratic Marxism of Plekenhov, Kautsky, Hilferding and others.[20] Orthodox Marxism at the time tended toward a reductionistic 'economism', which interpreted the dynamics of history primarily in terms of economic development in the 'base' that supposedly controlled developments within the 'superstructure'. This version of Marxism was deterministic in two dimensions: the economic base determined the superstructure, and laws of history, rooted in the economy, determined the trajectory of all social life. This 'orthodox Marxism' was also scientistic, claiming the status of a science of social development, and tended to be dogmatic as it congealed into a rigid system of categories, laws and positions.

By contrast, the Marxism of Lukács and Korsch (as well as Gramsci) developed a 'philosophy of praxis' which stressed the importance of subjectivity, culture and action, in opposition to objectivistic Marxism, which put more emphasis on economic laws and objective social conditions.[21] The philosophy of praxis was more action-oriented, insisting on the importance of the unity of theory and practice, and tended to stress the importance of workers' self-management and activity, as well as the institution of workers' councils over the party and the state bureaucracy as the agencies of the construction of socialism.

Horkheimer and his colleagues shared Korsch's and Lukács's dissatisfaction with orthodox Marxism and their commitment to a critical social theory that pointed to the importance of Hegel's dialectical method. Hegelian Marxists analysed capitalist society as a totality, as a system, and emphasized the relative autonomy of the superstructures and the importance of cultural and subjective factors in historical development. Their more philosophical, more sophisticated view of history ruled out a scientistic, determinist model thereof, and stressed instead complex, contradictory sets of social relations and struggles in a specific historical era, whose trajectory could not be determined with certainty in advance.

The individuals who would produce Critical Theory thus conceived of Marxism as an open-ended, historical, dialectical theory that required development, revision and modification, precisely because it was, they believed, a theory of contemporary socio-historical reality which itself was constantly developing and changing. The notions of historical specificity and dialectics are therefore the interpretive keys to the type of Marxism professed at the Institute – at least within the 'inner circle' of Horkheimer, Marcuse, Adorno, Pollock, Fromm and Lowenthal. During the 1920s and 1930s, most of the Institute members believed that Marxism provided a critical theory of a historically specific epoch which was superior to competing theories for both investigating and transforming social reality. Later we shall see that many members of the Institute questioned key aspects of the Marxian theory, and even abandoned Marxism in some cases, though others, like Marcuse, continued to identify with the Marxian tradition even while going beyond many of its classical positions.

The failures of the European revolutions in the early 1920s, accompanied by the emergence of fascism, produced a 'crisis of Marxism'.[22] Although a Marxist-inspired revolution took place in the Soviet Union in 1917, successful revolutions failed to materialize in the West – except for convulsions in Germany, Italy, Hungary and Central Europe which were suppressed by the early 1920s. Korsch, Lukács, Gramsci, Marcuse and most members of the Institute concluded that, although the objective conditions for revolution were present, the subjective conditions were lacking. Consequently, although European civilization had been going through protracted crises of war, economic depression, political conflict and so on – which confirmed Marxian views concerning the recurrent crises of capitalism – the prospects for revolution in Europe and the advanced capitalist countries did not seem bright, because revolutionary consciousness, culture and organization and a clear notion of socialism seemed to be lacking. Thus those individuals who became known as 'Western Marxists' saw the need to concern themselves with consciousness, subjectivity, culture, ideology and the concept of socialism precisely in order to make possible radical political change.

In this context it is significant that the Institute for Social Research was founded in 1923, the year marking the end of the period of revolutionary upheaval that began with the Russian revolution and the end of World War I, while also marking the beginning of the stabilization of capitalism and bourgeois rule. Consequently, while it was still possible to envisage a German or European revolution in the early 1920s, it became increasingly difficult as the decade progressed. At this time too, the Left became more and more fragmented and uncertain concerning revolutionary theory and politics. This crisis of the Left is evident in the fragmentation of political perspectives and an uncertain relation to revolutionary politics within the Institute itself.

1.3 The Institute for Social Research

In the aftermath of the German revolution of 1918, political ferment eventually erupted within the traditionally conservative German universities, and, for the first time, Marxism began to be taught and discussed in a university setting. Many Leftist intellectuals, disappointed by the collapse of the German revolutionary movement but hoping that a socialist revolution was still possible in Germany, returned to university life. At this time, Felix Weil, a committed sympathizer of the German revolution, undertook to establish the first Marxist-oriented research institute in Germany. Weil was the son of a wealthy grain merchant, and had studied with Karl Korsch, for whom he wrote a dissertation on the various plans for socializing the economy and the contemporary debates over socialism. Soon after, Weil's father agreed to contribute a substantial endowment to establish an institute for social research, and the liberal and Social Democrat education minister and administrators of Frankfurt University were receptive to the idea.[23]

An affiliation with Frankfurt University was officially realized in 1923, and Weil financed the construction of a building to house the Institute, its library and archives. After the premature death of its first director, Karl Albert Gerlach, the Austrian Carl Grunberg, who had edited a yearbook for the history of the workers' movement, took over the directorship. Grunberg was an authority on historical materialism and the first self-proclaimed Marxist to hold a chair in a German university. In his 1924 inaugural address, he disclosed his commitment, arguing that Marxism is at once a self-contained economic theory, a *Weltanschauung* and a method of research. Grunberg claimed that the materialist conception of history does not attempt to develop eternal categories or formulate universal laws of nature and history.[24] Rather, its object is 'the given concrete historical world in its change and development', or, more precisely, social life in its transformations. Historical materialism is thus conceptualized as a theory which can comprehend a changing, developing society.

For Grunberg, the aim of Marxist research was to discover the causes and laws of social change. Grunberg believed that social life in all its manifestations is a reflex of the existing economic system, and that the key to social theory can be found in the laws governing the economic system. Grunberg's methodology was more inductive than dialectical, and his view of history as an 'organic evolutionism' 'from the less perfect to the more perfect' would be rudely confronted with fascism and World War II. Likewise, his view that the present age was a 'period of transition' from capitalism to socialism would be put in question by the defeat of the revolutionary movements in Germany by the Right. Hence, it would be a

mistake to overemphasize his influence on his more philosophically sophisticated and politically skeptical successors who were to develop Critical
Theory.

Nonetheless, at least until the 1940s, the Institute was to follow his
Marxist program by placing the critique of political economy at the center
of a multidisciplinary program of research. Under Grunberg the Institute
specialized in empirical and historical research from the point of view of
historical materialism. It maintained close relations with the Marx-Lenin
Institute in Moscow, with which it worked to produce a critical edition of
the works of Marx and Engels. During the 1920s, the Institute adhered to a
rather orthodox Marxism on the whole. Many in the Institute were members
or sympathizers of the German Communist Party (KPD), although others
belonged to the Social Democratic Party (SPD) or remained unaffiliated.[25]
Furthermore, the Institute's most prominent economists, Henryk Grossmann and Friedrich Pollock, taught and utilized Marxian economics
(though Grossmann was considerably more orthodox than Pollock).

In Wiggershaus's view, the Institute had created a situation unparalleled
in European university life:

Marxism and the history of the workers' movement could now be taught and
studied at a university, and whoever wanted to could earn a doctorate in this field.
There was now established in Frankfurt a full professor in political economy who
advocated Marxism. There now existed in the University an affiliated Institute
whose speciality was research into the working class movement and socialism from a
Marxist standpoint, and in which Marxists like Karl Korsch or the Austro-Marxists
Max Adler, Fritz Adler, or Otto Bauer could hold lectures. . . . Editing of the works
of Marx and Engels was recognized as a task for scholarly work within the accepted
research tasks of the University.[26]

Grunberg had a serious heart attack and was forced to step down from
the directorship in 1929, however; and Max Horkheimer was named
director in 1930. Under Horkheimer's direction the Institute carried
through a unique synthesis of philosophy and social theory. Horkheimer
remained its guiding spirit during the troubled period in which fascism
forced the emigration of the Institute's members to other European countries and later to the United States. Horkheimer was the son of a bourgeois,
Jewish factory-owner who rebelled against his father's wishes that he take
over and run the family business.[27] Managing to avoid the fate of Engels,
who spent many years of his life running his father's factory in England,
Horkheimer studied philosophy and social theory at the best German
universities to prepare for a university career. A series of aphorisms written
between 1926 and 1931 and published in 1934 as *Dammerung* provides
insight into his thought and politics during that period.[28] The text is an
important document which shows why radical youth of the period broke

with family and class values and sought alternative positions in the socialist movement. In some ways the book provides an excellent introduction to Critical Theory; moreover, it contains many anticipations or articulations of later, key, defining positions.

The title *Dammerung* signifies both dawn and twilight, and its aphorisms suggest the twilight of a disappearing historical epoch dominated by capitalism and the bourgeoisie and the dawn of a new (socialist) era. The tone of the book is one of restrained revolutionary optimism, with Horkheimer proclaiming: 'The twilight (*Dammerung*) of capitalism does not need to lead to the night of humanity that today appears to threaten us' (*D&D*, p. 17). Stylistically it reads like a Marxist Nietzsche, and its positions are informed by a type of radical humanism reminiscent of the early Marx. *Dammerung* is distinguished by its thoroughgoing critique of capitalism and bourgeois ideology, traits that would distinguish Critical Theory throughout its trajectory. In Horkheimer's words, the text 'critically examines and re-examines the concepts of metaphysics, character, morality, personality and the value of the human being as they appeared in this period of capitalism' (*D&D*, p. 13).

Horkheimer's attacks on bourgeois society, capitalism and imperialism are relentless, and his commitment to socialism is unequivocal:

The capitalist system in the current phase is a world-wide system of organized exploitation. Its maintenance is the condition of immeasurable suffering. This society possesses in reality the human and technical means to abolish poverty in its crudest material forms. We know of no epoch in which this possibility would have existed to the extent that it does today. Only the property system stands in the way of its realization, that is, the condition that the gigantic apparatus of human production must function in the service of a small group of exploiters. (*D&D*, p. 46)

This passage is symptomatic of Horkheimer's early position, which was animated by a desire to alleviate human suffering by discovering its causes and suitable remedies.[29] At the time Horkheimer was convinced that the capitalist mode of production and the class society were the fundamental sources of human suffering, and that their elimination was a necessary condition for social progress. His early letters and *Dammerung* both express outrage over the misery of the working class and the poor, and blame it on the capitalist system and the class domination of the bourgeoisie. *Dammerung* is full of passages which depict the great differences between social classes and which point to the benefits for humanity that socialism would make possible (see, for example, *D&D*, pp. 62, 89, 98 and 100). Nevertheless, Horkheimer recognized that:

the assessment of any contemporary historical event can always stress aspects other than its nexus with class rule. But what counts today is precisely an insight into this nexus. The suspicion cannot be rejected out of hand that the antipathy to onesided-ness, crudeness, platitudes, banality, and ultimately to all explanation, derivation, investigation of causes and systematic theory is based on the fear that the social cause of our present regression might enter public consciousness. (*D&D*, p. 48)

Although Horkheimer was never an uncritical defender of the Russian revolution and Soviet communism, during this phase at least he was a sympathetic supporter of the Bolshevik revolution: 'Whoever has eyes for the senseless injustice of the imperialist world, will consider the events in Russia as the continuing, painful attempt to overcome this terrible social injustice, or will at least ask with a beating heart whether this attempt is still going on' (*D&D*, p. 72). Yet he was skeptical as to whether current forms of the working-class movement could produce a revolutionary upheaval in Germany. In a key analysis of 'The Impotence of the German Working Class', Horkheimer analyzed the fragmentations and divisions within the working class and between their parties, especially the Social Democrats and the Communists. Following Lenin's analysis of the 'working class aristocracy', Horkheimer suggested that employed workers, who tended to side with the Social Democrats, had much more to lose than their chains, and were fundamentally divided from the unemployed, from whom the Communist Party tended to draw many of its adherents. In regard to revolutionary theory, Horkheimer suggests, the movement is split between those who possess knowledge of the basic principles but lack adequate knowledge of existing conditions – the Communists – and those who possess reams of factual knowledge but lack 'the fundamental experience of the urgent need for change' – the Social Democrats.

Horkheimer himself was unable to affiliate with the dominant Leftist parties in Germany, and committed himself instead to theoretical work. He utilized his organizational abilities and political energies to guide the research and affairs of the Institute for Social Research. In effect this theoretical work was his politics. Consequently, while the Institute's members, in good Marxian fashion, constantly called for the unity of theory and practice, their own separation from practical politics ultimately contributed to Critical Theory's increasing distance from the political debates and struggles of the day – though this distance made possible the time and leisure to produce important theoretical works.[30]

Upon assuming the role of director, Horkheimer delivered his inaugural address, on 24 January 1931; it was entitled 'The Present Situation of Social Philosophy and the Tasks of an Institute for Social Research'.[31] In this address he defined social philosophy as an attempt to elucidate the 'fate of human beings, insofar as they are parts of a community, and not mere individuals. It concerns itself above all with the social life of people: state, law, economy, religion, in short, with the entire material and spiritual culture of humanity' (p. 33). Horkheimer's lecture provides the first major conception of his view of critical social theory as a synthesis of social science and philosophy, and therefore deserves careful scrutiny.

He begins by pointing to the limitations of the classical German social theories of Kant and Hegel and of contemporary metaphysical and positivist philosophies. This exercise typifies Horkheimer's method of clarifying his own position through criticism of opposing positions. Kant is criticized for grounding social philosophy in the experience and faculties of the particular individual (pp. 33ff.). Hegel's attempt to situate philosophy within the fields of society and history is presented as an improvement on Kant; yet Hegel's idealism and tendency to justify the existing order is rejected (pp. 34–7). Then Horkheimer criticizes the current forms of idealism in the neo-Kantian, neo-Hegelian, phenomenological and existential philosophies with their questionable speculative metaphysics and their tendencies to celebrate a higher, transcendental sphere of being (*Sein*) and meaning (*Sinn*) over concrete existence (pp. 38–9). The positivistic schools which root their theories in isolated facts are also criticized for their unsupportable metaphysical presuppositions and methodological limitations (p. 39).

Horkheimer concludes that none of the dominant philosophical schools contains an adequate social philosophy. He assumes that social philosophy encompasses 'the entire material and spiritual culture of humanity'. Consequently he rejects the claims of the specific social sciences such as 'material sociology' to provide adequate knowledge, since the specialized sciences abstract from the structure and organization of society as a whole and describe only limited domains of social experience. In opposition to the separation between social theory, science and philosophy which was dominant at the time and continues today, Horkheimer called for a new sort of synthesis between philosophy and the specialized sciences.

Horkheimer claims that the positivistic view that philosophy 'is perhaps beautiful, but scientifically fruitless because it is not subject to controls', verification, experiments and the like, must be rejected, as must the philosopher's prejudice that he or she is dealing with the essential, while the scientist is dealing with bare, trivial facts (p. 40). These conflicting claims to primacy must be overcome in favor of a 'dialectical penetration and development of philosophical theory and the praxis of the individual disciplines' (p. 40). For Horkheimer, the philosophical drive toward the universal and essential should be the animating spirit for social research; but at the same time philosophy must be 'sufficiently open to the world to allow itself to be impressed with, and transformed by, progress in concrete studies' (p. 41).

To fulfill these goals, Horkheimer envisaged a program of supradisciplinary research which would investigate current social and political problems. This project would unite

philosophers, sociologists, economists, historians, and psychologists in an ongoing research community who would do together what in other disciplines one individual does alone in the laboratory, – which is what genuine scientists have always done: namely, to pursue the great philosophical questions using the most refined scientific methods; to reformulate and to make more precise the questions in the course of work as demanded by the object; and to develop new methods without losing sight of the universal. (p. 41)

In effect, Horkheimer is calling for a *new synthesis* of philosophy and social theory. He claims that all philosophies contain an explicit or implicit social theory, but that such theories can be grounded and developed reliably only in a program of social research that will test and elaborate their claims and revise and modify their positions accordingly. Yet, in ascribing to philosophy such a central role within social theory, Horkheimer is sharply distinguishing his enterprise from the dominant forms of social theory and research which eschew philosophy, as well as from the project of his predecessor, Carl Grunberg, who grounded the Institute work solely in empirical and historical investigations.

Horkheimer signals this difference by pointing out that Grunberg's chair was in the faculty of political economy (*wirtschaftliche Staatswissenschaften*), while his chair will be in social philosophy (p. 41). One might also signal the differences between Horkheimer and Grunberg by reflecting on the titles of the journals which they edited. While Grunberg's journal provided an 'Archive for the History of Socialism and the Workers' Movement', Horkheimer's was called the 'Journal for Social Research'. Thus, while Grunberg grounded the Institute's work in a traditional Marxian framework and subordinated social theory to empirical and historical research, Horkheimer assigned a more fundamental role to philosophy and social theory.

After praising Grunberg's legacy and contributions, Horkheimer stresses that the Institute will now undergo a new start directed at 'new tasks' (p. 42). He claims that the Institute's new multidisciplinary program will allow its members to raise the question of 'the interconnections between the economic life of society, the psychic development of the individual and transformations in the realm of culture . . . including not only the so-called spiritual contents of science, art and religion, but also law, ethics, fashion, public opinion, sport, amusement, life style, etc.' (p. 43). This research program is somewhat unorthodox for Marxian social theory, which in the past had tended to neglect the dimension of individual and social psychology, and had also downplayed the study of culture and leisure. Attention to these topics would eventually produce many of the distinctive contributions of Critical Theory.

In his inaugural address Horkheimer distanced his conception of social theory from a crude Marxian materialism. He proclaimed that the Institute would not subscribe to any metaphysical thesis, such as idealism or materialism, on the relation between the economy, society, culture and consciousness. He noted that the attempt to derive all forms of life from one metaphysical substance was 'bad Spinozaism'. From the very beginning, therefore, Horkheimer rejected all metaphysical absolutism and all philosophical reductionism. He argued that an illusory idealism that derives everything from the Idea is 'an abstract and therefore badly understood Hegel'; just as the attempt to derive everything from an economy which is understood merely as material being is 'an abstract and therefore badly understood Marx' (p. 43). Such theses posit an 'uncritical, obsolete and highly problematic cleavage of spirit and reality into naive absolutes', and must be dialectically overcome (p. 43).

Critical social philosophy, by contrast, describes the complex set of mediations which interconnect consciousness and society, culture and economy, state and citizens. These relations can best be clarified and developed in concrete historical contexts in which one asks 'which interconnections exist in a definite social group, in a definite period of time and in a definite country, between the role of this group in the economic process, the transformation of the psychic structures of its individual members, and the totality of the system that affects and produces its thoughts and mechanism' (p. 44).

To begin this task, the Institute proposed to study technically qualified workers and employees in Germany by gathering empirical material on their psychological, social and political attitudes and interpreting these in terms of work done in theoretical economics, sociology and psychology. Horkheimer illustrated the project of the Institute's social theory by indicating that an empirical study of the white-collar working class would be its first research project. In addition, he indicated that his colleagues would undertake studies predominantly in 'theoretical economics, economic history, and the history of the working class movement' (p. 45). Thus, at least during the early Horkheimer years, the Institute sought to continue many of Grunberg's projects regarding topics central to classical Marxism and socialist politics, but from a more comprehensive theoretical vantage point.

Indeed, the first publications by the Institute under Horkheimer's directorship reflected a continuing commitment to Marxism. After the publication of Henryk Grossmann's *The Law of Accumulation and Collapse of the Capitalist System* and Friedrich Pollock's *The Attempts at a Planned Economy in the Soviet Union, 1917–1927*, both in 1929, the Institute published Karl Wittfogel's study of *Economy and Society in China* in 1931 and Franz Borkenau's *The Transition from the Feudal to the Bourgeois World View* in 1934.[32] During this time too, the Institute was preparing for publication a study of the German working classes' socio-political attitudes. Most of these works employed rather orthodox Marxian methods of analysis, and were focused on themes central to Marxian theory.

The initial multidisciplinary project undertaken during Horkheimer's directorship sought to confront an issue of central importance for Marxian theory and practice – namely, the political potential and situation of the German working class in the contemporary era. The Institute assigned Erich Fromm to head this project, and hired Hilde Weiss and Paul Lazarsfeld, who would later become a central figure in the development of communications research in the United States, to help with the research design and survey. Although this study was never published under the auspices of the Institute, the results were written up by Fromm and published for the first time as *Arbeiter und Angestellte am Vorabend des Dritten Reiches* after Fromm's death in 1980.[33]

The study was intended 'as a first attempt at investigating the social and psychological attitudes of two large groups in Germany – manual and white-collar workers' (p. 41). A comprehensive questionnaire with 271 questions was devised and distributed to 3,300 recipients through unions, political organizations and Institute workers. By the end of 1931, 1,100 had been returned, though only 584 were extant when Fromm began writing his report in 1934, due to loss of some of the material in the emigration. Publication was announced by the Institute for 1936, but severe differences over the value of the study delayed publication; and when Fromm left the Institute in 1939, he took the relevant documents with him.[34]

Fromm's text stated that:

The purpose of our questionnaire is to collect data about the opinions, life-styles and attitudes of manual and white-collar workers. We wanted to form a picture of what books they read, how they furnished their homes, and what their favourite plays and films were. We were interested in what and in whom they believed, in what they had to say about topics such as women's work, the upbringing of children and the rationalization of work in the workplace, and in how they regarded their colleagues and superiors. Finally we wanted to know their attitude towards lending money to friends, their view of the legal system, their opinion about the actual distribution of power in the state – and their views on many other subjects. (p. 42)

The primary goal of the study was to determine if the workers' character structure, disposition toward political action and values cohered with their stated political orientations. The study concluded that only 15 per cent of the members of the major Leftist political parties were consistent in their political affiliations, character structure and attitudes; 25 per cent manifested, tendentially or totally, authoritarian attitudes; and the rest exhibited rather contradictory attitudes and views. The analysis suggested that the actual revolutionary potential of the German working class was less than was usually assumed, and that, while the workers might resist a fascist attempt to take over the government, it was unlikely that they would undertake the sacrifices necessary for a socialist revolution. (For further discussion of the text, see 2.2.)

While the Institute pursued a rather explicitly Marxian research program, its relationship to the dominant forms of Marxism was rather ambivalent, and would become increasingly so during Horkheimer's directorship. By comparison with Grunberg's explicit identification with Marxism and his relatively orthodox Marxist program of research,[35] Horkheimer's inaugural address includes no positive reference to Marxism, only an indication that, under his direction, the Institute would pursue 'new tasks'. Neither Grunberg nor Horkheimer, however, explicitly related the theoretical work of the Institute to practical politics in any obvious fashion. Even Grunberg in his inaugural address goes out of his way to stress that the Institute's members would pursue strictly theoretical questions with scientific methods, and 'would distance themselves from the political issues of the day'. Indeed, Grunberg concluded his address with the assurance that he aimed simply to increase scientific knowledge; while Horkheimer concluded with a similar pledge to guide the Institute with the 'unchanging will to truth', rather than the promotion of social change or revolution.[36]

One might interpret such a self-conscious severing of theory and practice as stemming from the concern of the respective directors in their formal inaugural addresses to assure their academic colleagues that they would not be serving merely as a front for revolutionary politics, and that they would pursue academically respectable research. Indeed, in such addresses to colleagues and administrators, one does not usually call the troops to the barricades. Yet, as far as we know, most Institute members did in fact distance themselves from actual political involvement during the last years of the Weimar Republic and at least the first years of the emigration. An ambivalent relationship to Marxism and actual politics would therefore characterize the theory and practice of the Institute for the next several decades.

2

From Supradisciplinary Materialism to Critical Theory: The 1930s Program

Although Critical Theory was basically inspired by Marxism, from 1930 through 1936, members of the Institute used code words like 'materialism' and the 'economic theory of society' for their version of the Marxian theory. During the early 1930s, the Institute saw its purpose as reformulating Marxian theory 'under the historically changed conditions of capitalism and the labor movement'.[1] This involved moving beyond crude Marxian conceptions of the relation between base and superstructure and developing both a Marxist social psychology and a cultural theory, so as to better analyze the mediations, or connections, between the economic base and the realms of the superstructure, as well as the changed roles of culture and psychology within capitalist modernity.

In this chapter, I will first analyze the concept of a supradisciplinary, materialist social theory which defined the Institute's project (2.1). Then I will discuss its development of a materialist social psychology which synthesized Freud with Marx, thus producing some of the Institute's most distinctive innovations (2.2). These discussions set the stage for analysis of Horkheimer's and Marcuse's programmatic essays which articulate the concept of a Critical Theory of society (2.3).

2.1 Supradisciplinary Materialism

The Institute for Social Research developed a supradisciplinary, materialist social theory as a response to inadequacies within both classical Marxism and the dominant forms of bourgeois science and philosophy. Orthodox Marxism had congealed into a dogmatic, reductionist and objectivistic metaphysical materialism, while bourgeois social science was characterized by a fragmentation of the sciences, each cut off from the other and pursuing its own investigations in isolation from other disciplines. Both bourgeois science and scientistic Marxism utilized excessively objectivistic methods, and thus were not able to conceptualize current problems, such as the ways in which social and cultural conditions were inclining strata of the working class and other social groups toward fascism. Lacking a theory of the subject, orthodox Marxism could not really confront the failure of revolutionary consciousness to develop, and could not point to ways in which revolutionary consciousness and struggle could be produced.

To overcome this dual crisis of Marxism and bourgeois science, the Institute attempted to develop a materialist social theory that would be characterized by an integration of philosophy and the sciences. Accordingly, during the 1930s the Institute developed critiques of both the abstract, speculative and metaphysical philosophy dominant in Germany at the time and the methodological and substantive poverty of the various specialized sciences.[2] Thus the project of constructing a materialist social theory uniting philosophy and the sciences was conceived in opposition to both the specialized bourgeois sciences and academic philosophy, as well as to the scientism of many orthodox Social Democrats like Kautsky or Communists like Stalin. As Horkheimer stated at the time: 'Materialism requires the unification of philosophy and science. Of course, it recognizes technical differences between the more general research of philosophy and the more specialized research in the sciences, just as it recognizes differences in method between research and presentation but not between science and philosophy as such.'[3]

The philosophical component of the Institute's work included development of a sustained practice of ideology critique which involved theoretical confrontation and appraisal of the dominant ideological trends of the day. Thus 'critique' was first conceptualized by the Institute as a method of attacking the cognitive distortions produced by ideology – though it would later take on other connotations as well. From the beginning, members of the Institute excelled in the critique of ideology, and this practice remains one of their major contributions to critical social theory.

The Critique of Ideology

Max Horkheimer's first essay for the Institute, 'A New Concept of Ideology?', consisted of a critique of Karl Mannheim's widely acclaimed book *Ideology and Utopia*.[4] At the time, Mannheim was a rising star in German sociology who was obviously perceived as a leading challenger to the concept of critical social theory being developed by Horkheimer and his colleagues. While Mannheim – who had office space in the Institute building in Frankfurt – seemed to present a Marxian critique of ideology,

Horkheimer argues that the incorporation of Marx's doctrines into contemporary social science (by Mannheim and others) has led to a distortion of their meaning and a transformation into their opposites (p. 33).

Horkheimer sees Mannheim's work as the latest attempt to incorporate elements of Marx into an idealist philosophy of spirit. In particular, he cites Mannheim's attempt to transform the theory of ideology from an 'armament of a party' into a nonpartisan sociological instrument through a 'sociology of knowledge' which would demonstrate the partisan, contextual and existentially determined nature of *all* cognition, thought and theories (pp. 33ff.). In this way, the concept of ideology would be extended to all theories, not just those which supposedly mask ruling-class interests.

Mannheim distinguished between 'particular ideology', which specified that '"this or that interest is the cause of such and such a disguise"', and a 'total' concept, which calls into question '"the opponent's entire world-view (including his conceptual apparatus"' (p. 34). In this argument, one's entire cognitive apparatus, with all its categories and forms of perception, is constituted by historical and sociological conditions. For Mannheim theories are primarily expressions of the views of social groups which are structured by their conditions of life. Mannheim expressly formulated his conception as both an application of Marxism and an extension of the concept of ideology to Marxism itself, which is thereby relativized as the expression of the consciousness of a particular group (that is, socialists and the working-class movement).

Horkheimer did not claim that Marxism somehow was able to escape 'existential determination', but instead attacked Mannheim's conception of a sociology of knowledge and his attempts to produce a social theory that transcended the limitations of particular world views.[5] Horkheimer argues that Mannheim's thought moves within the framework of idealism, and does not adequately specify the relationships between social groups and their ideologies because it lacks an adequate theory of society. While Mannheim attempts to correlate ideas and social groups, he does not specify how the groups themselves are grounded in a structure of society and how their thoughts and activities are thus products of specific socio-historical conditions.

Horkheimer also objects to Mannheim's claim that assimilating and transcending the limitations of particular views will provide ever broader and more comprehensive perspectives on reality, which will eventually illuminate 'the essence of man' (p. 39). For Mannheim, as for Wilhelm Dilthey whom he follows in this respect, history is essentially the unfolding of humanity's essential nature.[6] Horkheimer believes that this position contradicts the premises of Mannheim's own sociology of knowledge, and represents an illicit smuggling of metaphysics into the sociology of knowledge. He concludes: 'If we take Mannheim's theory of ideologies seriously, then there is little reason why in a fundamentally contingent and change-able reality only the process of "becoming human" should be exempt from ideology; nor is it convincingly demonstrated why of all knowledge it is precisely anthropological knowledge that is seen as free of ideology' (p. 41).

In addition, Horkheimer criticizes Mannheim's quest for a foundation outside history for his supposedly historical theory of knowledge. He sharply criticizes Mannheim's notion that a 'realm beyond history' is the real cause of events, and that we should thus 'look for traces of the extra-historical (*des Aussergeschichtlichen*) in everyday history' (p. 42). Horkheimer claims that Mannheim's attempts to discover a higher meaning within history, along with his use of concepts like the 'ineffable', 'transcendent meaning' and 'the ecstatic element in human experience', disclose that idealist and spiritual metaphysics have permeated his theory.[7]

In opposition to Mannheim, Horkheimer argues that the project of undermining metaphysics was precisely the task of Marx's theory of ideol-ogy, which he believes Mannheim vitiates by smuggling metaphysical categories back into his theory. Throughout the 1930s, Horkheimer and his colleagues attacked the metaphysical assumptions of dominant modes of thought, and consistently applied the Marxian notion of ideology critique to dominant theories in the classical and contemporary philosophical traditions.[8] For Horkheimer,

It is indeed impossible for history as a whole to be the expression of any sort of meaningful configuration. History is, after all, the synopsis of processes which arise from the contradictory relations existing in human society. These processes reveal no psychic or spiritual unity. Neither are they simply the side effects of conflicts between opinions, attitudes, styles of thought or systems. It is entirely different forces, both human and extrahuman, that lead to their realization. In so far as history does not derive from the conscious intentions of individuals who bring it about in accordance with a systematic plan, it has no meaning. ... It is characteristic of Marx's materialism to describe as the true reality precisely the unsatisfactory condition of matters in this world, and to object to the hypostatization of any sort of thought as belonging to a higher sphere of existence. He is the sworn enemy of every attempt to comprehend reality merely in terms of ideas or a purely spiritual order. Such consolation about the world is no longer possible, according to Marx. (pp. 44-5)

Horkheimer's critique of Mannheim was written before he assumed the directorship of the Institute. After he became director, the central import-ance of the critique of ideology became even more fundamental to Institute activity. During the next decade, various Institute members would carry out ideology critiques of idealism, positivism, existentialism, philosophy of life and the emerging ideology of fascism, as well as of the ideological trends dominant in such disciplines as metaphysics and morality.[9] Yet the Institute was also concerned with developing a supradisciplinary theory of the contemporary epoch, and it is to this project that we shall turn in the following sections.

Zeitschrift für Sozialforschung

Horkheimer and his colleagues elaborated their concept of a materialist social theory in the context of a series of articles published in *Zeitschrift für Sozialforschung*, which was a medium for the presentation of their developing social theory. Specialists in philosophy and social theory like Horkheimer and Marcuse wrote articles on philosophy and intellectual history; Fromm sketched out a materialist social psychology; Leo Lowenthal and Walter Benjamin developed approaches to a sociology of literature, while Adorno contributed to developing a sociology of popular music and carried out ideology critiques of certain dominant modes of thought; Pollock, Grossmann and others contributed articles on political economy, while Franz Neuman, Otto Kirchheimer and others contributed articles on political sociology. The articles published by members of the Institute were collectively discussed, and represent the shared theoretical position of the Institute. The *Zeitschrift* also contained a full series of book reviews in every issue, edited by Lowenthal, which provided both critiques of new (or old) ideological trends and attempts to discern new material which might help in the production of a social theory of the present age.

The first issue of *Zeitschrift*, published in Germany in 1932 before the exile from fascism, exhibited the characteristic version of Marxism produced by the Institute and its distinctive features and focuses.[10] As Wiggershaus points out, all the contributors utilize the Marxian materialist theory of history – or economic theory of society, as Horkheimer sometimes called it – which they apply to various topics and disciplines.[11] All of them privilege the Marxian emphasis on the importance of the contradiction between forces of production and relations of production within capitalist society, and for the most part they emphasize the explosive potential of forces of production which, if unfettered, might make possible the establishment of a new (socialist) social order. All the contributors thus present themselves as critics of capitalist society and supporters of socialism – although they utilize somewhat different rhetoric, and are more or less explicit about their commitments to Marxism and specific political positions.

In some 'Remarks on Science and Crisis', Horkheimer indicated how the current world crisis of capitalism in the 1930s provided a fetter on science, industry and all productive forces, and argued that only with fundamental social transformation could science and industry be developed to their full potential. In a study of 'The Current Situation of Capitalism and the Outlook for a Planned Economy', Pollock documented the destruction of productive forces in the anarchic capitalist economy of the period, while arguing that only a planned economy could produce a solution to recurrent economic crises and fully develop productive forces. While Pollock believed that socialism presented more promising perspectives on a planned economy, he did not rule out the possibility that a planned economy could be developed under capitalism; and later he developed the concept of state capitalism, which he saw as a new stage of capitalism.

In his essays on social psychology, Fromm analyzed how bourgeois socialization obstructs full development of personality, and discusses how, through a synthesis of Marxism and psychoanalysis, productive human powers might be liberated and developed by combining social change and transformation of material conditions with new modes of education and socialization. In a study of 'The Social Situation of Music', Adorno criticized the restraints on musical production imposed by the commodification of music in a capitalist market situation, and pointed to how the modern music of Schönberg and others attempted to revolutionize music and musical production. Lowenthal demonstrated how application of the materialist theory of history could transform literary study; and all the contributors argued that the materialist theory of history could reconstruct the various academic disciplines and produce new critical perspectives throughout intellectual life.[12]

Consequently the Institute originally presented its work in a rather traditional Marxian framework, criticizing restrictions on the forces of production in a variety of fields and calling for their liberation and development. Thus 'critique' was coming to signify criticism of all material and intellectual constraints on production and other forms of human activity. It thus required a global, synthesizing theory of the present age to specify the various forms of oppression and constraint and to highlight perspectives for liberation and social change. Such general positions were often presented in the *Zeitschrift* in the form of programmatic statements from Horkheimer and others concerning the general goals of the Institute. For example, in an introduction to the first issue, Horkheimer claimed that social research from various academic fields in the journal would be part of an attempt to develop a 'theory of contemporary society as a whole' aiming at 'the entirety of the social process. It presupposes that beneath the chaotic surface of events one can grasp and conceptualize a structure of the effective powers.'[13] This theory would be based on the results of historical studies and the individual sciences, and would therefore strive for the status of 'science' (pp. 1 and 4). Yet these investigations would not exclude philosophy, 'for it is not affiliation to a specific discipline but its importance for the theory of society which determines its choice of material' (p. 2).

Materialism and Social Theory

Against all idealist modes of thought, the Institute theorists defended materialism. Rejecting both the mechanistic, metaphysical materialism already criticized by Marx and Engels in *The Holy Family*, as well as the current positivistic forms of materialism, Horkheimer and his colleagues defined the objects of materialist theory in terms of material conditions, human needs and social struggles against oppression. Furthermore, materialism did not signify for the Institute a specific metaphysical doctrine, but stood for a whole series of ideas and practical attitudes, which took different forms in different contexts.

In 'Materialism and Metaphysics', Horkheimer spells out what, for him, is involved in a materialist view of the world, and what sort of thought, research and action it requires (*CT*, pp. 10ff.). He begins by criticizing metaphysical materialism, which attempts to capture the totality of being in a universal philosophical system. In these remarks Horkheimer makes evident his hostility to metaphysical systems, absolutism and all foundationalist theories that attempt to discover a foundation for knowledge. He then argues that the specific views which a materialist holds at a given moment are not dictated by any unchanging metaphysical theses, but rather by the

tasks which at any given period are to be mastered with the help of the theory. Thus, for example, criticism of a dogma of religious faith may, at a particular time and place, play a decisive role within the complex of materialist views, while under other circumstances such criticism may be unimportant. Today the knowledge of movements and tendencies affecting society as a whole is immensely important for materialist theory, but in the eighteenth century the need for knowledge of the social totality was overshadowed by questions of epistemology, of natural science, and of politics. (*CT*, pp. 20–1).

Horkheimer claims that while idealist views generally aim at *justification*, and are advanced by ruling-class ideologues to affirm dominant-class interests, materialist theories aim at *explanation* with reference to material conditions, classes and specific historical situations (*CT*, pp. 22ff.). He especially objects to notions of metaphysical cognition and absolute truth, and argues that there is 'an irreducible tension between concept and being' (p. 27). Horkheimer rejects here metaphysical theses of the identity of thought and being, of knowledge and the known. He argues instead that concepts are not organs of absolute knowledge, but simply instruments for achieving certain goals, which are to be developed and modified constantly in the course of experience.

Horkheimer thus proposes a post-metaphysical conception of materialism, and stresses the different content of materialist theories in different contexts. He and his colleagues rejected both Hegel's identity theory, which posited an identity between thought and being within an idealist ontology, and the forms of epistemological realism held by many positivistic materialists then and now, which maintained that correct thought simply mirrored or reflected the object of thought. In addition, the Institute stressed the historical nature of both theories and their subject matter: 'The theoretical activity of humans, like the practical, is not the independent knowledge of a fixed object, but a product of ever-changing reality' (*CT*, p. 29). As historical conditions change, concepts and theories must also change; thus there is no stable foundation for absolutist metaphysical views.

For Horkheimer, concepts and theories therefore provided representations of the socio-material world, and not any absolute or indubitable knowledge. Horkheimer also criticizes theories that operate with a model which rigidly distinguishes between subject and object, arguing that 'the subject-object relation is not accurately described by the picture of two fixed realities which are conceptually fully transparent and move towards each other. Rather, in what we call objective, subjective factors are at work; and in what we call subjective, objective factors are at work' (*CT*, p. 29). Horkheimer's materialism is thus *dialectical*, utilizing a subject/object dialectic in which objective conditions help constitute the subject, while the subject in turn helps constitute objective (material, historical) conditions. For Horkheimer:

A dialectical process is negatively characterized by the fact that it is not to be conceived as the result of individual unchanging factors. To put it positively, its elements continuously change in relation to each other within the process, so that they are not even to be radically distinguished from each other. Thus the development of human character, for example, is conditioned both by the economic situation and by the individual powers of the person in question. But both these elements determine each other continuously, so that in the total development neither of them is to be presented as an effective factor without giving the other its role. (*CT*, p. 28).

Horkheimer and his colleagues would consistently follow this dialectical conception which stresses the relative autonomy of thought, culture and all other 'superstructural' phenomena in a process of reciprocal interaction with a socio-economic 'base'. Furthermore, the Institute version of 'dialectical materialism' is thoroughly *historical*, because it stresses that our experience, views of the world and concepts change in relation to historical development, and that therefore both our theories and perceptual apparatuses, as well as the objects of knowledge, are historical: 'Materialism, unlike idealism, always understands thinking to be the thinking of particular men within a particular period of time. It challenges every claim to the autonomy of thought' (*CT*, p. 32).

At bottom, for Horkheimer, 'materialism is not interested in a world view or in the souls of men. It is concerned with changing the concrete conditions under which humans suffer and in which, of course, their souls must become stunted. This concern may be comprehended historically and psychologically; it cannot be grounded in general principles' (*CT*, p. 32). Horkheimer believes that it is primarily materialist – that is, Marxist – theories which are currently concerned with human suffering and with transforming the material conditions that produce human suffering so as to produce a more rational society and a more humane form of existence. This analysis assumes that 'the wretchedness of our own time is connected with the structure of society; social theory therefore forms the main content of contemporary materialism' (p. 24). In particular, 'the fundamental historical role of economic relations is characteristic of the materialist position.... Understanding of the present becomes more idealist, the more it avoids the economic causes of material need and looks to a psychologically naive elaboration of so-called "basic elements of human existence"' (pp. 25–6).

Horkheimer's materialist social theory thus focused on human needs and suffering, the ways in which economic conditions produced suffering and the changes necessary to eliminate human suffering and increase human well-being. Such a project requires a critical social theory which focuses on the social problems of the present age: 'If materialist theory is an aspect of efforts to improve the human situation, it inevitably opposes every attempt to reduce social problems to second place' (*CT*, p. 26). The social theory in turn is produced by a synthesis of philosophy and the sciences (pp. 34ff.).

For the Institute, philosophy without empirical scientific research is empty, just as science without philosophy is blind. In the mid-1930s, Horkheimer's attempt at unification of science and philosophy seems to have involved a dialectical interpenetration and mediation of science and philosophy, without making one superordinate to the other.[14] Consequently Horkheimer rejected both metaphysics and positivist concepts of science which profess '"the dogma of the invariability of natural laws"' (*CT*, p. 36). Dominant positivist conceptions of science, according to Horkheimer, are 'unhistorical'; and 'science' is not to be privileged above philosophy and social theory, although 'materialism has in common with positivism that it acknowledges as real only what is given in sense experience, and it has done so since its beginnings' (p. 42). Sense experience is mediated through concepts, however, and both sense perception and cognition are subject to social conditions and historical change; thus notions of absolute intuition, whether through the senses or cognition, are to be rejected. Horkheimer and his colleagues therefore subscribe to a nontranscendental materialist theory of knowledge which acknowledges, with Kant and the idealists, that forms of cognition and theories determine our experience of the external world, and also that objective material conditions in turn condition forms of thought and knowledge. The results of materialist social theory are thus always provisional, contextual and subject to revision.

In an important essay entitled 'The Latest Attack on Metaphysics', Horkheimer continues his critique of metaphysics and positivistic science, while developing his materialist concept of social theory. Metaphysics is criticized for its attempts to grasp the totality of being through intuition, and Horkheimer sharply attacks its 'mere opinions, improbable statements, and outright fallacies' (*CT*, pp. 134ff.), as well as its attempts to provide illusory consolation and compensation (p. 137). In contrast, science is presented as 'a body of knowledge which a given society has assembled in its struggle with nature' (p. 133). Yet Horkheimer criticizes the (positivist) position that science provides 'the only possible form of knowledge' (pp. 136ff.), and defends instead 'critical, dialectical' thought which makes connections between various spheres of social reality (p. 145 and *passim*) and which contextualizes all the 'facts' of science 'as segments of the life process of society' in producing 'the right social theory' (p. 159).[15]

Horkheimer's dialectical social theory focuses on 'empirical material' and connects each particular to the fundamental processes of a given society (*CT*, pp. 161–2). Attacking the fetishism of isolated, unmediated facts in positivism, he says that 'within dialectical theory such individual facts always appear in a definite connection which enters into every concept and which seeks to reflect reality in its totality' (p. 161). In addition, 'Dialectical thought integrates the empirical constituents into structures of experience which are important not only for the limited purposes served by science, but also for the historical interests with which dialectic thought is connected' (p. 162). Dialectical social theory thus affirms the importance of values, while attacking notions of a value-free science, and criticizes existing society from the standpoint of specific values which the theory is concerned to defend and to fight for. Dialectical social theory thus involves a synthesis between social theory, morality and politics.

Materialism and Morality

Horkheimer's materialist social theory is marked by 'solidarity with suffering humans', and 'is formed by the presently prevailing state of affairs' (*CT*, pp. 44, 45). In an article on 'Materialism and Morality' published in 1933, Horkheimer criticized idealist and universalist ethical theories from the standpoint of a materialist theory rooted in a philosophical anthropology which would provide the basis for a socialist ethics and politics.[16] Against Kantian idealism, which rooted ethics in universal precepts of reason, duty and a 'good will', Horkheimer argued that ethics should be grounded in human needs and concrete human situations, denying that ethical principles could be grounded in either a transhistorical ideal realm of values or an unchanging nature: 'There is no eternal realm of values. Needs and desires, interests and passions of human beings are transformed together with the social process' (p. 104). Against Kantian idealist moral values, Horkheimer argued that human *happiness* was the highest ethical ideal and the proper province of morality. In the language of traditional ethical theory, Horkheimer is rejecting deontological, universal and rationalist ethics in favor of an eudaemonistic ethics grounded in the value of 'the striving of men for happiness', which is taken 'as a natural fact that needs no justification' (pp. 93ff.).[17]

For Horkheimer, however, the striving for happiness involves attempts to eliminate unhappiness and the conditions which produce human suffering. Suffering itself is conceived as a product of both natural conditions – scarcity, sickness, natural catastrophe and so on – and historical conditions – poverty, exploitation, war and so forth. The task for social theory (and society) is therefore to conceptualize and struggle to eliminate social and historical causes of suffering:

In the future society toward which the moral consciousness aspires, the life of the whole and of the individuals is produced not merely as a natural effect, but as the consequence of rational designs that take account of the happiness of the individuals in equal measure. In place of the blind mechanism of economic struggles which presently condition happiness and – for the greater part of humanity – unhappiness, emerges the purposive application of the wealth of human and material powers of production. (p. 100)

Horkheimer therefore conceptualizes morality as the life expression of problems suffered by determinate individuals, groups and societies at specific points in history. 'Materialism understands itself', Horkheimer proposes, 'as the effort to abolish existing misery' (p. 103). Motivated by a concern for human suffering, Critical Theory thus constituted itself as a critique of existing conditions which produce suffering and an instrument of social transformation which would serve the interests of increasing human freedom, happiness and well-being. More specifically in reference to ethical theory, in view of human suffering, Horkheimer proposed that sympathy and compassion were the appropriate moral responses. Present-day economic and political development atrophied and crippled those powers, however: 'The struggle of great economic power groups', Horkheimer wrote, 'played out on a world scale, is conducted amid the atrophy of kind human inclinations, the proclamation of overt and covert lies, and the development of an immeasurable hatred' (p. 106).

This is especially intolerable, Horkheimer believed, because at present humanity has become so rich and has at its disposal such great natural and human auxiliary powers, that it could exist united by worthy objectives. The need to veil this state of affairs, which is transparent in every respect, gives rise to a sphere of hyprocrisy which extends not only to international relations, but which penetrates into even the most private relations; it results in a diminution of cultural endeavors (including science) and a brutalization of personal and public life, such that spiritual and material misery are compounded. At no time has the poverty of humanity stood in such crying contradiction to its potential wealth, at no time have all powers been so horribly fettered as in this generation where children go hungry and the hands of the fathers are busy turning out bombs.... We view human beings not as subjects of their fate, but rather as objects of a blind occurrence of nature, to which the response of a moral sentiment is compassion. (pp. 106-7)

I have quoted this passage at length not only because of its relevance to the contemporary situation, but because it points to what Horkheimer takes as the basis of morality and – as we shall soon see – politics: concern for human suffering and human solidarity and compassion with suffering as the basis for morality. Yet Horkheimer is concerned not to reduce morality to either emotivism (which would conceive of ethics as the capricious expression of feeling unmediated by reason) or decisionism (which would ground ethics in arbitrary values or decisions). Rather, Horkheimer's ethic is grounded in a philosophical anthropology which focuses intensely on human needs, sufferings and potentialities in a given historical situation. Therefore ethics cannot be separated from anthropology and social theory or from political concern with the suffering of human beings in the present situation. Horkheimer is thus resolutely opposed to a separation of disciplines which would abstract philosophy from social theory and politics. Indeed, he argues that the 'other form in which morality today finds appropriate expression is politics. The happiness of the general public is consistently characterized as its proper aim by the great moral philosophers' (p. 107).

Consequently Horkheimer's political position is itself rooted in a philosophical argument concerning the nature of human beings and morality. For Horkheimer, moral sentiment is rooted not only in compassion for suffering human beings and solidarity with their predicament, but also in indignation and outrage over suffering, combined with a desire to eliminate its causes. Since, as Schnadelbach argues, compassion for Horkheimer is not interpreted as mere emotion or subjective feeling, but 'as an emotional impulse mediated by insight', Horkheimer is no mere emotivist.[18] Compassion thus unites the perspectives of the individual and society, and reason and emotion, because each individual can sympathize with the suffering of others, since pain and suffering are experiences accessible to all.

Moral concern for suffering and human compassion thus lead to a demand to eliminate the social sources of human suffering and to merge ethics with politics. Although Horkheimer believed that earlier philosophers deceived themselves by taking the contemporary form of society and experience as eternal and as the measure of the good society, nonetheless, such bourgeois ideals as freedom, equality and justice remain valid ideals for the contemporary era. Horkheimer argues that:

The battle-cries of the Enlightenment and of the French Revolution are valid now more than ever.... Politics in accord with this goal therefore must not abandon these demands, but realize them ... in conformity with their meaning. The content of the ideas is not eternal but is subject to historical change ... because the human impulses which demand something better take different forms according to the historical material with which they have to work. The unity of such concepts results less from the invariability of their elements than from the historical development of the circumstances under which their realization is necessary. (p. 108)

Horkheimer believed, for instance, that at the present time the ideal of equality took on forms and meanings different from those in the period of the bourgeois revolutions, when it signified such things as equality before the law or equality to pursue one's economic interests unimpeded by the state.

Today, however, the freedom of the individual demands submitting their economic independence to a plan. The presupposition of the ideas of equality and justice hitherto was the prevailing inequality of economic and human subjects.... Hitherto, these concepts took their determinate content from the relations of the free market, which with time were supposed to function to the benefit of all. Today they have transformed themselves into the concrete image of a better society, which will be born out of the present one, if humanity does not first sink into barbarism. (pp. 108-9)

Justice for Horkheimer is thus bound up with freedom, equality and morality. In a class society, however, inequality is linked not only with disparities in goods and services but with unequal divisions of pain, suffering, opportunities and possibilities. For Horkheimer, no form of inequality is to be seen as 'natural' or 'inevitable', but rather as 'something that should be overcome' (p. 111). In other words, political conceptions of justice, freedom and equality should be seen in relation to the present unequal distribution of wealth, goods, opportunities and power and to the sorts of suffering and deprivations that these forms of inequality produce. This requires new syntheses of ethics and politics and the constitution of an ethical politics devoted to eliminating human suffering and increasing happiness.

Yet, because there is no guarantee that history itself will increase justice and freedom (as in some versions of classical Marxism), morality and politics are themselves bound up with the indeterminacy and contingency of history, and must be modified in accord with ever-changing historical conditions:

Materialist theory certainly does not afford to the political actor the solace that he will necessarily achieve his objectives; it is not a metaphysics of history, but rather a changing image of the world, evolving in relation to the practical efforts towards its improvement. The knowledge of tendencies contained in this image offers no clear prognosis of historical development. (p. 114)

In Horkheimer's view, 'materialism does not lack ideals, then; its ideals are shaped with the needs of society as a starting point and are measured by what is possible in the foreseeable future with the human forces available' (*CT*, p. 46). Critical Theory does not offer any absolute foundation for morality and politics, yet it attempts to overcome relativism through its intense focus on human needs, sufferings and struggles in the present age. It holds out the hope that individuals will create a better social order which will fulfill human needs, develop human potentialities and struggle to eliminate the main causes of human suffering. It thus ascribes philosophy a major role in social critique and transformation, while attempting to make it an instrument of social emancipation and progress.

While the Critical Theorists defined their enterprise during the 1930s as a *materialist* theory, its most characteristic feature is probably its utilization of Hegel's dialectical method; it is thus a unique synthesis of materialism and idealism. The materialism of the Institute was closer in spirit to the early Marx and the position set forth in his *Theses on Feuerbach* than to the positivistic materialism of Engels, as set forth in texts like *The Dialectics of Nature*, which posited matter in motion as the primary metaphysical reality. Marxian materialism, of the sort taken over by Critical Theory, by contrast, assumed as its primary presuppositions the reality of human needs, class interests, and the constitutive role of the system of production in shaping social reality and experience. Consequently, against certain dismissals of Critical Theory as inherently idealist, one might point to the Critical Theorists' materialist self-understanding, which in turn should be qualified by emphasis on the extent to which Hegel's idealism and dialectics influenced their project. Consequently, it is more accurate to characterize Critical Theory as a mediation of materialism and idealism, philosophy and the sciences.

2.2   Toward a Materialist Social Psychology

The emphasis on psychological factors in the Institute theory was connected with the project of developing a Marxist social psychology which would describe how individual thought and behaviour are shaped by material conditions and socialization processes. The theory analyzes the mediations between material conditions and individual consciousness, and thus provides aspects of a materialist social psychology which the Institute members believed was lacking in orthodox Marxism. The synthesis of Marxism and psychology instantiates the Institute's transcendence of disciplinary boundaries and specializations and its belief that fruitful theoretical innovations can best be attained by supradisciplinary work.

There were several reasons why the members of the Institute for Social Research believed that it was important to develop a materialist social psychology.[19] From a theoretical point of view, one of the major deficiencies of classical Marxism was the lack of a socio-psychological theory which could describe in detail how society shapes the beliefs, values, aspirations and so on dominant among its members. This deficiency has major political implications, because without such a fully developed social psychology, it is impossible to discuss how either conservative or revolutionary consciousness is produced. In light of the failure of the German and European revolutions in the post-World War I period and in view of the emergence of fascism, it was obvious that an adequate radical psychology was needed to deal with the subjective conditions of revolution (or fascism) as an issue of both central political and theoretical importance.

Fromm's Freudian Marxism

The key theoretical essays outlining the Institute's materialist social psychology were published by Fromm in the *Zeitschrift für Sozialforschung*. Fromm was a practicing psychoanalyst who also held an academic position as lecturer in the Institute for Psychoanalysis at the University of Frankfurt. In addition, he was interested in Marxism and sociology, and joined the Institute as its psychology expert in 1929.[20] Fromm was one of the first to attempt to synthesize Marx and Freud, so as to develop a Marxian social psychology. Many other members of the Institute were to attempt similar syntheses, though the precise mixture and interpretations of Freud and Marx were often quite different.

Fromm sketches the basic outline of his project in an article entitled 'The Method and Function of an Analytic Social Psychology', subtitled 'Notes on Psychoanalysis and Historical Materialism'.[21] He begins by discussing the basic principles of psychoanalysis, and then indicates why he thinks Freud's theory, properly interpreted and reconstructed, is compatible with historical materialism. For Fromm, psychoanalysis is a materialist psychology which analyzes instinctual drives and needs as the motive forces for human behavior. It carries out an inventory of the basic instincts, and dissects the unconscious forces and mechanisms that sometimes control human behavior. Psychoanalysis also analyzes the influence of specific life experiences on the inherited instinctual constitution. Thus, in Fromm's view, Freud's theory is 'exquisitely historical: *it seeks to understand the drive structure through the understanding of life history*' (*CoP*, p. 139).

For Fromm the key conception of psychoanalysis is the '*active and passive adaptation of the biological apparatus, the instincts, to social reality*' (*CoP*, p. 141). Psychoanalysis is especially valuable for social psychology in that it seeks 'to discover the hidden sources of the obviously irrational behavior patterns in societal life – in religion, custom, politics, and education' (ibid.). Fromm therefore believes that an 'analytical social psychology' is thoroughly compatible with historical materialism, since both are materialist sciences which 'do not start from "ideas" but from earthly life and needs. They are particularly close in their appraisal of consciousness, which is seen by both as less the driving force behind human behavior than the reflection of other hidden forces' (p. 142). Although historical materialism tends to assume the primacy of economic forces and interests in individual and social life, whereas the psychoanalytic focus is on instinctual and psychological forces, Fromm believes that they can be fruitfully synthesized. In particular, he believes that an analytical social psychology can study the ways in which socio-economic structure influences and shapes the instinctual apparatus of both individuals and groups.

The psychoanalytic emphasis on the primacy of the family in human development can also be given a historical materialist twist, Fromm believes. Since 'the family is the medium through which the society or the social class stamps its specific structure on the child', analysis of the family and of socialization processes can indicate how society reproduces its class structure and imposes its ideologies and practices on individuals. Psychoanalytic theories which abstract from study of the ways in which a given society socializes its members into accepting and reproducing a specific social structure, Fromm suggests, tend to take bourgeois society as a norm, and to illicitly universalize their findings. Historical materialism provides a corrective by stressing the intrinsically historical nature of all social formations, institutions, practices and so on.

Fromm's essay is primarily programmatic, and does not specify in great detail *how* bourgeois capitalist society reproduces its structures within its members. Rather he is concerned to outline a research program and to argue for the compatibility of psychoanalysis and Marxism, proposing that psychoanalysis 'can enrich the overall conception of historical materialism on one specific point. *It can provide a more comprehensive knowledge of one of the factors that is operative in the social process: the nature of man himself*' (*CoP*, p. 154). For Fromm, natural instincts are part of the base (*Unterbau*) of society. He therefore believes that our understanding of human behavior and social processes will be enriched by knowledge of how society molds and adapts instincts to its structures, and how human beings shape and change their environments to meet their needs.

In certain fundamental respects, the instinctual apparatus itself is a biological given; but it is highly modifiable. The role of primary formative factors goes to the economic conditions. The family is the essential medium through which the economic situation exerts its formative influence on the individual's psyche. The task of social psychology is to explain the shared, socially relevant, psychic attitudes and ideologies – and their unconscious roots in particular – in terms of the influence of economic conditions on libido strivings. (*CoP*, p. 149)

Fromm also suggests that psychoanalysis can help to explain how socio-economic interests and structures are transformed into ideologies, as well as how ideologies shape and influence human thought and behavior. Such a merger of Marx and Freud will immeasurably enrich materialist social theory, in Fromm's view, by providing analysis of the mediations through which psyche and society interact and reciprocally shape each other. Every society, he claims, has its own libidinal structure and its processes whereby authority is reproduced in human thought and behavior. An analytical social psychology must thus be deeply empirical if it is to explain how domination and submission take place in specific societies and thereby provide an understanding of how social and psychological change is possible.

In an essay from the same period entitled 'Psychoanalytic Character-ology and Its Relevance for Social Psychology', Fromm applies his analytic social psychology to an investigation of how bourgeois society forms dominant character types which reproduce social structures and submit to social authority.[22] A theory of social character would become central to Fromm's work, though in this essay he assumes in rather orthodox Freudian fashion that the 'general basis of psychoanalytic characterology is to view certain character traits as sublimations or reaction formations of certain instinctual drives that are sexual in nature' (*CoP*, pp. 164–5). Fromm then discusses Freud's theory of oral, anal and genital characters and how specific social structures produce and reward certain types of character traits while eliminating others. In particular, drawing on Werner Sombart's study of the 'bourgeois' and on Benjamin Franklin's diaries, Fromm discusses how bourgeois society produced a character structure in which duty, parsimoniousness, discipline, thrift and so on became dominant traits of the bourgeois character structure, while love, sensual pleasure, charity and kindness were devalued.

Anticipating later Institute studies of the changes within personality in contemporary capitalism, Fromm writes of developments of character structure under monopoly capitalism and says:

It is clear that the typical character traits of the bourgeois of the nineteenth century gradually disappeared, as the classic type of the self-made, independent entrepreneuer, who is both the owner and the manager of his own business, was disappearing. The character traits of the earlier business man became more of a handicap than a help to the new type of capitalist. A description and analysis of the latter's psyche in present-day capitalism is another task that should be undertaken by psychoanalytic social psychology. (*CoP*, p. 185)

Fromm would later describe in detail the dominant character types within contemporary capitalist societies.[23] One of his most interesting attempts to develop a materialist social psychology in the early 1930s, however, is found in his study of Johann Jacob Bachofen's theory of matriarchy in an article 'The Theory of Mother Right and its Relevance for Social Psychology'.[24] Fromm shows how Bachofen's study had been appropriated by both socialist thinkers, such as Engels and Bebel, and conservative thinkers. After criticizing the conservative version of the theory of matriarchy, Fromm suggests how it can be appropriated by progressive thought. To begin with, Bachofen provides insights, Fromm believes, into how woman's nature develops from social practices; specifically, how the activity of mothering produces certain nurturing, maternal character traits associated with women, thus anticipating recent feminist theories of mothering.[25]

Moreover, Fromm suggests that Bachofen's theory of the matriarchal society reveals

a close kinship with the ideals of socialism. For example, concern for man's material welfare and earthly happiness is presented as one of the central ideas of matriarchal society. On other points, too, the reality of matriarchal society as described by Bachofen is closely akin to socialist ideals and goals and directly opposed to romantic and reactionary aims. According to Bachofen, matriarchal society was a primeval democracy where sexuality is free of christian depreciation, where maternal love and compassion are the dominant moral principles, where injury to one's fellowman is the gravest sin, and where private property does not yet exist. (*CoP*, pp. 118–19)

For Fromm, the crucial question concerning the theory of matriarchy is not whether a matriarchal society as described by Bachofen actually existed. Rather, in Fromm's view, the theory of matriarchy represents a certain set of institutions, attitudes and values opposed to capitalist patriarchal society. For this reason, it won wide approval 'from those socialists who sought, not reform, but a thoroughgoing change of society's social and psychic structure' (*CoP*, p. 120).

In Fromm's reading, Bachofen points out the relativity of existing societal relationships and institutions such as marriage, monogamy, private property and so forth. Fromm suggests that such views on the social con- structedness of social arrangements should 'be welcomed by a theory and political activity that advocated a fundamental change of the existing social structure' (CoP, p. 123). There were other political reasons as well why such a theory could appeal to progressives:

Aside from the fact that the theory of matriarchy underlined the relativity of the bourgeois social structure, its very special content could not but win the sympathy of Marxists. First of all, it had discovered a period when woman had been the authority and focal point of society, rather than the slave of man and an object for barter; this lent important support to the struggle for woman's political and social emancipation. The great battle of the eighteenth century had to be picked up afresh by those who where fighting for a classless society. (CoP, p. 123)

Fromm concludes the study by pointing to compatibilities between matricentric tendencies and Marxism, and hence between Marxism and feminism:

The psychic basis of the Marxist social program was predominantly the matricentric complex. Marxism is the idea that if the productive capabilities of the economy were organized rationally, every person would be provided with a sufficient supply of the goods he needed – no matter what his role in the production process was; furthermore, all this could be done with far less work on the part of each individual than had been necessary up to now, and finally, every human being has an unconditional right to happiness in life, and this happiness basically resides in the 'harmonious unfolding of one's personality' – all these ideas were the rational, scientific expression of ideas that could only be expressed in fantasy under earlier economic conditions: Mother Earth gives all her children what they need, without regard for their merits. (CoP, pp. 134–5)

While one might contest Fromm's reading of Bachofen and whether the theory of matriarchy can be put to progressive uses, it is interesting to note his concern for the emancipation of women and his attacks on patriarchy. One also notes his concern, shared by other key members of the Institute, for sensual gratification and happiness. He believes that Bachofen's emphasis on 'material happiness on earth' and 'social hedonism' in his theory of matriarchy helps to explain its appeal to socialist thinkers (CoP, p. 125). It also underlines Fromm's own commitment to material happiness and sensual gratification in a discussion of how sexuality 'offers one of the most elementary and powerful opportunities for satisfaction and happiness' (p. 126).

Studies on Family and Authority

Fromm also played a key role in the most substantial research project undertaken by the Institute for Social Research in the 1930s, a multidisciplinary inquiry into the connections between family and authority. The results of a five-year study were published in 1936 in a two-volume 'research report' Studien über Autorität und Familie.[26] The first section consisted of three theoretical studies, by Horkheimer, Fromm and Marcuse, and was edited by Horkheimer; the second part was edited by Fromm and consisted of studies of socialization in different classes, with special studies of sexual education, socialization of youth and socialization in unemployed families; the third part, edited by Lowenthal, consisted of individual studies of a variety of topics in the area of family and authority in different countries.

The Institute intended to combine its theoretical efforts with social research, in such a way that the theory would help guide the research, and the results of the empirical research would refine and modify the theory. Institute theorists intended to investigate an area of social life neglected by classical Marxism and to produce materialist theories of socialization which would contribute to both the materialist social theory and a materialist social psychology. In the Preface to the first volume, Horkheimer insisted that the studies published were but 'progress reports' which 'can have full meaning only in connection with a general theory of social life of which they form a part' (p. 899). The topics of authority and family arose within the framework of Institute research into the interconnections between various spheres of social life. In particular, the studies were concerned with how economic factors influenced the family and how family socialization constituted attitudes toward authority. They were also concerned with identifying changes within the family and authority, and with conceptualizing current socialization patterns in an attempt to explain why individuals were presently submitting to irrational authority in fascist countries.

Studies of authority convinced Horkheimer and his colleagues that 'the strengthening of the belief that there must always be a superior and an inferior, and that obedience is a necessity, constitutes one of the most important cultural factors in the dynamic forces that shape society' (p. 900). Since attitudes toward authority are shaped first and foremost within the family, Horkheimer suggested that study of how the family produced patterns of submission and obedience to dominant authorities would provide insight into how authority functions both within the family and within society at large.

In his introductory theoretical essay, Horkheimer provides a general overview of theoretical issues bearing on the themes of family and authority.[27] He polemicizes against both idealist theories which assume a unified, harmonious society and culture and vulgar materialist theories which reduce all institutions and social life to reflexes of the economic. Pointing to the dialectical approach characteristic of the Institute, Horkheimer argues that, as economic conditions evolve, new social and cultural forces emerge which may put in question patterns of traditional authority. While outmoded patterns of authority and ideas may persist (Horkheimer gives as examples ancestor worship and the caste system in

China and India), such 'unequal development' gives rise to new tensions and conflicts, which in turn produce new social and cultural configurations. Consequently, investigation of structures of authority and their 'changing significance, of the decay of the old and the birth of new forms of authority at the present time, constitutes an important task of sociology' (p. 903).

Horkheimer points to growing conflicts between previous bourgeois anti-authoritarian critiques of tradition and contemporary irrationalist submission to authority. He saw changes within the economy and the family as contributing to the growth of submission to irrational authority. Whereas, earlier, the father held authority through his role as economic provider, in a crisis economy patriarchal authority declines, and individuals are subject more directly to forces of social authority. Thus, while the family still plays a crucial role in producing authoritarian personalities, extra-familial socializing factors should also be taken into consideration.

In his theoretical essay, Fromm attempted to provide conceptual tools for analyzing the relations between authority and the family. He and his colleagues sought to specify 'the psychological impulses which cause people to submit to authority, and which make this submission pleasurable without regard to the nature of the commands' (p. 908). Fromm claims that Freudian theory provides 'by far the best approach for the understanding of the psychic dynamics of authority', and he uses the Freudian categories of the ego, superego and sado-masochism to elucidate the mechanisms of authority and submission.

Following Freud, Fromm presents the superego as the internalization of social authority,

and specifically of the father in the patriarchal family of modern times. Since the outer authority is internalized, the individual obeys its commands and prohibitions, not only because of real fear of external punishment, but also because of fear of that inner censor which he has created within himself. While the super-ego owes its existence to an internalization of authority, this existence is constantly reenforced by a projection of the super-ego upon the representatives of authority. The latter are endowed with the qualities of the super-ego, its morality, its wisdom and strength, in a manner largely independent of the realities of the case. In this way, these authorities become better and better adapted to further internalization and better suited to their role of bearers of the super-ego. In this manner a continuous circuit is established. The super-ego-authority relationship is hence dialectical. (p. 908)

Fromm then describes how the family is the key institution in the production of the superego and how development of a strong superego facilitates repression of rebellious impulses. Weak egos submit to superego authority; therefore Fromm calls for the production of stronger egos that will make possible more independent thought and action. He saw this as particularly urgent, since he believed that people's egos were becoming so weak that 'the masochistic character' appears almost 'normal'. 'Character' for Fromm refers to specific personality structures which result from repression and sublimation of instinctual drives, reaction formations and socialization processes.[28] 'Social character' refers to dominant character structures in different societies. The masochistic character, Fromm believes, is closely bound up with sadism. Fromm's main emphasis in this essay is on the sado-masochistic character which he believes is becoming a major aspect of the psychic apparatus of authoritarian societies. A sado-masochistic character submits to dominant authorities and higher powers, but in turn lords it over those below him or her in the social hierarchy. The masochistic character derives pleasure both from submission to higher authorities and from imposing authority on lower strata. This character type thus helps reproduce social authority, and contributes to an increase in social domination and aggression.

Fromm claimed that authoritarian societies produce those needs and satisfactions which in turn result in sado-masochistic character structures. Likewise, he believed that as economic conditions worsened, social anxiety grew, and that while the authority of the father in the family might decline, the power of social authorities often increased, subjecting individuals to more direct domination by society. In a concluding discussion of insubordination, Fromm calls for rebellion against irrational authority and development of strong egos which do not derive pleasure from either subordination or domination, and which are independent of dominant authority, yet able to recognize rational authority.

Other Institute members would later be more skeptical than Fromm concerning the possibilities of developing independent egos in contemporary capitalist societies; and eventually much more emphasis would be put on the institutions of mass culture and politics in directly socializing individuals (see Chapter 5). Yet concern with family, authority and socialization would continue to characterize the Institute's social theories in the following years. Such studies would contribute to their later theories of contemporary capitalism (see 3.2) and fascism (see 3.3). While working on these substantive projects, however, the Institute saw the need to distinguish more clearly its research program and theory from traditional theory and other contemporary theories and research. Its meta-theoretical discussions eventually led the Institute to present its theory as a Critical Theory of society.

2.3   Traditional and Critical Theory

While in exile at Columbia University in New York, the Institute explicitly adopted the term 'Critical Theory' to characterize its position. This period

(1937–40) was marked by the defeat of the labor movement in Germany, the triumph of fascism and increasing doubts about the Soviet Union as revelations of its trials, labor camps and Stalinist deformations became widespread. These crises of Marxism required new reflections on the relation between politics and theory, the role of the radical intellectual and the nature of socialism. In essays published at this time, both Horkheimer and Marcuse 'expressly emphasize that a change in property relations implies merely a negative precondition for the building of a socialist society'.[29] As Marcuse put it, 'Without freedom and happiness in the social relations of human beings, even the greatest increase in production, even the abolition of private property in the means of production, remains infected with the old injustices.'[30]

Critical Theory was thus animated by interests in freedom, happiness and justice, and attempted to synthesize the philosophical components of Marxism with a critique of political economy and socialist politics. The Institute adopted the term 'Critical Theory' to define its theoretical position in part because conditions of exile in the United States forced it to use code words to describe its project in order to cover over its commitment to Marxism in an environment that was quite hostile to a theory associated with socialist revolution and the Soviet Union. The label stuck, however, and many of the inner circle utilized it to define their theoretical position for the rest of their lives. Consequently the Institute's theoretical labors as a whole are frequently subsumed under the blanket concept 'Critical Theory', though, as we shall see, the term was eventually used to cover work in different contexts that was often quite different in character, intention and substance.

What, then, is the Critical Theory of society? The question can be answered by a careful examination of Horkheimer's essay 'Traditional and Critical Theory' in conjunction with other Institute publications of the 1930s.[31] In general, Critical Theory strives to provide both a substantive social theory of the present age and a meta-theory concerning theory and method. On the one hand, it involves a set of ways of looking at theory and the world and a set of investigative, research, textual and political practices. On the other, it provides a substantive, comprehensive theory of the present age, as well as a methodological orientation for doing social theory and research and for relating theoretical work to radical politics. Since its context, its starting point and frame of reference, is history and society – and thus macrotheory – Critical Theory is guided by the conviction that all inquiry, all thought, all political action and all informed human behavior must take place within the framework of a comprehensive and global Critical Theory of society which contains a synthesis of philosophy, the sciences and politics. Building on the Institute's research projects, ideology critiques of bourgeois philosophy and social theory and the meta-theoretical work of the past decade, Horkheimer attempts in 'Traditional and Critical Theory' to spell out the presuppositions of the Institute's project and its relation to traditional theory.

Traditional theory from Descartes through positivism is characterized by what is now called 'foundationalism', an attempt to ground theory in simple particulars, in basic 'facts' and theoretical postulates which form the foundation of the theory, which then builds its theoretical constructs on this foundation. Traditional theory tends to be deductive and to privilege science and mathematics; its goal, Horkheimer claims, is unity and harmony, with mathematics as its model (*CT*, p. 190). He suggests that traditional theory is thus a projection of the bourgeois ideal of the harmonious capitalist market unified by calculable laws of supply and demand.

Critical Theory frequently shows the relationships between ideas and theoretical positions and their social environment, and thus attempts to contextualize, or historicize, ideas in terms of their roots in social processes. Following this line of inquiry, Horkheimer suggests that traditional theory is itself in part a result of the social practices that constituted capitalism and bourgeois society. Its tendencies toward mechanistic materialism reproduced the mechanistic thought and practice of the industrial revolution, which conceptualized the world as a machine during an era in which machines came to dominate human beings. The dominant bourgeois trends of abstract and quantitative thought which informed traditional theory reproduced the tendencies toward abstraction and quantification based on exchange in the capitalist market, where value was expressed in quantitative terms. Just as a bourgeois society governed by exchange value abstracted from values, goals, sentiments and qualities, so too did traditional theory. Finally, the fragmentation and division of the sciences reproduces the bourgeois division of labor under capitalism whereby specialization and fragmentation are dominant features of the structure of society.

Social theories, for Critical Theory, are thus forms of social practice which reproduce dominant forms of capitalist activity.[32] Traditional theory, claims Horkheimer, is unaware of the ways in which it is bound up with social processes, and thus fails to see its lack of autonomy and its social determination. As it became increasingly involved in social processes of production and reproduction, it became increasingly conformist, uncritically submitting to the dominant instrumental, quantitative and capitalist values. Unaware of its social determination, 'theory was absolutized ... and became a reified, ideological category' (*CT*, p. 194). Consequently, 'The scholar and his science are incorporated into the apparatus of society; his achievements are a factor in the conservation and continuous renewal of the existing state of affairs, no matter what fine names he gives to what he does' (p. 196).

While traditional theory uncritically reproduces the existing society, Critical Theory, by contrast, is an expression of activity which strives to transform it. As Horkheimer put it,

There is a human activity that has society itself for its object. The aim of this activity is not simply to eliminate one or another abuse, for it regards such abuses as necessarily connected with the way in which the social structure is organized. Although it itself emerges from the social structure, its purpose is not, either in its conscious intention, or in its objective significance, the better functioning of any element in the structure. On the contrary, it is suspicious of the very categories of better, useful, appropriate, productive, and valuable, as these are understood in the present order, and refuses to take them as nonscientific presuppositions about which one can do nothing. (*CT*, pp. 206–7)

Critical Theory is thus rooted in 'critical activity', which is oppositional and involved in a struggle for social change and the unification of theory and practice. 'Critique', in this context, therefore involves criticism of oppression and exploitation and the struggle for a better society. Much of the last half of 'Traditional and Critical Theory' (*CT*, pp. 213–43) defines the relation between Critical Theory and Marxism, though the affinity is formulated in allusive code words and is not always immediately clear. Yet, in addition to its critique of vulgar, Marxian, mechanistic materialism and economic reductionism and determinism, Critical Theory also rejects efforts to ground Marxism in proletarian class consciousness and its embodiment in a Communist Party, a concept that governed Lukács's earlier work. Horkheimer argues that 'even the situation of the proletariat is, in this society, no guarantee of correct knowledge' (p. 213). While the proletariat may have knowledge of its exploitation and wretchedness, the fragmentation of the working class and the fact that many of its members are brutalized and undereducated, while others fall prey to conservative or reformist tendencies, means that there is no guarantee that its consciousness will be either theoretically correct or revolutionary.

Nonetheless, a careful reading of Horkheimer's 'manifesto' makes it clear that the Institute saw itself at the time as part of the tradition of Hegelian Marxism, and grounded its theory in the Marxian critique of political economy. Horkheimer and his associates firmly adhere to the Marxian position that the economy is the crucial determining factor for all social life and individual activity, and Critical Theory accepts the Marxian critique of capitalism which sees all social problems as ultimately rooted in the irrationality and contradictions of the capitalist mode of production. For example, Horkheimer writes: 'The categories which have arisen under its influence criticize the present. The Marxian categories of class, exploitation, surplus value, profit, impoverishment and collapse are moments of a conceptual whole whose meaning is to be sought, not in the reproduction of the present society, but in its transformation to a correct society' (*CT*, p. 218).

Critical Theorists insist on the necessity of a theory of society grounded in a theory of capitalism to make sense of socio-historical processes and developments, because the dynamics of capitalism play such a constitutive role in social life. Furthermore, to understand and explain social phenomena, one must contextualize one's topic of inquiry within a comprehensive theoretical framework for social analysis and critique, so as to avoid illegitimate abstraction which would analyze a political or cultural phenomenon apart from its constitution in socio-economic processes. Yet, while critics of totalizing modes of thought often attack Critical Theory's use of Hegelian-Marxian concepts of totality, I would argue that Critical Theory does not operate with either a fetishized or a reified concept of totality. Indeed, polemics against the concept of totality, or totalizing modes of thought, generally do not distinguish between varying senses and types of 'totality'.[33] Often 'totality' is identified with a harmonizing metaphysical mode of thought which stresses coherence, unity and order and in which all parts are seen as elements of a whole in which holistic harmony is posited as a normative value. The Institute sharply rejected such metaphysical concepts of totality, and used the term 'totality' in different ways in different contexts.

Frequently, Critical Theorists used the term in a synchronic sense to refer to the structure of society, defined by the Marxian critique of political economy, which provides the framework and context of inquiry and constitutes many social facts. They begin with the categories of economics and the Marxian critique of political economy precisely because the economy plays a constitutive role within all areas of social life and provides the framework for developing a theory of society. Marx's concepts of commodity, money, value and exchange characterize not only economics but also social relations when social relations and everyday life are governed by commodity and exchange relations and values. In this sense, Critical Theory utilizes totalizing concepts to describe a totalizing capitalist society which attempts to impose its values, structures and practices throughout society.

The concept of totality refers in other contexts to the diachronic, or historical, perspectives of Critical Theory, which both characterize the historical conditions that have produced the existing capitalist society and conceptualize the vicissitudes of capitalist development and the (hoped for) transition to socialism. Thus, rather than operating with a static or metaphysical notion of totality, the Institute utilized dynamic and historical modes of totalizing thought. The Institute's justification for its macrotheories of society were thus that: (1) capitalist society is organized as a system, and requires systematic theory to grasp its social organization; (2) the logic and social processes of capitalism penetrate into ever more domains of social life, requiring a theory of capitalist society as a whole to explain developments and processes in every domain of social reality; consequently, since capitalist society is totalizing, so too must social theory be totalizing; (3) capitalist society constantly changes and develops, and requires global historical analysis of its various stages and transformations; and (4) social critique and transformation require delineation of historical alternatives and normative values which can be used to criticize existing states of affairs and to argue for alternative values and organization of society.

Critical Theory is thus intrinsically global and historical, and attempts to provide the 'big picture' that portrays the fundamental outlines of socio-economic development and the ways in which the vicissitudes of capitalism structure social life and can in turn be replaced by a socialist society. Yet the Institute was constantly on the alert to avoid any sort of economic reductionism, and was especially concerned to trace the linkages between the economy and the political, social, cultural and psychic realms, while stressing the relative autonomy of the superstructure. They described the mediations between these spheres, as well as the contradictions, and thus produced what might be called a 'mediated totality'. That is, the Critical Theorists believed that the boundaries between the various realms of existence reproduced in the fragmentation of the scientific disciplines were artificial and abstract. Consequently, to pursue theoretical and political issues intelligently required supradisciplinary research and a dialectical method of presentation which demonstrated in concrete detail the interconnections and conflicts between the primary areas of the socio-historical totality that constitutes the context and framework for thought and action. Dialectics for the Institute involved cognitive mapping and making connections, or mediations. Social theory therefore involved construction of a model of the current society and a demonstration of the fundamental connections – as well as contradictions and conflicts – between the various domains of the current social system. The result was a theory of a mediated totality which described various relations between spheres of reality, rather than reducing all society to the dynamics of the economy.

Thus the Institute attempted to avoid reductionistic materialism, which would reduce all social and cultural phenomena to their economic base, and stressed instead the reciprocal interaction between base and superstructure and the relative autonomy of the various spheres. For example, in the introduction to the Institute's collective study of authority and the family, Horkeimer wrote that for many years their primary focus was on

the interconnections between the various spheres of civilization, material and intellectual. It was not merely a matter of investigating how changes in one field find expression also in other realms of social life. The problem was a more fundamental one: namely, to investigate the continuous inter-relationships between the various spheres of culture or civilization, how they are significantly related and how these interconnections are continuously modified and renewed.... Among all spheres of social life prevails a characteristic reciprocal interaction. Tensions and antagonisms arise which lead to new formulations within the social whole or to its decay.[34]

In fact, theory itself had a mediating function for Critical Theory, integrating science and philosophy and mediating between research (*Forschung*) and theoretical construction and presentation (*Darstellung*). Critical Theory would mediate between various domains of reality, between parts and whole, between appearance and essence, and between theory and practice. Pursuing such an ambitious research and political program required synthesizing empirical and historical research with the broader theoretical and critical perspectives often associated with philosophy. Yet, in his programmatic essay 'Traditional and Critical Theory', Horkheimer underplayed the role of philosophy; and apparently debates within the Institute led him to add a 'Postscript' to his original essay which highlighted in more detail the synthesis of philosophy, political economy and revolutionary politics which characterized Critical Theory.[35] Critical Theory's goal of a rational society, Horkheimer suggests, follows rationalist philosophy's demand that reason shape the totality of life and its activist concept of rational/critical activity (*CT*, pp. 244ff.). Yet 'the theory never aims simply at an increase of knowledge as such. Its goal is man's emancipation from slavery' (p. 245).

Critical Theory is thus motivated by a dual interest in a rational society and the liberation of the individual from bondage to a system of exploitation and domination. It also aims at the full realization and development of individual potentialities: 'The new dialectical philosophy, however, has held on to the realization that the free development of individuals depends on the rational constitution of society. In radically analyzing present social conditions it became a critique of the economy' (*CT*, p. 246). Note here how Horkheimer identifies his enterprise as a 'dialectial philosophy' related to the critique of political economy. The rest of the 'Postscript', in fact, sketches in some detail its specific relation to Marxism and the revolutionary struggle for a better society.

Yet there are some significant differences between Horkheimer's presentation of Critical Theory and classical Marxism. Marxism tends to be rooted in a primacy of production and to explain social phenomena and trends in terms of the dynamics of commodity production and capital accumulation.[36] Horkheimer, by contrast, tends to maintain the primacy of exchange – and thus distribution and circulation – over production, claiming that 'The Critical Theory of society begins with abstract determinations; insofar as it deals with the present epoch, with a characterization of an economy based on exchange' (*CT*, p. 225). Indeed, the Institute tended to downplay the process of production and to focus its analysis on exchange, consumption, distribution and so on.

Classical Marxism also tends to root its analysis of social contradictions in a historical theory, in a dynamic account of how contradictions generate change. While there are references to contradictions and conflicts within capitalism in Horkheimer's analysis, they tend to be abstract, inert and static. The relative lack of historical and political analysis in 1930s Critical Theory is in part a result of the excessively theoretical focus of the theory and in part a function of exile and the historical circumstances of the period. Despite their calls for the revolutionary transformation of society and for relating theory to practice to make social theory an instrument of emancipation, the Critical Theorists found themselves increasingly distanced from actual political struggles. Hence their calls for liberation or revolution during this period became increasingly paradoxical. From this vantage point, Critical Theory represents a stage in the development of neo-Marxian social theories during which radical intellectuals were separated from revolutionary socialist movements, while fascism steadily gained power throughout the world. The Institute theorists were among the first to describe this situation and to make explicit the problems for the Marxian theory of revolution when the working class was defeated or became integrated into capitalist societies. This remains one of the defining features of the trajectory of Critical Theory to this day and points to why the Institute felt it necessary to update and revise the Marxian theory and critique of capitalism, as well as the Marxian theory of revolution and the transition from capitalism to socialism.

Thus, as Dubiel puts it, 'By 1937, the subject and addressee of revolutionary theory are separated much more clearly in the Frankfurt Circle's political self-interpretation. Horkheimer maintains repeatedly that, for the sake of the adequacy of the theory, the critical intellectual must be able to endure marginalization from the addressee of his theoretical work.'[37] This situation came about in part because of the Institute's forced emigration to the United States during the era of fascism; and in the next chapter I shall present its analyses of the new stage of capitalism and of fascism, and shall reflect on the ways in which the experience of exile influenced its theory and politics.

3

Economy, State, Society: New Theories of Capitalism and Fascism

While in exile in the United States, the Critical Theorists produced analyses of the basic features of contemporary capitalist societies and of how capitalism shapes the dominant institutions, social processes, values and ideologies in the interests of profit and domination. In particular, Critical Theory explored the current relationships between the economy, state, society and culture and the transition from market capitalism to monopoly/state capitalism. As a consequence, the Institute for Social Research exploded the boundaries between fragmented academic disciplines and social sciences to provide a model of a comprehensive, supradisciplinary social theory grounded in a theory of the developments of capitalist society in the present age. Critical Theory is thus akin to Marxism during this period via its depiction of the fundamental interconnections and contradictions between various spheres of society and its analysis of the fundamental conflicts within a given historical period.

Critical Theory also conceptualizes borderlines between various stages of development of capitalist societies. It is a historical theory that analyzes socio-historical transformations and the transition from one stage of capitalist development to another. In this chapter, I shall explicate the general project of producing a Critical Theory of society of the contemporary era (3.1), and then discuss the Institute's account of the transition from liberal/market to monopoly/state capitalism (3.2), as well as its theory of fascism (3.3). The chapter will conclude with analyses of the contributions and deficiencies of the Institute's theories of contemporary capitalist and fascist societies and of the impact of the experience of emigration on the development of its theoretical and political perspectives (3.4).

3.1   Political Sociology and Political Economy

Recent scholarship has challenged the myth that the Critical Theorists were simply philosophers who had no knowledge of, or interest in, economics, politics, sociology or the other social sciences. In fact, not only did the Institute employ distinguished economists like Henryk Grossmann and Friedrich Pollock, but their work in political economy, or in what Andrew Arato calls 'political sociology', formed an important – indeed, foundational – component of Critical Theory.[1] Arato claims that the political sociology developed by Pollock, Neumann, Kirchheimer and others – specifically their theories of 'state organized industrial social formations' – provided 'part of the *groundwork* for the later (and better known) social philosophy of Horkheimer, Adorno, and Marcuse, *the missing complement* to Adorno's *cultural criticism*, and *the anticipation* of the much later critique of politics in the works of Jürgen Habermas and Claus Offe' (*FSR*, pp. 3–4).

Building on this position, I shall argue that one of Critical Theory's basic theoretical operations involved extension and transformation of Marxian categories derived from the critique of political economy into categories used to describe a wide range of economic, political, social and cultural processes and phenomena. In other words, I am suggesting that the early stages of Critical Theory can be read as an extension of the Marxian critique of political economy toward development of a comprehensive theory of society. It is congruent with classical Marxism in that it roots social theory in political economy, yet it goes beyond classical Marxism in expanding the critique to development of a theory of contemporary capitalist society in both its 'democratic' and fascist forms. Thus I am proposing that, while Critical Theory had a somewhat ambiguous relationship to the Marxist critique of political economy, the Institute's enterprise during the 1930s was grounded in a specific interpretation of the Marxian theory which Critical Theorists attempted to reconstruct in order to make it more appropriate to the conditions and demands of contemporary social theory and radical politics.

In particular, the members of the Institute were impressed with the critique of capitalism developed by Georg Lukács in *History and Class Consciousness*, and used his innovative analyses in original and illuminating ways.[2] Lukács, closely following Marx in *Capital*, argued that the *commodity* was the key unit of capitalist society, which should be defined as a system of commodity production. From this standpoint, all phenomena within capitalist societies should be interpreted from the point of view of the commodity and commodity production. Lukács claimed that capitalism was characterized by an expanding 'commodification' of the entirety of social life wherein everything from the worker to culture and sex becomes a commodity in the capitalist market. The process of commodification was closely connected with a process of 'reification' in Lukács's analysis. 'Reification' for Lukács described the process whereby individuals become like things, or more thing-like, and accordingly perceive themselves, other individuals, social processes and history as static, objectified entities detached from social and historical processes and the possibility of social and self-transformation.[3]

Lukács incorporated Max Weber's theory of bureaucracy and administration into his own theory.[4] He saw the growth of bureaucracies and administrations as intensifying the process of reification which classical Marxism rooted in production and the economic sphere, and thus fleshed out the political dimension of Marxian political economy. Both Lukács and the Institute used the categories of commodification, reification and administration to describe a wide range of social phenomena (see 3.2 and 3.3); and these concepts became basic to their repertoire.

Another major theoretical focus of the Institute was the category of exchange as a central form of social relations in capitalist society. Exchange, reification and commodification were in fact interconnected in capitalistic social processes. According to the Marxian theory, value in capitalist societies is constituted by exchange value, the worth of a person, object or service on the market. Market-constituted value is intrinsic to the commodification process, where everything becomes a commodity determined by its market value and price. In production, individuals exchange their labor power for a wage, and thus submit to wage slavery, and capitalists exchange the commodities produced for profit, and expropriate the surplus value produced to augment their own wealth and power.

The Institute extended the Marxian theory of exchange, arguing that capitalist market relations and values were penetrating ever more areas of life. For Critical Theory, exchange permeates labor, consumption and the ways in which individuals relate to themselves and the world. In contemporary capitalism, areas once separate from exchange and commodification, such as sex, love and culture, were becoming integrated into the system of exchange, and were increasingly becoming dominated by exchange values and relationships. In the Institute's view, then, exchange was becoming the primary way in which people related to and interacted with each other in a capitalist market society. Consequently reification, the turning of humans, culture, nature and everything else into commodities whose fundamental substance was exchange value, came to dominate relationships and activity within capitalist society.

In all these instances, categories used by Marx to describe economic processes were used by Lukács and the Institute to describe a wide range of social phenomena and processes, thereby transposing categories derived from the Marxian critique of political economy into categories of a theory of society. The Institute expanded the totalizing impetus of the Marxian theory to encompass areas of social life neglected by classical Marxism. It could justify doing so by arguing that capitalism itself was a totalizing system which attempted to penetrate every area of life from self-constitution to interpersonal relations to education, and that therefore totalizing concepts were necessary to describe the functioning of the capitalist system itself. Consequently, rather than neglecting the particular and reifying totalities as some critics claim, the Institute attacked totalizing social processes which themselves were destroying individuality and particularity.[5] From the beginning, Critical Theorists opposed all forms of totalitarianism, and saw the origins of modern totalitarian domination in the totalizing processes of capitalism and traditional theory. Consequently, against recent critiques of totalizing thought, I would argue that the Institute's use of totalizing categories was justified in the face of a society which, like its totalitarian counterparts in Nazi Germany and the Soviet Union, was itself attempting to control more and more aspects of life.

The Institute also utilized other totalizing categories in its Critical Theory of society, some of which were derived from traditional or contemporary theory and some of which they coined themselves. Both Lukács and the Institute, for instance, used the category of 'rationalization' – derived from Weber – to describe both fundamental tendencies of the economy and other regions of contemporary capitalist society. Lukács wrote in 1923: 'We are concerned above all with the *principle* at work here: the principle of rationalization based on what is and *can be calculated*. . . . Rationalization in the sense of being able to predict with ever greater precision all the results to be achieved is only to be acquired by the exact breakdown of every complex into its elements and by the study of the special laws governing production.'[6] The Institute described a variety of ways in which the economy, state, society, culture, everyday life, thought and theory were subject to processes of rationalization in their critiques of instrumental reason, which we shall discuss in the next chapter.

In addition, the Institute followed Weber and Lukács in perceiving rationalization as bound up with the growth of administration and bureaucracy.[7] Other totalizing categories developed by the Institute, which we shall examine and use in this and following chapters, include self-preservation, domination and homogenization, or massification. Such totalizing categories were deemed necessary, according to the Institute, because capitalist society was itself extending domination, massification, administration and so forth into ever more areas of social life. I shall introduce and expand discussion of these categories in the following chapters.

3.2   From Market to Monopoly/State Capitalism

One of the major focuses of the Institute in the 1930s was its development
of a theory of the transition from the stage of liberal/market capitalism to
the stage of monopoly/state capitalism. This process involved updating
and revising the classical Marxian theory of capitalism and the transition
to socialism, and this contributed to the eventual abandonment of key
aspects of Marxism by some members of the Institute. In this section, I
shall focus on some of the central essays by the Institute's chief economist,
Friedrich Pollock, and its director, Max Horkheimer, who generally took
on the responsibility of presenting the Institute's theoretical position in
synoptic form.

   In classical Marxism capitalism was defined as an economic system in
which commodity production, the market, private property and the private
appropriation of profit – that is of surplus value – determined the dynamics
of social life from labor through politics and law. For the Institute, 'liberal
capitalism' was characterized by the primacy of the supposed 'free market',
in which the individual entrepreneur was free to pursue his or her own
economic interests unimpeded by state regulation or interference. This
mode of economy was especially crisis-prone, and was harshly criticized by
classical Marxism as being anarchic, chaotic, destructive and doomed to
eventual demise. In the Marxian theory, the capitalist economy was subject
to periodic economic crises precisely because it lacked an economic plan,
and was plagued by falling rates of profit, overproduction and undercon-
sumption, uneven development between various sectors of capital and by
the contingencies of business cycles over which it had no control.[8] A
historical alternative to capitalism appeared to emerge with the Russian
revolution of 1917, which immediately instituted a planned economy with
the means of production socialized, supposedly belonging to the people and
to be administered and used in the people's interests. With the economic
crash of 1929, growing interest emerged in a planned economy. The
Institute studied the new economic developments and literature, including
the revision of liberal economics by Keynes and others.[9]

Pollock's Theory of State Capitalism

In 1929, Pollock traveled to the Soviet Union and undertook a study of
Soviet efforts to build a planned economy.[10] Pollock was a professionally
trained economist who was a close friend of Horkheimer and a key member
of the Institute, both as an administrator and as a theorist. Pollock and
some other Institute members carefully studied both the Russian and the
non-Communist literature on the planned economy, and participated in

the debates on the issue. In 1932 Pollock published his essay 'The Present Situation of Capitalism and the Outlook for an Economically Planned New Order'.[11] He argued that the 'liberal' phase of capitalism was coming to an end, following the collapse of the world economy in the late 1920s. Capitalist relations of production could no longer be counted on to develop the forces of production, as evidenced by the current massive unemployment, factory shutdowns, destruction or waste of raw materials, underutilization of machinery and productive capacity, and so on. Capitalism could only survive, Pollock claimed, if it inaugurated a planned economy. 'The manifest difficulties of the capitalist system, as well as the Russian planning efforts whose collapse was wrongly prophesied by nearly all experts, are the main reasons why today economic planning is being discussed everywhere' (p. 17).

However, different possibilities for state planning exist, and in his 1932 article Pollock outlined two basic types: (1) capitalist state planning of the type described by Hilferding in his study of how monopolies and economic cartels controlled markets which would preserve the capitalist relations of production; versus (2) a state model resting on collective ownership of the means of production such as in the Soviet Union. Both models entail replacement of a market economy by one governed by an economic plan, though state capitalism would operate in the interests of the capitalist class, whereas the alternative, socialist planned economy would presumably serve the interests of the entire population and be governed by satisfaction of human needs rather than imperatives to maximize capitalist profitability and domination.

It might be instructive to compare Pollock's analysis with classical Marxism at this point. According to a standard reading of Marxism, capitalist production and distribution through a market system were the essential features of Marx's model, which also delineated ways in which contradictions and disproportions between the circuits and sectors of capital would inevitably lead to crisis, which would then provoke a socialist revolution. Marx and Engels believed that the beginnings of state planning in capitalist societies would help to create the preconditions for socialism, although they and succeeding traditional Marxists envisaged a transition directly from market capitalism to socialism, and did not anticipate a form of state capitalism which would stabilize the capitalist economy.

Orthodox Marxian economics and crisis theory were represented within the Institute by Henryk Grossmann, who wrote one of the classical texts on crisis theory, published in 1929 as *The Law of Accumulation and Collapse of the Capitalist System*.[12] Grossmann subscribed to a rather orthodox version of Marx's economic theory, putting Marx's theory of accumulation at the center. He then attempted to show how unlimited capitalist accumulation was impossible by describing the obstacles that would eventually lead to the

collapse of the capitalist system. The book was published during the year of
the Great Crash of 1929, which it anticipated in its prognostic analysis.
Thus it was not able to draw upon the experiments in state planning in the
fascist countries or in Roosevelt's New Deal. Consequently, while Grossmann continued to be highly respected by some Institute members and to
maintain orthodox Marxian positions on capitalist crisis and collapse for
the most part, Horkheimer and his inner circle tended to side with Pollock,
who sketched out a theory in which the emergence of a capitalist state and
state planning would attempt to overcome the contradictions of the capitalist
market economy and to prevent its collapse.

Against orthodox Marxism, Pollock wrote in his 1932 essay: 'Without a
doubt it can be established that the crisis can be overcome by *capitalistic
means* and that "monopolistic" capitalism will be able to continue existing at
least for the foreseeable future' (p. 16). Pollock did not rule out the possibility that this new form of planned capitalism might contain its own crisis
tendencies; but he envisaged capitalism as capable of coming up with
survival strategies involving state planning and regulation and using at
least some features of a planned economy in its own interests. He wrote:
'There is considerable evidence, to be sure, that in this administered capitalism the depressions will be longer, the boom phases shorter and stronger,
and the crises more destructive than in the times of "free competition," but
its "automatic" collapse is not to be expected' (p. 16).

Pollock thus foresaw that an unregulated market capitalism would
inevitably produce ever worsening economic crises, and that a planned
economy of some sort was necessary for its very survival. Yet, against
Marxists who were proclaiming the imminence of the collapse of capitalism, Pollock argued that capitalism might come up with a type of planned
economy which would stabilize its crises, at least temporarily. Consequently, while socialism certainly provided an alternative to capitalism, the
transition to socialism was by no means automatic. Unlike Marx, however,
Pollock had no analysis of how the new stage of the capitalist economic
system was generating contradictions and crises that would produce socialist revolution as part of the immanent dynamic of the social system and
historical process itself. Likewise, he failed to indicate how the Depression
and new forms of capitalism were producing resistance and new forms of
struggle.

These lacunae in Pollock's analysis, lacunae that would be found in the
work of other Critical Theorists as well, become apparent in his 1933 article
'Remarks on Economic Crisis' and in his 1941 article 'State Capitalism'.[13]
In 'Remarks' Pollock argued that capitalism had proved itself 'incapable of
utilizing the forces that it had produced itself to serve the needs of all of
those belonging to the society' (p. 337). Massive intervention by the state,
however, might preserve the capitalist mode of production, temporarily at

least, and thereby save it from catastrophic collapse. Pollock described some of the ways in which the capitalist state was currently intervening in the economy to minimize contradictions between the forces and the relations of production, 'which had become more intense than ever before'. Such intervention involved forcible destruction of excess productive forces – that is, closing down factories where production surpassed consumption or where production was no longer especially profitable – which Pollock described as a 'procrustean adjustment process'. Or there might be a relaxation of the fetters by which capital binds relations of production. Both these methods 'leave the *foundations* of the capitalist system untouched'; and they can be 'differentiated sharply only in thought', since they are in fact united in the practice of state capitalist management (p. 338).

Pollock saw that there were limits to the extent to which capitalists could employ state planning and still retain a *capitalist* society; but he envisaged no strictly economic factors that would inevitably lead to collapse and revolution. The transition to socialism, in his view, would not follow automatically from economic collapse; only the power of resistance and the struggles of the masses would make possible a transition to socialism. As he put it in his 1932 article, 'There is no *purely economic* irrepressible compulsion to replace it with another economic system' (p. 16; my emphasis).

Pollock saw that conditions existed for the transition to socialism, but he could not envisage how that transition would take place. In 1932, he wrote that the economic preconditions

can be formulated as follows: the major weight of industrial production must be shifted to large-scale mass production enterprise and the process of centralization must reach a certain level; the technical and organizational means for mastering the tasks of a centralized economic administration must be already known; and a considerable reserve of productivity must be available to be utilized through the application of the methods of economic planning. It can be easily demonstrated that all these economic presuppositions are to a great extent at hand in the great industrial nations, as well as in the world economy. (p. 20)

But Pollock also saw clearly that capitalism had a response to the world economic crisis in the mechanism of state planning. Thus, while he and other Institute members maintained an ideal of democratic control of the production process by 'associated individuals' who would use economic resources for the welfare and happiness of the majority of the people, they believed that the fundamental tendency of the historical process was moving toward control and administration of the economy in the interests of the strongest monopolistic groups, who would arbitrarily decide on 'the weal and woe of all remaining economic subjects, owners of capital, and workers' (Pollock 1933, p. 349). Indeed, Pollock believed that revolutionary struggle on the part of the proletariat was unlikely in the foreseeable future, as a result of the diminished role of the working class in the process of production, improved weapons technology in the hands of the ruling class and new forms of social control, such as mass culture, used as instruments of class domination.

Consequently Pollock believed that a capitalist planned economy was a more likely result of the Great Depression than a socialist revolution: 'It is not capitalism that is coming to an end but just its liberal phase' (p. 350). From this point forward, one of the main tasks of the Institute would be to analyse the enormous changes in economic, political, social and cultural life brought about by the transformations in the capitalist economy as responses to the 1930s Depression. The Institute attempted to conceptualize the changes resulting from new modes of organization of the economy, new relationships between the economy and the state in neo-capitalist social formations and new modes of culture and social control.

One of its tasks was to develop new categories and new theories to describe the nature and prospects of the new socio-economic formations that were emerging. In a 1941 article, Pollock argued that the term 'state capitalism' best characterizes the current form of capitalism which has supposedly replaced market capitalism. Pollock proposes adoption of the term because 'it indicates four items better than do all other suggested terms: that state capitalism is the successor of private capitalism, that the state assumes important functions of the private capitalist, that profit interests still play a significant role, and that it is not socialism' (*FSR*, p. 72). In state capitalism, a system of direct controls replaces market mechanisms for pricing, distribution and so on, and the state assures full employment and utilization of facilities through allocation and control of markets. Some 'free market' sectors remain, which Pollock calls 'pseudo markets', but on the whole the state plays the primary role in directing and managing the economy.

By 'state capitalism', Pollock does not mean a system in which the state is the sole property-owner, for he distinguishes between two dominant forms:

Under a totalitarian form of state capitalism, the state is the power instrument of a new ruling group, which has resulted from the merger of the most powerful vested interests, the top-ranking personnel in industrial and business management, the higher strata of the state bureaucracy, (including the military) and the leading figures of the victorious party's bureaucracy. Everybody who does not belong to this group is a mere object of domination. (*FSR*, p. 73)

This form is contrasted to a 'democratic form of state capitalism' in which 'the state has the same controlling functions but is itself controlled by the people. It is based on institutions which prevent the bureaucracy from transforming its administrative position into an instrument of power, and thus laying the basis for transshaping the democratic system into a totalitarian one' (*FSR*, p. 73). The 'totalitarian form of state capitalism' obviously refers to fascist economies, though in a note Pollock also sub-sumes the Soviet economy under this form (p. 174).[14] The 'democratic form' refers to the kind of economy emerging in the United States during Roosevelt's New Deal and the developments in European capitalist democracies (though it seems somewhat naive to assume that in any state capitalist form, the state is 'controlled by the people').

Pollock attempted to describe 'the new set of rules' governing the economy in state capitalism. In state capitalism, by contrast with market capitalism, a general plan provides the direction for production, consump-tion, savings and investment: 'Prices are no longer allowed to behave as masters of the economic process but are administered in all important sections of it.' While the profit motive is still in effect, it is subordinated to the general plan; principles of scientific management, administration and rationalization are applied to ever more activities and realms; and imple-mentation of the plan is enforced by state power, so that 'nothing essential is left to the functioning of laws of the market or other "economic" laws' (*FSR*, pp. 75–8).

Pollock thus believed that fundamental changes had taken place within the capitalist economy, which required revision of both bourgeois and Marxist economic theory: 'Government control of production and distri-bution provides the means with which the economic causes of depressions, cumulative processes of destruction, and unemployment due to lack of capital can be eliminated. We can even say that economics as a social science has lost its object under state capitalism' (*FSR*, p. 87). Against bourgeois economics, Pollock's argument suggests that a new form of *political* economy is needed to grasp the new relations between the economy and the state. But his analysis also puts in question the Marxian theory of the primacy of economics over all social life, and presents instead a position which advocates a 'primacy of the political'.[15]

Pollock argues that:

Under state capitalism men meet each other as commander or commanded; the extent to which one can command or has to obey depends in the first place upon one's position in the political set-up and only in a secondary way upon the extent of one's property. Labor is appropriated directly instead of by the 'roundabout' way of the market. Another aspect of the changed situation under state capitalism is that the profit motive is superseded by the power motive. (*FSR*, p. 78)

He claims that under state capitalism, the state acquires power over money and credit, and regulates production and prices. Furthermore, manage-ment becomes separate from ownership: 'The entrepreneurial and capital-ist functions are interfered with or taken over by the Government' (*FSR*,

p. 78), and 'the will to political power becomes the center of motivation' (p. 81).

Pollock's notions of 'state capitalism' and 'the primacy of the political' seem questionable, as does his analysis of the end of market society, which has in fact survived longer than Pollock or most other Marxist economists of the day anticipated. Indeed, the history of capitalism (and some experiments in state socialism) have shown that markets and state economic planning are not incompatible. One might also question Pollock's claim that in state capitalism, although a market price and a wage system remain in place, they no longer serve the general function of regulating the economic process, and that this role is assumed by the state. In this view, the economic function of private property has been abolished, and 'the capitalist has been transformed into a mere rentier' (*FSR*, p. 86).

It can be argued that Pollock's model blurs the extent to which capital still controls the state in democratic capitalist countries, by creating a model that abstracts certain general features from fascism and from Keynesian theory and its application in the New Deal. Such an abstract model covers over differences between democratic capitalist and fascist societies and the ways in which the capitalist class continues to play a central role in both the economy and the state, however differently, in both systems. On this point, Pollock would be contested within the Institute by Neumann in regard to fascism,[16] and I shall take up this debate in the next two sections.

The question arises, therefore, as to whether the capitalist state has assumed as many economic functions and has as much power as Pollock suggests.[17] Although both German fascism and the New Deal and the wartime economy of the United States in the 1930s and 1940s allowed the state to assume many of the functions and powers that Pollock described, since then the relations between the state and the economy have been more contradictory. In fact, one could argue that to a great extent capitalist corporations have increased their powers and that market forces have continued to play a major role in determining economic development. Pollock indicated that under state capitalism 'pseudo-markets' were allowed (*FSR*, p. 73), but argued that the state plays the primary role in determining prices, wages and employment, and distribution. In fact, however, a more mixed set of corporate and governmental forces has developed since the end of World War II and continues to the present. Thus, while Pollock's model of state capitalism describes some trends in contemporary capitalist societies, on the whole it tends to exaggerate the role of the state in most contemporary capitalist societies. (I shall bracket here the hotly disputed question of whether the concept of state capitalism adequately describes the Soviet Union, since the Institute itself did not really systematically address this issue.)

In addition, as Brick and Postone have argued, Pollock tends to ignore production in his theory of state capitalism, which centers on distribution. This omission is significant, they argue, for without focusing on commodity production, socialism merely becomes a new form of distribution, rather than a new mode of production and a new type of society.[18] That is, if the basic industrial framework and values of capitalist commodity production are assumed as a given, then socialism becomes merely a question of a more equitable system of distributing goods and social wealth, rather than a new system of production in which workers control the productive process as well as their social and political life – as postulated by Marx as the goal of socialism in his writings on the Paris Commune and his *Critique of the Gotha Program*.

Consequently, while Pollock analyzed some of the economic, natural and noneconomic limitations of state capitalism (*FSR*, pp. 87ff.), he really did not provide either a theory of social change or clear guidelines for political intervention within and against the capitalist state. Part of the problem derives from his method of analysis, which uses Weberian ideal types, or models, of various sorts of social formation, such as state capitalism and totalitarian versus democratic state capitalism. The problem with Weberian ideal types is that they tend to provide a static model of society rather than a more dynamic Marxian model which would root social trends within existing social relations and struggles. While Pollock's theory of state capitalism generalizes from contemporary historical situations, it brackets the possibility of both a resurgence of political struggle and an intensified economic crisis. Consequently, in Pollock's theory there are no analyses of the contradictions, tendencies and struggles that might lead to a society beyond capitalism – as one finds in classical Marxism.

For example, Marx and Engels always analyzed the ways in which new forms of capitalist organization provided new forms of working-class struggle or produced possibilities that could aid in the struggle for socialism. Likewise, Lenin in his analysis of the new stage of monopoly capitalism and imperialism looked at how these new forms of capitalism produced new forces of revolution, new national liberation movements, and how World War I gave rise to the conditions for the Russian revolution and the Soviets. By contrast, such a two-sided, multidimensional historical dialectic is lacking in Pollock and in most of the Frankfurt School analysis, which tends to focus solely on mechanisms of capitalist power and domination, while downplaying types and strategies of working-class struggle.

Pollock's analysis of state capitalism exerted an enormous influence on Horkheimer, Marcuse and other Institute members, however, and provided an important component of their Critical Theory of society. Although Pollock's theses were sharply disputed by Grossmann, Neumann and the more orthodox Marxian members of the Institute (see 3.4), in various ways Horkheimer, Adorno and Marcuse built their theory of the transition to a new stage of capitalism on Pollock's analyses, while developing their Critical Theory of contemporary society from this vantage point.

Horkheimer and 'The End of Reason'

Horkheimer's 'The End of Reason' provides a striking anticipation of some of the theses of *Dialectic of Enlightenment* and later Critical Theory, while presenting key aspects of the Institute's theory of fascism.[19] One sees in this article for the first time the contours of the new theory of society that would henceforth be associated with the Institute. Horkheimer's focus is on the differences between compliance to social domination in the earlier bourgeois epoch, brought about by the internalization of conscience and duty through rationalist education, religion and bourgeois socialization, and compliance brought about by the new direct forms of domination characteristic of fascism. His argument is that 'The substance of individuality itself, to which the idea of autonomy was bound, did not survive the process of industrialization' (*FSR*, p. 36).[20] Furthermore, matters have grown even worse in fascism and other totalitarian societies which increase pressures for conformity while whittling away the ego, possibilities for autonomy and individual thought and action. At this point, Horkheimer's essay becomes somewhat confusing, for, having begun with a general theory of the decline of reason and individuality (*FSR*, pp. 26–34), he then launches into an attack on fascism as gangsterism (pp. 34–6), and subsequently carries out an analysis of current social trends which could refer to both fascist and neo-capitalist societies (pp. 36–43). The concluding pages (pp. 43–8) accelerate the critique of fascism, and contain a passionate denunciation of fascist injustice and oppression.

In this essay Horkheimer starts out by analyzing the changes in thought, language and consciousness which accompany the transition to a new stage of capitalist society. In addition to the new economic and political conditions, Horkheimer alludes to changes in the nature of the family and of socialization which he believes have helped to produce a decline in critical thought and action:

With the decline of the ego and its reflective reason, human relationships tend to a point wherein the rule of economy over all personal relationships, the universal control of commodities over the totality of life, turns into a new and naked form of command and obedience. No longer buttressed by small-scale property, the school and the home are losing their educational function of preparing individuals for life in society. (*FSR*, p. 39)

In previous essays on the family, Horkheimer and his colleagues tended to follow the Freudian and other theories which center socialization in the family, and in particular in the authority of the father over wife and children. This situation was bound up with traditional oedipal conflicts and revolts of the son against the father, and while it produced much misery due to excessive discipline and repression, it also provided a situation in which the child could revolt against the father and become an autonomous ego, capable of independent thought and behavior. In contemporary capitalist societies, however, society is more directly socializing people, Horkheimer suggested, and the role of both family and schooling is declining.

The result is increased social conformity and a decline in individuality: 'Today the child imitates only performances and achievements; he accepts not ideas, but matters of fact' (*FSR*, p. 37). Authority, previously rooted in the family or in teachers or religious figures,

is the authority of the omnipotent standards of mass society. The qualities which the child needs in this society are imposed upon him by the collectivity of the school class, and the latter is but a segment of the strictly organized society itself. . . . Education is no longer a process taking place between individuals, as it was when the father prepared his son to take over his property, and the teacher supported him. Present-day education is directly carried out by society itself and takes place behind the back of the family. (*FSR*, p. 40)

Authority thus becomes less personal and more anonymous and difficult to combat. In Horkheimer's view, the school and the home are losing their educational, civilizing and socializing functions: 'Living and being prepared have become one and the same thing, just as with the military profession. In school, the hierarchy of sport and gymnastics triumphs over the class-room hierarchy' (*FSR*, p. 39). In addition, the father is no longer the social authority and representative of society: 'The child, not the father, stands for reality' (p. 41). But it is social reality as a whole, 'the power of what is and the efforts of adjustment to it', that are the source of social domination. In this situation, the major emphasis is on adjustment and conformity: 'Previously, men were mere appendages to the machine, today they are appendages as such. Reflective thought and theory lose their meaning in the struggle for self-preservation' (p. 38). Increasingly, in a society of organization and administration, there is loss of deliberation, free time, leisure and the possibility of doing nothing productive or practical. Individual reflection and its offspring, theory and philosophy, suffer in this situation. The result is both the decline of individual rationality and the integration of all modes of thought and behavior into the prevailing mode of production.

Horkheimer also argued that human relationships were ruled by the economy and society (*FSR*, pp. 39ff.). Sexuality and love were subject to processes of rationalization and control from above: 'Today, sex seems to be emancipated and still oppression goes on. Social regimentation of the relations between the sexes had gone far before racial eugenics consummated this process; it was expressed by the standardized normalcy in all spheres of mass culture' (p. 42). The culture industries provide instruction in proper techniques of courtship and romance, and sex manuals teach individuals how to perform properly and achieve maximum gratification. What was once a sphere of individuality and rebellion becomes a sphere of integration and conformity: 'Sex loses its power over men [sic]. It is turned on and off according to the requirements of the situation. Men no longer lose themselves in it, they are neither moved nor blinded by love' (p. 42).

Horkheimer's essay manifests an aphoristic-epigrammatic style, which would henceforth become characteristic of Critical Theory, particularly the work of Horkheimer and Adorno. Both these authors frequently use metaphors to depict social conditions, presenting society as a concentration camp or prison and characterizing fascism as a form of gangsterism. Both also use critiques of fascism to provide insight into what they see as the emerging trends in *all* capitalist societies, totalitarian and democratic. 'The End of Reason' concludes with a powerful attack on fascism and its irrationality, injustice, inhumanity and wanton sacrifice of lives (*FSR*, pp. 44ff.). Horkheimer's passion heats up as he sharply criticizes fascist domination; but the ending shows the political impasse that Critical Theory was entering with the world-wide triumph of fascism, the defeat of the working-class movement and the expansion of war and barbarism by the early 1940s.

Horkheimer concludes by arguing that in an irrational society, the chief function of reason becomes simply to call 'things by their name', to describe and denounce the barbarism taking place (*FSR*, p. 47). Clearly, Horkheimer and his colleagues were attempting to do precisely this in the 1930s and 1940s. Yet they were unable to formulate an appropriate political response, and they were coming to see their previous theoretical strategies as increasingly questionable. In the absence of a revolutionary proletariat and an emancipatory socialist alternative to state capitalism and fascism, the Institute found it increasingly difficult to advocate the Marxian politics of its 1930s essays. Cut off from addressees of the theory, it became ever more difficult to see Critical Theory as part of a revolutionary movement, to ground it in revolutionary practice.

The crux of the dilemma was that the triumph of fascism seemed to signal the end of the era of revolutionary politics. Resolutely confronting this historical impasse, the Critical Theorists increasingly focused their analysis on fascism itself and on the obstacles that it presented to socialist revolution and human freedom. The result was some of the Institute's most original and provocative work.

3.3   Fascism

The experience of fascism had a major impact on the thought, style, language and politics developed by the Institute of Social Research in the 1930s and 1940s. Its origin, nature and effects were a major topic of debate within the Institute from the time of the rise of Hitler and National Socialism to power. The triumph of German fascism drove the Institute into exile for the next several decades, and it devoted much energy to analyzing the fascist phenomenon. I would suggest that the Institute's direct experience of fascism, its hatred thereof, its intense concern with it over the next decades and the fact that it could analyze it from a distance in the United States all contributed to providing insights into fascism and the ways in which it was both a product of, and a rupture with, previous European civilization.

Marcuse's 'The Struggle against Liberalism in the Totalitarian View of the State' was one of the first Institute studies of fascism, and focused, characteristically, on fascist ideology and the ways in which it was both similar to and different from classical liberalism. Marcuse tells of how after a speech by Hitler at Dusseldorf's businessmen's club one day, Horkheimer and his colleagues decided that a study should be carried out of the origin and nature of fascist ideology, and assigned the task to him.[21] Arguing for a direct continuity between the previous liberal/market form of bourgeois society and fascism, Marcuse claimed that both liberalism and the totalitarian ideology provide successive defenses of the capitalistic economy and organization of society (N, p. 10). Whereas liberalism, Marcuse suggests, provided an adequate defense of 'European industrial capitalism in the period when the actual economic bearer of capitalism was the "individual capitalist, the private entrepreneur in the literal sense of the term" ' (p. 9), fascism corresponds to the 'monopoly capitalist requirements of economic development' (p. 10).

The Institute's theory and critique of fascism began with ideology critique, moved to socio-psychological analysis of the cultural roots of fascism in attitudes toward the family and authority (see 2.2) and eventually took the form of inquiries into the economic and political structure of fascism and the relative importance of economic versus political factors in its constitution. Discussion in this section will focus on the latter dimension, which increasingly preoccupied the Institute during the late 1930s and early 1940s.

Horkheimer and his colleagues agreed that there were important connections between liberal capitalism and fascism, and that fascism was the outcome of capitalist development, which had been going through phases of imperialism, monopoly, periodic crisis and challenges from the working-class movement. In his 1939 article completed on the first day of World War II, 'Die Juden und Europa', Horkheimer begins by stating that 'Whoever wants to explain anti-semitism must speak of National Socialism,' and then says: 'Whoever is not willing to talk about capitalism should remain silent about fascism as well.'[22] He argues that fascism should be perceived as a successor to liberal capitalism which consolidates and expands the trends toward monopoly and imperialism and which also uses the state to overcome the crisis tendencies and periodic mass unemployment, inflation and depressions endemic to market capitalism. The result is a new synthesis of monopoly capitalism and the totalitarian state which threatens to dominate the world and to eliminate its opponents and all vestiges of the earlier forms of liberal economy and politics.

While there was general agreement within the Institute that fascism could best be explained and understood as a product of monopoly capitalism in crisis, there was a debate as to whether fascism should be interpreted primarily from a classical Marxian perspective as a stage of capitalist development which saved capitalism from the dual threats of economic collapse and political upheaval or as a new type of post-capitalist social order in which the state assumed functions previously carried out by a market economy and thus became the primary arbitrator of socio-economic development. In the Institute debates, Pollock argued for 'the primacy of the political' in fascism, and claimed that it did constitute a new order; whereas Neumann argued that fascism preserved central features of the capitalist economy and should be interpreted as a new form of 'Totalitarian Monopoly Capitalism'.[23] Within the Institute, Horkheimer tended to side with Pollock, while Kirchheimer, Gurland and others tended to side with Neumann, though there were also attempts to mediate between the two sides, especially by Marcuse.

At stake in the debate was whether Marxian theories of 'determination in the last instance' by the economic were still relevant in the era of fascism. In the following discussion I will suggest that a Marxian approach which allows the 'relative autonomy of the superstructure' and the 'reciprocal interaction of base and superstructure' provides a viable framework for analysis of the new forms of neo-capitalist societies, including fascism, and that most Institute members adopted this dialectical approach – whichever side they took in the Pollock-Neumann debate. I will also show that arguments and material within both Pollock's and Neumann's works of the period often support the other's position, and that 'deconstructive' readings of both positions would show that Pollock himself constantly refers to the capitalist nature of fascism and the continuing importance of economic factors in the 'new order', while similar readings of Neumann show that he frequently documents the primacy of the political in fascism and the new relationships between state and economy.

In the early 1930s, during the period of the rise and triumph of fascism in Germany, Pollock shared the Institute position that a new form of monopoly capitalism was superseding liberal/market capitalism, and that National Socialism represented a phase within the development of capitalism that was not so much an irrational regression to an earlier, more barbaric state of humanity, but rather the logical process by which capitalist development proceeded from severe economic crisis to state management of the economy.[24] In Pollock's 1933 'Remarks on Economic Crisis', he argued that: 'The analysis of the causes of economic crisis . . . leads to the conclusion that it would be false to predict the necessary end of capitalism in the near future. . . . What is coming to an end is not capitalism, but its liberal phase. Economically, politically, and culturally the majority of human beings will have less and less freedom in the future' (p. 350). Turning to comment on fascism near the end of his article, Pollock concluded:

As a consequence of the release from the constraints of parliamentarianism and having at their disposal the entire apparatus of the psychic domination of the masses, the governments that are appropriate for this period appear to be independent from classes and to stand above society without partisanship. A sociological analysis of the new state-form is an indispensable task of the present; the economic problems just discussed provide the key to understanding. (p. 353)

In his article 'State Capitalism' Pollock carried out a dialectical analysis of the interaction between economic and political factors in the constitution of fascism (see 3.2 above). Yet in his 1941 article 'Is National Socialism a New Order?' Pollock unambiguously maintained that National Socialism *does* constitute a 'new order', a new type of socio-political formation, in which the 'primacy of the political over economics . . . is clearly established' (p. 453), a position that he attempted to document in an analysis of the ruling class, the role of market, prices and profits, the relationship between government and the governed and the role of the individual.

In effect, Pollock is suggesting that Marxian categories cannot adequately characterize the new social formations of fascism, which, for him, constitute a qualitative break with both market and monopoly capitalism, and thus require new categories and theories to capture its specificity. Neumann, by contrast, aggressively polemicizes against the notion of the primacy of the political in fascism and the belief that fascism is a 'new order' in his monumental study *Behemoth*, a book soon accepted as a classic account of German fascism, in which he discusses 'The Structure and Practice of National Socialism 1933–1944'.[25] I shall argue here that a dialectical Marxian analysis, such as Neumann and other Institute members offer, provides a more comprehensive, more adequate conceptual framework which allows a better historical contextualization of fascism and a better analysis of its structural components and eventual trajectory and defeat than Pollock's ultimate position. For, by allowing 'the relative autonomy of the political' in certain cases, Neumann can account for the features which Pollock alludes to, without abandoning the earlier Institute position which saw the origins of fascism in the crisis of capitalism. He can thus present it as both a socio-economic formation which preserves capitalist relations of production and a new political formation which transforms relations between the economy and the state.

Neumann and Behemoth

Neumann begins by presenting fascism as an expression of capitalism in a crisis rooted in the need to carry out further imperialist expansion and to defeat the socialist threat (B, pp. 3ff.). After comprehensive and illuminating sections on 'The Collapse of the Weimar Republic' and 'The Political Pattern of National Socialism', Neumann analyzes what he calls the 'Totalitarian Monopoly Capitalism' which underlies German fascism. He argues that fascism basically left the capitalist economic order intact and developed the tendencies toward monopoly and imperialism which had characterized the German state for decades. In studies of 'The Monopolistic Economy' (pp. 255ff.), Neumann depicts the ways in which National Socialism encouraged cartels and monopolies, while maintaining central features of capitalism such as private ownership of the means of production, the profit motive, exploitation and wage labor more or less intact. In studies of 'The Command Economy', he indicated how National Socialism diminished the nationalized sector of the economy, introduced compulsory labor that ended a free labor market but served the interests of capital, and promoted policies that destroyed much small business but served the interests of big business. Thus Neumann believes that the term 'Totalitarian Monopoly Capitalism' best characterizes the fascist economic order, which combines a totalitarian state apparatus with a monopoly capitalist economy in which political and economic elites direct the society.

Neumann concludes that the German economy is both a 'monopolistic economy – and a command economy' (B, p. 261), but primarily emphasizes how Nazi intervention in the economy benefited big capital (and groups like the Goering Combine in which Nazi officials established their own combines from expropriated businesses). Neumann argues that despite Nazi interventions in the economy and transformations of relationships between the state and the economy, fascism nonetheless serves the interests of big capital. He claims that the Nazi economy is by and large capitalist, with monopoly economic interests continuing to play a major role. He documents this argument in discussions of price control and the market (pp. 305–16), profits, investments and finance capital (pp. 316–27), foreign trade, imperialism, the control of labor and the fight for higher productivity (pp. 327–63). Yet Neumann, too, employs a dialectical analysis of the interaction between political and economic factors; and despite his rejection of Pollock's thesis of the primacy of the political, he recognizes the importance and new autonomy of the political sphere in the constitution of fascism, and refrains from engaging in a reductionist economic analysis which would derive fascism solely from economic factors.

Neumann concludes *Behemoth* with an analysis of the antagonisms within National Socialism and the prospects for its elimination. He discusses antagonisms among the rulers themselves, between the rulers and the ruled, and between fascism and the democratic countries, suggesting that the system is flawed and that military defeat of fascism is possible. He concludes, however, by warning that only increased democratization within the countries that are fighting Germany and only the eventual elimination of anti-democratic forces and a profound alteration of its political and economic structures can ultimately produce the demise of fascism (*B*, pp. 475–6).

From the standpoint of a theoretical analysis of how the economy is organized and functions under fascism, I think it is fair to say that Neumann has put forward some extremely persuasive arguments of the extent to which the fascist economy remains capitalistic.[26] Yet, from the standpoint of analyzing the nature, structure and policies of German fascism as a whole, one could conclude that in many cases political factors predominate over economic ones to an extent rarely seen before in capitalistic societies, so that Pollock's notion of the primacy of the political has at least some validity in its application to German fascism. However, Neumann described many of the mechanisms of political domination, and agreed with other Institute members that domination under fascism was even more direct, immediate and repressive than in the earlier stages of capitalist society.

Dialectics of the Economic and the Political

In general, I believe it is a mistake to employ too rigid a model, either one which maintains the supposed primacy of the economic or one which assigns primacy to the political. For dialectical thought, political and economic factors are interconnected, and it is frequently difficult to ascertain which factors are primary in specific instances. From this perspective, among the main contributions of the Institute's theories of fascism and the new developments within capitalism are the analyses of how new configurations of the political require increased focus on the state and on political factors in the constitution of various types of capitalist societies, as well as a focus on interaction between the economic and political spheres.

In general, the analyses of fascism by Horkheimer, Marcuse and Kirchheimer in the early 1940s exhibit features of a dialectical and historical analysis which avoids the reduction of fascism to either primarily political or primarily economic factors. The typical mode of argumentation by the Institute during this period was by way of social analysis and critique in terms of historical stages that were continuous with but different from previous stages. This mode is evident in Kirchheimer's article 'Changes in the Structure of Political Compromise'.[27] In one of a series of lectures on fascism at Columbia University in 1941, Kirchheimer analyzes both the shifting relationships between forms of the economy and 'political compromise' and the respective weight of economic and political forces in determining the direction of socio-historical development. He gives several examples of how banks exerted power over both domestic and international politics from the end of World War I into the fascist era. Generally speaking, banks could grant credits and loans to countries and parties that they favored and withhold such favors from governments they opposed. Examples from Germany in the 1920s and the Macdonald government in England indicate that banks generally granted favorable credit when conservative governments were in power and withheld credit when liberal or working-class governments held power; this is particularly obvious, Kirchheimer suggests, in France in the 1920s and 1930s (*FSR*, pp. 53–5).

Kirchheimer's analysis suggests that in the previous liberal and demo-cratic eras, capitalist economic interests were generally able to exert power over the state through the instrument of finance capital. By the 1930s, however, 'Successive devaluation in different countries, the control of foreign commerce and exchange, and the abandonment of the cherished doctrine of budget equilibrium in favor of deficit spending have done away with the dependence of the government upon the whim of private bankers' (*FSR*, p. 55). In this situation, Kirchheimer suggests, the balance of power is definitely shifting in favor of the state, marking a world-wide tendency that has been consummated in the authoritarian countries. Within fascism, 'leadership' replaces political compromise, and imperialist expansion provides the booty to satisfy the ruling circles.

Kirchheimer's article provides insight into the particular ways in which Critical Theory does political analysis. The first task is to explore relation-ships between economic and political forces in investigating a phenomenon like political compromise and to put the topic into historical perspective. The next task is to specify which economic and political forces are playing a crucial role in the phenomenon under investigation and in the general trends of historical development. (In other analyses, cultural, legal, religious or any number of other factors might also play a key role.) Changes in the nature of political compromise, for example, provide insight into the nature of fascism, which in turn is interpreted in terms of the general trends of previous economic and political development. Although in the passages cited Kirchheimer seems to agree with Pollock's position concerning the primacy of the political in constituting fascism, in his analysis of the demise of democracy and political compromise in fascism, he specifies ways in which it serves the interests of German business (*FSR*, pp. 62ff.) arguing: 'Business, trade, and the independent ranks of agriculture became a closed monopoly. Government and party not only accepted its inner power distribution as they found it but actively helped to drive it still more pointedly in the direction of oligarchic combine' (p. 68). Kirchheimer concludes with indications that the relations between these groups and the army and party hierarchy are 'in flux'.

Consequently Kirchheimer employs a dialectical analysis of the interplay between economic and political forces in the constitution of fascism, rather than deriving fascism from political or economic factors alone. Horkheimer and Marcuse also consistently employed such a dialectical approach. In his article 'Some Social Implications of Modern Technology', Marcuse analyzes the increasingly important role of technology in the constitution of contemporary capitalist societies, including fascism.[28] He writes:

National Socialism is a striking example of the ways in which a highly rationalized and mechanized economy with the utmost efficiency in production can operate in the interest of totalitarian oppression and continued scarcity. The Third Reich is indeed a form of 'technocracy': the technical considerations of imperialistic efficiency and rationality supersede the traditional standards of profitability and general welfare. (*FSR*, p. 139)

This analysis would seem to support Pollock's account; yet Marcuse then situates the analysis of the new functions of technology in contemporary societies within the context of an analysis of capitalist development, and attempts to demonstrate how 'Business, technics, human needs, and nature are welded together into one rational and expedient mechanism. . . . Expediency in terms of technological reason is, at the same time, monopolistic standardization and concentration' (*FSR*, pp. 143ff.).

Thus, for Marcuse, contemporary industrial societies are a synthesis of certain (capitalist) economic factors, political bureaucracy and technology. In a more specific reference to fascism, Marcuse then describes the various mergers

between private, semi-private (party) and public (governmental) bureaucracies. The efficient realization of the interests of large-scale enterprise was one of the strongest motives for the transformation of economic into totalitarian political control, and efficiency is one of the main reasons for the fascist regime's hold over the regimented population. At the same time, however, it is also the force which may break this hold. Fascism can maintain its rule only by aggravating the restraint which it is compelled to impose upon society. It will ever more conspicuously manifest its inability to develop the productive forces, and it will fall before that power which proves to be more efficient than fascism. (*FSR*, pp. 154–5)

On this analysis, although fascism involves political control over the economy and the populace, economic factors continue to play an autonomous role in the constitution of society and its potential demise. In an Introduction to the 1941 issue of the *Zeitschrift* which contained articles by Pollock, Gurland and Kirchheimer on fascism, Horkheimer also tended to take a dialectical approach which attempted to analyze the historical origins of fascism in 'the transition from liberalism to authoritarianism in continental Europe'.[29] In his analysis he attempts to specify at once the economic and political roots and structures of fascism without reducing it to one dimension or the other:

Competition among independent entrepreneurs eventually culminated in the giant concerns of monopolist industry. Under their hegemony competition assumed a different form. . . . Individuals have become less and less independent of society, while society has fallen to the mercy of mere individual interests. . . . Rigid discipline such as ruled inside the factory has now spread throughout the hinterland, borne forward by elites who in their composition and function have combined economy and politics. The leaders of industry, administration, propaganda, and the military have become identical with the state in that they lay down the plan of the national economy as the entrepreneur before them had laid down policy for his factory. At the same time the state manifests its private character in that the enormous power wielded by the elites inevitably segregates them from the whole as bearers of very special interests. (pp. 195–6)

Against Pollock's analysis, which suggested that National Socialism had largely overcome major antagonisms, Horkheimer claimed that fascism was, rather, a primarily antagonistic social form full of conflicts and contradictions:

The big industrialists attack the fuehrers for their expensive political apparatus; the fuehrers blood purge the underfuehrers because of their radical claims; the generals would like to get rid of all of them. To counterbalance their antagonisms, no common faith exists, as among the medieval clergy, no belief in chivalry and princely blood, as among the seigneurs of absolutism, – ideals which had combined with their material interests to hold these groups together. The unity of fascist leaders is cemented merely by their common fear of the people they tyrannize, by their dread of ultimate doom. This clique does not become the dupe of its own ideologies; it shuffles them about freely and cynically according to the changing situation, thus finally translating into open action what modern political theory from Machiavelli and Hobbes to Pareto has professed. (p. 196)

Consequently, while Horkheimer believed that Pollock's theory of state capitalism provided insights into the new combination of economics and politics in capitalist states of various sorts, he never completely assented to Pollock's thesis concerning the primacy of the political and his suggestions that fascist societies were 'post-capitalist', arguing instead that 'Under

National Socialism the distribution of goods is carried on by private means, though competition has become even more one-sided than in the era of the 200 families. . . . Under its totalitarian set-up big industry is in a position not only to impose its plan upon its former competitors, but to order the masses to work instead of having to deal with them as free parties to a contract' (pp. 196–7).

In his 1942 article 'Authoritarian State', Horkheimer also carries out a dialectical analysis of the interpenetration of the play of economic and political factors in the constitution of fascism and the ways in which fascism is both continuous and discontinuous with earlier stages of capitalism.[30] Like Pollock's article 'State Capitalism', Horkheimer's analysis operates on a level of generality which moves from more specific analyses and critiques of fascist, capitalist and Soviet societies (the last described as 'integral statism') to more general analyses of the 'authoritarian state' which attempt to delineate factors common to all these dominant socio-political formations. As in his article 'The End of Reason', Horkheimer tends to allude to similarities between fascist and capitalist societies without clearly and explicitly analyzing the differences.

The article is striking for its sharp critique of all forms of the authoritarian state and for Horkheimer's affirmation of his own democratic and humanistic brand of socialism. It is one of the Institute's few 'positive' statements of its political position during the period, and is perhaps Horkheimer's last uncompromising affirmation of a version of critical Marxism. Defining his last position in proximity to Pollock's, Horkheimer argues that '*state capitalism is the authoritarian state of the present*' (*FSR*, p. 96). He then articulates a somewhat orthodox Marxist position on the transition from capitalism to socialism:

For the natural course of the capitalist world order, theory prescribes an unnatural end: the united proletarians will destroy the last form of exploitation, state-capitalist slavery. The rivalry of the wage-laborers among themselves had guaranteed the prosperity of the private entrepreneurs. That was the freedom of the poor. . . . But to the same extent that capital concentrated the workers in the large factories, it came into crisis and made its own existence a hopeless prospect. The workers cannot hire themselves out yet another time. Their interests push them inexorably to socialism. When the ruling class 'must feed the workers, instead of being fed by them,' revolution is at hand. (*FSR*, p. 96)

Yet, while Engels claimed that intensifying economic crisis would require more state management of the economy and provide the transition to socialism, it appeared to Horkheimer that the authoritarian state had itself emerged as a stabilizing form for capitalism, one which could avoid the destructive effects of economic crisis, and that '*state capitalism does away with the market and hypostatizes the crisis for the duration of eternal Germany*' (*FSR*, p. 97). Horkheimer attempts to explain how this frightening situation came about by means of a sharp critique of working-class unions and parties, arguing that they replicated the bureaucratic structures of organization and administration under capitalism:

Whatever seeks to exist under a state of domination runs the danger of reproducing it. Insofar as the proletarian opposition in the Weimar Republic did not meet its downfall as a sect, it fell victim to the spirit of administration. The institutionalization of the top ranks of capital and labor have the same basis: the change in the form of production. Monopolized industry, which makes the mass of stockholders into victims and parasites, pushes the masses of workers into supporting passivity. They have more to expect from the protection and assistance of the organizations than from their work. (*FSR*, p. 98)

Consequently, in Horkheimer's view, the unions and working-class parties merely reproduced the passivity and subordination of the workers previously produced by the capitalist organization of labor and society. Furthermore, the Soviet Union, described here as defined by an 'integral statism' in which the state presumably owns and controls the means of production, is no better:

In the Western democracies the leaders of the big working class organizations find themselves in the same relationship to their membership as the executives of integral statism [i.e. the Soviet Union] have to the society as a whole: they keep the masses, whom they take care of, under strict discipline, maintain them in hermetic seclusion from uncontrolled elements, and tolerate spontaneity only as the result of their own power. (*FSR*, p. 98)

In his criticism of working-class organizations for falling prey to bureaucracy, Horkheimer presents the first extensive Institute critique of the Soviet Union, which is interpreted as a form of the authoritarian state:[31]

Integral statism or state socialism is the most consistent form of the authoritarian state which has freed itself from any dependence on private capital. It increases production at a rate only seen in the transition from the mercantilist period to the liberal era. The fascist countries create a mixed form. Though here too surplus value is brought under state control and distributed, it flows under the old name of profits in great amounts to the industrial magnates and landowners. Through their influence, the organization is destroyed and deflected. In integral statism, socialization is simply decreed. . . . Integral statism is not a retreat but an advance of power. It can exist without racism. However, the producers, to whom capital legally belongs, 'remain wage workers, proletarians,' no matter how much is done for them. Factory regimentation is extended to the entire society. . . . In integral statism, even apart from the militaristic encroachment, the absolutism of bureaucracy, whose authority the police enforce to the utmost in all phases of life, stands opposed to the free structuring of society. No economic or juridical measures, only the will of the ruled can lead to a democratization of the system of control. (*FSR*, pp. 101–2)

Against state socialism, Horkheimer advocates a democratic and revolutionary concept of socialism. He suggests that only renewed revolutionary activity by the masses can lead to genuine socialism, which he characterizes in terms of a system of workers' councils, or Soviets, where the workers themselves democratically control the workplace, community and other forms of socio-political life.[32] Yet Horkheimer also suggests that the authoritarian states are themselves creating the conditions for a future potential socialist society by centralizing and planning the economy, creating full employment, training workers and reducing economic and political issues to technical ones that presumably all workers could conceivably solve (*FSR*, p. 104). Horkheimer warns, though, that Critical Theory offers no guarantees that authoritarian states can be replaced by democratic socialist ones (p. 106), and argues that only a radical rupture with the present form of the authoritarian state might make possible 'the end of exploitation' and 'the break with class society' (p. 107).

This is the last essay in which Horkheimer envisaged the possibility and desirability of socialist revolution. It was written during a period when the entire world was plunged into a barbaric war and the prospects for democratic socialism appeared extremely bleak. In this era the Institute concentrated on developing theories and critiques of fascism which would clarify its ideological and historical origins, analyze its political, economic and social structure, and explain its appeal to the masses. Yet at the same time, Institute theorists continued to radicalize their critiques of contemporary capitalist societies, although some of them, especially Adorno and Horkheimer, would soon break with their previous conceptions of theory and politics. Before examining these developments (in Chapter 4), however, let us sum up some of the contributions and limitations of the Critical Theory of society as it developed from the mid-1930s to the early 1940s.

3.4   Fragments of a Theory of Society

I have suggested that Critical Theory is of interest to radical social theory today because of its methodological conception of a supradisciplinary social theory which combines philosophy, the social sciences, history and politics, as well as the contributions of its substantive social theory. In this chapter I have suggested that its theorization of the new social trends, developments and transformations in the transition from an earlier stage of market capitalism to a later stage of monopoly/state capitalism provides illuminating perspectives on the central trends of social development at the time. These insights were made possible, I believe, by a unique conjuncture of three sets of conditions which distinguished Institute theorists from other social theorists: (1) their independent version of critical Marxism; (2) their supradisciplinary research institute which combined philosophy and the social sciences; and (3) their exile in the United States and ability to experience both the rise of fascism and the transition to a new stage of capitalism in the United States at first hand.

Marxism and the Debate over State Capitalism

The Institute theorists' training in Marxism led to their rooting all social phenomena in the fundamental socio-economic processes which determine the trajectory of social life, and to seeing commodification, exchange, reification, fetishism and other aspects of capitalism as permeating all social domains. Their dialectical Marxian method also gave them a way of conceiving and representing the relations between the spheres of the economy, state, culture and society and of conceptualizing how new developments in these areas impacted on the other spheres, on everyday life and on human thought and behavior. Transgressing the boundaries of traditional thought and the academic division of labor enabled them to perceive interconnections and relations ignored by traditional theory and to put forward a broad, comprehensive macrotheory of contemporary society that provides accounts of fascism and the new stage of monopoly/state capitalism.

In effect, the Critical Theorists' sharp historical consciousness allowed them to perceive historical changes and transformations, to analyze the borderline from the previous stage of capitalism and to chart trends toward new stages of socio-political development. Here their adherence to a nondogmatic form of Marxism enabled them to depart from and move beyond Marxian orthodoxy in a number of areas, and to both update and reconstruct the Marxian theory, while showing the limitations of classical Marxism when faced with new social developments. Yet they never really developed their social theory systematically. Fragments of a new theory of society appear in Horkheimer's 'The End of Reason' and other Institute publications of the period; but they are never developed into a fully developed social theory. Consequently one must turn to a variety of publications to grasp aspects of their social theory of the new configurations of capitalism and fascism.

Moreover, some of their theoretical constructions were of questionable validity, especially Pollock's concept of 'state capitalism', coined to characterize the new phase of capitalism which, in its totalitarian form, allegedly went beyond capitalism while manifesting the primacy of the political. This concept, as I have argued in this chapter, is flawed theoretically, empirically and politically; and while many Institute members strongly contested Pollock's concept of state capitalism and his notion of the primacy of the political, Horkheimer adopted at least a modified version of the theory of state capitalism, absorbing it into his analysis of the authoritarian state.[33]

Others in the Institute sharply contested Pollock, however. After reading Pollock's article 'State Capitalism', Adorno wrote to Horkheimer: 'I can best formulate my views of this essay by perceiving it as an inversion of Kafka. Kafka presented the hierarchy of the bureaucracy as hell. Here, however, hell is transformed into a hierarchy of bureaucracy.' Crucially, Adorno thought that Pollock's essay was marred by the 'undialectical position that in an antagonistic society a non-antagonistic economy was possible'.[34] Although Adorno claimed that he did not object to Pollock's pessimism, he did reject the notion that state capitalism actually stabilized the capitalist economy. Instead, he maintained that 'what perpetuates itself appears to me not so much a relatively stable and in a certain sense even a rational condition, but rather appears as an incessant procession of catastrophes, chaos, and cruelty for an incalculably long period but that also allows of course the chance for upheaval'.

Neumann was the most aggressive public critic of the concept of state capitalism, claiming that it is self-contradictory in that it suggests that the state has taken over the means of production and therefore cannot be capitalistic (*B*, pp. 224ff.).[35] Neumann also criticized the concept on empirical grounds, claiming that the term was an ideal type which was nowhere fully instantiated in reality and thus 'violates the principle that the model or the ideal type must be derived from reality and must not transcend it' (p. 224). Moreover, while Pollock wrote an article arguing that the features of state capitalism were instantiated in National Socialism, neither he nor any of the other Institute members ever produced a comprehensive study of 'democratic state capitalist' societies; so it is not clear what insight, if any, such an analysis might provide into their structure and function.

Neumann also objected to the notion of state capitalism on political grounds, claiming that it projected a hopeless situation in which capitalism could extend itself indefinitely by overcoming its contradictions, and that such a notion occluded the antagonisms within capitalism that continued to exist.[36] Indeed, the term 'state capitalism' generally signified for both Pollock and Horkheimer a new type of socio-economic formation which transcended the classical contradictions of capitalism and utilized a planned economy to prevent or minimize the effects of economic crisis endemic to an unplanned market economy. In such a social order, radical social change could thus be avoided indefinitely through techniques of administration, planning, rationalization and the like. Ultimately, such a conception became central to the Institute's post-World War II Critical Theory of society, so that Pollock's analysis, in different forms and with different names, eventually became a fundamental constituent of the Institute's social theory. Yet, as I shall argue later, 'the primacy of the economic' has continued to play a major role in the trajectory of contemporary capitalist societies from the end of World War II to the present. In a sense, the 'primacy of the political' referred more to the configurations of fascist and state socialist societies than to those of democratic capitalist ones. Consequently I believe that merging Pollock's analysis of state capitalism and the primacy of the political with a concept of a new type of global social formation, as he himself tended to do, would be a conceptual error; for surely a dialectic of economic, political and technical factors played a major role in the development of succeeding capitalist and state socialist societies (see Chapter 7 for an elaboration of this argument).

It is indeed one of the weaknesses of the first stage of Critical Theory that Institute theorists never carried out a detailed analysis of the allegedly new forms of democratic capitalist societies and never presented a comprehensive analysis of the political structure and relations between the state and the economy in the constitution of the state in democratic capitalist societies.[37] Instead, their analysis moved on a high level of conceptual generality where 'state capitalism' and the 'authoritarian state' were presented as concepts which described the structure and dynamics of fascist, democratic and even Soviet society in the era of the Depression and World War II. Despite lip service to the importance of historical analysis, their own empirical and historical analysis was too thin and underdeveloped.

Consequently the Institute never really came through with the systematic, comprehensive theory of society intended in its original program and in frequent comments throughout the period.[38] Instead, it produced fragments of such a theory and utilized concepts at a high level of abstraction to characterize the new stage of capitalist society. But such a level of generality, combined with the conditions of exile, severed the relationship between theory and politics which at one time was presented as the cornerstone of the Institute position.[39] In fact, the Institute rarely participated publicly in the political debates of the 1930s over the Popular Front, the Soviet Union, the Spanish civil war, the New Deal or the role of the Communist Party, and rarely advocated specific political courses of action or goals beyond that of the elimination of fascism. Consequently, the political dimension of Critical Theory was severely desiccated in the 1930s and 1940s, and would not return to the forefront of the theory until the efforts of Marcuse, Habermas and others of the second generation in the 1960s (see Chapter 8).

In a sense, Pollock's analysis of state capitalism provided a foundation for the pessimism that would characterize Critical Theory from the 1940s through the next decades. For, as Horkheimer stated in his Introduction to the *Zeitschrift* issue on state capitalism: 'The opening article [by Pollock] of this issue draws a picture of an authoritarian society that might embrace the earth, or one that is at least autarchic. Its challenging thesis is that such a society can endure for a long and terrifying period.'[40] Soon the Critical

Theorists were arguing that contemporary societies were not only producing new configurations of economic, political, technical and cultural
factors, but were integrating the working class and other potential sources
of opposition as well, at the same time constituting a society immune to
crisis, explosive antagonisms and political conflicts. Such a conception
carried the Institute far from its original Marxian synthesis of theory and
politics, and produced a new stage of Critical Theory during the 1940s. I
shall discuss the Institute's development of its new social theory in the next
several chapters. First, however, I want to reflect on the impact of
emigration on its theory and politics.

Critical Theory and Emigration

In my view, the experience of political emigration played a crucial role in
influencing the nature, form and politics of Critical Theory, a role that has
been downplayed or not perceived in many previous studies. The initial
interpretations of Critical Theory in the English-speaking world have
tended to claim that it was the Institute's German-Jewish bourgeois ethnic
and class roots and situations which provided the primary influences on
Critical Theory. Martin Jay, for instance, claims that the Institute's Jewish
origins constituted the 'common thread running through individual biographies'.[41] Zoltan Tar goes even further by claiming that 'The impact of
Judaism . . . can be traced in Frankfurt throughout its 50-year history,'
and he attempts – albeit unsuccessfully – to show how Judaism constituted
key elements of characteristic Institute positions.[42] And George Friedman
claims that Jewish concern for redemption and the sacred informed the
Institute's theory.[43]

Taking this common Jewish heritage as the key constitutive feature of
Critical Theory is misleading, however, because not all Institute members
were Jewish, nor did they all identify with Judaism. While one can easily
connect some of the positions of Horkheimer, Adorno and Fromm with
Jewish traditions, this is not the case in any profound way with many of the
central positions of Critical Theory. Moreover, Tar and most Marxist-
Leninist critics of Critical Theory emphasize the bourgeois class origins of
the Critical Theorists, using them to explain their deviations from orthodox
Marxism or allegiance to modes of 'bourgeois' thought and politics.
Against these attempts to specify the key contextual determinants of
Critical Theory, I would argue that the experience of emigration played a
central, often underemphasized, role.

The Institute had only been under Horkheimer's directorship a couple of
years when the Nazis came to power in Germany. It had cautiously – and
wisely as it turns out – deposited much of its funds in banks outside
Germany, and had also made connections to open branches in Geneva and

Paris. After Hitler's rise to power, Horkheimer and his colleagues left Germany almost immediately, and were, in effect, political emigrés until the end of World War II, when some of them returned to Germany.[44] Consequently Critical Theory, like much modern philosophy and contemporary social theory, is exile theory, the product of thinkers forced by adverse circumstances into emigration.

Although the situation of political refugees is often not a happy one – and, as Henry Pachter points out, many German exiles at the time could not adjust to conditions of exile – it can be conducive to producing critical and original thought and writing.[45] For the political emigrant is often fueled by a passion to criticize and unburden himself or herself of anger and frustration. Consequently, the thought and writings of political refugees often contain a sharp critical edge and a polemical passion and intensity. Further, those in exile from their homeland often find themselves in a land that is strange, and are sometimes able both to view conditions in their home country from a different perspective and to gain original perceptions of conditions in the country in which they find themselves exiled.

Such is the case, I shall argue, with the members of the Institute for Social Research, whose Critical Theory amply manifests such polemical passion and intensity, as well as containing original and often striking ideas and perceptions concerning both the European situation from which they were exiled and the situation in the United States in which they found themselves. Accordingly, in the following chapters, I will argue that both the Institute theory of the transition from the stage of market capitalism to a new stage of state and monopoly capitalism and its theory of fascism were shaped in crucial ways by the exile experience.

Testimony by members of the Institute themselves indicates the extent to which their experience of exile influenced their choice of language, modes of expression and development of their social theory. Throughout *Minima Moralia*, written by Adorno from 1944 through 1947 while in exile in California, there are signs of how emigration shaped Adorno's thinking. Indeed, Adorno points out that the starting point of his inquiries is 'the intellectual in emigration'; and throughout the book there are reflections on the exile experience and how the conditions of emigration affected everyday life, thereby requiring new modes of thought and action (see Chapter 3 for further discussion).[46]

By conceptualizing the novel conditions of contemporary capitalism from their vantage point as European refugees, the Institute members focused attention on how it differed from the earlier stage of capitalism. Because 'the new' was so novel to them, the Critical Theorists were able to perceive differences between older and newer social conditions more sharply than those to whom such things were simply natural parts of their environment which were both familiar and habitual. Thus we see that there were some advantages to what might be called 'exile thought'. But there were also problems that I shall allude to now and then elaborate in the following chapters.

Indeed, it is probable that the limitations, as well as the insights, of Critical Theory are related to the theorists' status as exiles. While an emigrant may gain insights into his or her new domicile which are not readily apparent to those totally immersed in the society, his or her position as an outsider may also lead to distortions or oversimplifications. Thus, while the experiences of Institute theorists as refugees may have enabled them to perceive that mass communications and culture, for instance, were being used to an unparalleled extent as instruments of indoctrination and social control in the United States, they may have missed some of the ideological contradictions within mass culture and the socially critical and potentially progressive possibilities of the new media such as film, radio and television (see the discussion in Chapter 5). Yet, unlike most inhabitants of the United States, they were able to perceive sharply the extent to which the culture industries were functioning as instruments of social control and domination. Furthermore, they also perceived how changes in the labor process, the rise of consumerism, the integration of the state and the economy, and new uses of science and technology as instruments of domination and so on were producing a new social order, an order which they saw as a 'totally administered society' marked by a decline of democracy and individuality – themes of 1940s and 1950s Critical Theorists which were rooted, I believe, in their status as outsiders and refugees.

4

From *Dialectic of Enlightenment* to *The Authoritarian Personality*: Critical Theory in the 1940s

One of the most significant developments in the trajectory of Critical Theory was the shift from the project of producing multidisciplinary social theory rooted in the Marxian critique of political economy to that of a new philosophical critique of science, technology and instrumental reason. The new phase of Critical Theory found classical expression in Horkheimer's and Adorno's *Dialectic of Enlightenment* (1947), which combined a novel critique of Western civilization and rationality with a powerful critique of 'the administered society', which became the new target of their social criticism.[1] On a methodological level, Horkheimer and Adorno shifted the focus of Critical Theory to philosophy of history, philosophical anthropology and a philosophical critique of culture. This project, as we shall see, differed significantly from their earlier efforts to produce a comprehensive theory of contemporary society rooted in a synthesis of philosophy, politics and the social sciences. For, while Horkheimer and Adorno extended their critique of fascism and capitalism, they distanced themselves from the Marxian theory of history and critique of political economy, subordinated science and politics to philosophy, and tended to make the domination of nature the fulcrum of their analysis, rather than such classical Marxian themes as political economy, social relations, class struggle or the transition to socialism.

Horkheimer's and Adorno's critical questioning of Marxism was induced in part by historical conditions, such as the demise of the labor movement, the spread of fascism and war, and oppressive developments in the Soviet Union which made it difficult to envisage Critical Theory as part of a revolutionary movement or to unproblematically call for socialist revolution. But the new developments of Critical Theory were also occasioned by experience of conditions in the United States and by the dispersion of the Institute's multidisciplinary group. This break-up happened because Horkheimer was forced to go to California, in part for health reasons and in part because of a desire to write a major book on dialectics which he had envisaged for decades but was unable to begin while burdened with duties as director of the Institute.[2] In California, Horkheimer was joined by Adorno, who henceforth became his closest collaborator. By contrast, many of the Institute's inner circle and other colleagues joined the United States government as part of their struggle against fascism – perhaps also in part because Horkheimer intimated that financial difficulties within the Institute would make it increasingly difficult, if not impossible, to support them. At this time, Horkheimer and Adorno thus took over the development of Critical Theory.

It would be difficult to overestimate the crucial role that Adorno played in the formulations of the new stage of Critical Theory.[3] Many of its primary motifs are already apparent in his earlier works, and the new positions developed in the 1940s exhibit traces of Adorno's philosophical ideas and literary-philosophical style. Adorno was always more committed to philosophical discourse and the superiority of philosophy over other theoretical modes than most of his Institute colleagues, and he was also more critical of the social sciences. Under his influence, Horkheimer also championed the importance of philosophy more aggressively. Thus, during the 1940s, Critical Theory became more 'philosophical'; and the earlier attempt to integrate philosophy and the social sciences was replaced by more uninhibited philosophical theorizing and speculation.

Given that both Horkheimer and Adorno were trained as philosophers and that there was no longer a multidisciplinary research institute, it is not surprising that Critical Theory should have become more philosophical or that its critique of science and instrumental reason should have become radicalized. This development was also conditioned by the instrumentalization of science and technology in the Nazi and other war machines and by Horkheimer's and Adorno's growing aversion to the sort of scientific philosophy and positivistic science dominant in the United States.

At this time, there was also a political transformation and a changing conception of the relationship between Critical Theory and politics. The distancing of Critical Theory from political practice and the refusal to advocate a more 'positive politics' (such as Horkheimer and Marcuse occasionally did previously) might be attributed in part both to Horkheimer's reluctance to take explicitly political positions for fear that this would endanger the status of the Institute and to Adorno's skeptical, critical temperament which was always suspicious of too direct a mediation between Critical Theory and practical politics. Indeed, Horkheimer's and Adorno's work during this period is addressed to 'critical intellectuals', and they surrendered the pretense that they were writing for a temporarily defeated revolutionary movement.

It appears that the defeat of revolutionary forces and movements by fascism in the 1930s and the gradual surrender of the hopes that after World War II a revolutionary working-class and socialist movement would produce more rational, just and democratic societies led to significant revisions of Critical Theory and reformulations concerning the relationship between theory and politics. Henceforth in Horkheimer's and Adorno's work, the critique of instrumental reason and the 'dialectic of enlightenment' would replace the earlier Marxian emphasis on class struggle and the transition to socialism. From now on, Horkheimer's and Adorno's theories focus on the primacy of the relation between humans and nature. Moreover, Marxism, enlightenment rationality, science and technology, the culture industries and the trends of development of both capitalist and socialist societies are interpreted under the rubric of the 'dialectic of enlightenment' and as part of 'the administered society'. In this theory of the trajectory of modernity, projects like Marxism and science, intended to contribute to the domination of nature, are interpreted as more powerful instruments for the domination of human beings. Yet, as we shall see below, many Marxian themes and categories remain in the new stage of Critical Theory.

4.1 Science, Reason and *Dialectic of Enlightenment*

Dialectic of Enlightenment seeks to discover 'why humanity, instead of entering into a truly human condition, is sinking into a new kind of barbarism' (*DoE*, p. xi). Horkheimer and Adorno indicate that they were forced to abandon trust in the disciplinary sciences and turn to critical philosophy in part because of the integration of science and scientific thought into the apparatus of the current systems of domination, fascist and capitalist. They perceived that scientific method and thought had become increasingly formalist, conformist, instrumental and in thrall to the interests of the existing social system, and thus were losing their potentialities for social insight and critique. Yet, since philosophy also has become implicated in the existing system of domination and fallen prey to contemporary modes of conformist thought, it too must distance itself from traditional forms, become critical and develop new concepts and methods of inquiry, thought and expression: 'There is no longer any available form of linguistic expression which has not tended toward accommodation to dominant currents of thought; and what a devalued language does not do automatically is proficiently executed by societal mechanisms' (i.e. censorship, editing, the current system of education, publishing, the media, etc.) (pp. xxi–xiii).

Another problem is that the current dominant form of supposedly critical thought, positivism, sticks so closely to verification of facts and formal presentation of mathematically calculable results that it is incapable of providing models for social theory and critique. Indeed, 'the self-destruction of the Enlightenment' in positivism is one of the major themes of their book. Horkheimer and Adorno believed that science, scientific reason and technology were part and parcel of existing processes of production and social domination, and thus should be mistrusted. From the beginning, Critical Theory defined itself as an attitude and practice characterized by mistrust, skepticism, reflexivity and 'negative thinking', which made social critique a central part of its theoretical practice (see 2.3). In *Dialectic of Enlightenment*, this attitude ballooned to epic proportions, and the book is informed by critical distance from prevalent modes of thought and expression as well as from current social developments at a point in history when the world was, in their view, falling into barbarism. Yet the authors – and this is more Horkheimer's position than Adorno's – occasionally seemed to contrast a form of critical reason to positivism's instrumental and formal reason. And while they affirm that the philosophical fragments which they present 'will contribute to the health of that theoretical understanding' (*DoE*, p. xiii), they really do not spell out what form critical reason might take; thus their focus is almost completely critical and negative.

Horkheimer and Adorno conclude that traditional and contemporary modes of thought and writing have become absorbed into the present system of administration and domination, and that new modes of radical thought, writing and critique are therefore required. *Dialectic of Enlightenment* breaks with standard discursive methods of presentation and modes of argumentation, while employing a new style of writing that juxtaposes material from philosophy, history, cultural studies and contemporary experience in a unique mixture of disciplines and topics which are usually separated in theoretical discourse, thereby exploding the boundaries of the established academic disciplines. The book consists of long studies of 'The Concept of Enlightenment' and the culture industry, with two excurses on enlightenment, a shorter series of 'Theses on Anti-Semitism', and some notes and drafts on major themes of their emerging Critical Theory of the 'administered society'. The text has a fragmentary structure, and the various sections are written and presented in quite different ways, employing different themes and subject matter to illuminate the major positions of the book.

The subtitle 'Philosophical Fragments' (which was the original working title of the book, and which was omitted from the English translation) points to both the philosophical and the fragmentary nature of their studies.

The language and mode of presentation are often esoteric and highly demanding, requiring sustained concentration and knowledge of the Enlightenment, Kant, Hegel, Marx, Sade, Nietzsche, Homer and Greek philology, as well as the previous works of Critical Theory on which the authors build. Consequently, in what is arguably *the* quintessential distillation of the new stage of Critical Theory, Horkheimer and Adorno move beyond their previous thought into new problematics, new modes of thought and expression and new ways of seeing. In general, they employ the method of juxtaposing often heterogeneous subject matter to illuminate the topics in question, rather than utilizing the more explanatory, systematic, structured method of presentation typical of the 1930s essays.[4]

Toward an Epic Philosophy of History

Dialectic of Enlightenment presents an epic philosophy of history which encompasses the history and pre-history of the bourgeois subject and its attempts to dominate nature. Indeed, *Dialectic of Enlightenment* can be read as a narrative theorization of the origins and anticipation of the bourgeois subject in Homer's *Odyssey*, of its heroic stage in the Enlightenment and its decline in fascism and administered neo-capitalism. Every such project has an origin and an end-point, and usually the end-point – which for Horkheimer and Adorno is the current state of social domination and barbarism – determines where one seeks the beginning. In interpreting various stages of the relationship between human beings and nature – and the corresponding forms of culture, thought and action – Horkheimer and Adorno begin with the triumph of what they call 'enlightenment', trace its origins to the Greeks and then describe current forms of social domination in the totally administered society.

In their analysis, 'enlightenment' (with a small 'e') refers to that mode of 'enlightened' thought which emancipates human beings from the despotism of myth and helps them to control and dominate nature. Thus 'enlightenment' (without the definite article) is to be distinguished from the period of 'the Enlightenment', and the 'dialectic of enlightenment' refers to the ways in which supposedly enlightened, rational thought contains traces of myth and irrationality, which in turn contain a rational core. Their critique of enlightenment encompasses critiques of science, technology and instrumental reason, and will be the focus of this chapter; I will present their critiques of the culture industry, the consumer society and the totally administered society, as well as other elements of their social and cultural critique of the present age in following chapters.

Here, I propose that *Dialectic of Enlightenment* is best read as a history and pre-history of the bourgeois subject and that subject's project of the domination of nature, rather than as an ontological history of the relationship between the human species and nature. In other words, I am proposing that the authors' philosophy of history is best read as a philosophical analysis of a certain epoch of history, rather than an essay in universal history and ontology. Such a reading is signaled in the Introduction, where Horkheimer and Adorno indicate that they will interpret enlightenment as part of 'the actual movement of civil society as a whole', and will thus interpret all their categories as forms of life, social phenomena, and not just abstract cognitive forms (*DoE*, p. xiv). Indeed, the authors attempt to show that even the most abstract, formal categories of thought, such as mathematical logic, are related to social processes, practices and behavior (and thus should not be interpreted as anthropological universals or products of pure reason). Consequently I would suggest that the social processes which are central to *Dialectic of Enlightenment* are those connected with the origins and development of bourgeois society.[5]

Although *Dialectic of Enlightenment* is often described as the dark side of Critical Theory and as a basically negative, pessimistic vision of history, nonetheless a residue of social optimism remains that will soon diminish. The authors begin with a formulation of the dialectic of enlightenment which points to both its contributions and its limitations: 'The fallen nature of modern man cannot be separated from social progress. On the one hand the growth of economic productivity furnishes the conditions for a world of greater justice; on the other hand it allows the technical apparatus and the social groups which administer it a disproportionate superiority to the rest of the population' (*DoE*, p. xv). Such hopeful possibilities are not really developed and thought through, however, either in the book or in the authors' later work. Instead, primarily pessimistic implications are drawn from current social trends and developments: 'The individual is wholly devalued in relation to the economic powers, which at the same time press the control of society over nature to hitherto unsuspected heights. Even though the individual disappears before the apparatus which he serves, that apparatus provides for him as never before. In an unjust state of life, the impotence and pliability of the masses grow with the quantitative increase in commodities allowed them' (p. xv).

The first study, 'The Concept of Enlightenment', attempts to show the ways in which myth and enlightenment are entangled and are themselves implicated in social domination. This enables Horkheimer and Adorno to carry through critiques of various modes of bourgeois thought from *The Odyssey* through logical positivism, including critiques of representatives of enlightenment thought like Bacon, Descartes and Kant, as well as counter-enlightenment figures like Nietzsche and Sade. Horkheimer and Adorno suggest that the first manifestations of enlightenment in Bacon already reveal the project of the domination of nature: 'What men want to learn from nature is how to use it in order wholly to dominate it and other

men. That is the only aim. Ruthlessly, in despite of itself, the Enlightenment has extinguished any trace of its own self-consciousness. The only
kind of thinking that is sufficiently hard to shatter myths is ultimately self-
destructive. . . . Power and knowledge are synonymous' (*DoE*, p. 4).

Horkheimer and Adorno undertake a critique of what they consider the
'totalitarian' nature of enlightenment reason. Building on their earlier
critiques of the extent to which bourgeois thought is ruled by the bourgeois
values of calculation, quantification, exchange, equivalence, formalization,
harmony and unity, they now indicate how these modes of thought are
themselves part of social processes of the domination of nature. On this
view, enlightenment reason serves the interests of domination by virtue of
its embeddedness in the existing society, its supplanting of more radical
modes of thought and its application to the domination of human beings.[6]

It is not clear whether Horkheimer and Adorno intend to carry out an
immanent critique of enlightenment thought or break with enlightenment
rationality altogether. In general, within Critical Theory, Marcuse,
Lowenthal, Habermas and sometimes Horkheimer attempt to base critiques
of instrumental and formal rationality on a concept of critical reason.
Adorno, however, consistently refuses to posit a positive concept of reason,
and Horkheimer in *Eclipse of Reason* is ambiguous (see 4.2 below). One can
accordingly read *Dialectic of Enlightenment* as an attempt to defend the
progressive tradition of the Enlightenment – the disenchantment of the
world, the dissolution of myth, superstition and ignorance, the ways in
which science and technology have contributed to human well-being and so
forth – against its more repressive, conformist heritage. Or, from the
vantage point of Adorno's later philosophy, one can read it as a more
radical critique of enlightenment rationality which breaks with enlightenment thought, discourse and reason altogether.[7]

Either way, one of the salient characteristics of the text is a radicalization
of the Institute critique of science and technology, a critique that was later
contested by Habermas and his school, who sought to rehabilitate science,
technology and enlightenment rationalism (see note 7). Horkheimer and
Adorno argue that from the beginning science and enlightenment reason
have aimed at the domination of nature, and have thus valorized modes of
thought and methods of verification that served these ends. Since Bacon
science has been conceptualized in terms of power over nature, and those
methods that were most effective and successful in the domination of nature
were celebrated as the sole road to truth, while competing theories were
rejected. Criteria of utility, efficiency and success thus guided intellectual
and practical endeavor; and modes of calculation, quantification and formalization proved so successful that enlightenment rationality eventually
championed the systems of mathematical physics and logic as privileged
models of truth.

All other modes of thought, ranging from myth and religion to critical and speculative philosophy, were deemed by enlightenment rationality as inferior and ineffective in the struggle to dominate nature. Against this position – which would rule out their own preferred modes of thought and inquiry – Horkheimer and Adorno argue that, while enlightenment is often posed against myth, enlightenment itself becomes myth, and myth is itself permeated with enlightenment rationality. Their argument is that both myth and enlightenment were motivated by attempts to abstract from and control nature. In myth, individuals try to gain power over nature and the spirit world through naming, ritual and magic. In science, domination of nature takes place through discovery of scientific laws based on causal connections and regularities in nature. In both cases identity-thinking (that is, the belief that one's concepts are identical with reality), mimesis and calculation are methods of control and domination, and both modes of thought are governed by the drive for self-preservation.

The concept of mimesis plays an especially important role in the theory of the domination of nature. Horkheimer and Adorno claim that:

Like science, magic pursues aims, but seeks to achieve them by mimesis – not by progressively distancing itself from the object. It is not grounded in the 'sovereignty of ideas,' which the primitive, like the neurotic, is said to ascribe to himself. . . . The 'unshakeable confidence in the possibility of world domination,' which Freud anachronistically ascribes to magic, corresponds to realistic world domination only in terms of a more skilled science. (*DoE*, p. 11).

Mimesis seeks 'to seize the identical in the flux of phenomena, to isolate the same species in the alternation of specimens, or the same thing in altered situations' (*DoE*, p. 246). Both thought and mimesis therefore aid the species and individuals in adapting to nature, in controlling natural processes.

But mimesis also contains residues of participation in nature, of primordial happiness and unity, which may later return in contradictory ways to revolt against rationalization and modernity.[8] Memories of former happiness may foster revolt against domination and alienation: 'Whatever the anguish men suffered then, they may not conceive any happiness now that does not draw its virtue from the image of that primal time' (*DoE*, p. 64). Domination of nature can thus never be complete without destruction of the nature which still resides within human beings. This issue of the repression of nature and the goal of reconciliation with nature raises the issues of sexuality and gender.

Critical Theory and Sexual Politics

In Excursus I on 'Odysseus or Myth and Enlightenment', Horkheimer and Adorno trace the rise of individual subjectivity from myth and nature while presenting a pre-history of bourgeois consciousness, discovering many features and principles of later bourgeois thought in Homer's Odysseus. The point of their brilliant hermeneutical reading of *The Odyssey*, described as 'the basic text of European civilization' (*DoE*, p. 46), is to show the interconnections between myth and enlightenment and the emergence of the modern self from the mythic past. Homer's text is read as an allegorical journey in which Odysseus overcomes primitive natural forces (immersion in pleasure, sexuality, animal aggressivity and violence, brutal tribalism and so forth) and asserts his domination over the mythic/natural world. In his use of cunning and deceit, his drive toward self-preservation and refusal to accept mythic fate, his entrepreneurial control over his men and his patriarchal power over his wife and other women, Odysseus is presented as a prefiguration of bourgeois man who reveals the connections between self-preservation, the domination of nature and the entanglement of myth and enlightenment.

The Odyssey can therefore be read as an allegory concerning the nature and social functions of patriarchy. This issue raises the controversial problem of the relationship between Critical Theory and feminism. To some extent, it was their focus on the relations between humans and nature that took Critical Theorists into the arena of sexual politics, to reflections on the nature and value of sexuality and desire, the role of repression and renunciation in the formation of personality, the establishment of relations between the sexes and the nature of authority, the family and patriarchy – all themes which had previously been ignored by Marxism.[9] Yet, while Critical Theory and contemporary feminism share certain problematics, the relationship between them is itself quite problematical. On the one hand, the Critical Theorists focus on issues central to feminism, and frequently use the terms 'patriarchy' and 'patriarchal' to designate modes of thought and behavior bound up with social domination, the domination of men over women and children, which they consistently criticize. On the other hand, as Patricia Mills has argued, they tend to analyze sexuality and gender from a male point of view and to reproduce what are arguably sexist representations of women in their reading of *The Odyssey*.[10]

In all cases, Mills argues, it is male identity that is the focus of Horkheimer's and Adorno's reading, and women are represented as either threats or handmaidens to male power. No positive image of women as autonomous subjects of desire and identity are projected, and woman is thus erased from the text of patriarchal myth. Yet Mills's reading should be qualified in light of Horkheimer's and Adorno's discussion of Odysseus, which presents aspects of a critique of the male bourgeois subject and patriarchy. Furthermore, Horkheimer and Adorno might respond that they are simply presenting a reading of a myth which itself should be seen as an allegory of how patriarchy is part of the project of the domination of nature. But a feminist could still counter that *Dialectic of Enlightenment* at best presents a male-centered critique of patriarchy which focuses on male desire, power and identity, and that Critical Theory should provide room for discussion of *female* desire, subjectivity, identity and so on.

This is indeed Mills's demand, and it points to a one-sidedness which has informed Critical Theory so far in its trajectory. While recognizing the validity of the feminist critique, however, I would suggest that Critical Theory's project, method and categories allow – demand even – feminist supplementation. Moreover, against suppression of gender and nature in some versions of Marxism, Critical Theory has consistently made the dialectics between history and nature, as well as the individual and society, and men and women, a focus, and has thus provided the conceptual space in which a synthesis of Critical Theory and feminism could be articulated.

In fact, many elements of *Dialectic of Enlightenment* anticipate elements of feminism. In Horkheimer's and Adorno's reading, for instance, Odysseus's story also illustrates the price paid for domination over nature and for the emergence of the sovereignty of the self over the totality of being which is the mark of enlightenment (*DoE*, pp. 3ff. and *passim*). For, as Odysseus overcomes all the challenges to his sovereignty and power through mythic, natural and human forces, he is increasingly separated from nature, other humans and even the capacity for pleasure and relaxation in his body. Like later bourgeois society and individuals, Odysseus is alienated from nature, his body and other people as he sets up boundaries between these domains, and even establishes a boundary within his own body between reason and passion, mind and body – a division and opposition that would later be the foundation of classical and modern philosophy.

It is precisely these boundaries which much contemporary feminist thought is concerned to criticize,[11] and it can be argued that Horkheimer and Adorno contribute to this project. The study of 'Juliette or Enlightenment and Morality' also contains elements of a proto-feminist critique of sexual objectification. The discussion of the Marquis de Sade focuses on his application of enlightenment principles of instrumentality, calculation and system to sexual practice, in which the body is organized as an instrument of sexual pleasure so that every orifice, position and possibility for sexual stimulation is diligently pursued. Horkheimer's and Adorno's critique thus parallels feminist critiques of sexual objectification and the ways in which the body and sexuality are objectified in pornography, mass culture, advertising and so on.

In any case, the excurses into both Homer's *Odyssey* and enlightenment and morality demand multivalent, or multidimensional, readings to flesh out their major themes. As noted, Horkheimer's and Adorno's interpretation of *The Odyssey* can be read as a study of the pre-history of the bourgeois subject, as well as an allegory of the nature of patriarchy which itself is arguably a patriarchal narrative about women and gender. But both the study of *The Odyssey* and the following excursus on enlightenment and morality also exhibit features of a more strictly psychoanalytic reading of history which show how certain traits and behavior that the authors deem undesirable have their origins in the childhood of Western experience.

Consequently, while Horkheimer's and Adorno's philosophy of history can be read as a negative, rather than a positive, theodicy, their tracing of the phenomenology of spirit can also be read as an attempt at a psychoanalytic therapeutic whereby the psyche can become reintegrated and healed by working through past sufferings. Like Freud and the Hegel of *The Phenomenology of Spirit*, Horkheimer and Adorno show the scars, wounds and suffering endured in history. Yet their story does not have a happy ending. The defeats and sufferings are not subsumed in a higher state of absolute knowledge and progress, as in Hegel; and though their odyssey might produce emancipatory 'enlightenment' for a few individuals or for themselves, it is not clear what therapeutic effects their philosophy of history will produce.

Finally, Critical Theory intersects with a tradition of feminist thought in its critique of the ways in which science and technology serve the interests of human domination and with its positing of alternative values of reconciliation, gratification and peace.[12] In fact, a major theme of *Dialectic of Enlightenment* is the radical critique of science, technology and instrumental rationality that continues to be of value during an epoch in which the tendencies described by Horkheimer and Adorno are increasing in both scope and intensity.

Science, Reason and Domination

Building on Lukács's critique of science and the reification which results from the capitalist division of labor, Horkheimer and Adorno point to the interrelationships between the developments of society, science and scientific modes of thought (see 2.3). They were among the first to present a critique of science and technology from a Left, radical point of view; previously most critiques had come from the Right and from irrationalist positions. Their critique rests on theoretical observations concerning the roles of science and technology in contemporary social life and the ways in which they further social domination, combined with an epistemological critique which specifies the limitations of scientific modes of thought. This position is obviously provocative in an era in which quantitative thought, logic and the computerization of the mind are gaining in prestige and power; and the thoroughgoing comprehensiveness of their critique distinguishes the Horkheimer-Adorno-Marcuse position within Critical Theory from that of Habermas and his followers, who are more sympathetic to science and technology.[13]

Previously Marxists had tended to separate science and technology from society, perceiving them as progressive forces of production that could be used to criticize irrational relations of production and as forces leading to the creation of a more rational society.[14] During the 1930s the Institute also seemed to share this positive appraisal of science. It called for a synthesis of science and philosophy in the production of critical social theory and the emancipation of science from capitalist relations of production, which were perceived as a fetter to its full development and use to benefit humanity.[15] By the 1940s, however, Institute theorists were conceptualizing the inter-relationships between science, technology and society more critically, following Georg Lukács, who was probably the first within the Marxian tradition to specify the relationships between science and capitalism.

Lukács suggests that natural science 'distills "pure" facts and places them in the relevent context by means of observation, abstraction, and experiment', and that it is precisely the 'social structure of capitalism which encourages such views'.[16] In producing commodities for the sake of their exchange value and in the exchange relationships which permeate bourgeois society, there is abstraction from qualitative needs, values and uses. The division of labor under capitalism fragments and isolates sectors of reality; capitalism promotes quantitative and calculative modes of thought governed by interests in profit, control, measurability and predict-ability, and thus constitutes science as a tool of its interests. Lukács concludes:

There is something highly problematic in the fact that capitalist society is pre-disposed to harmonize with scientific method, to constitute indeed the social premises of its exactness. If the internal structure of the 'facts' of their inter-connections is essentially historical, if, that is to say, they are caught up in a process of continuous transformation, then we may indeed question when the great scientific inaccuracy occurs. (pp. 95–6)

For Lukács, the 'inaccuracy' and 'the unscientific nature of this seemingly so scientific method' consist 'in its failure to see and take account of the *historical character* of the facts on which it is based' (p. 98).

Here Lukács anticipates the Institute's argument concerning the historical nature of theories and their objects (see 2.3). Since Lukács is sometimes dismissed as an 'irrationalist' and as a 'romantic' enemy of science whose work 'represents the first major irruption of the romantic anti-scientific tradition of bourgeois thought into Marxist theory',[17] it should be noted that he grants natural science a certain limited validity, but claims that its methods are inappropriate when applied to society and history: 'When the ideal of scientific knowledge is applied to nature it simply furthers the progress of science. But when it is applied to society it turns out to be an ideological weapon of the bourgeoisie' (p. 104). Hork-heimer and Adorno go one step beyond Lukács's social and epistemological critique of science by arguing that interests in objectification and quantification – which are intimately linked with interests of capitalist profit and social control in the contemporary era – constitute science and technology as instruments of domination:

Even the deductive form of science reflects hierarchy and coercion. Just as the first categories represented the organized tribe and its power over the individual, so the whole logical order, dependency, connection, progression, and union of concepts is grounded in the corresponding conditions of social reality – that is, of the division of labor. But of course this social character of categories of thought is not, as Durkheim asserts, an expression of social solidarity, but evidence of the inscrutable unity of society and domination. Domination lends increased consistency and force to the social whole in which it establishes itself. (*DoE*, p. 21)

Horkheimer and Adorno also argue that logic has its origins in processes of substitution wherein human sacrifices gave way to animal sacrifices, and eventually totems and rituals. On this view, modern logic is rooted in processes of abstraction bound up with the social practices of substitution, calculation and equivalence. They argue that conformity of thought is rooted in social conformity and 'fear of social deviation' (*DoE*, p. xiv). Such a relationship of concepts and modes of thought to social processes is one of the basic positions of Critical Theory that distinguishes its mode of inquiry and critique. This analysis of the relation between the categories of enlightenment rationality and social domination parallels in interesting ways Nietzsche's derivation of moral categories in *The Genealogy of Morals*.[18] Just as Nietzsche claimed that moral phenomena were rooted in pain, sacrifice and punishment, so Horkheimer and Adorno propose that substitution, equivalence and universal interchangeability are rooted in *sacrifice* (*DoE*, pp. 10ff.), with rituals, prayers and so forth eventually being substituted for human sacrifices in the effort to please the gods. Tribal sacrifices were an attempt to gain power over nature and desire, whereas efforts to dominate nature manifest an 'introversion of sacrifice', a renouncing of one's own instinctual demands for pleasure, which Horkheimer and Adorno claim is a key to 'the history of civilization' (p. 55). That is, the price paid for engaging in the attempt to dominate nature is ultimately alienation from it and from the nature that exists within all of us: 'Humans pay for the increase of their power with alienation from that over which they exercise their power. Enlightenment behaves toward things as a dictator toward men. He knows them in so far as he can manipulate them' (p. 9).

Exchange of equivalents requires abstraction from concrete particularities and conceiving of value in terms of abstract, exchangeable quantities like money. For Critical Theory, exchange of equivalents is one of the central features of a capitalist market economy, and pervades the realm of economics, politics, law, culture and everyday life. This argument goes beyond the standard Marxian claims that in capitalist society exchange value predominates over use value, and that all phenomena are turned into commodities which receive their value through exchange in the market-place.[19] Instead, Critical Theorists present a historical argument that thinking in equivalences necessarily leads to sacrifice of individuality and particularity in both modes of thought and social processes. From the early 1930s through the 1960s, Horkheimer and Adorno argued that abstract, quantitative modes of thought are not capable of grasping the complexity of social processes or offering critical perspectives on social development (see 2.3 above). But, beginning with *Dialectic of Enlightenment*, they began arguing as well that quantitative, abstract modes of thought are ruled by principles of equivalence and substitution whereby dissimilar things become comparable by reduction to abstract quantities which exclude individual quality on principle. Against these practices and modes of thought, Horkheimer and Adorno call for discourse and writing which preserve individuality while illuminating the particular and the universal, the individual and the social, and demonstrating the dialectical inter-penetration of the individual and the social, the subject and the object.

For Horkheimer and Adorno, the enlightenment principle that all valid thought and knowledge must conform to principles of calculation, equiv-alence and systemization is suspect and promotes conformist modes of thought: 'For the Enlightenment, whatever does not conform to the rule of computation and utility is suspect. . . . Enlightenment is totalitarian' (*DoE*, p. 6). Enlightenment banishes all myth, subjectivity, value, quality, aesthetics, feelings and particulars from valid thought; for 'its ideal is the system from which all and everything follows' (p. 7). Both its rationalist and empiricist versions aim at a principle of scientific unity whereby the 'multiplicity of forms is reduced to position and arrangement, history to fact, things to matter' (ibid.). In addition, 'Formal logic was the major school of unified science. It provided the Enlightenment thinkers with the schema of the calculability of the world. The mythologizing equation of Ideas with numbers in Plato's last writings expresses the longing of all demythologization: number became the canon of the Enlightenment' (ibid.).

Such quantitative modes of thought presuppose an identity between concept and object, word and thing, and privilege mathematical logic as alone capable of grasping the essence of things. For the Institute, however, there is always a nonidentity between thought and being. Every object has its own particularity and uniqueness, which cannot be subsumed in cat-egories, and it is totalitarian to believe that a specific mode of thought can systematize all being. The social implications of this mind-set concern attempts by social organization and administration to control individuals in ways that abstract from individuality and uniqueness through the imposition of formal rules and regulations.

Modernity and the Totally Administered Society

In an excursus on 'Juliette or Enlightenment and Morality', Horkheimer and Adorno carry out a brilliant analysis of the ways in which enlightenment rationality leads logically to fascism, which applies enlightenment principles of order, control, calculability, domination and system to the totalitarian administration of society: 'For the rulers, men become material, just as nature as a whole is material for society. After the short intermezzo of liberalism, in which the bourgeois kept one another in check, domination appears as archaic terror in a fascistically rationalized form' (*DoE*, p. 87). This study illustrates the ways in which enlightenment can 'sink into barbarism' (p. xi) and how a 'fully enlightened earth radiates disaster triumphant' (p. 3).

Such positions are reminiscent of Walter Benjamin's discussions of the interconnections between mythology and modernity, nature and history, the old and new, and progress and regression in the contemporary world.[20] Horkheimer's and Adorno's argument is that Kant intensified the critique of religion, morality and metaphysics – all of which provided alternatives to the modes of instrumental thought which eventually triumphed. Then Sade demonstrated what a world without morality and religion might look like, while Nietzsche allegedly destroyed the lingering illusions connected with metaphysical modes of thought. From the beginning of Western history, they imply, rulers always used enlightenment in their interests, from the times of Odysseus's domination of his men and wife to fascist attempts to dominate the world. Horkheimer and Adorno find the psychological origins of modernity in Odysseus's attempts to escape from domination by mythic forces (which metaphorize forces of nature) and to dominate nature himself. Another stage in the connection between modernity and the totally administered society is evident in Kant's systemization of the categories of rational thought and in his conception of philosophy as a closed rational system that contains all truth and appearance, while banishing everything outside the system to the unreal, irrational, 'noumenal' realm (*DoE*, pp. 81ff.). Kantian reason projects an ideal of a subject who transcends nature and history, and who contains within himself perfect order, hierarchical supervision and administration of all concepts and experiences by a super-bureaucrat, the transcendental ego.

Kant's system of pure reason is transposed by the capitalist class into its factories and then prisons, by Sade into his organization of sexual orgies and by the Nazis into their totalitarian social order epitomized by their concentration camps. Enlightenment rationality shares a love of system, order, administration and organization in which everything finds its place and everything is hierarchically ordered and administered. Deviations are invariably punished by Kant's conscience for those who break the moral law, by unemployment and deprivation for those who refuse to work, by imprisonment for those who refuse to obey the judicial law and by death for those who radically challenge the laws of the system. According to Horkheimer and Adorno, Sade systematizes and organizes deviance in his celebrations of immorality, criminality and otiosity, but in the same calculating, ordered and administered fashion in which enlightenment rationality organizes its totally administered society which excludes what Sade celebrates in his inversion of enlightenment.

Horkheimer and Adorno, like their colleague Karl Wittfogel, see the ways in which forms of organization and administration are part of the productive forces and relations of bourgeois capitalist society.[21] Rather than abandoning Marxism in *Dialectic of Enlightenment*, they add a new dimension to radical social theory of the important ways in which organization and administration and their corresponding modes of thought contribute to producing social domination and exploitation. Although they withdraw attention from production and labor, they show the ways in which the imperatives and organization of capitalist modernity permeate social life and lead to social domination. Their argument is that while enlightenment rationality has its origins in the pre-history of bourgeois society, its development is intimately bound up with the triumph of capitalism, industrialism and the bourgeoisie. Consequently, all principles and modes of thought connected with enlightenment reason can be conceptualized and criticized as forms of bourgeois ideology:

The system the Enlightenment has in mind is the form of knowledge which copes most proficiently with the facts and supports the individual most effectively in the mastery of nature. Its principles are the principles of self-preservation. Immaturity is then the inability to survive. The burgher, in the successive forms of slaveowner, free entrepreneur, and administrator, is the logical subject of the Enlightenment. (*DoE*, p. 83)

The administrator abstracts from particulars in favor of universal rules and regulations, and thus forces individuals to conform to the system of administration and domination. The result is a leveling off of differences and the production of a mass society. Horkheimer and Adorno suggest that enlightenment thought moves naturally from being an instrument for the domination of nature to becoming an instrument for the domination of human beings, and that therefore there is a logical progression from the factory to the prisons to the concentration camps of the totally administered society. The notion of the totally administered society recurs constantly throughout *Dialectic of Enlightenment*, and will be interrogated in the next several chapters. The themes of societal regression, growing standardiz-ation, massification and rationalization are central to the 'Notes and Drafts' which conclude the book. Here Horkheimer and Adorno adopt a literary strategy, already in use in Horkheimer's *Dammerung*, of presenting their ideas in short drafts and aphorisms which are intended to illuminate contemporary social reality. This method, influenced by Nietzsche's aphoristic method of presentation, provides constellations of images designed to shock and disturb the reader and so lead to new insight and new ways of seeing. For example, Horkheimer and Adorno use aphoristic meta-phors to present their view of contemporary society: 'The punishment of imprisonment is nothing when set against the social reality in which we live' (*DoE*, p. 229).

The notes and drafts also tend to be apocalyptic and to express their dark view of history, as in 'Avalanches', in which the authors compare con-temporary history to natural catastrophe and express their view that, even after the defeat of fascism, things may still grow worse (*DoE*, pp. 220–1). Relatively new motifs also appear in this section, such as fragments toward a dialectical anthropology and reflections on the relations among humans, animals and nature. Yet no 'positive' politics emerges, even in aphoristic form; nor do any fissures in consciousness or society appear that would allow opposition to surface. Thus *Dialectic of Enlightenment* ends on a rather gloomy note with a series of visions of catastrophe, followed by reflections on human stupidity which refrain from pointing to any positive hopes for a way out of the current impasse of Western civilization.

In their magnum opus, Horkheimer and Adorno therefore carry out an extremely radical, negative, multidimensional critique of the relationships between humans, thought and nature, utilizing Marxian, Nietzschean, Freudian and varying philosophical modes of analysis. While the book as a whole exhibits a distancing from the Marxian perspectives that dominated their 1930s works, I have suggested that Adorno and Horkheimer fre-quently make use of Marxian methods of analysis in which modes of thought are interpreted in terms of their implication in social processes and their social functions. In the absence of political economy in the book, however, it is not clear how the imperatives of capitalism enter into the production of science, technology and instrumental rationality or how the complex interaction between socio-economic systems and modes of thought and inquiry takes place. While their philosophy of history provides a critical perspective on science and instrumental rationality full of important insights, it is not clear that abandonment of Marxist perspectives on history and political economy aids in comprehending the dialectics of production, science, technology and instrumental rationality in the constitution of contemporary societies.

Another problem is that Horkheimer and Adorno have a rather undifferentiated critique of science, rationality and Enlightenment, and seem to assume that *all* science and reason are bound up with the domination of nature, and are thus intrinsically connected with domination. Such a position equates objectification with reification, and covers over the social factors whereby certain forms of science, technology and thought serve interests of domination and reify objects, nature and people, while other modes of thought and activity may be governed by other interests and do not necessarily reify their objects. Against Horkheimer's and Adorno's undifferentiated critique of enlightenment rationality, Habermas calls for developing more differentiated critiques of the various sciences and discourses, in opposition to the global critique of science and scientific discourses per se by Horkheimer and Adorno in *Dialectic of Enlightenment* and their later works.[22]

Furthermore, Horkheimer and Adorno also tend to have undifferentiated concepts of commodification, rationalization, administration, bureaucracy and exchange. In later discussions, I shall argue for more differentiated views of enlightenment, the media, consumption, culture and so on, while attempting to preserve the radical core of Horkheimer's and Adorno's critique of fundamental societal processes which reproduce human domination. At this point, one might also note the similarities between the critiques of modernity developed by Horkheimer and Adorno in *Dialectic of Enlightenment* and the critiques of the German sociological tradition that includes Tonnies, Simmel and Weber, which also characterizes advanced industrial society as a totally administered system of domination.[23] This tradition interprets the fate of modernity in terms of growing heteronomy, whereby individuals are progressively dominated by the technological bureaucratic apparatus and its mode of work, politics, everyday life and thought. The Institute thus came to share the 'tragic pessimism' which marked the theory of modernity developed by German sociology, and its theories of the totally administered society and the end of the individual can be read as a pessimistic response to the developmental trends of modernity, which posit no real hope of reversing the direction of historical development.

Yet as I shall argue in the following chapters, the Institute made many original contributions to contemporary social theory, and it would be a mistake to see its theory as no more than a tragic, pessimistic response to the trajectory of modernity. In addition, one might note that their experiences of the rise of fascism in Germany and its ensuing horrors gave Institute theorists quite good reasons for responding to contemporary history in a pessimistic manner. Conditions of life in exile in the United States also provided good reasons for questioning certain postulates of the Marxian theory of history and revolution, as I shall indicate in the following sections.

4.2 Eclipse of Reason

Dialectic of Enlightenment was concluded in 1944 and published in Holland in 1947. In the Spring of 1944, Horkheimer presented some of the key ideas in lecture form, and published them in 1947 in English as *Eclipse of Reason*.[24] The method of presentation, style and, in many cases, substance of the ideas is strikingly different in the two books, however. Yet I would propose reading *Eclipse of Reason* as a valuable clarification of, and supplement to, many of the key ideas in *Dialectic of Enlightenment*, rather than simply as a repetition, a watering down or even a break with the radicalism of *Dialectic of Enlightenment*. While the style of Horkheimer's and Adorno's book was elusive, epigrammatic and often esoteric, *Eclipse of Reason* is relatively lucid and accessible to a general audience. The text is organized and argued in a rather traditional systematic fashion by comparison with *Dialectic of Enlightenment*, which consists of philosophical fragments with only a rather disjointed and often puzzling connection and organization. A comparison of the two texts suggests that Adorno played a central role in the idiosyncratic mode of presentation of *Dialectic of Enlightenment*, while Horkheimer still felt comfortable with more traditional modes of thought and presentation.

Eclipse of Reason is more superficial and less fascinating than its predecessor, and it has been somewhat neglected in the literature on Critical Theory. This is unfortunate, however, since it presents a cogent introduction to Critical Theory for readers in the English-speaking world, and contains a strong critique of positivism, pragmatism and other modes of thought dominant in the United States. Horkheimer argues that an 'eclipse of reason' is apparent in contemporary thought, mass culture, the union movement and working-class parties, and contemporary modes of social organization. The text is informed by a distinction between subjective and objective reason, or instrumental and substantive reason, and expounds a critique of positivism and Enlightenment rationality.

Horkheimer sees objective reason as connected with the philosophical tradition in which reason is to produce a comprehensive theory of nature, society and human beings and is to develop on this basis theories of values, goals and the purposes of human life so that inadequate social conditions can be criticized. Subjective reason, by contrast, limits reason to the calculation of means within a predefined system in which goals and values are accepted and not criticized. Subjective reason

is essentially concerned with means and ends, with the adequacy of procedures for purposes more or less taken for granted and supposedly self-explanatory. It attaches little importance to the question whether the purposes as such are reasonable. If it concerns itself at all with ends, it takes for granted that they too are reasonable in the subjective sense, i.e. that they serve the subject's interest in relation to self-preservation. (*EoR*, pp. 3–4)

Eclipse of Reason carries through a careful, lucid critique of dominant theories of science and philosophy, to which Horkheimer opposes the conception of Critical Theory. The first two studies, 'Means and Ends' and 'Conflicting Panaceas', present detailed critiques of dominant modes of contemporary thought, while the second half of the book presents many of Critical Theory's criticisms of contemporary society and culture, restating many of the central ideas of *Dialectic of Enlightenment* with the addition of examples culled from the author's experiences in the United States. In general, Horkheimer illustrates some of the most difficult concepts of Critical Theory in an illuminating way or provides interesting supplemental analyses.

For instance, in 'The Revolt of Nature', he argues that the drive toward self-preservation leads to the repression of internal nature. He then suggests that the 'repressed mimetic impulse' returns as a destructive force manipulated by fascism and other systems of social domination (*EoR*, pp. 115ff.). He claims that if humans become dissatisfied with the process of civilization, the repressed mimetic impulses lie ready to emerge and 'break out as a destructive force' (p. 115). Such repressed urges, he suggests, help explain phenomena like pornography, sadistic laughter and the persecution of Jews. Horkheimer ends this study with an analysis of how Darwinism serves the interests of the domination of nature by stressing adaptation and survival of the fittest. In the final two studies of the book, 'Rise and Decline of the Individual' and 'On the Concept of Philosophy', he presents aspects of his social theory and his conception of philosophy as social critique.

In attempting to assess the differences between the two most important Institute presentations of the critique of Enlightenment and instrumental rationality, one should be aware that *Dialectic of Enlightenment* and *Eclipse of Reason* were aimed at quite different audiences and had somewhat different purposes. *Dialectic of Enlightenment* requires a high level of learning and culture, as well as familiarity with many of the central figures in Western thought; whereas *Eclipse of Reason* requires only some familiarity with contemporary trends in philosophy, science and American society and culture. It appears that Horkheimer had more confidence in using vernacular vocabulary and in presenting his positions in an accessible way than Adorno, who feared that such modes of exposition would only foster conformity and assimilation to dominant modes of thought.

There are also other interesting theoretical differences between the two books. While Adorno was highly suspicious of bourgeois humanism and generally attempted to avoid its discourses, Horkheimer is aggressively 'humanistic' in his text.[25] In the Preface, he writes that, as the people of the democratic nations consummate their victory over fascism, they

must work out and put into practice the principles of humanity in the name of which the sacrifices of war were made. The present potentialities of social achievement surpass the expectations of all the philosophers and statesmen who have ever outlined in utopian programs the idea of a truly human society. Yet there is a universal feeling of fear and disillusionment. The hopes of mankind seem to be farther from fulfillment today than they were even in the groping epochs when they were first formulated by humanists. It seems that even as technical knowledge expands the horizon of man's thought and activity, his autonomy as an individual, his ability to resist the growing apparatus of mass manipulation, his power of imagination, his independent judgment appear to be reduced. Advance in technical facilities for enlightenment is accompanied by a process of dehumanization. Thus progress threatens to nullify the very goal it is supposed to realize – the idea of man. (*EoR*, p. vi)

Contrasting this Preface with the Introduction to *Dialectic of Enlightenment*, one notices the frequent use of categories of humanism in the first and their absence in the second. Horkheimer's text is also more 'positive' in the role it assigns to philosophy and reason, and claims that philosophy can provide direct access to truth (see below). It is also more optimistic regarding the possibilities for social transformation and progress than *Dialectic of Enlightenment*, which takes a more skeptical position; and it contains a more positive appraisal of potentialities for progressive social change and a clearer statement of Critical Theory's notion of reconciliation with nature as opposed to domination of nature. Thus, while there is almost nothing on the theme of reconciliation with nature in *Dialectic of Enlightenment*, *Eclipse of Reason* frequently calls for a reconciliation of reason and nature, subject and object, practical and theoretical reason, individual and society, the particular and the universal, mind and body, thought and being (*EoR*, pp. 123, 126). The general position has to do with a conception of dialectical thought, to which Horkheimer was especially attracted, which conceives of it as undoing and resolving contradictions and antinomies which are shown to be one-sided and incomplete. Nondialectical thought is binary, and opposes one factor to another, with one side of the opposition privileged, the other denigrated.

Indeed, in the final section, 'On the Concept of Philosophy', Horkheimer assigns philosophy an important role in promoting social progress: 'An underlying assumption of the present discussion has been that philosophical awareness of these processes may help to reverse them' (*EoR*, p. 162). Philosophy is assigned the task of 'adequate description' and calling things by their 'proper names'. 'Philosophy helps man to allay his fears by helping language to fulfill its genuine mimetic function, its mission of mirroring the natural tendencies. . . . Philosophy is the conscious effort to knit all our knowledge and insight into a linguistic structure in which things are called by their right names (p. 179). The whole notion of philosophy as a vehicle for discovering and articulating truth – 'the adequation of name and thing' (p. 180) – and the notion that philosophy should organize ideas systematically into a structure that corresponds to the structure of reality is quite foreign to the position of *Dialectic of Enlightenment* and to Adorno's philosophy in general.[26]

In addition, Horkheimer assigns philosophy the role of fostering a mutual critique of subjective and objective reason, and 'if possible', preparing in the intellectual realm the reconciliation of the two in reality' (*EoR*, p. 174). Here Horkheimer ascribes to philosophy the role of overcoming opposites in thought, while preparing for an eventual transcendence of oppositions in reality – the traditional utopian function of philosophy. Yet, while Horkheimer ascribes philosophy an essential role in the process of genuine enlightenment and emancipation, he hesitates to assign it a direct political role, consciously warning against philosophy degenerating into propaganda (pp. 184ff.).

At this phase, Critical Theory is almost identical with critical philosophy, which assigns the functions of critique, negation and reconciliation to philosophy; though Adorno, as we shall see in Chapter 5, also privileges 'authentic art', and will eventually privilege its claims to truth over those of philosophy. The relationships between Critical Theory and science and politics are problematized and distanced, and Critical Theory appears to be reconstructed as a mode of philosophy. Yet, in its succeeding stages, with the empirical studies of anti-Semitism and the 'authoritarian personality', Critical Theory would once again attempt syntheses of philosophy and the social sciences, although philosophy henceforth would arguably play the key role in the work of Adorno, Horkheimer, Marcuse and, later, Habermas.

4.3   Critical Theory, the Proletariat and Politics

In this section, I will reflect upon changes in Adorno's and Horkheimer's political positions and their relationship to classical Marxism during the 1940s, and will contrast their positions with Marcuse's stance at the time. We have seen that, with the break-up of the interdisciplinary Institute during World War II, Horkheimer and Adorno transformed Critical Theory from a supradisciplinary theory of society into a philosophy of history and a critique of instrumental rationality. Critical Theory cut itself off, at least temporarily, from both the sciences and political struggle and developments. Consequently the Critical Theory developed by Horkheimer and Adorno in the 1940s and 1950s became more philosophical, literary and at times hermetic.

The Institute's exile experience once again played a major role in shifting the focus and substance of Critical Theory. With Critical Theorists dispersed as a result of the war, Critical Theory suddenly became the concern of individuals, and in particular of Horkheimer and Adorno who were the only major theorists among the inner circle who did not go to Washington to work for the United States government. Yet experience of life in the United States obviously had a major impact on the development of Critical Theory. The emergence of the culture industry and the consumer society were especially pronounced in the United States – and above all in California where Horkheimer and Adorno lived – and struck the Institute members as providing a crucial development and strengthening of capitalism. Administration and bureaucracy were also growing in the United States with the vast expansion of the government during the war and the expansion of corporations, universities, the Civil Service, and local bureaucracies after the war.

During the 1940s, the Institute in effect anticipated the major themes of 1950s social theory: the affluent society, the consumer society, conformity, the media, the administered society, science and technology and domination, and so forth. I propose that it was precisely their status as emigrés that led to their experiencing these new developments as especially crucial, changes that were transforming the very nature of capitalism while putting in question some of the tenets of Marxian revolutionary theory. Radicals in exile, the Critical Theorists thus attempted to revise and develop radical social theory in the light of the new social conditions in which they found themselves.

Striking changes emerge during this period in their political orientation. As late as 1942, in his essay 'Authoritarian State', Horkheimer continues to use Marxist categories and to commit himself to a Marxian revolutionary socialist politics. Such overt theoretical and political commitments to Marxism soon disappear, however. In particular, Horkheimer and Adorno begin to lose faith in the revolutionary potential of the working class in the face of the triumph of fascism and the integration of labor into the capitalist system in the democratic capitalist countries. Although the Institute began questioning the Marxian theory of capitalist crisis in the 1930s, while postulating a new form of state capitalism which might protect it from the contradictions and antagonisms within the capitalist system through state management of the economy, no questions were raised – at least in published writings – concerning the privileged role of the working class in the Marxian theory of revolution.

Doubts as to the revolutionary potential of the working class begin to appear in Adorno's letters, notebooks and essays during the 1940s, some of

which were published in 'Reflections on Class Theory' and *Minima Moralia*.[27]
Adorno's questioning of the Marxian theory of the proletariat as *the* revolutionary subject begins in 'Reflections on Class Theory'. In this essay, Adorno scrutinizes the Marxian theory of class and the theory of the proletariat as a revolutionary class, and raises the question of their continuing relevance in the current situation. He points out that even in Marx's day the theory of class contained a contradiction in that it was supposed to designate what a group had in common, its features of identity and common interests. Yet even the bourgeois class had different interests and different degrees of capital and power, which created fundamental differences and inequalities even within the ruling class.

At this time, the proletariat shared a situation of oppression and exploitation, and thus had discernible class interests, as well as an interest in ending exploitation and capitalism. Yet the proletariat's vocation as a revolutionary class was directly related to its pauperization. If it had nothing to lose but its chains, then 'poverty could become the force of revolution, which would overcome poverty' (p. 383). Yet today, Adorno claims,

> the proletariat has more to lose than its chains. Its standard of living in comparison with the English conditions of one hundred years ago – which the authors of *The Communist Manifesto* had before them – has not become worse but has improved. Shorter working hours, better nutrition, housing and clothing, protection of family members and the aged, and a higher average life expectancy have – along with the development of the technical productive forces – all accrued to the workers. There can no longer be any talk of hunger necessarily bringing them together and driving them to revolution. (p. 384)

Adorno also discusses ways in which reification and dehumanization further disqualify the proletariat from its revolutionary vocation while at the same time preserving the actual structure of class society and making its abolition all the more necessary for the dehumanized and oppressed (pp. 388ff.). In *Dialectic of Enlightenment*, and throughout the decade, not only did Horkheimer and Adorno question certain postulates of the Marxian philosophy of history; they did not affirm any revolutionary class politics at all. Indeed, they constantly used the term 'masses', rather than 'working class' or 'proletariat', in their writings. And against the masses, they affirmed that radical opposition was located primarily in critical intellectuals and radical thought and discourse. This position was aggressively formulated in Adorno's *Minima Moralia*, and henceforth became the centerpiece of Horkheimer's and Adorno's political position. Adorno writes: 'In the face of the totalitarian unison with which the eradication of difference is proclaimed as a purpose in itself, even part of the social force of liberation may have temporarily withdrawn to the individual sphere. If Critical

Theory lingers there, it is not only with a bad conscience' (*MM*, p. 18). Further, 'For the intellectual, inviolable isolation is now the only way of showing some measure of solidarity. All collaboration, all the human worth of social mixing, and participation, merely masks a tacit acceptance of inhumanity' (p. 26).

Horkheimer and Adorno came to accept this position during World War II, when they were unable to identify with any specific political tendency or movement. At this time revolutionary politics had all but disappeared in the effort to provide a popular front against fascism. This was a period of extreme pessimism for Adorno and Horkheimer, during which they felt especially isolated and depressed over the monstrous crimes of fascism. The allies' victory over fascism did not cheer them up, however; nor did it lead them to modify their radical individualism or their rejection of Marxian revolutionary perspectives. There is no evidence in any of Horkheimer's and Adorno's correspondence or other writings that they expected any exciting new political possibilities from the defeat of fascism; and Marcuse informed them from Washington that the supposed de-Nazification program was quickly returning former Nazis to positions of economic, political and cultural power.[28]

Nor did Horkheimer and Adorno initiate any sustained efforts to regroup the old multidisciplinary team of the Institute for Social Research. Both Marcuse and Neumann wrote from Washington inquiring into the possibility of a revival of Institute activity, and were constantly proposing the renewal of the journal and various collective projects.[29] Horkheimer and Adorno did not seem particularly interested in reviving the project of developing an interdisciplinary social theory of the contemporary epoch, however; indeed, they no longer seemed to believe that such a theory could be grounded in the Marxian critique of political economy or serve as a springboard for revolutionary politics.

Recent material from the Marcuse archives reveals that, not only was Marcuse eager to resume the multidisciplinary project of the previous years, but that he continued to concern himself with Marxian theory and revolutionary politics. In a 1946 letter to Horkheimer, he wrote:

What I have written and collected in the last years 'off duty' is envisaged as pre-liminary work for a new book. . . . It is – naturally – centered on the problem of the 'unrealized revolution.' You might remember the drafts on the transformation of language, of the function of scientific management, and on the structure of regimented experience that I wrote in Santa Monica. These drafts will be rewritten as part of the book.[30]

Marcuse could not be aware of the changes that had taken place in Horkheimer's and Adorno's interests and thought during the years after he left California to work in Washington during the war. On a trip to Europe later in 1946, his first since his exile in 1934, Marcuse enthusiastically wrote to Horkheimer concerning the great interest in the Institute's work. He describes meetings with Karl Mannheim, Richard Lowenthal and others in London and Raymond Aron, Jean Wahl and young existentialists and surrealists in Paris, noting:

All of them asked me why in heaven's name the *Zeitschrift* does not come out again. It was – so they said – the only and the last publication which discussed the real problems on a really 'avant-garde' level. The general disorientation and isolation now is so great that the need for the reissue of the *Zeitschrift* is greater than ever before. Even if the *Zeitschrift* could not be officially introduced into Germany, the public outside Germany is large enough and important enough to justify its appearance.[31]

Marcuse then proposed a special issue on Germany, incorporating analyses of the diverse political, economic and cultural programs of the most import-ant German parties and groups at present.

Later in the year Marcuse met Horkheimer in Washington, and they agreed to sketch out a theoretical orientation to the problems of the current historical epoch which could serve as a framework for renewed publication of the *Zeitschrift*. While no manuscript by Horkheimer exists, Marcuse sent a twenty-four-page typewritten draft outlining his perspectives on the postwar situation in Germany in the context of a theory of the present age. Dated February 1947 and consisting of thirty-three 'Theses', it included a detailed analysis of the decline in revolutionary consciousness and activity among the working class and the socialist parties and unions (*Verburger-lichung*). What is striking about Marcuse's text is the overt use of Marxian categories and continued commitment to Marxian revolutionary politics. The text opens:

After the military defeat of Hitler-fascism (which was a premature and isolated form of capitalistic reorganization) the world is being divided into neo-fascist and Soviet camps. The still existing remains of democratic-liberal forms will be pulverized between both camps or will be absorbed by them. The states in which the old ruling class survived the war economically and politically will in foreseeable time become fascistic, while the others will enter the Soviet-camp.

In the second thesis, Marcuse writes:

The neo-fascistic and the Soviet society are economically class enemies and war between them is probable. Both are, however, essentially forms of domination which are anti-revolutionary and hostile to a socialist development. . . .'. Under these conditions there is only one position for revolutionary theory: without compromise to represent the orthodox Marxist teaching against both systems relentlessly and without disguise.[32]

Interestingly, this would be precisely Marcuse's strategy and position during the next three decades.[33] Since Adorno and Horkheimer were rapidly abandoning such orthodox Marxian perspectives, however, they must have perceived their growing distance from Marcuse, which no doubt contributed to their reluctance to bring him back into the inner circle. Indeed, they, along with Lowenthal and Pollock, were becoming increasingly involved in a study of anti-Semitism, funded by the, at best, liberal American Jewish Committee (see 4.4).[34] Moreover, they would never again return to the sort of revolutionary Marxian perspectives which, it can be argued, characterized their earlier work and would continue to characterize Marcuse's work.

Some of the reasons for Adorno's and Horkheimer's increasing distance from orthodox Marxism are found in the aphorisms of Adorno's *Minima Moralia*. Entries collected under the rubrics '1944' and '1945' contain almost exclusively individualistic critique of culture, with little political analysis or concern with classical Marxian themes. The pessimism and distance from both American society and Leftist politics is striking. Adorno writes:

There is nothing innocuous left. The little pleasures, expressions of life that seemed exempt from the responsibility of thought, not only have an element of defiant silliness, of callous refusal to see, but directly serve their diametrical opposite. Even the blossoming tree lies the moment its bloom is seen without the shadow of terror; even the innocent 'How Lovely!' becomes an excuse for an existence outrageously unlovely, and there is no longer beauty or consolation except in the gaze falling on horror, withstanding it, and in unalleviated consciousness of negativity holding fast to the possibility of what is better. Mistrust is called for in face of all spontaneity, impetuosity, all letting oneself go, for it implies pliancy towards the superior might of the existent. . . . It is the sufferings of men that should be shared: the smallest step towards their pleasures is one towards the hardening of their pains. (*MM*, pp. 25–6)

Yet Adorno was also aware that

He who stands aloof runs the risk of believing himself better than others and misusing his critique of society as an ideology for his private interest. While he gropingly forms his own life in the frail image of a true existence, he should never forget its frailty, nor how little the image is a substitute for true life. . . . Private existence, in striving to resemble one worthy of man, betrays the latter, since any resemblance is withdrawn from general realization, which yet more than ever before has need of independent thought. There is no way out of entanglement. The only responsible course is to deny oneself the ideological misuse of one's own existence, and for the rest to conduct oneself in private as modestly, unobtrusively and unpretentiously as is required, no longer by good upbringing, but by the shame of still having air to breathe, in hell. (*MM*, pp. 27–8)

Minima Moralia represents a continuation and a radicalization of many of the positions of *Dialectic of Enlightenment*. It centers on, and is written for, intellectuals, and contains uncompromising radical critiques of bourgeois society, culture and thought. It contains 'reflections from damaged life' (its subtitle), and is written from the standpoint of 'the intellectual in emigration'. Adorno's suspicion of the existing world extends to critical reflections on the working class, Leftist parties, revolutionary politics and the Marxian theory. One aphorism, 'Cat out of the Bag', expresses a growing mistrust of Marxian political language and organizations. Adorno complains that the term 'solidarity' has become a slogan, and claims that party entreaties to sympathetic intellectuals to sign petitions or support party causes make individuals dupes of party manipulation. Profession of solidarity 'has turned into confidence that the Party has a thousand eyes, into enrollment in workers battalions – long since promoted into uniform – as the stronger side, into swimming with the tide of history' (*MM*, p. 51). For Adorno, however, such submission merely increases the power of party bureaucracy, and such optimism ultimately leads to destructive political illusions.

Adorno's own position is set forth in a section entitled 'Sur l'eau', which concludes the 1945 entries and sets forth some sharp critiques of Marxism, while projecting quite different perspectives on emancipation and the good society:

He who asks what is the goal of an emancipated society is given answers such as the fulfilment of human possibilities or the richness of life. . . . The naive supposition of an unambiguous development towards increased production is itself a piece of that bourgeois outlook which permits development in only one direction because, integrated into a totality, dominated by quantification, it is hostile to qualitative difference. If we imagine emancipated society as emancipation from precisely such totality, then vanishing lines come into view that have little in common with increased production and its human reflections. . . . *Rien faire comme une bête*, lying on water and looking peacefully at the sky, 'being nothing else, without any further definition and fulfilment,' might take the place of process, act, satisfaction, and so truly keep the promise of dialectical logic that it would culminate in its origin. None of the abstract concepts comes closer to fulfilled utopia than that of eternal peace. Spectators on the sidelines of progress like Maupassant and Sternheim have helped this intention to find expression, timidly, in the only way that its fragility permits (*MM*, pp. 156-7)

Henceforth 'emancipation' for Adorno would signify freedom from anxiety, misery, hunger and conformity – rather than, say, liberation of the oppressed from capitalism or imperialism. Moreover, the word 'capitalism' was rarely used in the subsequent works of Horkheimer. Indeed, Wiggershaus reports that central Marxian categories were edited out of the 1944 typescript of *Dialectic of Enlightenment* when it was published in 1947: ' "capitalism" became "the existing society," "capital" became "the economic system," "capitalist oppression" became "industrial power," "class society" became "domination," . . . and a sentence like "That would be a classless society" was crossed out.'[35]

By the 1940s Horkheimer and Adorno had apparently abandoned all faith in the working class as the instrument of emancipation. Henceforth they would constantly cite tendencies toward the integration of the working class into the technical apparatus of the capitalist system and ways in which workers were co-opted into the system by hopes of advancement. In this situation, 'despite a historical development that has reached the point of oligarchy, the workers are less and less aware that they are such' (MM, p. 193). Decline of class consciousness was a result both of the war, which reduced class struggle and opposition, and a technical apparatus which reduced the burden of heavy industrial labor, raised wages and provided at least some opportunities for workers to advance in the system and better themselves. For Adorno – as for Marcuse, who would later develop this position – exploitation continued to exist, and in a way the workers became even more powerless against the system; yet their perception of their class interests is diminishing, posing 'the grimly comic riddle: where is the proletariat?' (p. 194).

In contrast to Horkheimer's and Adorno's abandonment of Marxian revolutionary perspectives in the 1940s, Marcuse, in his 1947 manuscript, was still proposing systematic inquiry into the situation of the working class, and was rethinking (rather than abandoning) the Marxian theory of revolution in the light of changed class composition and conditions of labor under contemporary conditions. Marcuse stressed that the full weight of exploitation was falling more and more on marginal and nonintegrated groups: 'outsiders', unorganized and unskilled workers, agricultural workers, minorities, colonial groups and regions, prisoners and so on.[36] Moreover, Marcuse proposed taking specific political positions – something increasingly foreign to Adorno and Horkheimer – and even proposed support of Communist political parties:

The communist parties are and remain the single anti-fascist power. Their denunciation must be purely in the theoretical sphere. For one knows that realization of theory is only posssible through communist parties and requires the help of the Soviet Union. This consciousness must be contained in our concepts. Further: in all of our concepts denunciation of neo-fascism and Social Democracy must surpass that of communist politics. Bourgeois democratic freedom is better than totalitarian regimentation, but it is literally purchased with decades of continued exploitation and the hindrance of socialist freedom.[37]

These passages reveal again Marcuse's continuing commitment to Marxian revolutionary politics, and point to the growing distance between him and his colleagues. His claims concerning communist parties reflect the vanguard roles which they played in countries like France and Italy in battling fascism and a post-World War II hope, shared by Sartre and others, that a renewal of Popular Front politics with Communist participation could bring socialism to Europe.

Yet a certain sort of Marxian orthodoxy is also visible in Adorno's theoretical position. In the Introduction to *Minima Moralia*, he grounds his theory in the Marxian position that production in capitalist society comes to dominate every area of social life:

What the philosophers once knew as life has become the sphere of private existence and now of mere consumption, dragged along as an appendage of the process of material production, without autonomy or substance of its own. He who wishes to know the truth about life in its immediacy must scrutinize its estranged form, the objective powers that determine individual existence even in its most hidden recesses. (*MM*, p. 15)

Indeed, Adorno continued to use the Marxian categories of production, commodification and exchange to describe the fundamental social processes of contemporary society. Further, he affirms that, 'Only by virtue of opposition to production, as still not wholly encompassed by this order, can men bring about another more worthy of human beings. Should the appearance of life, which the sphere of consumption itself defends for such bad reasons, be once entirely effaced, then the monstrosity of absolute production will triumph' (ibid.).

Adorno would continue to use many Marxian categories and to affirm certain Marxian positions throughout his life, while distancing himself from Marxian class politics and theoretical orthodoxy.[38] By contrast, Marcuse would attempt to update and revise Marxian positions in the light of historical and political changes in the present epoch. Yet Horkheimer would distance himself from classical Marxism almost completely, while becoming increasingly conservative (see Chapter 8). In any case, it is interesting that during the 1940s the theoretical and political positions that would come to be identified with the later phase of Critical Theory were apparent, as were some of the differences among the Critical Theorists. Wiggershaus reports that Horkheimer never responded with any specific comments to Marcuse's sketch of the current world situation, and that Marcuse never provided any commentary on *Dialectic of Enlightenment* when he was sent a copy in 1948. In Wiggershaus's words:

The 'orthodox Marxist' theorist of the unrealized revolution [Marcuse] and the authors [of *Dialectic of Enlightenment*] no longer shared the same conception of Critical Theory. . . . Marcuse spoke of the emancipation from exploitation and oppression and meant the emancipation of the exploited and the oppressed. When Adorno spoke of emancipation he was thinking rather of emancipation suggested by his own situation – namely freedom from anxiety, from violence, from the indignity of conformity. . . . Marcuse attempted, with utopian means, to preserve orthodox

Marxism. Adorno attempted to justify the distanced and isolated social critic. The 'existentialist' Marcuse made himself spokesperson for outrage over social injustice. Adorno made himself 'philosophy of life' advocate for the non-conformist intellectual.[39]

From this point on, Horkheimer distanced himself somewhat from Marcuse, and was also nervous concerning reports that one of his former students in Germany, Heinz Maus, was presenting Critical Theory as a Marxist alternative to the dominant paradigms of social theory in postwar Germany.[40] At this point, Horkheimer hesitated in response to requests that he publish his and other Institute texts from the 1930s; and Habermas later reported that by the 1950s, after his return to Germany, Horkheimer kept copies of the *Zeitschrift* hidden in the basement of the Institute.[41]

Horkheimer was coming more and more to subscribe to the tenets of pragmatic liberalism. Taking the position of Cold War liberals, without sharing their fanatic anti-communism, he came increasingly to counterpose 'democratic' politics to 'totalitarianism' and to advocate 'education' rather than revolutionary politics as the instrument of social change. Although in the 1940s and at least some of the 1950s, Horkheimer warned against the dangers of anti-communism, his position henceforth was defense of the individual against all collective powers – be they capitalist or socialist. Never again would Horkheimer explicitly criticize capitalism or enthusiastically defend any form of socialism.[42]

Horkheimer's theoretical and political decline represents one of the enigmas of the history of Critical Theory. During the 1930s he was clearly the theoretical mentor and leader of the Institute, and was one of its most productive writers and thinkers. His work from the mid-1920s to the mid-1940s was of consistently high theoretical quality, and was informed by both Marxian theoretical conceptions and a passion for radical change. As interdisciplinary manager of the Institute, he played a key role in organizing and carrying through the various projects undertaken, as well as articulating the common methodology and social theory. Although from the late 1940s until his retirement in the late 1960s, Horkheimer continued to play something of an organizational and entrepreneurial role within the Institute, he did not publish a major book, and his essays became increasingly pedestrian.

While Horkheimer made hardly any contributions during this period, Adorno and Marcuse, by contrast, had their most productive periods in the 1950s and 1960s. Horkheimer's decline is therefore something of a mystery. In 1945 he celebrated his fiftieth birthday, and, despite some health problems, appeared to be at the height of his intellectual powers, impressing individuals in both the United States and Germany with his breadth and depth of knowledge.[43] Yet his chief accomplishment during the remaining decades of his life was his editing of the series *Studies in Prejudice* to which we shall now turn.

4.4   *Studies in Prejudice* and the Return to Germany

The Institute's major project during the late 1940s was a five-volume series of books which investigated prejudice, anti-Semitism and the authoritarian personality. At the time when Horkheimer and Adorno were completing the draft of what became *Dialectic of Enlightenment*, Neumann, Lowenthal and other members of the Institute in New York began developing grant proposals and a prospectus for a series of studies of anti-Semitism.[44] As early as 1939, the Institute prepared a prospectus for a study of anti-Semitism, and in 1942 Horkheimer had contacted the American Jewish Committee and had discussed funding for the study with John Slawson, its vice-president.[45] The American Jewish Committee provided an initial grant which made possible an interdisciplinary conference on prejudice in May 1944, when an ambitious research program was elaborated and discussed.

The projects enabled the Institute to return to empirical research and begin testing the viability of combining their (German-European) theoretical approach with research methods utilized in the social sciences in the United States. With the entry of the United States into World War II, however, many of the Institute's key members went to work for the government in Washington; so the studies in prejudice did not really represent the sort of multidisciplinary project envisaged in the 1930s. Instead, various Institute members – especially Adorno, Pollock and Horkheimer, who played a supervisory role for the project as a whole – worked with various research groups which were recruited for the various projects funded by the American Jewish Committee.

The project is described in the 'Foreword to Studies in Prejudice', written by Horkheimer and Samuel Flowerman of the American Jewish Committee, which accompanied each of the five volumes. Three of the books focus on psychological elements which predispose individuals toward prejudice and racial hatred. The most elaborate and impressive volume, *The Authoritarian Personality*, contains systematic examination of correlations between personality traits and overt prejudice. *Dynamics of Prejudice* considers the connection between personality traits and prejudice among war veterans, while *Anti-Semitism and Emotional Disorder* analyzes case studies of individuals from different walks of life who had undergone psychotherapy and who exhibited marked traits of anti-Semitism.[46] Leo Lowenthal's and Norman Guterman's *Prophets of Deceit* analyzed techniques of mass persuasion and manipulation, while Paul Massing's *Rehearsal for Destruction* described the historical roots and genesis of anti-Semitism in Germany.

In the following discussion I shall focus on those aspects of *The Authoritarian Personality* which provide tools for the analysis of the personality structure of the potential fascist character type. I believe that this analysis, along with concepts put forward in a study by Adorno of 'Freudian Theory and the Pattern of Fascist Propaganda', give important insights into the authoritarian personality, insights which I believe are still useful in analyzing the mind-set of contemporary conservatism. In the research lying behind *The Authoritarian Personality*, Adorno worked with a group of Berkeley psychologists; together they devised an elaborate set of questionnaires which were sent to 2,099 respondents, along with a set of interpretive techniques which allowed them to determine a potentially fascist mind-set from the answers tabulated.[47] The answers were classified to correlate individuals on a scale of A-S (anti-Semitism), an E (enthnocentrism), a PEC (political-economic conservatism) and an F (potentially fascist). The research group then conducted interviews with a large number of the individuals who scored both highest and lowest on the potentially fascist scale, so as to be able to draw further conclusions about the mind-set, patterns of ideas and behavior, and personality structure of the authoritarian personality. Questionnaire and interview results were tabulated, analyzed and published in the various studies that make up *The Authoritarian Personality*.

The authors indicate in the Introduction that their 'major concern was with the *potentially fascistic* individual, one whose structure is such as to render him particularly susceptible to anti-democratic propaganda' (*AP*, p. 1). They are convinced 'that no politico-social trend imposes a graver threat to our traditional values and institutions than does fascism, and that knowledge of the personality forces that favor its acceptance may ultimately prove useful in combating it' (ibid.). Their research disclosed that 'individuals who show extreme susceptibility to fascist propaganda have a great deal in common', and 'exhibit numerous characteristics that go together to form a "syndrome" although typical variations within this major pattern can be distinguished' (ibid.).

Although this focus was criticized by people like Edward Shils, who saw communism as a greater threat to traditional American values than fascism,[48] the lack of a Communist presence in the United States over the last several decades and the strong presence of the Right suggest that Adorno and his colleagues focused on the psychological mind-set and political tendencies that indeed posed the greatest threat to democracy and civil society in the United States. Consequently, in the following analysis, I wish to suggest how the analysis of the authoritarian personality by Adorno and his colleagues provides insights into the sort of New Right conservatism that has become dominant in the United States and elsewhere in the 1980s.

I believe that the variables which constituted the basic content of the

F scale and which were thus the defining characteristics of the authoritarian personality provide an analytical framework particularly suitable for describing and criticizing contemporary conservatism. This suggests that Adorno and his colleagues grasped certain fundamental features of the authoritarian personality which would continue to play an important and highly destructive role in American life over the next decades. The following characteristics are said to constitute a 'more or less central trend' in the authoritarian personality, which expressed itself in enthnocentrism and various forms of political-economic conservatism which, together with anti-Semitic and racist tendencies, pointed to a fascist potential in American life:

a. *Conventionalism.* Rigid adherence to conventional, middle-class values.

b. *Authoritarian submission.* Submissive, uncritical attitude toward idealized moral authorities of the ingroup.

c. *Authoritarian aggression.* Tendency to be on the lookout for, and to condemn, reject, and punish people who violate conventional values.

d. *Anti-intraception.* Opposition to the subjective, the imaginative, the tender-minded.

e. *Superstition and stereotypy.* The belief in mystical determinants of the individual's fate; the disposition to think in rigid categories.

f. *Power and 'toughness'.* Preoccupation with the dominance-submission, strong-weak, leader-follower dimension; identification with power figures; overemphasis upon the conventionalized attributes of the ego; exaggerated assertion of strength and toughness.

g. *Destructiveness and cynicism.* Generalized hostility, vilification of the human.

h. *Projectivity.* The disposition to believe that wild and dangerous things go on in the world; the projection outwards of unconscious emotional impulses.

i. *Sex.* Exaggerated concern with sexual 'goings-on.' (*AP*, p. 228)

It was Adorno who set forth the analysis of the fundamental character traits and modes of thought characterizing the potentially fascist personality. In Part 4 of the study, he analysed the dominant forms of prejudice in the interview material (*AP*, pp. 606ff.) and the formal constituents of the political mind-set of the authoritarian personality. Such a character type had a deep psychological need for an 'imaginary foe' on whom to project all forms of evil and aggression, a foe who would serve as a scapegoat for explaining the world's (and individual's) major problems, fears and obsessions. This foe could be Jews, blacks, Communists or a combination thereof, and such a mind-set was generally based on ignorance, confusion and stereotyped perception.

In his analysis 'Politics and Economics in the Interview Material', Adorno indicated that an overall ideological pattern was evident in those who scored high on the F scale, and that this could be correlated with conservative trends in the 'general cultural climate' and public opinion

(*AP*, pp. 654ff.). He noted a 'widespread ignorance and confusion in political matters' in those interviewed, 'a phenomenon which might well surpass what even a skeptical observer should have anticipated' (p. 658). This correlated with a 'general "anti-intellectual" attitude of high scorers', and pointed to 'a susceptibility to fascist propaganda' in the United States (ibid.). 'In addition, the official optimism of the high scorer tends to exclude that kind of critical analysis of existent conditions on which rational political judgment depends (ibid.). Such ignorance, Adorno notes, 'works in favor of general reactionary trends' (ibid.).

Ignorance about the complex conditions of modern societies leads to a general uncertainty and anxiety, while creating favorable conditions for the projection of paranoid fears onto imaginary enemies. It also leads to what Adorno calls 'ticket thinking' and 'personalization in politics', whereby the confused, anxious authoritarian personality buys into an entire political agenda and projects hostile and aggressive tendencies on personalized enemies, while idealizing authoritarian leaders. Such ideological stereotyping and personalization produces 'stereopathy', a stultified political mind-set that is '*inadequate to reality*' because it dodges the concrete and takes refuge in a 'preconceived, rigid, and overgeneralized' set of ideas 'to which the individual attributes a kind of magical omnipotence. Conversely, personalization dodges the real abstractness, that is to say, the "reification" of a social reality which is determined by property relations and in which the human beings themselves are, as it were, mere appendages' (*AP*, pp. 665–6).

Adorno goes on to analyze the contradictions in the authoritarian personality, the differences between surface ideology and real opinion, the superficial adherence to traditional democratic ideas and the readiness to abandon such ideas when prejudices are aroused. The result is a form of 'pseudo-conservativism' which is characterized by conventionality and 'authoritarian submissiveness on the ego level, with violence, anarchic impulses, and chaotic destructiveness in the unconscious sphere' (*AP*, p. 675). Further, 'the pseudoconservative is a man who, in the name of upholding traditional American values and institutions and defending them against more or less fictitious dangers, consciously or unconsciously aims at their abolition' (p. 676). 'Pseudo-conservatism' is accompanied by a 'usurpation complex' which sees the government illegitimately usurping power or wealth that should be left to the private sector, or sees Communist governments or leaders 'usurping' power and authority that should be left to traditional sources (ibid.).

Conservative resentment at the time was particularly mobilized against bureaucrats and politicians, and while anti-communism had not yet assumed the demonized role that it would play from the 1950s to the present in the conservative mind, evidence was already appearing that the authoritarian personality was gaining a new enemy upon which to project its anxieties, aggression and hostilities. Such a conservative mind-set was also extremely pessimistic about the possibility of bettering the world, had a low regard for human nature and had little pity for the poor or dispossessed. It was anti-labor and anti-working class, and believed absolutely in the virtues of the capitalistic market economy: 'To them . . . the concept of the free market coincides with the moral law, and any factors which introduce, as it were, an extra-economic element into the business sphere are regarded by them as irregular' (*AP*, p. 709).

Adorno documented his claims with abundant material from the interviews, and it is uncanny how such positions and the mind-set that characterized the authoritarian personality have remained relatively stable from the 1940s through the Reagan/Bush era among Right-wing conservatives in the United States and elsewhere. While Horkheimer and Flowerman stressed the need for education to combat the formation of authoritarian personalities in the Foreword to the volume (*AP*, p. vii), Adorno and his colleagues concluded with a call for social change, on the grounds that authoritarian personalities are the 'products of the total organization of society and are to be changed only as that society is changed' (p. 975).

The Authoritarian Personality ends on an upbeat political note, nonetheless.

It would be foolish to underestimate the fascist potential with which this volume has been mainly concerned, but it would be equally unwise to overlook the fact that the majority of our subjects do not exhibit the extreme ethnocentric pattern and the fact that there are various ways in which it may be avoided altogether. Although there is reason to believe that the prejudiced are the better rewarded in our society as far as external values are concerned (it is when they take shortcuts to these rewards that they land in prison), we need not suppose that the tolerant have to wait and receive their rewards in heaven, as it were. Actually there is good reason to believe that the tolerant receive more gratification of basic needs. They're likely to pay for this satisfaction in conscious guilt feelings, since they frequently have to go against prevailing social standards, but the evidence is that they are, basically, happier than the prejudiced. Thus, we need not suppose that appeal to emotion belongs to those who strive in the direction of fascism, while democratic propaganda must limit itself to reason and restraint. If fear and destructiveness are the major emotional sources of fascism, *eros* belongs mainly to democracy. (*AP*, p. 976)

Adorno developed his critique of the authoritarian personality further in his important article 'Freudian Theory and the Pattern of Fascist Propaganda'.[49] This study uses Freudian psychology to study the patterns of fascist propaganda in speeches and discourses of Right-wing politicians, and once again the patterns remain extremely stable from Hitler to Reagan and Bush. Fascist (and Rightist) propaganda is predominantly abstract, and is not concerned with its audience's real needs. Its stock repertoire is both systematic and highly repetitive, utilizing 'a rigidly set pattern of clear-cut "devices" ' (*FSR*, p. 119). The propaganda material forms 'a structural unit with a total common conception' based on irrational fears and a simplistic distinction between good and evil. The psychological pattern is paranoid and projective, resulting in an often imaginary enemy upon which one's own aggressive and immoral traits are projected.

Adorno builds his analysis on Freud's *Group Psychology and the Analysis of the Ego*, which he takes as an acute analysis of the mechanisms of fascism. In particular, Freud's theory explains the ways in which fascist (or Rightist) propaganda and leaders are able to form their followers into a mass with common libidinal ties and bonds (*FSR*, pp. 120ff.). The fascist leader allows the unleashing of socially repressed aggressive instincts, which provides pleasurable release and group cohesion. The key psychological mechanisms are *personalization* and *identification*. Fascist leaders are personalized as attractive authority figures, and they in turn personalize their discourse with 'incessant plugging of names and supposedly great men, instead of discussing objective causes' (p. 124). The follower is able to identify with the leader through identification with an idealized version of him or herself. The leader represents a highly superior person, yet one who is similar enough to the follower that he or she can identify with this idealized version of self cleansed of all the stains of frustration and failure: 'Accordingly, one of the basic devices of personalized fascist propaganda is the concept of the "great little man," a person who suggests both omnipotence and the idea that he is just one of the folks, a plain red-blooded American, untainted by material or spiritual wealth' (p. 127).

Fascist or Rightist propaganda also reproduces the structure of hierarchical groups, inducing their followers to respect those above them and revile those below them or outside the in-group. Consequently, the authoritarian personality exhibits a sado-masochistic character. Thus the 'tendency to tread on those below, which manifests itself so disastrously in the persecution of weak and helpless minorities, is as outspoken as the hatred against those outside' (*FSR*, p. 128). This produces, Adorno suggests, both narcissistic in-group identification and projection of aggressive tendencies toward the out-group.

The *Studies in Prejudice* series was published during a period when the Institute was considering returning to Germany. Both Adorno and Horkheimer periodically visited Germany during the mid- and late 1940s, and eventually an offer was made to re-establish the Institute in Frankfurt that was too attractive to refuse.[50] Consequently Adorno, Horkheimer and Pollock returned to Germany to re-establish the *Institut für Sozialforschung*, while Marcuse, Lowenthal and others decided to remain in the United States. This permanently destroyed the possibility of re-establishing the sort of multidisciplinary research program begun in the early 1930s and continued to some degree or another in the 1940s. For, while Horkheimer talked in his inaugural address of merging American social science research methods with speculative social theory, the Institute undertook few multidisciplinary projects, and never really returned to serious work on developing a systematic social theory of the current epoch.

Instead, Adorno and Horkheimer turned once again to philosophy, which they taught in most of their lecture and seminar courses upon resettling in Gemany. Horkheimer, as already noted, hardly produced any independent work of value thereafter; and while Adorno became the most prolific and fascinating writer of his generation, his work is highly idiosyncratic and cannot be taken as an expression of a multidisciplinary research program, even though he continued to express his ideas concerning social research and theory and to defend Critical Theory against positivism.[51]

In the following four chapters, I shall focus on the contributions of the Critical Theorists to theories of art and mass culture and communication (Chapter 5), the consumer and administered society (Chapter 6) and developments within contemporary capitalist societies and their perspectives on social change (Chapters 7 and 8). The reason for a more systematic focus than in previous chapters is that, in the absence of Institute attempts to develop a systematic and comprehensive social theory of the present age, the elaboration of Critical Theory henceforth took place in a variety of essays, books and lectures produced by various members of the Institute at different times, which often exhibit great differences, even conflicts.

Critical Theory also became more highly theoretical, for the most part, and less closely connected with either empirical research or radical politics than in the earlier phases. The major contributions of Critical Theorists would now be to philosophy and cultural analysis and critique, rather than to social theory per se – though I shall attempt to show that fragments of a theory of society are still evident in their works. Consequently I shall focus on those aspects of Critical Theory which I believe constitute some of its central contributions to radical social theory and cultural criticism. Since the work of Critical Theorists at this stage is even more fragmented and less systematic than in preceding stages, I shall draw on a variety of works, often from different periods, to present what I consider their major contributions and deficiencies. The following chapters will thus be especially concerned with what aspects of classical Critical Theory are most useful for radical social theory and politics today, and what elements should be discarded or significantly modified and developed.

5

From 'Authentic Art' to the Culture Industries

Critical Theory's analyses of the functions of culture, ideology and the mass media in contemporary societies are among its most valuable legacies. The Critical Theorists exceled as critics of both 'high culture' and 'mass culture', and produced many important texts in these areas. Their work is distinguished by the close connection between social theory and cultural critique and by their ability to contextualize culture within social developments. In particular, their theory of culture was bound up with analysis of the dialectic of enlightenment. Culture, once a refuge of beauty and truth, was falling prey, they believed, to tendencies toward rationalization, standardization and conformity, which they saw as a consequence of the triumph of the instrumental rationality that was coming to pervade and structure ever more aspects of life. Thus, while culture once cultivated individuality, it was now promoting conformity and was a crucial part of 'the totally administered society' that was producing 'the end of the individual'.

This pessimistic analysis of the fate of culture in modernity was part and parcel of Institute pessimism concerning the rise of the totally administered society in its fascist, democratic state capitalist, and state Communist forms. Yet the Institute continued to privilege culture as an important, and often overlooked, source of social knowledge, as well as a potential form of social criticism and opposition. As Adorno wrote:

The task of [cultural] criticism must be not so much to search for the particular interest-groups to which cultural phenomena are to be assigned, but rather to decipher the general social tendencies which are expressed in these phenomena and through which the most powerful interests realize themselves. Cultural criticism must become social physiognomy. The more the whole divests itself of all spontaneous elements, is socially mediated and filtered, is 'consciousness,' the more it becomes 'culture'.[1]

This passage points both to the position of Critical Theory that administered culture was coming to play ever more fundamental roles in social production and reproduction, and that analysis of culture can provide crucial insights into social processes. Critical Theory thus assigned a central role to cultural criticism and ideology critique precisely because of the central role of culture and ideology within contemporary capitalist societies. This focus on culture – which corresponded to some of the Institute members' deepest interests – took the form of a systematic inquiry into the different types, forms and effects of culture and ideology in contemporary capitalist societies. These ranged from theoretical reflections on the dialectics of culture – that is, the ways in which culture could be both a force of social conformity and one of opposition – to critiques of mass culture and aesthetic reflections on the emancipatory potential of high art.

In this chapter I shall discuss some of the cultural phenomena with which the Critical Theorists were concerned, though, given the wealth of material in this field, I shall necessarily have to be selective. I begin with a discussion of the Institute's distinction between 'high art' and 'mass culture' (5.1), and continue with more detailed analyses of its critique of the culture industries (5.2). Then I offer some alternative perspectives on mass communication and culture and some criticisms of the Institute's cultural theory (5.3). Focus will be on the extent to which classical Critical Theory continues to be valid and useful for cultural criticism today.

5.1   Dialectics of Culture

In the first issue of the *Zeitschrift für Sozialforschung*, articles appeared by Lowenthal and Adorno which set forth, respectively, programs for a sociology of literature and a theory and critique of mass culture.[2] In 'On Sociology of Literature', Lowenthal argues against dominant idealist and philological approaches in favor of a practice which analyzes texts and other cultural objects within their social and historical contexts. Refusing to study literature as a self-contained object, Lowenthal would become a pioneer in the development of the sociology of literature, as well as a trenchant critic of mass culture.

Rejecting a positivistic historicism which would putatively produce a 'science of literature', as well as all metaphysical and idealist approaches to art which would see it as an autonomous expression of creative genius, Lowenthal proposes a historical and sociological approach based on the principles of historical materialism:

Such concern with the historical and sociological dimensions of literature requires a theory of history and society. . . . the historical explanation of literature has to address the extent to which particular social structures find expression in individual literary works and what function these works perform in society. Man is involved in specific relations of production throughout his history. These relations present themselves socially as classes in struggle with each other, and the development of their relationship forms the real basis for the various cultural spheres. The specific structure of production, i.e. the economy, is the independent explanatory variable not only for the legal forms of property and organization of state and government but, at the same time, for the shape and quality of human life in each historical epoch. . . . A genuine, explanatory history of literature must proceed on materialistic principles. That is to say, it must investigate the economic structures as they present themselves in literature, as well as the impact which the materialistically interpreted work of art has in the economically determined society. (pp. 247-8)

Lowenthal stresses the importance of a theory of mediations which will articulate the interconnections between society and the work of art, including class, psychology, ideology and the artistic materials currently available. These and other mediations constitute the aesthetic object; though for a historical materialist approach, 'the concept of ideology will be decisive for the social explanation of all phenomena of the superstructure from legal institutions to the arts. Ideology is false consciousness of social contradictions and attempts to replace them with the illusions of social harmony. Indeed, literary studies are largely an investigation of ideologies' (p. 248).

Lowenthal illustrates his position by addressing issues of form, motif and content central to literary analysis. He shows how a historical materialist approach provides access to aspects of a work of art overlooked by conventional literary theories, and thus enriches our approach to literature without necessarily being reductive. He concludes with a call for an 'aesthetics of reception' as part of this problematic which would analyze the reception and social functions of literature:

It has always been of great interest to me why a task as important as the study of the reception of literature among various social groups has been so utterly neglected even though a vast pool of research material is available in journals and newspapers, in letters and memoirs. A materialistic history of literature, unhampered by the anxious protection of the literary arts by its self-styled guardians and without fear of getting stranded in a quagmire of routine philology or mindless data collection, is well-prepared to tackle this task. (p. 254)

In addition to pioneering attempts to develop a sociology of literature, the Institute was among the first to apply the Marxian method of ideology critique to the products of mass culture. Whereas Critical Theorists like Horkheimer and Marcuse never really analyzed any artifacts of mass culture, others, like Adorno and Lowenthal, developed global theories and critiques, while carrying out detailed studies of what they came to call the 'culture industries'. Adorno began the Institute critique of mass culture in his 1932 article 'On the Social Situation of Music', and continued it in a series of studies of popular music and other forms of mass culture over the next decades.[3] Initially Adorno criticized popular music production for its commodification, rationalization, fetishism and reification of musical materials – thus applying the key neo-Marxist social categories to culture – while subsequently criticizing as well as the 'regression' in hearing produced by popular music. The framework for his critique was thus the Institute theory of the spread of rationalization and reification into every aspect of social life and the resultant decline of the individual.

A remarkable individual on the margins of the Institute, Walter Benjamin, contested the tendency to sharply separate 'authentic art' from mass culture and to valorize one at the expense of the other.[4] For Benjamin, mechanical reproduction – his term for the processes of social rationalization described by Adorno and others in the Institute – robbed high art of its 'aura', of the aesthetic power of the work of art, related to its earlier functions in magic and religious cults and as a spiritual object in the religions of art celebrated in movements like Romanticism or 'art for art's sake'. In these cases the 'aura' of the work derived from its supposed authenticity, its uniqueness and individuality. In an era of mechanical reproduction, however, art appeared in the form of commodities like other mass-produced items, and lost its special power as a transcendent object, especially in mass-produced objects like photographs and films with their photo negatives and techniques of mass reproduction. Benjamin regarded this process – which he believed to be irreversible – ambivalently:

For the first time in world history, mechanical reproduction emancipates the work of art from its parasitical dependence on ritual. To an even greater degree the work of art reproduced becomes the work of art designed for reproducibility. From a photographic negative, for example, one can make any number of prints; to ask for the 'authentic' print makes no sense. But the instant the criterion of authenticity ceases to be applicable to artistic production, the total function of art is reversed. Instead of being based on ritual, it begins to be based on another practice – politics. (p. 224)

Whereas Adorno tended to criticize precisely the most mechanically mediated works of mass culture for their standardization and loss of aesthetic quality, while celebrating those works that most steadfastly resisted commodification and mechanical reproduction, Benjamin saw progressive features in high art's loss of its auratic quality and its becoming more politicized. Such art, he claimed, assumed more of an 'exhibition value' than a cultic or religious value, and thus demystified its reception. Furthermore, he believed that proliferation of mass art, especially through film, would bring images of the contemporary world to the masses, and would help raise political consciousness by encouraging scrutiny of the world, as well as by bringing socially critical images to millions of spectators:

By close-ups of the things around us, by focusing on hidden details of familiar objects, by exploring commonplace milieus under the ingenious guidance of the camera, the film, on the one hand, extends our comprehension of the necessities which rule our lives; on the other hand, it manages to assure us of an immense and unexpected field of action. Our taverns and our metropolitan streets, our offices and furnished rooms, our railroad stations and our factories appeared to have us locked up hopelessly. Then came the film and burst this prison-world asunder by the dynamite of the tenth of a second, so that now, in the midst of its far-flung ruins and debris, we calmly and adventurously go traveling. (p. 236)

Benjamin claimed that the mode of viewing film broke with the reverential mode of aesthetic perception and awe encouraged by the bourgeois cultural elite who promoted the religion of art. Montage in film, its 'shock effects', the conditions of mass spectatorship, the discussion of issues which viewing films encouraged, and other features of the cinematic experience, produced, in his view, a new sort of social and political experience of art, which eroded the private, solitary and contemplative aesthetic experience encouraged by high culture and its priests. Against the contemplation of high art, the 'shock effects' of film produce a mode of 'distraction' which Benjamin believed makes possible a 'heightened presence of mind' and cultivation of 'expert' audiences able to examine and criticize film and society (pp. 237–41).

In some essays on popular music, and later in his famous studies (with Max Horkheimer) of the culture industries, Adorno attempted to provide a critical response to Benjamin's optimistic appraisal of the socially critical potential of popular art. In a 1938 essay entitled 'On the Fetish-Character in Music and the Regression of Listening', Adorno analyzed in detail the various ways in which performers of music, conductors, instruments, technical performance and arrangement of works were fetishized, and how this signified the ways in which exchange value was predominating over use value in musical production and reception, thus pointing again to how capitalism was able to control aspects of life once resistant to commercial concerns. In Adorno's words:

The works which are the basis of the fetishization and become cultural goods experience constitutional changes as a result. They become vulgarized. Irrelevant consumption destroys them. Not merely do the few things played again and again wear out, like the Sistine Madonna in the bedroom, but reification affects their internal structure. They are transformed into a conglomeration of irruptions which are impressed on the listeners by climax and repetition, while the organization of the whole makes no impression whatsoever. (*FSR*, p. 281)

In this situation, musical listening regresses to mere reaction to familiar and standardized formulas (*FSR*, pp. 285ff.), which increases social conformity and domination. Regression closes off the possibility of a different and oppositional music. Regressive, too, is the role which contemporary mass music plays in the psychological household of its victims. They are not merely turned away from more important music, but they are confirmed in their neurotic stupidity, quite irrespective of how their musical capacities are related to the specific musical culture of earlier social phases. The assent to hit songs and debased cultural goods belongs to the same complex of symptoms as do those faces of which one no longer knows whether the film has alienated them from reality or reality has alienated them from the film, as they wrench open a great formless mouth with shining teeth in a voracious smile, while the tired eyes are wretched and lost above. Together with sport and film, mass music and the new listening help to make escape from the whole infantile milieu impossible. The sickness has a preservative function. (*FSR*, p. 287)

Adorno's infamous attack on jazz should be read in the context of his theory of musical fetishism and regression.[5] For Adorno, the often faddish taste for jazz also exhibited features of fetishism, reification and regression that he observed in other forms of popular music. Contrary to popular belief, Adorno argued, jazz was as standardized, commercialized and formulaic as other kinds of popular music, and encouraged cultural conformity (to dominant models, tastes and so on) in its devotees as much as did other forms of mass culture. Its seeming spontaneity and improvisation are themselves calculated in advance, and the range of what is permissible is as circumscribed as in clothes or other realms of fashion.

Horkheimer and Adorno also attempted to counter Benjamin's optimistic appraisal of the progressive elements of film through critique of Hollywood film production. Film in the culture industries was organized like industrial production, and utilized standardized formulas and conventional production techniques to mass-produce films for purely commercial – rather than cultural – purposes. Films reproduced reality as it was, and thus helped individuals to adjust and conform to the new conditions of industrial and mass society: 'they hammer into every brain the old lesson that continuous friction, the breaking down of all individual resistance, is the condition of life in this society. Donald Duck in the cartoons and the unfortunate in real life get their thrashing so that the audience can learn to take their own punishment' (*DoE*, p. 138). Finally, films

are so designed that quickness, powers of observation, and experience are undeniably needed to apprehend them at all; yet sustained thought is out of the question if the spectator is not to miss the relentless rush of facts. Even though the effort required for his response is semi-automatic, no scope is left for the imagination. Those who are so absorbed by the world of the movie – by its images, gestures, and words – that they are unable to supply what really makes it a world, do not have to dwell on particular points of its mechanics during a screening. All the other films and products of the entertainment industry which they have seen have taught them what to expect; they react automatically. (*DoE*, pp. 126–7)

During the late 1930s and the 1940s, when Adorno was developing his critique of popular music (and culture), he was working with Paul Lazarsfeld on some of the first academic studies of the communications industry, and was thus being exposed to some of the more debased and commercialized forms of popular music.[6] Yet, while the Institute generally criticized mass culture, it did not surrender its belief in the emancipatory potential of high culture. In an important essay entitled 'On Affirmative Culture', Marcuse provides a dialectical analysis of bourgeois high culture and the ways in which it is a vehicle of both emancipation and mystification of existing social reality. In his view, culture provides a higher, compensatory realm for escape and diversion from the cares of everyday life, as well as a refuge which preserves higher ideals and claims to freedom, happiness and a better life denied in the existing organization of society.[7] Hence bourgeois culture is 'affirmative' of higher cultural ideals which provide both ideological and potentially critical and emancipatory functions.

Many later analyses of high culture within Critical Theory preserve this tension, seeing both regressive and progressive elements within the aesthetic dimension. Yet the Institute tended to ascribe the higher, more progressive functions of culture to 'art' – that is, 'high culture' – and its more debased ideological functions to mass culture. For example, Max Horkheimer argued in 'Art and Mass Culture' that 'authentic art' was diametrically opposed to 'mass culture', a position shared by most in the Institute. He begins by describing the concept of aesthetic experience as the product of a highly individualized society, in which the private subject abstracts from prevailing social conditions and standards to make what appears to be a pure 'aesthetic judgement':

In his aesthetic behavior, man so to speak divested himself of his functions as a member of society and reacted as the isolated individual he had become. Individuality, the true factor in artistic creation and judgment, consists not in idiosyncrasies and crotchets, but in the power to withstand the plastic surgery of the prevailing economic system which carves all men to one pattern. Human begins are free to recognize themselves in works of art in so far as they have not succumbed to the general leveling. The individual's experience embodied in a work of art has no less validity than the organized experience society brings to bear for the control of nature. Although its criterion lies in itself alone, art is knowledge no less than science is. (*CT*, p. 273)

For Critical Theory 'authentic art' is thus a preserve of both individuality and happiness, as well as a source of critical knowledge. Further, an 'element of resistance is inherent in the most aloof art. Resistance to the restraints imposed by society, now and then flooding forth in political revolution, has been steadily fermenting in the private sphere' (*CT*, p. 274). Art resists incorporation into existing society, while providing standards and ideals by which to criticize its limitations:

Works of art – objective products of the mind detached from the context of the practical world – harbor principles through which the world that voice them appears alien and false. Not only Shakespeare's wrath and melancholy, but the detached humanism of Goethe's poetry as well, and even Proust's devoted absorption in ephemeral features of *mondanité*, awaken memories of a freedom that make prevailing standards appear narrow-minded and barbarous. Art, since it became autonomous, has preserved the utopia that evaporated from religion. (*CT*, p. 275)

Horkheimer celebrates the classics of bourgeois high culture as 'authentic art'. With the advance of industrialism and mass society, however, the private sphere and the individual to whom bourgeois art appealed have become steadily threatened, as has the family, which once provided a sphere of intimacy and support. With the rise of industrial society, the family in turn loses its power, and 'even well-to-do parents educate their children not so much as their heirs as for a coming adjustment to mass culture' (*CT*, p. 276). At this point, Horkheimer begins a critique of mass culture that will subsequently characterize the Institute's work:

The gradual dissolution of the family, the transformation of personal life into leisure and of leisure into routines supervised to the last detail, into the pleasures of the ball park and the movie, the best seller and the radio, has brought about the disappearance of the inner life. Long before culture was replaced by these manipulated pleasures, it had already assumed an escapist character. Men had fled into a private conceptual world and rearranged their thoughts when the time was ripe for re-arranging reality. The inner life and the ideal had become conservative factors. But with the loss of his ability to take this kind of refuge – an ability that thrives neither in slums nor in modern settlements – man has lost his power to conceive a world different from that in which he lives. This other world was that of art. (*CT*, pp. 277–8)

Henceforth, with some qualifications, Critical Theory would make a sharp distinction between authentic art and mass culture, between 'high' and 'low' culture, ascribing all culture's emancipatory powers to authentic art and its ideological functions to mass culture. Lowenthal, for example, writes:

The counterconcept of popular culture is art. Nowadays artistic products having the character of spontaneity more and more are being replaced by a manipulated reproduction of reality as it is; and, in so doing, popular culture sanctions and glorifies whatever it finds worth echoing. Schopenhauer remarked that music is 'the world once more.' This aphorism exhibits the unbridgeable difference between art and popular culture: it is the difference between an increase in insight through a medium possessing self-sustaining means and mere repetition of given facts with the use of borrowed tools.[8]

As far as the Institute was concerned, mass culture merely reproduced the status quo, and thus helped reproduce personality structures which would accept the world as it is. By contrast, high culture is conceptualized as at least a potential force of enlightenment and emancipation. For Adorno, however, only the most radically avant-garde works could provide genuine aesthetic experience. Against the false harmonies of kitsch and affirmative art, Adorno defended the 'de-aestheticization' (*Entkunstung*) of art, its throwing off of false veils of harmony and beauty in favor of ugliness, dissonance, fragmentation and negation, which he believed provided a more truthful vision of contemporary society and a more emancipatory stance for socially critical art. In Adorno's view, art had become increasingly problematical in a society ruled by culture industries and art markets; and to remain 'authentic', art must therefore radically resist commodification and integration. This required avant-garde techniques which would enhance art's shock value and its critical, emancipatory effects. In his volumes of critical writings, Adorno always championed precisely the most negative, dissonant artists: Kafka and Beckett in literature, Schönberg and Berg in music, Giacometti in sculpture and Celan in poetry. Through de-aestheticization, autonomous art would undermine specious harmonization and reconciliation with the existing world, which could not legitimately take place, Adorno believed, until the world was radically changed.

In 'Commitment', his well-known critique of 'politically committed art', for example, Adorno writes:

It is not the office of art to spotlight alternatives, but to resist by its form alone the course of the world, which permanently puts a pistol to men's heads. . . . Kafka's prose and Beckett's plays, or the truly monstrous novel *The Unnameable*, have an effect by comparison with which officially committed works look like pantomimes. Kafka and Beckett arouse the fear which existentialism merely talks about. By dismantling appearance, they explode from within the art which committed proclamation subjugates from without, and hence only in appearance. The inescapability of their work compels the change of attitude which committed works merely demand.[9]

Thus, for Adorno, 'authentic art' provided insight into existing reality, expressing human suffering and the need for social transformation, as well as providing an aesthetic experience which helped to produce critical consciousness and awareness of the need for individual and social transformation. Art for Adorno was thus a privileged vehicle for emancipation. Aesthetic experience alone, he came to believe, provided the refuge for truth and a sphere of individual freedom and resistance. The problem was that only authentic art could provide aesthetic experience, and it was precisely authentic art which was disappearing in the administered society.

It is impossible here to go into the complexities of Adorno's theory of authentic art, or even to discuss the full range of the various Institute contributions to the sociology of culture, ideology critique and aesthetic theory and political aesthetics. Before appraising and criticizing the Institute's celebration of 'authentic art' and its identification with high culture (5.3), however, I wish to discuss in more detail its critique of mass culture and the important effects which its theory of the culture industry had on theories of mass culture, communications and society.

5.2   Critical Theory and the Culture Industry

The origins of the Critical Theorists' approach to mass culture and communications are visible in Adorno's early writings on music (see 5.1), though the Institute did not really develop a theory of the culture industries until its emigration to the United States in the 1930s.[10] During their exile period from the mid-1930s through the 1940s, members of the Institute witnessed the proliferation of mass communications and culture and the rise of the consumer society, experiencing at first hand the advent to cultural power of the commercial broadcasting systems, President Roosevelt's remarkable use of radio for political persuasion and the ever growing popularity of cinema during a period in which from 85 to 110 million Americans paid to see 'the movies' each week.[11] They also experienced the widespread popularity of magazines, comic books, cheap fiction and the other flora and fauna of the new mass-produced culture.

From their vantage point in California, where many of their exiled compatriots worked for the film industry, Adorno and Horkheimer were able to see how business interests dominated mass culture and to observe the fascination which the entertainment industries exerted within the emerging media and consumer society. Marcuse, Lowenthal and others, who worked in Washington during this period for the Office of War Information and the United States Intelligence services, were able to observe government use of mass communications as instruments of political propaganda. The Critical Theorists thus came to see what they called the 'culture industries' as a central part of a new configuration of capitalist modernity, which used culture, advertising, mass communications and new forms of social control to induce consent to the new forms of capitalist society. The production and transmission of media spectacles which transmitted ideology and consumerism by means of allegedly 'popular entertainment' and information were, they believed, a central mechanism through which contemporary society came to dominate the individual.

Adorno and Horkheimer adopted the term 'culture industry', as opposed to concepts like 'popular culture' or 'mass culture', because they wanted to resist notions that products of mass culture emanated from the masses or the people.[12] They saw the culture industry as involving administered culture, imposed from above, as an instrument of indoctrination and social control. The term 'culture industry' thus contains a dialectical irony typical of the style of Critical Theory: culture, as traditionally valorized, is supposed to be opposed to industry and expressive of individual creativity while providing a repository of humanizing values. In the culture industries, by contrast, culture has come to function as a mode of ideological domination, rather than of humanization or emancipation.

The culture industry was perceived as the outcome of a historical process in which technology and scientific organization and administration came to dominate thought and experience (see 4.1). Although Horkheimer and Adorno carried out a radical questioning of Marxism and the development of an alternative philosophy of history and theory of society in *Dialectic of Enlightenment*, their theory of the culture industry provided a neo-Marxian account of the mass media and mass culture which helps to explain both the ways in which the culture industries reproduce capitalist societies and why socialist revolutions have failed to take place in these societies. In this sense, the Institute theory of 'culture industry as mass deception' provides a rebuttal of both Lukács's theory of revolution and 'class consciousness' and Brecht's and Benjamin's belief that the new forces of mass communications, especially radio and film, could serve as instruments of technological progress and social enlightenment which could be turned against the capitalist relations of production and used as instruments of political mobilization and struggle.[13]

By contrast, Horkheimer and Adorno saw these new technologies as instruments of ideological mystification and class domination. Against Lukács and others who argued that capitalist society necessarily radicalized the working class and led to class consciousness, Adorno and Horkheimer argued that the culture industries inhibit the development of class consciousness by providing the ruling political and economic forces with a powerful instrument of social control. The conception of the culture industry therefore provides a model of technically advanced capitalist society which mobilizes support for its institutions, practices and values from *below*, making class consciousness more difficult to attain than before. In Gramsci's terminology, the culture industries reproduce capitalist hegemony over the working class by engineering consent to the existing society, thereby establishing a socio-psychological basis for social integration.[14] Whereas fascism destroyed civil society (or the 'public sphere') through politicizing mediating institutions or using force to suppress all dissent, the culture industries coax individuals into the privacy of their homes or the movie theaters, where they produce consumer-spectators of media events and escapist entertainment while subtly indoctrinating them with dominant ideologies.

The analysis of the culture industry stands, therefore, in a quite ambivalent relationship to classical Marxism. On one hand, the theory is part of the foundation for the Critical Theory of society, replacing the critique of political economy which had previously been the foundation for social theories in the Marxian tradition. It also served as an important part of the explanation of why the Critical Theorists no longer placed faith in the revolutionary vocation of the proletariat. Yet, in other ways, the analysis of the culture industry employs Marxian arguments by stressing capitalist control of culture, the commodification and reification of culture, its ideological functions and the ways in which it integrates individuals into capitalist society.

For example, Horkheimer and Adorno utilize a model that pits the individual against its 'adversary – the absolute power of capitalism' (*DoE*, p. 120), and describe the tendencies toward conformity, standardization and deception in the culture industry in terms of its control by monopoly corporations, which themselves are central to the capitalist system (pp. 120ff.). The very processes of production in the culture industry are modeled on factory production, where everything is standardized, streamlined, coordinated and planned down to the last detail. Indeed, Adorno and Horkheimer use their analysis of the culture industry to call attention to what they perceive as the fundamental traits of the administered society and to carry out a radical critique of capitalism. They suggest that reflection on the culture industries illuminates the processes promoting standardization, homogenization and conformity that characterize social life under what they call 'totalitarian capitalism'. The tendencies toward manipulation and domination in the culture industry illuminate similar trends throughout capitalist society.

The mass deception present in the culture industries is similar to the deception, false promises and manipulation in the economic, political and social spheres. In this conception, one of the main trends of contemporary capitalist societies is the synthesis of advertising, culture, information, politics and manipulation that characterizes the culture industries.[15] This dialectical focus on the relationship between the culture industry and capitalism points to a basic methodological position within Critical Theory that in turn marks its affinity with Marxian dialectics. For Critical Theory, every social phenomenon must be interpreted in terms of a theory of society which itself is part of a theory of capitalism. The theory of the relationship between society and the economy illuminates phenomena like the culture industry, and analysis of the latter in turn sheds light on the economy and society. Consequently, Critical Theory operates with a dialectic between its topics of analysis (the culture industry or anti-Semitism or whatever) and its theory of society. In this dialectic, the theory of society illuminates the topic under investigation, which in turn illuminates the fundamental social trends – commodification, reification and so on – described in the social theory.

After describing the style of culture industry products and the formulas, conventions and stereotypes that constitute them, Adorno and Horkheimer analyze several of the strategies used to indoctrinate consumers into accept-ance of the existing society. 'Entertainment', they claim, accustoms audiences to accept existing society as natural by endlessly repeating and reproducing similar views of the world which present the existing way of life as the way of the world. The eternal recurrence of the same in the culture industry changes the very nature of ideology, they suggest.

Accordingly, ideology has been made vague and noncommittal, and thus neither clearer nor weaker. Its very vagueness, its almost scientific aversion from commit-ting itself to anything which cannot be verified, acts as an instrument of domination. It becomes a vigorous and prearranged promulgation of the status quo. The culture industry tends to make itself the embodiment of authoritative pronouncements, and thus the irrefutable prophet of the prevailing order. It skillfully steers a winding course between the cliffs of demonstrable misinformation and manifest truth, faithfully reproducing the phenomenon whose opaqueness blocks any insight and installs the ubiquitous and intact phenomenon as ideal. Ideology is split into the photograph of stubborn life and the naked lie about its meaning – which is not expressed but suggested and yet drummed in. To demonstrate its divine nature, reality is always repeated in a purely cynical way. Such a photological proof is of course not stringent, but it is overpowering. . . . The new ideology has as its objects the world as such. It makes use of the worship of facts by no more than elevating a disagreeable existence into the world of facts in representing it meticulously. (*DoE*, pp. 147–8)

The culture industry thus tries to induce the individual to identify with society's typical figures and models:

Pseudo-individuality is rife: from the standardized jazz improvization to the excep-tional film star whose hair curls over her eye to demonstrate her originality. What is individual is no more than the generality's power to stamp the accidental detail so firmly that it is accepted as such. The defiant reserve or elegant appearance of the individual on show is mass-produced like Yale locks, whose only difference can be measured in fractions of millimeters. (*DoE*, p. 154)

The culture industry thus serves as a powerful instrument of social control, which induces individuals to accept their fate and conform to existing society. Advertising progressively fuses in style and technique with the entertainment of the culture industry (*DoE*, pp. 156–67), which in turn can be read as a series of advertisements for existing society and the established way of life (see Chapter 6 for further discussion of this point).

Like every theoretical conception, the notion of the culture industries was a product of its historical period, and its insights and limitations result primarily from the fact that it theorized features of a past historical con-juncture. The Institute theorists' conception of the role of mass culture and communications was first shaped in the period of Nazi Germany, where they witnessed Hitler's extraordinary use of mass communications and fascist spectacles. Obviously the experience of fascism shaped the Critical Theorists' views of the rise of a behemoth state and cultural apparatus combined with an eclipse of democracy, individuality and what they saw as authentic art.[16] And in exile in the United States, they observed Roosevelt's impressive use of the media and the propagandist uses of the mass media during World War II. Consequently political use and control of the media during conditions of warfare, with an enlarged war-time state and a sub-ordinate war-time economy, coupled with capitalist control of the enter-tainment industries, provided the historical roots of the Institute model of the culture industries as instruments of social control. Indeed, the media under this type of militarized social system and war conditions – whether liberal democratic, fascist or state socialist – are bound to be rather one-dimensional and propagandist. Moreover, the Critical Theory model of the media and society described rather accurately certain dominant trends and effects during the post-World War II Cold War period, when the media were enlisted in the anti-Communist crusade and when media content was subject to tight control and censorship, a situation signaled by Adorno's and Horkheimer's allusions to 'purges' (DoE, p. 123).[17]

Critical Theory, Communications Research and Social Theory

The culture industry theory was thus developed in the United States during the heyday of the Press, radio and cinema as dominant cultural forms; and it was published just before the first wave of the introduction of television, whose importance Adorno and Horkheimer anticipated and whose forms and effects were analyzed by Adorno in a classic article originally entitled 'How to Look at Television'.[18] Interest in the new communications media was growing, and a new discipline was emerging to study its social effects and functions. Research into media communications in the United States was largely inaugurated by the Institute for Social Research, then located at Columbia University, and by Paul Lazarsfeld and his associates in the 'Radio Research Project' and later the 'Bureau of Applied Social Research' at Princeton and then Columbia. Lazarsfeld was connected with the Institute in various ways, and for several years the groups interacted and undertook common projects.[19]

Not only did the Institute provide an early model of critical communi-cations research, but Institute theorists were among the first to see the importance of mass communications and culture for social theory, and influenced some of the early attempts to incorporate such themes into critical social theory. In his major works of the 1950s, C. Wright Mills, for instance, tended to utilize the Institute models of the media as agents of manipulation and social control, although, in the spirit of Lazarsfeld, he sometimes qualified its power to directly and consistently manipulate the public. In *White Collar* (1951) Mills stressed the crucial role of the mass media in shaping individual behavior and inducing comformity to middle-class values.[20] He argued that the media were increasingly shaping individual aspirations and behavior, and were above all promoting values of 'individual success'. He believed that entertainment media were especially potent instruments of social control, because 'popular culture is not tagged as "propaganda" but as entertainment; people are often exposed to it when most relaxed of mind and tired of body; and its characters offer easy targets of identification, easy answers to stereotyped personal problems' (p. 336).

Mills analyzed the banalization of politics in the media due to the fact that 'the mass media plug for ruling political symbols and personalities'. Perceiving the parallel between marketing commodities and selling politicians, Mills analyzed tendencies toward the commodification of politics; and in *The Power Elite*, he focused on the manipulative role of the media in shaping public opinion and strengthening the power of dominant elites.[21] In an analysis that anticipated Habermas's theory in *Structural Changes in the Public Sphere*, Mills discusses the shift from a social order consisting of 'communities, of publics', in which individuals participate in political and social debate and action, to a 'mass society' characterized by the 'transformation of public into mass' (pp. 298ff.). The impact of the mass media is crucial in this 'great transformation', for it shifts 'the ratio of givers of opinion to the receivers' in favor of small groups of elites who control or have access to the mass media. Moreover, the mass media engage in one-way communication which does not allow feedback, thus obliterating another feature of a democratic public sphere. In addition, the media rarely encourage participation in public action. In these ways, they foster social passivity and the fragmentation of the public sphere into privatized consumers.

Like the Institute, Mills makes *manipulation* the central feature of his theory of the media. He paid explicit homage to the Institute in a 1954 article in which he described the dominant types of social research as those of the scientists (quantitative empiricists), the Grand Theorists (structural functionalists like Talcott Parsons) and those genuine sociologists who inquire into '(1) What is the meaning of this – whatever we are examining – for our society as a whole, and what is this social world like? (2) What is the meaning of this for the types of men and women that prevail in this society? and (3) how does this fit into the historical trend of our times, and in what direction does this main drift seem to be carrying us?'[22] Mills then comments:

I know of no better way to become acquainted with this endeavor in a high form of modern expression than to read the periodical, *Studies in Philosophy and Social Sciences*, published by The Institute of Social Research. Unfortunately, it is available only in the morgues of university libraries, and to the great loss of American social studies, several of the Institute's leading members, among them Max Horkheimer and Theodore Adorno, have returned to Germany. That there is now *no* periodical that bears comparison with this one testifies to the ascendancy of the Higher Statisticians and the Grand Theorists over the Sociologists. It is difficult to understand why some publisher does not get out a volume or two of selections from this great periodical. (ibid.)

Following the lead of Adorno and Horkheimer, other Critical Theorists like Fromm, Marcuse and Habermas also attributed a fundamental role to the culture industries in their critical social theories. Their books helped lead many social theorists to perceive the importance of mass culture and communications in social reproduction. Fromm's first book published in the United States, *Escape from Freedom* (1941), applied the culture industry model to a critique of advertising, mass culture and political manipulation. After discussing some of the techniques of modern advertising, Fromm writes: 'All these methods are essentially irrational; they have nothing to do with the qualities of the merchandise, and they smother and kill the critical capacities of the customer like an opiate or outright hypnosis. They give him a certain satisfaction by their daydreaming qualities just as the movies do, but at the same time they increase his feeling of smallness and power-lessness.'[23]

Fromm then calls attention to how mass communications dull the capacity for critical thinking and contribute to the decline of the individual (pp. 128ff.). Summarizing his argument, he writes:

Vastness of cities in which the individual is lost, buildings that are as high as mountains, constant acoustic bombardment by the radio, big headlines changing three times a day and leaving one no choice to decide what is important, shows in which one hundred girls demonstrate their ability with clocklike precision to eliminate the individual and act like a powerful though smooth machine, the beating rhythm of jazz – these and many other details are expressions of a constellation in which the individual is confronted by uncontrollable dimensions in comparison with which he is a small particle. All he can do is to fall in step like a marching soldier or a worker on the endless belt. He can act; but the sense of independence, significance, has gone. (pp. 131–2)

In *Escape from Freedom* Fromm also analyzes how public opinion is shaped by news media (pp. 192ff.) and how socialization patterns contribute to the decline of the individual (pp. 250ff.). The Institute critique of the culture industries also played a central role in Fromm's book *The Sane Society* and Marcuse's *Eros and Civilization*, both published in 1955.[24] Using Freudian and Marxian categories, Marcuse described the process by which sexual and aggressive instincts are tamed and channeled into socially necessary, but unpleasant, labor. Following the Institute analysis of changes in the nature of socialization, Marcuse notes the decline of the family as the dominant agent of socialization and the rise of the mass media:

The repressive organization of the instincts seems to be *collective*, and the ego seems to be prematurely socialized by a whole system of extra-familial agents and agencies. As early as the pre-school level, gangs, radio, and television set the pattern for conformity and rebellion; deviations from the pattern are punished not so much in the family as outside and against the family. The experts of the mass media transmit the required values; they offer the perfect training in efficiency, toughness, personality, dream, and romance. With this education, the family can no longer compete. (p. 97)

In Marcuse's view, the mass media were becoming dominant agents of socialization which were displacing the primacy of the family – the role of the mass media in both Freudian and many United States social science theories. The result was the decline of individual autonomy and the manipulation of mind and instincts by mass communications: 'With the decline in consciousness, with the control of information, with the absorption of individuals into mass communication, knowledge is administered and confined. The individual does not really know what is going on; the overpowering machine of education and entertainment unites him with all the others in a state of anaesthesia from which all detrimental ideas tend to be excluded' (p. 104). Marcuse continued to stress the manipulative effects of the culture industries in his major works, and contributed to the widespread adoption of the so-called manipulation theory of the media by the New Left and others in the 1960s. In *One-Dimensional Man*, Marcuse claims that the inanities of commercial radio and television confirm his analyses of the decline of the individual and the demise of authentic culture and oppositional thought in 'advanced industrial society'.[25] Throughout the book, he assigns an important role to the media as 'new forms of social control' which engender 'false needs' and the 'one-dimensional' thought and behavior necessary for the smooth reproduction of advanced capitalism.

In his first major work, *Strukturwandel der Öffentlichkeit* of 1962, Habermas analyzed the rise of the culture industries and the decline of the public sphere within liberal democracy.[26] He provided a historical analysis of the transition from a form of liberal capitalism that contained a democratic public sphere in which 'public opinion' was formed by debate and consensus and in which an educated public critically discussed political and social issues to a form of monopoly capitalism in which public opinion was formed by the mass media, and culture was passively consumed by culture industry spectators.

The Critical Theorists therefore were among the first to see the important role of mass culture and communications in social reproduction, and deeply influenced social theorists like C. Wright Mills, David Riesman,

Alvin Gouldner, Stanley Aronowitz and a later generation of the New Left.[27] Furthermore, critical communications researchers like George Gerbner were directly influenced by Adorno and Critical Theory, and continued to work in this tradition to some extent.[28] Yet, what eventually became the dominant tradition of critical communications research in the United States (the work of Dallas Smythe, Herbert Schiller, Eric Barnouw and others) focused more on the political economy of the media, and engaged in historical and empirical communications research.[29] Consequently the impact of Critical Theory on critical communications research is often indirect. Yet a direct influence on theories of society and on United States debates over 'popular culture' can be attributed to the Institute for Social Research.

Critical Theory and the Debates over Mass Culture

Despite problematical elements of the Institute critique of mass-mediated culture, there is no question that its radical attacks provoked a lively discussion of its merits and deficiencies that is still important and topical.[30] Institute theorists' critiques of mass culture helped shape the first major anthology published in the United States on *Mass Culture* (1957), which in turn helped foster an important debate over its nature and effects. The anthology contained articles by Adorno, Lowenthal, Kracauer and Lazarsfeld, as well as many other studies influenced by the Critical Theory model. One of the editors, Bernard Rosenberg, attacked mass culture in terms reminiscent of Adorno and Horkheimer, while the other editor, David Manning White, defended it as the culture of the people appropriate to a democratic society, a culture which has made significant contributions to modern society, which in White's view would increase in the future.[31]

Lowenthal, in an essay in *Mass Culture* entitled 'Historical Perspectives of Popular Culture', outlines the theoretical, historical and critical approach toward mass culture which he defends against mainstream approaches.[32] In a sharp polemic, he attacks the contemporary 'modern social science' approach to culture and communication:

Empirical social science has become a kind of applied asceticism. It stands clear of any entanglements with foreign powers and thrives in an atmosphere of rigidly enforced neutrality. It refuses to enter the sphere of meaning. A study of television, for instance, will go to great heights in analyzing data on the influence of television on family life, but it will leave to poets and dreamers the question of the actual human values of this new institution. Social research takes the phenomena of modern life, including the mass media, at face value. It rejects the task of placing them in a historical and moral context. In the beginning of the modern era, social theory had theology as its model, but today the natural sciences have replaced theology. This change in models has far-reaching implications. Theology aims at salvation, natural science at manipulation; the one leads to heaven and hell, the other to technology and machinery. Social science is today defined as an analysis of painstakingly circumscribed, more or less artificially isolated, social sectors. It imagines that such horizontal segments constitute its research laboratory, and it seems to forget that the only social research laboratories that are properly admissible are historical situations. (*LPCS*, p. 52)

Against the critiques of mass culture by Institute theorists and others, Edward Shils attacked its critics as elitist, socialist radicals who had no sympathy for the tastes of the common people. Shils designated Horkheimer and his circle as 'Marxian socialists' who were leading the onslaught against mass culture:

It is not accidental that most of the recent critics of mass culture are, or were, Marxian socialists, some even rather extreme, at least in their past commitment to the socialist ideal . . . Prof. Max Horkheimer, who is the leading exponent of the 'critical' philosophy of the Frankfurt circle, is an apolitical Marxist whose Hegelian sociological terminology obscures his Marxism. Prof. T. Wiesengrund-Adorno and Prof. Leo Lowenthal, the former at Frankfurt University, the latter at the University of California, are both leading adherents of this school in which a refined Marxism finds its most sophisticated expression. Dr. Erich Fromm is a psychoanalyzing Marxist.[33]

Shils claimed that disappointed Marxian hopes led these radicals to turn with fury on mass culture, which they blamed for seducing the proletariat away from its revolutionary vocation. Shils insinuated that these 'European anti-American intellectuals' were full of unjustified contempt for the common people and do not understand the culture, people or society which they so vehemently criticized.

If one were to take seriously the two fountainheads of the interpretation of mass culture, namely, the Frankfurt *Institut für Sozialforschung*, led by Professor Horkheimer, and *Politics* under the editorship of Mr. MacDonald, one would believe that the ordinary citizen who listens to the radio, goes to films and looks at television is not just *l'homme moyen sensuel* known to past ages. He is something new in the world. He is a 'private atomic subject,' utterly without religious beliefs, without any private life, without a family which means anything to him; he is standardized, ridden with anxiety, perpetually in a state of 'exacerbated' unrest, his life 'emptied of meaning,' and 'trivialized,' 'alienated from his past, from his community, and possibly from himself,' cretinized and brutalized. (pp. 596–7)

This picture of the victims of mass culture has its parallel, Shils claims, in the German romantic, elitist and Marxian attacks on industrialism. All the critics, Shils confidently maintains, were 'ideologists, hostile to human beings as they are' (p. 598), and their critique is fueled, he claims, by 'the frustrated attachment to an impossible ideal of human perfection, and a distaste for one's own society and for human beings as they are' (p. 606). In short, their critiques are 'unrealistic' and should be rejected by men of 'sound common sense and good judgement' (ibid.).

The Institute never responded to Shils directly, and I shall indicate to what extent his critique is justified in the next section. There is a suggestion of an answer to Shils, however, in a later essay by Adorno, in which he writes: 'The bourgeois is tolerant. His love for men as they are arises out of hate for the correct man.'[34] Critical Theory maintained that accepting people 'as they are' and 'realistically' accepting the status quo precluded conceiving of potentialities for a higher mode of human being and a better society. Critical Theorists claimed that the uncritical acceptance and celebration of mass culture promoted a conformist attitude toward established society. Critique of mass culture was perceived as an important part of social critique by Institute theorists, and they believed that renouncing this task by either celebrating or failing to take seriously mass culture simply strengthened the power of existing society. They believed that theory could help break the hold of mass culture by de-naturalizing it, by developing critical perspectives that would interrogate and criticize the forms, messages and effects of mass culture and communications.

5.3   New Critical Perspectives on Mass Communications and Culture

The critique of the culture industries was one of the most influential aspects of Critical Theory, and its impact on social theory and on theories and critiques of mass communications and culture accounts in part for the continuing interest in Critical Theory today. In particular, from the 1960s to the present, there has been renewed interest in Critical Theory and a wealth of radical critiques of mass culture, many of them influenced by Institute theories or quite similar in intent and practice.[35] There have also been critiques of the Institute's theory of mass culture, which stressed the similarity of the Critical Theory analysis to conservative critics of mass culture, and which condemned the Institute for its cultural elitism.[36]

Despite its limitations, which I shall outline in this section, the Institute theory of the culture industries contains several novel features, and makes many important contributions to the study of mass communications and culture. Critical Theory conceptualizes culture and communications as part of society, and focuses on how socio-economic imperatives helped constitute the nature, function and effects of mass communications and culture. By conceptualizing these important social forces as part of socio-economic processes, Critical Theory integrates study of culture and communications with study of the economy and society. And by adopting a critical approach to the study of all social phenomena, Critical Theory is able to conceptualize how the culture industries function as instruments of social control, and thereby serve the interests of social domination.

On the whole, later critical approaches to the media and culture tended to separate communications research from the study of mass culture, thus failing to provide a unified account of cultural production, distribution and reception. Consequently, Critical Theory is more than a piece of history, because it contains a unified, critical approach to the study of culture and communications within the context of critical social theory. Likewise, its mode of cultural criticism situates artifacts of analysis within the context of their social environment, and uses social theory to help interpret cultural artifacts, while using culture to help decipher social trends and processes. Critical Theorists' use of psychoanalytic theory leads them to decipher cultural works as exhibiting traits of individual and social psychology, as well as socio-historical content. Yet, despite its contributions, the Critical Theory model has serious limitations, for much of the criticism of popular culture is limited to denunciation of its ideological features. Since much in popular culture deserves and demands severe condemnation, Critical Theory's method of ideology critique provides some useful tools for cultural criticism; but it also suffers some limitations.

In contrast to the mode of condemnatory criticism associated with Critical Theory, radical cultural criticism today should develop more complex strategies, and should attempt to develop a more multidimensional approach to mass culture. Rather than seeing its artifacts simply as expressions of hegemonic ideology and ruling-class interests, it is preferable to view popular entertainment as a complex product that contains contradictory moments of desire and its displacement, articulations of hopes and their repression. In this view, popular culture provides access to a society's dreams and nightmares, and contains both ideological celebrations of the status quo and utopian moments of transcendence, moments of opposition and rebellion and its attempted containment.[37] Recent studies of popular culture also show how social struggles and conflicts enter into works of popular entertainment, and see culture as a contested terrain, rather than a field of one-dimensional manipulation and illusion.[38]

New Critical Theories of culture and communications must therefore be able to develop more complex methods of cultural interpretation and criticism which pay attention to and conceptualize the contradictions, the articulation of social conflicts, the oppositional moments, the subversive tendencies and the projection of utopian images and scenes of happiness and freedom that appear within mainstream commercial culture. The classical Critical Theory approach, especially Adorno's work, generally limits itself to attacking the ideology and purely retrogressive effects of radio, popular music, films, television and so forth. In this sense, the model of cultural interpretation and criticism is remarkably similar to the crude Marxian critique of ideology which restricts cultural analysis to denunciation of ideology. Part of the problem is that for Adorno and many of his colleagues, the artifacts of the culture industry are simply beneath contempt. In *Minima Moralia*, Adorno writes: 'Every visit to the cinema leaves me, against all my vigilance, stupider and worse' (*MM*, p. 25). Such an arrogant, grandiose gesture of absolute disdain, however, precludes understanding what gratifications popular culture actually provides and what needs it serves, in however distorted a fashion. This attitude also leads Critical Theorists to neglect, albeit with some exceptions, analysis of specific films, television programs or artifacts of popular culture, since they presume in advance that such artifacts are merely a debased form of culture and a vehicle of ideology which are not worthy of detailed study or critique. Thus, when Adorno does analyze examples of popular music and television, he generally limits himself to arraigning their ideologies and 'retrogressive' effects on consciousness, without analyzing their contradictions, critical or oppositional moments, or potential to provide insight into social conditions or to elicit a critical response.[39]

But while popular music may, as Adorno argued, exhibit features of commodification, reification and standardization, which may in turn have retrogressive effects on consciousness, such a theoretical optic cannot adequately account for the genesis and popularity of many forms of popular music such as the blues, jazz, rock and roll, reggae, punk and so on. Since music is the most nonrepresentational of all arts, it provides vehicles for the expression of pain, rage, joy, rebellion, sexuality and so forth, which might have progressive effects. Historically, the production of certain types of popular music was often carried out by oppressed groups, like blacks or hispanics, or by working-class whites or marginalized youth. Much popular music thus articulates rebellion against standardization, conformity, oppression and so on, however much this oppositional articulation is expressed in standard musical forms and types. Moreover, the forums of reception of popular music have frequently been dances and festivities in a context of transgression of propriety through drinking, making love, wild dancing, communal singing and the rest. Ragtime, jazz, bop, swing and rock have been more at home in the brothel, dance-hall or bedroom than within His Master's Voice in the living room. Though contemporary forms of punk and hard rock may provide background for young fascists and conservatives, they may also provide the social cement for a culture of political mobilization and struggle, as the Rock against Racism and Rock against the Right concerts in England and Germany proved. And music like reggae can be bound up with a subculture of protest as much as with the commodification of culture for profitability and harmless catharsis.

Adorno's model of the culture industry does not allow for the heterogeneity of popular culture and contradictory effects. Instead it sees popular culture in terms of reification and commodification and hence as a sign of the total triumph of capital and the total reification of experience. To be sure, much popular culture lends itself to Adorno's categories and critique, though as suggested, other examples resist his categories and require a more nuanced approach to cultural interpretation and critique. Yet occasionally, Adorno qualified his one-dimensional condemnation of popular culture, and allowed for the possibility of audience resistance to media manipulation. In 'Transparencies on Film'[40] Adorno uncharacteristically indicated that a certain sort of film might contain socially critical potential, and that mass culture itself reproduces existing conflicts and antagonisms: 'In its attempts to manipulate the masses, the ideology of the culture industry itself becomes as internally antagonistic as the very society which it aims to control. The ideology of the culture industry contains the antidote to its own lie' (p. 202). In particular, Adorno believed that the technique of montage (the juxtaposition of images to create multiple effects of meaning and socially critical associations) developed by Sergi Eisenstein and the revolutionary Soviet cinema provides models for a socially progressive cinema: 'Film is faced with the dilemma of finding a procedure which neither lapses into arts-and-crafts nor slips into a more documentary mode. The obvious answer today, as forty years ago, is that of montage which does not interfere with things but rather arranges them in a constellation akin to that of writing' (p. 203).

Yet Adorno believed that pure montage and cinematic shock effects (such as were celebrated by Benjamin) 'without the addition of intentionality in its details, refuses to accept intentions merely from the principle itself' (p. 203). Progressive film would thus have to combine montage in image construction with other effects, like advanced music (and progressive political intentions and insights?), to turn the images of film in a socially critical direction: 'The liberated film would have to wrest its *a priori* collectivity from the mechanisms of unconscious and irrational influence and enlist this collectivity in the service of emancipatory intentions' (pp. 203–4).

In another late article, 'Leisure', Adorno pointed to limitations in the ability of the culture industry to manipulate spectator consciousness. Reflecting on a study of the media's presentation of the marriage of a Dutch princess to an upper-class German, Adorno stressed that the audience saw through the media hype of this event, and realistically perceived its insignificance. He thus concluded: 'The integration of consciousness and leisure is obviously not yet entirely successful. The real interests of the individuals are still strong enough, at the margins, to resist total control.'[41]

Following these models, new critical approaches to popular culture should not simply limit themselves to denouncing bourgeois ideologies and escapist functions. Even conservative mass culture often provides insights into forms of dominant ideologies, and sometimes unwittingly provides images of social conflict and opposition. Recent studies of Hollywood films, for instance, reveal that this form of commercial culture exhibits a confict of representations between competing social ideologies over the last several decades.[42] Particularly in the period from around 1967 to the present, a variety of competing ideological standpoints have appeared in mainstream Hollywood film. Consequently there is no one, monolithic, dominant ideology which the culture industries promote; indeed, the conflicting ideologies in contemporary culture industry artifacts point to continuing and intensifying social conflict within capitalist societies.

Yet in the Institute critique of mass culture, there is no consideration of oppositional and emancipatory uses of the media and cultural practices. There is neither a strategy for cultural revolution, as is found in Brecht, Benjamin and Enzensberger, nor a media politics to overcome the harmful effects that Horkheimer and Adorno describe.[43] In an era of media saturation, however, such withdrawal would only further marginalize already marginalized critical intellectuals (or the Left, feminists and others). Consequently, a radical media politics should replace the pessimistic denunciation found in classical Critical Theory, a point I shall take up in 8.2.

Part of the problem is that most Critical Theorists rigidly pit their concepts of 'authentic art', modeled on masters of the avant-garde like Schönberg, Kafka and Beckett, against mass culture, which they denounce for failing to have the qualities that they find in their preferred aesthetic models. But the very distinction between 'high culture' and 'popular culture' has come under attack, and it seems perverse to expect products of the culture industries to have the qualities of works of previous 'high culture' or the avant-garde. Yet, by limiting his model of authentic art to those few avant-garde examples of highly negative art, Adorno rules out in advance the possibility of any broad-based cultural politics, and his model of emancipatory aesthetics is intolerably ascetic and narrow, limited to those avant-garde productions which resist assimilation and co-optation.

In a sense, Adorno's aesthetics is completely undialectical. He operates with a binary contrast between 'authentic' art and mass culture, in which the latter is completely debased, and emancipatory effects are limited to the former. This stance reproduces the German religion of high art and its inevitable elitism, and completely excludes the 'popular' from the domain of the 'authentic', thus falling behind the critiques of Brecht and Benjamin – and Adorno's own critique of 'the authentic' in his book *Jargon of Authenticity*. Indeed, Adorno's own esoteric aesthetic theory itself becomes a jargon motivated by a dual fear of co-optation and regression.[44] Yet his uncompromising radicalism provides a healthy antidote to all affirmative and idealist aesthetics, and his obstinate obsession with art provides a wealth of insights into the mediations between art and society which might become productive for materialist social theory and cultural criticism of the future.[45]

I would propose in conclusion that Critical Theory today should take mass culture as seriously as Adorno and his colleagues previously took high culture, by applying the same sophisticated arsenal of critical strategies and categories to the reading of contemporary mass culture as it once applied to 'high culture'. While cultural discrimination can be made, the absolute dichotomy between so-called 'high' and 'low' culture should be overcome; and radical cultural criticism today should pursue articulation and critique of ideological and emancipatory qualities – and their contradictory imbrication – with regard to a vast range of cultural artifacts.

Adorno's cultural criticism also helped produce the first neo-Marxian theory and critique of the consumer society, and it is to this theme that we shall now turn.

6

From the Consumer Society to Postmodernism

For the Critical Theorists, 'mass culture' included both media culture and consumer culture. The term 'culture industries' referred to the industrialization of culture and the similarities between mass-produced consumer products and the productions of the entertainment industry. Both types of commodities were produced for mass consumption, and were characterized by standardization and highly rationalized mass production which allegedly eliminated individual creativity from the processes of production and consumption – or at least severely restricted it. Both domains were criticized by Critical Theorists for 'reifying' human beings. People were reified in production by being forced to submit to domination by a mechanical and fragmented labor process which turned human beings into appendages of machines and the apparatus. Going beyond standard Marxism, Critical Theory argued that individuals were also reified in the process of consumption, by means of passive viewing of media spectacles or attempts to buy happiness or solve problems through consumer goods.

Mass culture was thus an integral part of the consumer society, which the Institute described as a new configuration of capitalist modernity. In the consumer society, culture and aesthetics blended with production and advertising to create a way of life focused on consumption of goods, services, mass images and spectacles. The proliferation of these phenomena led theorists in the 1970s to speak of 'mass-mediated culture', and eventually a 'postmodern society' defined by a condition in which images, codes and models became primary determinants of everyday life.[1] Yet, in contrast to postmodernists who tend to describe developments in contemporary society in abstraction from political economy, Critical Theory characteristically described significant social changes in terms of developments within capitalist modernity. In this chapter, I will therefore discuss the Critical Theorists' formulations and critiques of the new configuration of capitalism centrally shaped by mass culture, consumption and the cultural industries (6.1), offer some critical perspectives on their classical formulations (6.2) and discuss their responses to the debate over postmodernism (6.3).

6.1   Critical Theory and the Consumer Society

One of the main functions of the culture industries is to shape the needs, attitudes and behavior of individuals so as to integrate them into the consumer society. The Critical Theorists were among the first to develop systematic critical reflections on the consumer society as the matrix for new configurations of contemporary capitalism which provided new modes of social integration and control. They anticipated current debates over needs, commodities and consumer policies, and were among the first to see the import of these issues for critical social theory and public policy.

Following Marx and Lukács, Critical Theory from the beginning characterized capitalist society as a commodity-producing society, and took the commodity as the basic social unit and key to the functioning of capitalism. In the new configurations of capitalism, everything – goods and services, art, politics and human life – became a commodity, while commodity exchange became the basic form of relationship in the consumer society. The Critical Theorists concluded that commodification and consumption were playing fundamental, constitutive roles in the contemporary development of capitalist modernity, and attempted to theorize its new configurations in the consumer society.

From around the 1920s, the problem of managing consumer demand became an increasingly important challenge to capitalist society. The 'captains of industry' had in place an apparatus of mass production, and needed to become 'captains of consciousness' to manage and administer a new order of mass consumption.[2] There were few references to consumption in 1930s Critical Theory, however, and no real critique of the consumer society. Indeed, in the 1930s depression, consumerism was not an important mode of social integration, and it was not until the post-World War II economic boom that consumption became widespread in the more developed capitalist societies. Consequently, references to the consumer society grew in number and importance in the Critical Theorists' writings during the 1940s and 1950s. In this section, I shall discuss the first perceptions and critiques of the consumer society in the writings of Adorno, Horkheimer, Lowenthal, Fromm and Marcuse.

Adorno on the Consumer Society

Adorno's early studies of music showed how the production and consumption of popular music followed the logic of commodity production. In a 1938 article entitled 'On the Fetish Character of Music and the Regression of Listening', he throws a characteristic swipe at consumer culture in the midst of his critical reflections on popular music:

> The couple out driving who spend their time identifying every passing car and being happy if they recognize the trademarks speeding by, the girl whose satisfaction consists solely in the fact that she and her boyfriend 'look good,' the expertise of the jazz enthusiast who legitimizes himself by having knowledge about what is in any case inescapable: all this operates according to the same command. Before the theological caprices of commodities, the consumers become temple slaves. Those who sacrifice themselves nowhere else can do so here, and here they are fully betrayed.[3]

After his arrival in the United States in 1938, Adorno observed the extent to which commodity production pervaded culture and how the new culture of consumption was colonizing everyday life, while producing a consumer society. One of Adorno's 1940s essays analyzed the diagnosis of an early critic of the culture of consumption, Thorstein Veblen.[4] He begins: 'Veblen's *Theory of the Leisure Class* became famous for its doctrine of conspicuous consumption, according to which the consumption of goods, from the very early 'predatory' stage of history to the present, has served not so much to satisfy men's true needs or to provide what Veblen chooses to call the 'fullness of life' as to maintain social prestige – status' (*P*, p. 75). Adorno sets out Veblen's theory of history, his sources and his method, and finds salutary elements of a critique of the consumer society. For Adorno, 'Veblen's basic experience may be characterized as that of pseudo-uniqueness' (p. 78). In an era of mass production and consumption, standardization reigns, and individuation (of goods and individual thought and behavior) declines. Pseudo-individuality emerges, to compensate for the actual decline of individuality, and takes the forms of kitsch for the middle classes and conspicuous consumption for the upper classes. Veblen sees both the pathetic attempts of the middle classes to emulate upper-class ostentation with kitsch reproductions, ornaments and artifacts and the waste and excess involved in conspicuous consumption as fundamentally irrational signs of modern 'barbarism'. Veblen championed a rational technocratic organization of society in opposition to a society organized around conspicuous consumption, while presenting cultivation of 'the work instinct' as an alternative to the emerging world of consumer capitalism. Competition, lust for acquisition and conspicuous consumption are attacked by Veblen as remnants of a primitive, 'predatory spirit', and he criticizes 'pecuniary capital' as a wasteful, irrational economic form.

Adorno sharply criticizes Veblen's idolization of production and his failure to see that the mode of consumption which he criticizes is integrally part of the mode of production and that the industrial capital whose 'instincts' Veblen praises is interconnected with 'pecuniary capital' and conspicuous consumption, as part of the same capitalist system. Yet Adorno appreciates many insights in Veblen's work concerning the structure and façade of the emerging consumer society. For example, he is impressed by Veblen's analysis of how the ostentation and ornamentation of contemporary architecture express a predatory capitalist (and in some cases imperialist) spirit, and applauds Veblen's characterization of sports in terms of a predatory regression to barbarism (*P*, pp. 78–81). Adding some thoughts of his own to Veblen's critique of sports, Adorno concludes: 'Modern sports, one will perhaps say, seek to restore to the body some of the functions of which the machine has deprived it. But they do so only in order to train men all the more inexorably to serve the machine. Hence sports belong to the realm of unfreedom, no matter where they are organized' (p. 81).

Adorno also appreciates Veblen's concern with the 'woman question' and his analyses of the ways in which women are oppressed by a society which enslaves them so that they can serve and become ostentatious elements of display to enhance their husbands' status and prestige. Adorno believes that there is a rudimentary 'dialectic of women' in Veblen's analysis, which presents women both as relatively independent of the economic system, and thus free from the 'predatory spirit', and as potentially conservative by virtue of exclusion from the production process and the public sphere. Reflecting on this situation, Adorno writes:

Following this line of thought, one might reach the conclusion that women have escaped the sphere of production only to be absorbed all the more entirely by the sphere of consumption, to be captivated by the immediacy of the commodity world no less than men are transfixed by the immediacy of profit. Women mirror the injustice masculine society has inflicted on them – they become increasingly like commodities. Veblen's insight indicates a change in the utopia of emancipation. Hope cannot aim at making the mutilated social character of women identical to the mutilated social character of men; rather, its goal must be a state in which the face of the grieving woman disappears simultaneously with that of the bustling, capable man, a state in which all that survives the disgrace of the difference between the sexes is the happiness that difference makes possible. (*P*, p. 82)

Adorno especially objects to Veblen's image of the good life, which 'is based not on the ideal of happiness but on that of work. Happiness enters his field of vision only as the fulfillment of the "work instinct," his supreme anthropological category. He is a puritan *malgré lui-même*. While he never tires of attacking taboos, his criticism stops at the sacredness of work' (*P*, p. 83). Adorno defends the values of leisure, happiness and freedom from utility, whereas Veblen criticizes the waste, luxury and irrationality of the leisure class, while celebrating the values of work, utility and industry. These values, Adorno points out, are fundamental values of the capitalist economic system itself. Thus, while Veblen powerfully denounces the 'residues' and 'culture' of capitalism, he fails to provide adequate critical perspectives on capitalism itself. Against Veblen's undialectical and splenetic denunciation of the epiphenomena of conspicuous consumption, Adorno concludes: 'The only adequate response to the present technical situation, which holds out the promise of wealth and abundance to men, is to organize it according to the needs of a humanity which no longer needs violence because it is its own master. . . . Today, adjustment to what is possible no longer means adjustment; it means making the possible real' (pp. 93–4).

Adorno assumed here a distinction central to Critical Theory between the possible and the actual, between the possibility of meeting needs and fulfilling potentialities with existing social wealth, contrasted with the actual suffering and inequality in current society. The problem was that existing wealth was utilized in the interests of maintaining the current organization of society and class domination, rather than in fulfilling human needs. In an article on Aldous Huxley's *Brave New World*, Adorno intensified his own critique of the consumer society.[5] For Adorno, Huxley's dystopia depicts the ways in which standardization and homogenization massify and destroy individual thought and action. In Huxley's sketch of a society constituted by mass reproduction, massive social conditioning and controlled consumption and sexuality:

'Community, Identity, and Stability' replaces the motto of the French Revolution. Community defines a collectivity in which each individual is unconditionally subordinated to the functioning of the whole (the question of the point of this whole is no longer permitted or even possible in the New World). Identity means the elimination of individual differences, standardization even down to biological constitution; stability, the end of all social dynamics. (*P*, p. 99)

Huxley attacks the eradication of culture, tradition, individuality and spirituality from a society which worships only production and consumption. Adorno's analysis and critique of Huxley provide some revealing insights into his own complex views of the consumer society. On one hand, the consumer society comes to control even thought and communication:

The degeneration of talk is due to objective tendencies. The virtual transformation of the world into commodities, the predetermination by the machinery of society of everything that is thought or done, renders speaking illusory. . . . The ladies of *Brave New World* – and in this case extrapolation is hardly required – converse only as consumers. In principle, their conversation concerns nothing but what is in any case to be found in the catalogues of the ubiquitous industries, information about available commodities. Objectively superfluous, it is the empty shell of dialogue, the intention of which was once to find out what was hitherto unknown. Stripped of this idea, dialogue is ripe for extinction. (*P*, p. 102)

In a subtle critique of Huxley's harsh condemnation of the hedonism of *Brave New World*, Adorno suggests that Huxley fails to perceive that the sexual libertarianism and gratification of individual impulses with which individuals are integrated into Huxley's dystopia contain a utopian potentiality of genuine gratification of individual needs. Adorno fears that Huxley's negative portrayal of admittedly socially administered happiness contains a puritan condemnation of happiness as such (*P*, pp. 103ff.). Crucially, 'His anger at false happiness sacrifices the idea of true happiness as well' (p. 103). Adorno also objects to Huxley's implicit celebration of ideal values – spiritual transcendence in this case – over material ones. Against such ascetic condemnation of the consumer society, Adorno maintains an uncompromising defense of the importance of satisfying material needs. Quoting a passage by Horkheimer, Adorno concludes:

'We criticize mass culture not because it gives men too much or makes their life too secure – that we may leave to Lutheran theology – but rather because it contributes to a condition in which men get too little and what they get is bad, a condition in which whole strata inside and out live in frightful poverty, in which men come to terms with injustice, in which the world is kept in a condition where one must expect on the one hand gigantic catastrophes and on the other clever elites conspiring to bring about a dubious peace'. (*P*, p. 109)

Adorno thus defends the value of happiness against ascetic attacks, but insists that true happiness can be envisaged only in a new social order. In his essay on Huxley, Adorno provides one of only a few glimpses into how he envisages human life might be when 'existing property relations' and 'the market and competition' – that is, capitalism – are abolished:

When this static situation comes to an end needs will look completely different. If production is redirected towards the unconditional and unlimited satisfaction of needs, including precisely those produced by the hitherto prevailing system, needs themselves will be decisively altered. The indistinguishability of true and false needs is an essential part of the present phase. . . . One day it will be readily apparent that men do not need the trash provided them by the culture industry or the miserable high-quality goods proferred by the more substantial industries. The thought, for instance, that in addition to food and lodging the cinema is necessary for the reproduction of labour power is 'true' only in a world which prepares men for the reproduction of their labour power and constrains their needs in harmony with the interests of supply and social control. (*P*, pp. 109–10)

In this passage Adorno combines critique of the culture industries with critique of consumption in his attack on the consumer society. He envisages a condition which would at once satisfy individual needs and provide true happiness. Such a social order would require an economy (socialism) oriented toward the satisfaction of the material needs of all its members and aimed at the abolition of scarcity, poverty and human suffering. If material needs could be satisfied, Adorno imagines a condition in which the antithesis between production and consumption would be overcome and individuals could attain happiness in all dimensions of their lives. Such a society would also transcend the obsession with material goods and imperatives toward productivity and utility that define the capitalist social order (that is, that productivity is an end in itself, and that only goods and activities that have a market value and utility are valuable per se).

Consumption, Mass Culture and Social Integration

In *Dialectic of Enlightenment*, written during the same period as the essays on Veblen and Huxley, Horkheimer and Adorno focus their critique of contemporary society on mass culture. In a key passage they indicate how technological and material forces of progress can be used to foster domination and regression:

The fallen nature of modern man cannot be separated from social progress. On the one hand the growth of economic productivity furnishes the conditions for a world of greater justice; on the other hand it allows the technical apparatus and the social groups which administer it a disproportionate superiority to the rest of the population. The individual is wholly devalued in relation to the economic powers, which at the same time press the control of society over nature to hitherto unsuspected heights. Even though the individual disappears before the apparatus which he serves, that apparatus provides for him as never before. In an unjust state of life, the impotence and pliability of the masses grow with the quantitative increase in commodities allowed them. (*DoE*, pp. xiv–xv)

Horkheimer and Adorno point to similarities between industrial and cultural production and a growing social unification based on increasing homogenization and control:

The ruthless unity in the culture industry is evidence of what will happen in politics. Marked differentiations such as those of A and B films, or of stories in magazines in different price ranges, depend not so much on subject matter as on classifying, organizing, and labelling consumers. Something is provided for all so that none may escape; the distinctions are emphasized and extended. The public is catered for with a hierarchical range of mass-produced products of varying quality, thus advancing the rule of complete quantification. Everybody must behave (as if spontaneously) in accordance with his previously determined and indexed level, and choose the category of mass product turned out for his type. Consumers appear as statistics on research organization charts, and are divided by income groups into red, green, and blue areas; the technique is that used for any type of propaganda. (*DoE*, p. 123)

Later in the chapter Horkheimer and Adorno describe the blend between mass culture, advertising and consumption in the consumer society (*DoE*, pp. 156ff.). They argue:

The assembly-line character of the culture industry, the synthetic, planned method of turning out its products (factory-like not only in the studio but, more or less, in the compilation of cheap biographies, pseudodocumentary novels, and hit songs) is very suited to advertising: the important individual points, by becoming detachable, interchangeable, and even technically alienated from any connected meaning, lend themselves to ends external to the work. The effect, the trick, the isolated repeatable device, have always been used to exhibit goods for advertising purposes, and today every monster close-up of a star is an advertisement for her name, and every hit song a plug for its tune. Advertising and the culture industry merge technically as well as economically. In both cases the same thing can be seen in innumerable places, and the mechanical repetition of the same cultural product has come to be the same as that of the propaganda slogan. In both cases the insistent demand for effectiveness makes technology into psycho-technology, into a procedure for manipulating men. In both cases the standards are the striking yet familiar, the easy yet catchy, the skillful yet simple; the object is to overpower the customer, who is conceived as absent-minded or resistant. (*DoE*, p. 163)

Throughout *Minima Moralia*, written just after the completion of *Dialectic of Enlightenment* in the mid-1940s, Adorno presents frequent criticisms of the culture industry and the consumer society – which are two aspects of the same new configuration of capitalism and have similar effects on personality structure and behavior. This text is full of criticisms of the new forms of mass culture which were emerging in the United States. Adorno reflects on conspicuous consumption and advertising, travel, the media and obsession with new products:

The fascinated eagerness to consume the latest process of the day not only leads to indifference towards the matter transmitted by the process, but encourages stationary rubbish and calculated idiocy. It confirms the old kitsch in ever new paraphrases as *haute nouveauté*. The concomitant of technical progress is the narrow-minded determination at all costs to buy nothing that is not in demand, not to fall behind the careering production process, never mind what the purpose of the product might be. Keeping up, crowding and queuing everywhere take the place of what were to some extent rational needs. (*MM*, p. 118)

While Adorno's melancholy reflections on a bad social order were deeply pessimistic, they occasionally included glimpses of the positive values by means of which Critical Theory criticized the current state of capitalism, principal of which was the fulfillment of basic needs and values such as peace, security and freedom from anxiety, as well as freedom from the competition and the administered consumption and production which define the contemporary stage of capitalism. In a revealing passage,

Adorno attacks the values of hustle and bustle associated with capitalism and affirms opposing values:

The concept of dynamism, which is the necessary complement of bourgeois 'a-historicity', is raised to an absolute, whereas it ought, as an anthropological reflex of the laws of production, to be itself critically confronted, in an emancipated society, with need. The conception of unfettered activity, of uninterrupted pro-creation, of chubby insatiability, of freedom as frantic bustle, feeds on the bourgeois concept of nature that has always served solely to proclaim social violence as unchangeable, as a piece of healthy eternity. It was in this, and not in their alleged levelling-down, that the positive blue-prints of socialism, resisted by Marx, were rooted in barbarism. It is not man's lapse into luxurious indolence that is to be feared, but the savage spread of the social under the mask of universal nature, the collective as a blind fury of activity. (*MM*, pp. 155–6)

Other Critical Theorists developed critiques of the consumer society as well, including Lowenthal in an article, first published in 1944, entitled 'The Triumph of Mass Idols'.[6] Through a comparison of biographies in popular magazines during the twentieth century, Lowenthal found a remarkable shift in emphasis from what he calls 'idols of production' to 'idols of consumption'. The overwhelming majority of magazine biographies during the first two decades of the century focused on 'idols of production', which

stem from the productive life, from industry, business, and natural sciences. There is not a single hero from the world of sports and the few artists and entertainers either do not belong to the sphere of cheap or mass entertainment or represent a serious attitude toward their art as in the case of Chaplin. . . . The first quarter of the century cherishes biography in terms of an open-minded liberal society which really wants to know something about its own leading figures on the decisive social, commercial, and cultural fronts. (*LPCS*, pp. 112–13)

Lowenthal claims that these earlier biographies exemplify 'opportunities open to every individual' and 'are to be looked upon as examples of success which can be imitated. These life stories are really intended to be educational models' (*LPCS*, p. 113). Sociologically, they attest to a confidence that 'the social ladder may be scaled on a mass scale' (*LPCS*, p. 114), and celebrate a self-made individualism. By the 1940s, however, the majority of magazine biographies shifted to 'idols of consumption', who belong to the sphere of leisure centered on entertainment and sports. This shift suggests that production has been displaced by consumption as the center of interest in everyday life, and that consumption involves not only purchase and use of goods and services, but appropriating mass fantasies as well. Lowenthal comments:

If a student in some very distant future should use popular magazines of 1941 as a source of information as to what figures the American public looked to in the first stages of the greatest crisis since the birth of the Union, he would come to a grotesque result. While the industrial and professional endeavors are geared to a maximum of speed and efficiency, the idols of the masses are not, as they were in the past, the leading names in the battle of production, but the headliners of the movies, the ball parks, and the night clubs. (*LPCS*, p. 116)

Lowenthal's content analysis shows that contemporary magazine biographies focused on their subjects' private lives, and devoted much space to discussing their hobbies, consumption habits and leisure activities, attesting to the increased importance of consumption and leisure in the consumer society. Lowenthal speculates that the superlatives invariably used to describe the success of the individual serve both to give the reader the illusion of being 'conversant with people who are paragons of human accomplishment' and to overwhelm the reader with a sense of his or her own insignificance:

What on first sight seems to be the rather harmless atmosphere of entertainment and consumption is, on closer examination, revealed as a reign of psychic terror, where the masses have to realize the pettiness and insignificance of their everyday life. The already weakened consciousness of being an individual is struck another heavy blow by the pseudo-individualizing forces of the superlative. Advertisement and terror, invitation to entertainment, and summons to humility form their unity in the world of superlatives. The biographer performs the functions of a side show barker for living attractions and of a preacher of human insignificance. (*LPCS*, p. 131)

Although Fromm left the Institute in 1939, he too developed critiques of the consumer society and contemporary capitalism which were quite close to the positions of Critical Theorists. While his 1940s texts, *Escape from Freedom* and *Man for Himself*,[7] tended to focus on alienation in the sphere of labor and political and social life, his 1955 text *The Sane Society* developed a thoroughgoing critique of alienated consumption and the consumer society. Although *Man for Himself* put forward a critique of what Fromm called the 'marketing personality', his analysis tended to focus on the ways in which certain character types package and market their 'personality' in order to sell themselves in the labor market, and contains almost no mention of consumption or consumerism. *The Sane Society*, by contrast, contains a detailed critique of alienated consumption as exemplified in the 'social character' of 'Man in Capitalistic Society'.[8]

Closely following analyses of the early Marx, Fromm discusses how the exchange of commodities through the medium of money separates use value from exchange value and makes it possible to purchase and consume anything as long as one can pay for it, thus linking money and consumption. By contrast, consumption should, Fromm suggests, be a 'concrete human act' which is a 'productive activity' that develops personality and fulfills human needs. Instead, he claims, consumption is in fact linked more to acting out mass-produced fantasies, gaining social prestige, compulsively and irrationally buying and consuming new models and gadgets and passively consuming the fantasies of the entertainment industries. Indeed, he suggests that consumption itself is becoming a new dominant character trait and personality type:

Having fun consists mainly in the satisfaction of consuming and 'taking in'; commodities, sights, food, drinks, cigarettes, people, lectures, books, movies – all are consumed, swallowed. The world is one great object for our appetite, a big apple, a big bottle, a big breast; we are the sucklers, the eternally expectant ones, the hopeful ones – and the eternally disappointed ones. How can we help being disappointed if our birth stops at the breast of our mother, if we are never weaned, if we remain overgrown babies, if we never go beyond the receptive orientation? (SS, p.166)

Fromm contrasts alienated consumption and what he calls receptive and marketing orientations with the 'productive orientation', which develops individual potential and fulfills human needs. Near the end of *The Sane Society*, he makes some proposals for overcoming both alienated labor and consumption:

If our aim is to change alienated into human consumption, changes are necessary in those economic processes which produced alienated consumption. It is the task of economists to devise such measures. Generally speaking, it means to direct production into fields where existing real needs have not yet been satisfied, rather than where needs must be created artificially. This can be done by means of credits through state-owned banks, by the socialization of certain enterprises, and by drastic laws which accomplish a transformation of advertising. (SS, p. 332)

In other words, Fromm is proposing that neither alienated labor nor consumption can be eliminated without significant socio-economic transformation in the direction of socialism; and he briefly sketches some of the transformations of the economy – including a universal subsistence guaranteed income – needed to eliminate alienated production and consumption (SS, pp. 270ff.).[9] He also proposes an alternative to what he sees as alienated consumption under capitalism, arguing that consumption should involve active and productive behavior, 'in which our senses, bodily needs, our aesthetic taste – that is to say, in which *we* as concrete, sensing, feeling, judging human beings – are involved. . . . In our culture, there is little of that. Consuming is essentially the satisfaction of artificially stimulated phantasies, a phantasy performance alienated from our concrete, real selves' (p. 122).

For Fromm, nonalienated consumption involves an autonomous, active use and development of human powers. Alienated consumption, by contrast, is passive and manipulated: 'We drink labels. With a bottle of Coca-Cola we drink the picture of the pretty boy and girl who drink it in the advertisement, we drink the slogan of "the pause that refreshes," we drink the great American habit; least of all do we drink with our palate' (*SS*, p. 121). To combat passive consumption, Fromm championed active, autonomous appropriation of objects and exercise of human faculties. Yet – as Adorno and Marcuse would argue – such championing of production and attacks on consumption within contemporary capitalist and patriarchal societies might reproduce capitalist 'productivist' ideologies, while defaming passive leisure and idleness, thus recapitulating Adorno's earlier critique of Veblen. And feminists might criticize Fromm for championing active, 'masculine', productivist activity, while defaming passive, 'female', domestic behavior.

Although there are differences among the Critical Theorists over the character of the consumer society, they agree that one should not criticize consumption and mass culture without also criticizing capitalism. Parallel to Horkheimer's admonition not to speak of fascism without speaking of capitalism, one could say that according to Critical Theory one should not critique the consumer society without critiquing the capitalist mode of production of which it is an expression. This linkage is consistently argued in Marcuse's 1964 text *One-Dimensional Man*.[10] Marcuse claimed that 'mass production and mass distribution claim the *entire* individual', and that the production of commodity needs is the key to social integration in contemporary society.[11] Marcuse had a powerful influence on the New Left and the 1960s counterculture, which often opposed the culture of consumption, as well as the ethos, values and behavior of the consumer society. Many in the New Left began investigating and tracing the origins and rise of the consumer society, while others carried through the critique of advertising, media, consumerism and commodity culture developed by Critical Theory.[12] These studies flesh out with historical and empirical detail the theories of the commodity, commodity fetishism and the consumer society of Lukács and Critical Theory. They provide powerful critical indictments of the commodification, standardization and human impoverishment of everyday life developed earlier by the Institute for Social Research (and in France by Henri Lefebvre, Guy Debord and the Situationists, Jean Baudrillard and others).[13]

For example, Stuart and Elizabeth Ewen argue in an article entitled 'Americanization and Consumption' that advertising, mass images and the consumer society served to initiate emigrants, rural dwellers and others into *modernity*.[14] The consumer society was thus the modernism of everyday life, which brought new images, experiences and practices into being. Henceforth money and commodities became the new sources of ultimate value, and the marketplace replaced the bonds of family, tradition, nature and community as the social cement by means of which individuals were bound to each other and their environment. By the 1920s, the Ewens argue, advertising, the culture industries and marketing were producing 'a new capitalist cosmos. It was here that industrial-bureaucratic rationality was fused with the aesthetic sphere.' The fusion of advertising and aesthetics became 'the aphrodisiac by which a submission to corporate advances could be achieved'.[15]

Yet, despite these powerful critiques and indictments of the consumer society and despite countercultural attacks on the culture of consumption, consumption has, if anything, proliferated further, and commodity fascination has continued to be a major source of social integration and stability. A large number of 1960s radicals who shared Marcusian perspectives on the consumer society have become 'yuppies', and have become integrated into consumerist life-styles, while the 'culture of narcissism' and the 'go for it' generations of the 1970s and 1980s have also become thoroughly immersed in consumer culture and its multifarious, ambivalent pleasures. In addition, demands for more consumption have become major factors within socialist societies and developing societies over the last decade.

Consequently, while Critical Theory's analysis of the consumer society provide illuminating historical and critical perspectives on the development of the consumer culture and the ways in which it has produced social integration, global denunciations of consumption have little political resonance, and provide a very weak basis for political radicalization and struggle today. Thus Critical Theory must now deepen and expand its critiques of the consumer society to demonstrate the failures and limitations of contemporary capitalism. Yet it must also develop more differentiated theories and critiques of commodities, needs and consumption. This project will concern us in the following section.

6.2   New Critical Perspectives on Commodities, Needs and Consumption

One major flaw of many neo-Marxist theories of the consumer society, evident sometimes, but not always, in Critical Theory, is a totalizing view and denunciation of the commodity, consumer needs and consumption. On this view, *all* commodities are *uniformly* seductive instruments of capitalist manipulation, which engineer homogeneous false needs and false consciousness. Hence, needs for commodities are produced by the capitalist system and implanted in the consumers, much as individuals were programmed from birth in Huxley's *Brave New World*. Commodities are thus conceptualized as alluring sirens whose symbolic qualities and values seduce the consumer into purchase and consumption. Commodity fetishism and false needs, then, supposedly enchain willing consumers into the institutions, practices and values of consumer capitalism.

There is, however, a latent Manichaeism and puritanism in this perspective. Commodities and consumption are negatively presented, simply as means of class domination, and the model also assumes a magical, diabolical power on the part of capital to create unreal false needs which it is then able to manipulate in its own interest.[16] It assumes that if individuals submit to (bad) consumption, they are weak, malleable and deficient as human beings – precisely the puritan attitude toward sex and pleasure. This perspective implies – although this is never articulated explicitly – that *all* consumption, needs and the commodities that supply them enslave the individual in the chains of capitalist-produced desire. But as Enzensberger has argued: 'The attractive power of mass consumption is based not on the dictates of false needs, but on the falsification and exploitation of quite real and legitimate ones without which the parasitic process of advertising would be quite redundant. A socialist movement ought not to denounce these needs, but take them seriously, investigate them, and make them politically productive.'[17]

Following Enzensberger's lead, I would propose that Critical Theory today needs to develop new theories of commodities, needs and consumption; and I will make some proposals for new perspectives in the following discussion. To begin, we need to break with totalizing and homogenizing theories which take a monolithic, puritanical view of consumption, and instead acknowledge that commodities can be what Marx described as 'objects of enjoyment and activity', as well as instruments of social integration and manipulation.[18] We need a more discriminating perspective which differentiates between artificial and real needs, useful and useless commodities, and nonfulfilling and life-enhancing consumption. Marcuse's distinction between 'true' and 'false' needs can be reconstructed and applied, I believe, to evaluate different types of commodities and varieties of consumption.[19] 'False needs', on this account, are those for commodities that do not fulfill 'vital needs' (to be defined below), and which produce expectations that the products cannot possibly fulfill. For instance, needs are false if they are for commodities which people do not really need or if they rest on expectations and make promises that can be demonstrated to be false. Advertisements which promise commodity solutions to problems or associate the product with the 'good life' can therefore be criticized if they make the sort of false promises projected, for example, by ads for certain shampoos or mouthwashes which promise popularity and intensified sex appeal or ads for soft drinks which promise fun, youth and community. In a similar manner, automobile ads promise power and social prestige; worthless tonics promise health and vitality; mass-produced clothes promise individuality and style; and a bevy of products of dubious worth promise solutions to a variety of problems. If it can be shown that these expectations and anticipations are, for the most part, 'false promises', then needs for products based on these expectations can be said to be 'false needs'.

It is more difficult, however, to define commodities which people really need against those which are intrinsically worthless. Marcuse characterizes 'true needs' as 'vital needs' which 'have an unqualified claim for satisfaction . . . nourishment, clothing, lodging at the attainable level of satisfaction' (*ODM*, p. 4). He insists that individual and social needs can be evaluated by objective 'standards of *priority*', which 'refer to the optimal development of the individual, of all individuals, under the optimal utilization of the material and intellectual resources available to man' (p. 6). On a social level, the goal would be maximum satisfaction of vital needs with a rational use of resources; this could be calculated as the Government calculates the needs of its budget and allocates resources accordingly. In a rational society, for instance, people could decide that 114 models of cars and 89 brands of toothpaste were unnecessary, or that certain children's games were either educational or harmless fun, whereas others were of dubious or negative worth, such as war toys or video-games that program kids for nuclear war. Other evaluations and discriminations must be made by the individual. I may genuinely need and benefit from a new word-processor, for instance, whereas nonwriters or others may find it of little use, or even confusing and oppressive.

In order to liberate one's self from the universe of prevailing false needs, one must become conscious of one's conditioning and recondition one's self so as to be able to discern one's true needs. The process of liberation aims at 'the replacement of false needs by true ones, the abandonment of repressive satisfactions'. But the 'distinguishing feature of advanced industrial society is its effective suffocation of those needs which demand liberation – liberation also from that which is tolerable and rewarding and comfortable – while it sustains and absolves the destructive power and repressive function of the affluent society' (*ODM*, p. 7). Hence liberation from false needs involves the rejection and refusal of a whole system of needs and the affirmation of other needs that contradict the established ones.

Making this distinction is logically dependent on our theory of the commodity and consumer practices. If a commodity, after critical scrutiny and use, reveals itself to be life-enhancing, truly useful, well constructed and fairly priced, then a need for it can be said to be a 'true need'. If the commodity fails to offer the satisfactions promised and is not beneficial, life-enhancing and useful, but is, on the contrary, poorly constructed, overpriced or not really useful, then a perceived need for it can be said to be a 'false need'. Note that the distinction between true and false needs proposed here rests on empirical grounds. Experience and careful critical scrutiny can determine, at least to some extent, whether needs are true or false on both an individual and a societal level. This is, I take it, one of the dominant challenges to a socialist society, which must determine what the society really needs. Therefore, I would submit that the concept of 'false needs' rather than being an idealist, metaphysical and obscure concept which is impossible to specify – as so many of Marcuse's critics and even friends have argued – is an important concept which is relevant to materialist revolutionary practice in both the critique of capitalism and the transition to socialism.

In determining the difference between true and false needs, we also need new perspectives on consumption. Critical Theory tends to sharply criticize consumption itself as the dominant means of integrating individuals into contemporary capitalism, and denounces it as a primary constituent of 'false consciousness'.[20] The global denunciations of consumption in classical Critical Theory tend to assume either implicitly (Lowenthal) or explicitly (Fromm) the superiority of production over consumption. In opposition to this position, I would propose a distinction between *consumption*, as the life-enhancing use and enjoyment of commodities, and *consumerism*, as a way of life dedicated primarily to the possession and use of consumer goods. Consumerism as a way of life falls prey completely to the 'commodity fetishism' first described in Marx's theory. Consumer addicts do 'find their soul' in the purchase, consumption and use of commodities, and are integrated into capitalist society through commodities and consumption. But does everyone engaged in consumption fall prey to false consciousness and false needs, and engage in alienating activity? Are all who participate in consumption dehumanized 'happy consumers' and 'one-dimensional' men and women?

While Critical Theorists tend to criticize consumption per se as fetishistic activity and commodities as intrinsically seductive and manipulative, more differentiated investigations of various types of consumption reveal a wide variety of uses of commodities, attitudes toward them and individualized consumer practices. Many individuals are quite inventive and creative in their consumer activities, and may well grow and develop as human beings through consumption. Individuals can use commodities for ends unforeseen by the corporate managers and captains of consciousness. Consumption can thus be a rational, life-enhancing activity that increases one's human powers and fulfills genuine human needs. Consequently, rather than denouncing commodities and consumption per se, we should try to discriminate between valuable and worthless or dubious commodities, and dehumanized, fetishized consumption as opposed to creative, life-enhancing consumption.[21]

There are also problems with the sort of valorization of production over consumption which we observed in Fromm's theory; and perhaps we should even question the fundamental dichotomy between production and consumption, which is a reified product of capitalism and not an anthropological constant, or universal distinction. That is, we should 'deconstruct' the opposition 'consumption-production' which usually covertly implies that production is a superior, distinctly human, beneficial activity, whereas consumption is supposedly debased, dehumanizing and inferior. In fact, as many neo-Marxists point out, *both* production and consumption tend to be alienated under capitalism, but the solution to this historical disaster is not to elevate one side of the dichotomy over the other. Instead we must discover how to create a social order and a way of life in which there is no radical opposition between production and consumption, and activity in both spheres is liberated from alienating features. To move beyond this historical stage, we need, I believe, new critical perspectives on the commodities, needs and consumption which contemporary Critical Theory should try to provide if it wishes to be relevant to progressive social transformation in the future, where, among other things, the rigid dichotomy between production and consumption may well be overcome.[22]

Evaluation of commodities and consumption – and everything else – is ultimately dependent on one's values and conceptions of the so-called good life. Critical Theory has never shied away from making normative judgments on capitalist society, and part of its attack on positivism and academic social science is that the pretense of value-free 'objectivity' serves the existing society by eschewing the practice of evaluation and critique. But Critical Theory has rarely – with the exception of Fromm and to some extent Adorno and Marcuse – spelled out in much detail the values, normative standards and conception of the good life by virtue of which it condemns capitalism. Moreover, Marcuse's flirtation with the 'philosopher king' argument (see, for example, *ODM*, pp. 39–40) has created the suspicion that Critical Theory wants its own theorists to make normative decisions and legislate the good society and the good life, thus eliciting critiques of its supposed elitism and utopianism.

Reacting against this tendency in Critical Theory, Habermas has been proposing sustained public discussion of needs, values and public policy.[23] His argument that we must revitalize the public sphere and engage in debate about crucial social, political and ethical issues is relevant to the topic at hand. Following Habermas, Critical Theory can help to promote public debate on needs, commodities and consumer practices so as to aim for democratic consensus on these issues. Such debate could be connected with discourse on values and the good life, and could help raise public consciousness on consumption and consumer politics both in advanced capitalism and in 'actually existing socialist' societies.

Part of this debate would involve what aspects of the consumer society are basically worthless and harmful and what social transformations would be necessary to eliminate, for example, the harmful impact on human health and the environment of certain commodities and types of production. Various health groups and movements have raised awareness of the harmful impact on the human body of a variety of chemicals and substances in food and of the dangers of eating junk food or other non-nutritious foods. Organized labor is becoming increasingly aware of the dangers to workers of producing various chemicals and substances whose production, or use in production, causes industrial diseases. Environmentalists have been pointing out that certain synthetic industrial substances are nonbiodegradable or are dangerous pollutants.[24] The near epidemic of cancer and other industrial and environmentally related diseases has made it mandatory to become aware of the impact of certain commodities on health and environment (one out of four people in the United States today gets cancer, and one out of five dies of it). Governments sometimes try to regulate the worst excesses of capitalist production, and frequently document a variety of abuses of different types of commodity production and products. Building on such empirical critiques of the production and consumption of specific commodities, Critical Theory could then focus its critique of the consumer society on those types of production and consumption which pollute and deplete the environment and waste resources, are potentially dangerous to human health and are obviously useless or harmful.

A rational society would, on this view, regulate production and consumption to curtail production that has harmful effects on health and environment, and would ascribe a much more important role to consumer politics. Critical Theory should thus be more aware of the importance of environmental and consumer politics, and should make clear how the capitalist mode of production as such is responsible for a variety of these threats to human well-being and the environment.[25] Thus radicals should not, as they have often tended to do in the past, see these health and environmental issues as superfluous to the struggle for socialism or irrelevant to the task of party building. Critical Theory can contribute to these struggles by showing how certain commodities and consumer activities are harmful to health and environment and should be regulated or eliminated, rather than by simply globally denouncing all consumption and commodities as alienating per se (see Chapter 8 for more systematic proposals for the repoliticization of Critical Theory along these and other lines).

On the other hand, initiatives of consumer, environment and health movements may be absorbed and used by the capitalist state or the consumer industries themselves. These movements might rationalize and strengthen the capitalist system by forcing correction of its worst abuses. They might also further technocracy and instrumental domination by making people dependent on 'experts' who define their consumer or health needs. Building on Foucault's work, Zygmunt Bauman, for instance, argues that consumer movements, jogging, health foods and injunctions toward rational consumption produce more disciplined workers and consumers, and thus could serve the interests of capital. Moreover, excessive emphasis on consumption and health may increase narcissism and individualism, driving individuals to be more absorbed in their own bodies and consumer practices.[26]

Nonetheless, with these problems in sight, risks must be taken, and the Left should try to take more seriously consumer, health, environmental and other new social movements. In particular, after the era of conservative hegemony in many capitalist countries during the 1980s, consumer, environmental and health movements provide a useful corrective to the trends toward deregulation and de-emphasis of these issues during the last decade. Critical Theory can contribute discriminating perspectives on the commodity and consumption, as well as insights into how the production of needs and consumer practices provides crucial mechanisms through which the consumer society reproduces itself. Indeed, in addition to criticism of certain commodities, corporations, needs and consumer practices, Critical Theory can move from partial critiques of aspects of the consumer society to critiques of the consumer society and contemporary capitalism as a whole. For the very notion of a society organized around production and consumption of commodities is highly peculiar and problematical, as is the assumption that the marketplace alone should dictate what is to be produced and consumed. The capitalist mode of production and organization of society should be perceived as the main cause of the irrational allocation of resources and goods and the waste and production of needs which have been a historical disaster, resulting in overproduction, injustice, inequalities and a system which rests on false priorities (profits over people, exchange value over use value and so forth).

From this perspective, one could argue that the rise of the consumer society has meant the homogenization and standardization of life and consumption in the United States, and has contributed to the incredible power enjoyed by corporations, which have come to control all facets of economic, political and even cultural life. In his history of life in the United States after World War II, Jezer points out, for instance, that as recently as the 1950s there were about 450 breweries selling their own local brands of beer, and that there were hundreds of brands of soft-drinks, locally produced by small businesses. But with the development of corporate capitalism, these smaller companies were driven out of business, and by 1970 the number of breweries was down to 70, with the 10 largest controlling 70 per cent of the market.[27]

Thus, more detailed study of the commodity world and consumption could concretize the thesis developed by Critical Theory in the 1940s concerning the trends toward standardization and massification of life in contemporary capitalist societies. Indeed, corporate control of the economy has made the United States look the same all over: drive down Anystreet, USA, and you will see generic America in the form of filling stations selling the same brands of gas, fast-food chains selling the same junk food, video stores renting the same (quite small) selection of films and chain stores selling the same goods everywhere. Consequently, the trends toward monopolization and conglomerization of the economy have led to standardization, homogenization and central control of both production and consumption – standard accusations against socialism! As a result of the triumph of corporate capitalism, there are thus fewer products that originate locally, less crafts and artisan production, and thus less variety and diversity of goods accessible to most individuals.

One can likewise move from critiques of specific advertising and consumer practices to global critiques of advertising, on the grounds that the industry is parasitical, duplicitous and serves no real social needs or purposes. Advertising is a tremendous social drain which a rational society would either eliminate or radically restructure from an instrument of manipulation predicated on waste to an instrument of socially necessary and beneficial information. Indeed, while 6.5 billion dollars were squandered on advertising in the United States in 1950, the figure was 40 billion dollars by 1970 and 56 billion dollars by 1980 – far more money cumulatively than was spent on schooling![28] Advertising is a waste of resources, talent and time, and a rational society would limit advertising to providing consumer information.

Critical Theory might also learn how to perceive the ways in which consumption itself is a source of conflict and contestation that affects the vicissitudes of capitalism and the trajectories of the economy. Classical Critical Theories of the consumer society tend to conceive of the production and consumption of commodities as the social cement that integrates individuals into the consumer society, and often fail to see that constantly increasing production of commodities and the drive toward ever increasing consumption may be either functional or dysfunctional for capital as a whole or for various sectors of capital. Part of the problem of the current crisis of American capitalism lies in the difficulties that capital has experienced over the past decades with workers' demands for higher wages, declining productivity and overproduction. For instance, workers' struggles for higher wages have cut into capitalist profitability, and have led multinational corporations to export production to Third World countries which have lower wage scales and less regulation; this process in turn has contributed to unemployment which means, among other things, less money in circulation for consumption. Consequently in almost every sector of American industry, overproduction has caused large stockpiles of commodities that forced industry either to cut back production and lay off workers or to go out of business.

In addition, as Marcuse argued, the consumer society produces needs for consumption, happiness, individuality and a good life that it may not be able to satisfy, and thus risks producing dissatisfaction and potential social opposition which might become explosive during an era of scarcity and growing structural unemployment.[29] An approach to the history of the consumer society that simply sees it as a successful attempt by capital to integrate the working class thus fails to see contradictions in the process of capital reproduction. Advertising and the production of consumer needs are certainly functional for capitalism, but, if the system cannot deliver the goods, they may be dysfunctional as well. Similarly, we should see the expansion of the sphere of consumption as both a result of working-class struggle and a project of corporate capitalism to increase its power and profitability. Likewise, we must attempt to see the contradictions generated within the sphere of consumption by commodity struggle in the market-place of consumer allegiance, and begin devising strategies and tactics of subversion in consumer practices.[30]

Critical Theory should therefore begin conceptualizing consumption and the use of commodities as a *contested terrain*: people may resist capital's entreaties for increased consumption or demand higher wages to make this possible, which capital may not want to, or be able to, grant. Commodities and businesses compete for consumer allegiance, and consumers frequently reject and negate products or models. Investments in new sectors of industry, such as electronics or computers, may destabilize older industrial sectors (see Chapter 7 for details). Closing down American plants in order to produce cheaper products in Third World countries may reduce consumer demand through the resulting unemployment, and may elicit new political demands to control corporate investment and movement. Contradictions between countries struggling for world trade may destabilize particular capitalist societies and even the world system as a whole. Critical Theory needs to investigate the ramifications of these contradictions and conflicts between different sectors of capital and to abandon the monolithic model of 'one-dimensional society' which fails to grasp the vulnerabilities of advanced capitalism. It needs to see how these crises and conflicts are played out in the media and to conceptualize the media and consumption as providing both stabilizing and destabilizing functions for contemporary capitalism that provide both obstacles to, and possibilities for, social change.

Thus, while Critical Theory has provided powerful global critiques of the consumer society, it has not, I believe, provided useful perspectives on the commodity and consumption which will help in the vast process of social reconstruction that is the task of the present age. The need to repoliticize Critical Theory will be discussed in Chapter 8. To conclude this chapter, I want to move on to discussions of what is seen by some theorists as the current stage of the consumer society and an outgrowth of a society in which image, culture, consumption and spectacle become organizing principles of life – postmodernism.

6.3   Critical Theory, Modernity and Postmodernity

By the 1980s, a debate over 'postmodernism' emerged in Western intellectual circles which eventually engaged the attention of the second and
third generation of Critical Theorists. Discussions of postmodernism first
appeared in the arts, and concerned whether contemporary architecture,
literature and other cultural forms decisively went beyond the forms and
practices of modernism and thus constituted a new type of 'postmodernist
art'.[31] The debate emerged next in philosophy, with a series of attacks by
Derrida, Rorty and others on the tradition of modern philosophy and calls
for breaks with this tradition.[32] The discussions over postmodernism then
migrated into social theory, where French writers like Lyotard and Baudrillard proclaimed that we had entered the 'postmodern condition', and
Jameson presented postmodernism as the 'cultural logic of late capitalism',
followed by Kroker's and Cook's description of *The Postmodern Scene*.[32]

These latter theories of postmodernity proclaimed the emergence of a
new historical epoch which constituted a new type of culture, and in some
cases new forms of society, experience and history, that required new
theories, methods and politics. Whereas the first generation of Critical
Theorists – Horkheimer, Marcuse, Adorno and the rest – had attempted to
update and revise the Marxian theory to incorporate the new social conditions, the response of Habermas and his followers to the discourse of postmodernity was defensive and hostile. Habermas, in an article on 'Das
Moderne – ein unvollendes Projekt', translated in *New German Critique* as
'Modernity versus Postmodernity', argued that the various theories of postmodernity were a form of attack on modernity which had their ideological
precursors in various irrationalist and counter-enlightenment theories and
their contemporary equivalents in conservative attacks on modernity.[34] In a
series of 'Lectures on the Philosophical Discourse of Modernity', Habermas
continued to attack the (primarily French) theories of postmodernity.[35] He
used standard methods of ideology critique, and suggested that the theories
of postmodernity which had their roots in Nietzsche and Heidegger were
aligned with the counter-Enlightenment and irrationalism, while exhibiting
a disturbing kinship with fascism. Against theories of postmodernity,
Habermas defended 'the project of modernity' which he believed was 'an
unfinished project' containing unfulfilled emancipatory potential.[36]

Habermas begins 'Modernity versus Postmodernity' by indicating that,
until recently, 'the modern' signified 'the new', thereby designating the
present epoch as distinct from the past, from 'antiquity' and then 'tradition'.
During the Enlightenment, the 'modern' came to take on significations of
development and innovation within science, technology and industry,
while the 'aesthetic modernity' of the nineteenth century equated the

modern with both innovations in art and aesthetic novelty. Aesthetic modernity took to an extreme rebellion against tradition, and valorized highly charged aesthetic experiences of novelty, dynamism, singularity and intense presence.

Habermas cites some sources which claim that this aesthetic modernity is dead, and then raises the question of whether this decline in the sphere of culture signals 'a farewell to modernity' and the 'transition to a broader phenomenon called postmodernity' (p. 6). To address these issues, he makes a distinction between aesthetic modernity and societal modernization, which he interprets in the Enlightenment (and Weberian) sense of a process of cultural differentiation. In particular, Habermas defends the differentiation of cultural spheres and the development of autonomous criteria of rationality and universality in the fields of knowledge, morality, law and justice, and art (p. 8). He refers to this as the 'project of modernity', which he interprets

as the efforts to develop objective science, universal morality and law, and autonomous art, according to their inner logic. At the same time, this project intended to release the cognitive potentials of each of these domains to set them free from their esoteric forms. The Enlightenment philosophers wanted to utilize this accumulation of specialized culture for the enrichment of everyday life, that is to say, for the rational organization of everyday social life. (p. 9)

While the project of modernity resulted in part in the colonization of the life-world by the logic of scientific-technological rationality and domination by a culture of experts and specialists, it also for Habermas has 'unrealized potential' to increase social rationality, justice and morality. He defends the project of modernity by citing what he considers some failed aesthetic revolts – that is, surrealism – and then defends a type of modern art which he believes could illuminate conditions in the life-world while providing progressive cognitive and moral effects – his example here is Peter Weiss (pp. 10–12).

From the standpoint of this qualified defense of modernity, Habermas then criticizes what he considers to be 'false programs of the negation of culture', or overly negative attacks on modernity, which fail to recognize its positive contributions and potential. Here he distinguishes – not very successfully – between the antimodernism of the 'young conservatives', the premodernism of the 'old conservatives' and the postmodernism of the 'neoconservatives'. He categorizes Bataille, Foucault and Derrida as critics of modernity who capitulate to the experience of aesthetic modernity and reject the modern world as 'young conservatives' – a procedure that has elicited spirited controversy.[37] Habermas concludes by expressing a fear that 'ideas of anti-modernity, together with an additional touch of premodernity, are becoming popular in the circles of alternative culture', and advances his own defense of modernity in opposition to these tendencies (p. 14) – a position that became central to his *Lectures on the Philosophical Discourse of Modernity* (1987).

Critical Theory versus Postmodern Culture

In his *Lectures* Habermas defends species of contemporary art as containing emancipatory potential; yet he breaks decisively with Adorno's conception of the autonomy of art by linking art with communicative rationality, morality and the project of emancipation. Habermas therefore rejects Adorno's normative valuation of authentic art as negation and his defense of modernist art forms that resist communication and assimilation to conventional discourse (see 5.1). Habermas did not discuss the forms and nature of postmodern art and culture currently being debated, however, and did not intervene in the debates over their alleged flaws or progressive features – with the exception of discussion of postmodernist architecture.[38] However, his colleague Albrecht Wellmer and several North American members of the third generation of Critical Theorists did intervene; and their contributions range from Wellmer's defense of the communicative potential of contemporary art to the attacks on postmodern culture of some American followers of Adorno who tend to dismiss postmodern culture as kitsch, ideology, trash and worse, while carrying out aggressive, often uninformed broadside polemics against French post-structuralism, which they see as complicit with postmodernism, or simply (and wrongly) identify with it.

In response to some recent critiques of Adorno, Wellmer, like Habermas, reconstructs Adorno's aesthetic theory in the direction of an open, non-dogmatic theory of autonomous art which stresses its 'communicative potential'.[39] For Wellmer: 'If one expands communicatively Adorno's concept of rationality, then his truth aesthetics may also be expanded "pragmatically." The inclusion of aesthetically experiencing, communicating, and acting subjects into the categorical schema of art, reality, and utopia produces an effect of "multidimensionality" as against Adorno's dialectical one-dimensional constructs' (p. 110). In other words, just as Habermas attempts to expand the concept of rationality through a theory of 'communicative rationality', so too one could expand the concept of authentic art to include art that links aesthetic experience with moral education and politics, and which thus produces a wealth of potential effects. Wellmer thinks that this schema – which makes certain concessions to postmodern demands for openness, plurality and the play of differences – produces openings for new theories and practices, though he does not provide any specific examples or analyses or criticize forms of postmodern culture.

In a pair of articles in the same special issue of *Telos* dedicated to 'Debates

in Contemporary Culture', Russell Berman and Richard Wolin reproduce
Adorno's and Horkheimer's denunciation of the culture industry, and
defend the distinction between high and low culture in which all emancipatory potential is assigned to the sphere of high culture.[40] Both authors
rigidly defend 'autonomous art' against allegedly 'heteronomous' art,
which is contaminated by commodification and ideology. They thus intervene in the postmodern debate to replay the old Frankfurt School attack on
the culture industry and to reassert the ideal of the 'autonomy of art'.

Both express almost hysterical fear concerning 'the end of the individual'
and barbaric cultural and societal regression (see Wolin, pp. 27ff., and
Berman, pp. 31ff.). Wolin fears that 'impending barbarism' and 'whole-
sale regression' are producing an 'eclipse of subjectivity' in a 'diabolical
turn of events' which can be contested, if at all, only by autonomous art
and a rebirth of subjectivity from the spirit of (Adorno's) Critical Theory.
Yet, while Wolin distinguishes between various forms of modernist art,
which he contrasts with postmodern culture, Berman, in a tirade against
the alleged regressive and irrational features which pervade contemporary
culture, attacks key moments of both modernist *and* postmodernist culture
as engaging in 'barbaric' (his favorite term) 'desublimation.' Berman links
a crisis in aesthetic modernity with political and moral crises, and goes so
far as to suggest that the decline of autonomous art contributed to social
catastrophes like World War I (pp. 31ff.), fascism (pp. 38ff.), a new
'recrudescent nationalism' (pp. 33, 51), the Grenada invasion (p. 53) and
'the "menace" that now hangs over the head of more than just Europe'
(p. 33).

In portentously overheated prose, Berman attacks a panorama of forms
of contemporary culture, as either blatantly advancing social domination or
unleashing destructive erotic and aggressive instincts. Neo-expressionism
'regularly limits itself to a nebulously emotional rage' (p. 42), while postmodern art manifests 'a breathtaking commercialization' (ibid.). Muzak
'tends to obliterate communication and to break down individual resistance, constructing instead the beautiful illusion of a collective, singing
along in dictatorial unanimity' (p. 45). Body building, health cults, jogging
and so on manifest an 'expectation of catastrophe, a fixation on death'
(p. 47), while ubiquitous commodification and the aestheticization of
everyday life incorporate all potential emancipatory impulses into the world
of commodification and social integration.

Berman's polemics emote unrelenting hostility to all forms of contemporary culture, resurrecting with a vengeance the method of cultural
denunciation wielded at times, but not always, by Adorno.[41] He resuscitates
Adorno's notion of the 'negative totality' – 'the whole is untrue' – to attack
a panoply of forms of contemporary culture as 'desublimated aggression'.
Such conceptualization, however, yields a monolithic totality which

assimilates all cultural and social forms in a negative essence, and thus fails to discriminate between opposing and different currents of contemporary society and culture. Against efforts to develop new theories and perspectives to conceptualize contemporary culture, Berman attempts to reassert an outmoded (by the 1960s and subsequent theoretical development) Frankfurt orthodoxy in the face of postmodern, or neo-Marxian, feminist and other projects to rethink, reconceptualize and hopefully reconfigure contemporary culture and society. Even Adorno, by contrast, is concerned to redeem and portray emancipatory features, à la Walter Benjamin, of some of the most debased and ideological forms of contemporary culture. By contrast, contemporary neo-Adornoians negate everything, forgetting immanent critique, redemptive criticism or dialectical negation.

Another problem with contemporary North American neo-Adornoism is that not only does it tend to reject almost everything on the contemporary cultural scene, but it has serious trouble in specifying any examples of contemporary 'autonomous art' which could be counterposed to postmodern culture industry material. Berman merely posits, without any examples, an empty call for the 'reauraticization of art'; and, when pressed, neo-Adornoians usually recite the names of Adorno's models Schönberg, Kafka and Beckett as paradigms of autonomous art.[42] Moreover, they seem to restrict the production of the "aesthetic experience" which they valorize to these modern masters and deny the traits of "authentic art" to anything else.

Critical Theory versus Postmodern Philosophy and Social Theory

Most of the Critical Theory focus in the postmodern debate has concerned the attacks on reason, enlightenment, universality and other concepts which have traditionally been used by New French Theorists such as Foucault, Derrida and Lyotard.[43] The discussion has for the most part focused on postmodern theory, or forms of knowledge, and its allegedly irrationalist proclivities. With the exception of Habermas, who takes on a broad panorama of postmodern theory, the Critical Theory response has focused on critiques of Lyotard's *The Postmodern Condition*, and on defenses of reason, universality and normativity against the postmodern attack.

In one of the most comprehensive discussions of the postmodernism debate to emerge from the Critical Theory camp, Wellmer provides an overview of some of the issues in the current debates:

The concept of postmodernism has become one of the most elusive concepts in aesthetic, literary and sociological discussion of the last decade. The word 'postmodernism' belongs to a network of 'post' concepts and thinking – 'post-industrial society,' 'post-structuralism,' 'post-empiricism,' 'post-rationalism' – in which, so it seems, the consciousness of an epochal threshold seeks to articulate itself, the contours of which are still unclear, confused and ambivalent, but whose central experience – that of the death of reason – appears to announce the end of an historical project: the project of modernity, the project of the European Enlightenment, or finally also the project of Greek and Western civilisation. (p. 337)

Wellmer claims that the postmodern critique of reason, enlightenment, universality and so on 'has found its most pregnant expression yet in Lyotard's philosophy' (p. 341). He characterizes this position as a synthesis of 'a post-empiricist epistemology (Feyerabend), a modernist aesthetic (Adorno) and a post-utopian political liberalism' (p. 340). Lyotard wishes to break with all the 'grand narratives' – for example, 'the emancipation of mankind or the becoming of the idea' – which have legitimated various previous theories and politics, as well as foundationalism, which privileges a specific mode of knowledge or discourse. Against the privileged 'language games' of philosophy or science, he calls for an 'irreducible plurality' of language games, each with its local rules, legitimations and practices. This also leads him to reject consensual theories of knowledge or justice, for which Habermas is famous.

Rather than systematically polemicizing against Lyotard's position,[44] Wellmer concentrates on showing how the earlier positions of Adorno and Horkheimer – especially in *Dialectic of Enlightenment* – anticipate postmodern critiques of the subject, representation, reason and so on (pp. 346ff.). He claims that both the earlier Critical Theory and contemporary postmodern critiques of the subject and its reason, and instrumental reason and societal rationalization, have their roots in Freud's theory of the unconscious and Nietzsche's theory of the will to power. He indicates that the New French Theory critique of how discourses produce subject effects is a novel addition to the earlier Critical Theory analyses, but claims that it is precisely reflection on the constitutive roles of language and communication which open the way to conceive of subjectivity and social relations in more productive modes. Rather than seeing subjectivity as a self-enclosed, completely manipulated atomistic monad – which is solely a product of language – Wellmer recommends that the subject of language can be conceived as an active agent of communication, self-reflexion, and self- and mutual understanding, thus opposing Habermas's program of communicative rationality to New French Theory's attacks on reason.

Wellmer concludes with some reflections on the 'death of modernity' proclaimed by the extreme postmodernists and celebrated by them as a positive development (pp. 355ff.). He proposes some Critical Theory perspectives on aesthetics, theory and politics which would transcend the limitations of the tradition of modernity while preserving its progressive features. He concludes: 'What is at stake here is not a "reconciliation of the language games" in Adorno's sense but the mutual "openness" of the discourses to each other: the "sublation" of the *one* reason in the interplay of plural rationalities' (p. 360).

Wellmer thus seems to be one of the few Critical Theorists to tentatively provide an opening to a dialogue with postmodernism and New French Theory. Most Critical Theorists, by contrast, have simply dismissed New French Theory while reasserting previous or present positions within Critical Theory. Some of their critiques of the discourses of postmodernity assume a guilt by association (with Nietzsche, Heidegger and fascism). Further, their defenses of modernity, the Enlightenment and the universalist heritage of philosophy and reason often fail to answer the strongest critiques of these discourses by Foucault, Derrida, Lyotard, Baudrillard and others. In addition, Adornoesque use of ideology critique as negation fails to redeem in a Benjaminian redemptive hermeneutic those positive contributions found in New French Theory which Critical Theory might make use of.[45]

Indeed, Critical Theory has previously distinguished itself by being at the cutting edge of radical social theory, by conceptualizing new social conditions, practices and experiences, and by rethinking radical social theory and politics in the light of these new socio-historical conditions. Critical Theory always presented itself as a dialectical and historical social theory which attempts to capture and conceptualize historical changes in terms of theories and concepts and to appraise the impact of such changes for the socialist project and the possibilities of human emancipation.

If it is the case that new socio-historical conditions, forms and experiences have emerged, then Critical Theory today should obviously analyze, critique and conceptualize these phenomena, and should develop and rethink radical social theory and politics in the light of these changes. Most Critical Theorists have not really confronted these challenges, however, and have either attacked postmodernist culture *en masse* from traditional Critical Theory positions (mostly Adorno's) or, like Habermas, have presented ideology critiques of the theories of postmodernism while defending modernity. This is unfortunate, for Critical Theory provides the framework, methodology and positions which could be used to develop a theory of the new social conditions which postmodern social theory points to, but does not, arguably, adequately theorize.

Complete dismissal of New French Theory by Critical Theory covers over important similarities and lines of contact. Both Critical Theory and New French Theory agree, by and large, in their critiques of the boundaries of the academic division of labor, of traditional philosophy and of ideology, though Critical Theory generally wants to draw and defend some boundaries, some categorical distinctions, which most postmodernists reject. For instance, Baudrillard rejects out of hand many categories of radical social theory that Critical Theorists would want to hold onto – class, dialectics, alienation/disalienation, domination/emancipation and so forth – while Lyotard rejects all totalizing theories of history and society.[46] Yet both traditions have been engaged in debates concerning the mapping of historical stages, though some French postmodernists claim that we are in a new stage of *post-histoire* in which it no longer makes any sense to engage in historical periodization, while many Critical Theorists deny that any major historical changes have taken place which would justify the label 'postmodernism' or the other 'post' concepts currently in circulation.[47]

Thus the tradition of Critical Theory has yet to develop a theory of postmodernism beyond its denunciations of postmodern theory and culture. Yet, from a position similar in many ways to the Hegelian-Marxian and Lukácsian perspectives that defined the first generation of Critical Theory, Jameson has argued that there is a fundamental rupture in social development, and thus something like a new historical stage of which postmodernism is the cultural expression. Jameson believes that postmodernism can be theorized most adequately within the framework of a neo-Marxian social theory, and in his article 'Postmodernism – or the Cultural Logic of Late Capitalism', he attempts to provide an account of its features, contours, genesis and possibilities.[48] In a panoramic sweep, he presents postmodernism as the 'cultural logic of late capitalism', which constitutes a new 'cultural dominant' within a new socio-economic stage of capitalism; his studies expand the discussion concerning postmodernism to include a wide range of cultural, social, economic and political phenomena.

For Jameson – as for Ernest Mandel in *Late Capitalism* (1975) upon which he draws – contemporary capitalism is an even purer, more developed, more realized form of capitalism than those earlier stages described by Marx's critique of market capitalism and Lenin's theory of imperialism.[49] On this account, contemporary capitalism has colonized and penetrated ever more domains of life, and commodification and capitalist exchange relations have penetrated the spheres of information, knowledge, computerization, and consciousness and experience itself to an unparalleled extent. Jameson thus proposes interpreting postmodernism as the cultural logic of a new type of capitalist society, and thus, in effect, carries out the earlier Critical Theory program of developing the categories of critical social theory in response to important transformations within society.

In another article related to his work on postmodernism, 'Cognitive Mapping', Jameson spells out more of what is included in a postmodern aesthetic of cognitive mapping.[50] The term derives from Brecht scholar Darko Suvin's emphasis on the cognitive function of art and aesthetics, Kevin Lynch's attempt to discover how people map images of the city and Althusser's theory of ideology as 'the Imaginary representation of the subject's relationship to his or her Real conditions of existence'. Just as Jameson argued in *The Political Unconscious* (1981) that narrative was a fundamental function of human being, he now seems to argue that individuals need some sort of image or map of their society and the world as a whole.[51] 'Cognitive mapping' thus involves the task of individuals, artists and theorists in providing orientation, a sense of place and a theoretical model of how society is structured. Jameson claims that this sort of mapping is of crucial importance for both social theory and politics, for 'the incapacity to map socially is as crippling to political experience as the analogous incapacity to map spatially is for urban experience. It follows that an aesthetic of cognitive mapping in this sense is an integral part of any socialist political project.'[52]

Jameson is thus attempting to answer the post-structuralist/postmodernist critique of representation by stressing that we need representations of our society, however imperfect, to get about in the world. As a theoretical model, Jameson's own sketches can be taken as cognitive maps of postmodern space; and from this perspective he poses the challenge to social theory to provide similar cognitive mapping of the transformations and developments within contemporary society. Indeed, in a Hegelian-Marxian fashion, Jameson is in effect providing a defense of the concepts of representation and totality against postmodern and post-structuralist attacks, and is offering his own totalizing theory of the present age – precisely the traditional function and important contribution of Hegelian Marxism. Jameson points to the debilitating effects of living in the fragments and just gaming with the remnants, and argues that new cognitive mapping is needed to contextualize and critique our present social environment.

Jameson's project therefore parallels the 1930s project of Critical Theory which attempted to develop a supradisciplinary theory of the new stage of capitalism which it saw emerging (see Chapters 2 and 3). His studies replicate Critical Theory's Hegelian-Marxian and Lukácsian attempt to provide a theory of contemporary capitalism, which Jameson contrasts with earlier forms of culture, society and experience in capitalist societies. Let us, then, in dialogue with the present generation of Critical Theorists, undertake an exercise in cognitive mapping which will address the debate on postmodernism and contribute to the discussion of where we are now and where we are heading. In the next chapter, I shall provide a framework, congruent with the tradition of Critical Theory, for interpreting the new social conditions and phenomena focused on by the postmodernists (and the theorists of the 'post-industrial society'). The concluding chapter will discuss some possible political responses to our current problems and crises.

7

Techno-Capitalism

The postmodernism debate poses in dramatic fashion the issue of historical borderlines from one historical epoch to another. Although Critical Theory has traditionally attempted to conceptualize new historical conditions in theories which go beyond old orthodoxies, so far most Critical Theorists have been reluctant to postulate anything like a new type of postmodern or post-capitalist society, or a new stage of capitalist society beyond the stage of monopoly/state capitalism whose defining traits they delineated in their works from the 1930s through the 1960s. To be sure, Habermas raised the question concerning a 'postmodern' society as early as 1973 in *Legitimation Crisis*, but never systematically pursued the issue.[1] Yet he has frequently argued that contemporary capitalist societies produce *new* types of conflicts, crises and pathologies, and in a discussion of 'new social movements' he contrasts the 'new politics' with the 'old politics' (see 7.3 and 8.2 below). Furthermore, Habermas's colleague Claus Offe has attempted to provide new theories of the capitalist state and the changing relations between state and economy in the contemporary era, and to analyze the contradictions and crises of 'disorganized capitalism' (see 7.2 and 7.3). With the exception of some of Habermas's and Offe's works, however, there have been no comprehensive attempts within post-1960s Critical Theory to characterize the contemporary era in terms that systematically elaborate the changes and developments within capitalist society which go beyond the configurations of capitalist society theorized by the first generation of Critical Theorists.

At stake is whether we are currently in a new phase of capitalism beyond the configurations of 'organized', or 'monopoly/state', capitalism described by earlier Critical Theory, as well as whether there are sufficiently decisive social changes and novelties to warrant theories of epochal boundaries between allegedly previous and current epochs of social development – that is, whether we are in a post-capitalist or postmodern era. On this latter point, I want to distinguish my position from certain theories of 'the post-industrial society', or of postmodernity, which either deny or occlude continuities between earlier and later socio-historical epochs by suppressing the fact that in the United States, Western Europe and parts of the so-called Third World we are still living in a predominantly capitalist society. Whereas theorists of postmodernity, or the post-industrial society, often argue that the key features of capitalism are no longer the central principles of social organization, I would argue that capitalist relations of production and the imperative to maximize capital accumulation continue to be central constitutive forces. For, despite changes that have taken place in the economy, in the relations between the economy and the state, in class structure, culture and so on, commodity production and wage labor for capital still exist as fundamental organizing principles, as does the control of the economic surplus by a corporate elite, the exploitation and alienation of labor, production for profit rather than use, and capitalist market, exchange relations.

Consequently, contemporary societies in the West continue to be organized around commodity production and capital accumulation, and capitalist imperatives continue to dominate production, distribution and consumption, as well as other cultural, social and political domains.[2] Workers continue to be dominated and exploited, and the entire social system continues to exist and reproduce itself as a capitalist society. Consequently – and against certain postmodernist, post-industrial and post-capitalist social theories – I believe that the concepts utilized by the earlier generation of Critical Theorists (commodification, production, exchange, reification, alienation, capital, class and so on) continue to be of central importance for radical social theory today, and shall consequently develop a sketch of a theory of *techno-capitalism* as an alternative to all post-capitalist social theories.

Yet, while I shall resist the claims that there is a completely new stage of postmodern or post-industrial society which has transcended capitalism, I shall acknowledge that there have been fundamental, dramatic changes in contemporary capitalism which require significant development of Critical Theory if it wishes to continue to be relevant to contemporary socio-historical conditions. In the following discussions I shall take up these issues by analyzing relations between the capitalist economy and technology (7.1), between the economy and the state (7.2), and between current forms of crisis and political struggle and conflict in contemporary capitalist societies (7.3 and Chapter 8). At stake is whether the methods, theories and concepts developed by Critical Theory and other neo-Marxian traditions still provide adequate tools and perspectives on contemporary social developments, and to what extent previous aspects of Critical Theory need to be revised in the light of contemporary developments.

7.1   Technology, Capitalism and Domination

The debates over postmodernity and the post-industrial society pose a serious challenge to Critical Theory today *as a social theory*, and I will argue in this and the concluding chapter that Critical Theory should begin developing a comprehensive theory of the present age to account for the new social conditions, tendencies and possibilities for social transformation beyond capitalism, in order to return Critical Theory to the cutting edge of radical social theory and politics. I believe that such a project is possible in terms of a theory of what I call 'techno-capitalism'. The term points to a configuration of capitalist society in which technical and scientific knowledge, automation, computers and advanced technology play a role in the process of production parallel to the role of human labor power, mechanization and machines in earlier eras of capitalism, while producing as well new modes of societal organization and forms of culture and everyday life.

During the 1950s, theorists from various traditions and standpoints began discussing a 'second industrial revolution' characterized by new types of production, new energy sources and new technologies.[3] Whereas the first industrial revolution was characterized by manufacture in which machines replaced hands, and in which mechanization replaced manual labor, in the second industrial revolution machines and new technologies replaced brains and played a major role in the restructuring of the labor process and other domains of social life. On Ernest Mandel's account, the capitalist mode of production described by Marx consisted primarily in 'machine-industrial production of commodities by means of hand-made machines', while the later configuration of capitalist production consisted in machines producing machines, as well as consumer goods, which increasingly led to the industrialization and automation of almost all capitalist production.[4] The first stage of this revolutionizing of production took place, in Mandel's view, from 1857 to 1873 through 'the progressive introduction of machine-made steam-driven machines . . . combined with the growing generalization of railway construction' (p. 187). The rising amount of capital needed to invest in new machine-directed production of the means of production led to increasing concentration of capital in big businesses and aided the 'transition from freely competitive to monopoly capitalism' (p. 188). A technological revolution through the introduction of electric motors (1873–93) was followed by a long period of 'broken accumulation and relative economic stagnation' until a new revolutionizing of production through automation fueled what Mandel calls a ' "long wave with an undertone of expansion," from 1940 (1945) to 1965' (pp. 189–90).

In this new configuration of capitalism, which we can now see as the early phase of techno-capitalism, technology, automation and information came to play increasingly important roles in the production process, and helped produce a wide range of new social and economic effects. What I am calling 'techno-capitalism' is thus characterized by a new synthesis of technology and capitalist social relations and by production of new techno-commodities and techno-culture. In terms of Marx's categories in *Capital*, this development can be interpreted in terms of a shift in the relative quantities and importance of what he called 'constant' and 'variable' capital in the production process, or a shift from 'labor-intensive' to 'capital-intensive' production. 'Constant capital' for Marx referred to all the inputs into the production process independent of labor, which included raw materials, machines and technologies; 'variable capital' referred to human labor power invested in the productive process which alone, for Marx, was the source of the capitalist's surplus value.

From this perspective, techno-capitalism thus describes a form of social organization in which what Marx calls the 'organic composition of capital' shifts toward a preponderance of constant over variable capital, as machines and technologies progressively and often dramatically replace human labor power in the production process. Under industrial capitalism, Marx postulated tendencies toward homogenization of variable capital or human labor power, as industrialization, standardization and the fragmentation of the productive process imposed similar types of work tasks and/or de-skilled labor so that literally any worker could fulfill any task within the production process. During this stage of capitalism, human labor power thus played the fundamental role within the production process, both in terms of the production of value and the extraction of surplus value.

Under techno-capitalism, however, constant capital progressively comes to replace variable capital, as the ratio between technology and labor increases at the expense of the input of human labor power. In other words, under techno-capitalism, as machines, automation of production, new technologies and computerization replace human labor power, both manual and mental, the source of surplus value shifts from extraction from humans to extraction from machines, and accumulation is fueled by technological development and automation, and not just by more efficient organization of human labor power, as during the era of scientific management and Taylorism. The various phases of this process are described by Harry Braverman in *Monopoly and Labor Capital*, in which he analyses the progressive de-skilling and homogenization of labor and the replacement of humans by machines, leading to dramatic transformations of the labor process and the recomposition of class.[5] Braverman describes the 'degradation of work in the twentieth century', and indicates how the capitalist division of labor, scientific management, fordism and the assembly line, and industrial psychology were geared both to increase productivity and to rob the workers of their labor skills. As the machine apparatus of production and its managers and supervisors came to control the labor process, workers were progressively de-skilled, and are now being rapidly displaced.

The process of automation continued throughout the 1950s and 1960s, during an era of unprecedented economic growth and affluence (see below). Yet automation was accelerated in certain sectors of the economy even more dramatically after the 1967 economic slowdown and 1973–4 recession, which put severe pressures upon profitability.[6] Higher labor and energy costs, increased international competition, and declining productivity and profitability forced corporate capital to introduce new technologies and to further rationalize the production process. The result was a proliferation of new technologies which were seen both as a mode of reorganizing and revitalizing previous industrial sectors and as a new high-tech sector which promised new opportunities for increasing capitalist profitability and power.

Consequently, new technologies, electronics and computerization came to displace machines and mechanization, while information and knowledge came to play increasingly important roles in the production process, the organization of society and everyday life. One immediate result of these shifts was that the role of manual labor – and thus the industrial working class – decreased, while new, white-collar, service, professional-managerial and technical classes emerged (in the following sections, I document and expand on these changes). Labor tended to be segmented into a diminishing sector of relatively unskilled, unionized and well-paid labor within the large corporate (and state) sectors, contrasted with generally low-paid and non-unionized clerical, service, and part-time labor (bolstered by a growing army of the unemployed or underemployed underclass).[7] Consequently, exploitation of labor intensified under techno-capitalism, while the working class was progressively fragmented, disorganized and brutalized.

The political economy of techno-capitalism is rooted in the forms of corporate and monopoly capital analyzed by Hilferding in *Finance Capital* and by Baran and Sweezy in *Monopoly Capital*, though it has become increasingly global and multinational.[8] Techno-capitalism exhibits growing concentration and centralization of capital, organized in transnational conglomerates in a global system in which new advanced technologies like satellite television, computers and information, scientific and technological knowledge, and forms of consumer and mass culture are international in scope, disseminated throughout the world by transnational capital and techno-elites. Techno-capitalism depends on an increasingly high-velocity form of capital in which money, ideas, images, technologies, goods and services can be rapidly moved from one part of the world to another and in which an international division of labor segments production and distribution in different regions and countries connected by new forms of global organization.[9]

Techno-culture represents a configuration of mass culture and the consumer society in which consumer goods, film, television, mass images and computerized information become a dominant form of culture throughout the developed world which increasingly interpenetrate developing countries as well.[10] In this techno-culture, image, spectacle and aestheticized commodification, or 'commodity aesthetics', come to constitute new forms of culture which colonize everyday life and transform politics, economics and social relations. In all these domains, *technology* plays an increasingly fundamental role, and new forms and organizations of technology play key constitutive functions in producing new configurations of economy, politics, society and culture. Yet a theory of techno-capitalism should resist temptations toward either the technological or the economic determinism which plague many classical and contemporary social theories. Instead, we should conceptualize what might be seen as a new dialectic of technology and capitalist social relations in which technology plays a more important role than previously in structuring and organizing production and everyday life. Yet, at bottom, *techno*-capitalism remains a form of *capitalism*, for technology continues to be employed, for the most part, under capitalist auspices, imperatives and control – though, as I shall suggest in 7.3 and 8.2, we should begin envisaging ways in which technologies could be used against capitalist interests and relations.

Such an approach avoids, I believe, the economic determinism and reductionism associated with classical Marxism, as well as the technological reductionism and determinism which I find characteristic of existing theories of post-industrial and post-capitalist societies.[11] Therefore I reject terms like 'post-industrial society', 'the information society', 'mode of information', 'media society', 'high-tech society' and the like, all of which assign a fundamental constitutive role to technology which in most cases covers over the economic factors and forces involved in the constitution of societies in the more technologically advanced countries.[12] Yet I am also resisting interpreting techno-capitalism as a new *stage* of capitalism, for the concept of what constitutes a 'stage' of capitalism has not been specified adequately. In addition, I suspect that, despite the novel conditions and transformations that we are currently experiencing, many systematic features of the phenomena of 'organized capitalism' analyzed by Hilferding and the environment of capitalism analyzed by Critical Theory (see Chapters 3–6), remain the same. That is, the state capitalist synthesis of the economic and political spheres, the growth of technological rationality, mass culture, and consumer society and so forth continue to be key constituents of the current constellation of capitalism. I would thus propose that analysis of the new conditions of techno-capitalism can best be interpreted at this point as theorization of new *configurations*, or *constellations*, of capitalism, rather than a new 'stage' of capitalism. Borrowing a term from Horkheimer, I would suggest that techno-capitalism refers to a 'society in transition' from previous configurations and constellations of capitalism to new ones, the contours of which I shall sketch out in this chapter and future studies.

Perceived from the dialectical perspectives of Marx and Critical Theory, techno-capitalism should be seen as a form of both progress and domination. It is a form of progress in that it produces new technologies and modes of information which have a potentially beneficial impact on human life. Yet it is a system of domination in that it forfeits many of these potentialities by employing new technologies primarily as a continued imposition of commodification and wage labor which exacerbates class inequalities while intensifying misery and suffering for millions of people throughout the world. That is, rather than introducing new technologies to benefit human life, techno-capitalism continues to attempt to monopolize new technologies in the interest of corporate domination and profitability, and thus continues to follow the imperatives of capitalist logic. Yet in so doing, techno-capitalism aggravates classical contradictions between and within capital as a whole – that is, the ruling elites and corporations – and labor as a whole – those forced to sell themselves for a wage and those who must continue alienated labor even during an epoch when it is no longer socially necessary. This aggravated conflict-potential forces techno-capitalism to attempt to manage and control these tensions and conflicts with new corporate and political strategies (see 7.2 and 7.3).

Therefore, I propose conceptualizing the new socio-economic, political and cultural developments within the framework of Critical Theory's dialectic of rationalization and irrationality, and progress and domination. Accordingly, in the following sections I shall indicate the ways in which techno-capitalism produces both new forms of rationalization and domination, new crises and irrationality, and new possibilities for progress and emancipation. I build on some works by the first generation of Critical Theorists, and then on Habermas and his colleagues, but shall draw on other sources as well. My argument will be that Critical Theory provides unique and powerful perspectives to conceptualize, explain and critique recent socio-economic developments, and that many elements of Critical Theorists' analyses of the administered society, the culture industries, science and technology as domination and the consumer society form an indispensable starting point for a theory of techno-capitalism.

Automation and Domination: Pollock and Marcuse

In the 1950s Pollock carried through studies of the impact of automation on the organization of the labor process and structures of class composition.[13] In this important and neglected study, Pollock attempted to describe the changes in the labor process and class composition which automation was producing and their economic and social consequences. He defined automation as 'a technique of production the object of which is to replace men by machines in operating and directing machines as well as in controlling the output of the products that are being manufactured' (*A*, p. 5). Pollock described the changes effected by the replacement of human labor power by machines, and analyzed the various optimistic and pessimistic prognoses of the effects of automation on workers and society. On the whole, he criticized the optimistic assessments which held that automation was a predominantly progressive force that would cause only minor suffering and disruption. Defenders of automation argued that it was being introduced at a sufficiently slow rate that changes and adjustments could be made without major problems or hardships, and that the introduction of automation would produce more prosperity and jobs which would ultimately benefit the workers, who would then be freed from oppressive manual or tedious mental labor and could anticipate shorter working hours, better jobs, higher wages and a better life. Against such (ideological) views, Pollock argued that the introduction of automation was proceeding at an extremely rapid pace that, in the absence of social planning, would cause great suffering and dislocation for the industrial working class, who would lose relatively high-paying jobs.

Pollock seemed especially concerned to analyze the (confused and ultimately inadequate) approaches of organized labor and the (ideological) responses of business to automation. In so doing, he tended to deflate the positive appraisals of business, while suggesting that it did not appear that automation would be in the interests of the working class when introduced within the confines of the existing capitalist system. On the other hand, he seemed to perceive automation as inevitable and as potentially beneficial to the working class, and thus argued for the need to plan and regulate automated production, so as to avoid serious technological unemployment and oppression. To avoid excessive suffering would require, Pollock claimed, more economic planning, a shortened work week and overcoming the problems of technological unemployment through state welfare measures. He feared that introduction of automation in a so-called free market environment would cause much unemployment and suffering: 'Our own belief is that if automation is introduced in an unregulated manner in a "free" economy there are serious dangers to the stability of both the economic and social structure' (*A*, p. 164).

Pollock feared that in the absence of regulation and state planning, automation would increase tendencies toward rationalization and domination, which would widen 'the gulf between a small group of highly qualified "managers", engineers and specialists on the one hand and the vast mass of wage-earners on the other' (*A*, p. 83). He believed that a 'new sort of society, based upon authoritarian or military principles, might be evolved' (ibid.). Automation might thus intensify class differences and exploitation and might produce 'an *economic general staff* – the real masters of both machines and men – at the apex of the social pyramid' (ibid.). This new class might 'ride roughshod over the vast mass of the workers', and greatly increase social domination and exploitation.

Building on current discussions of automation cybernetics, while extending earlier Institute theories of domination, Pollock thus projected the possibilities that automation and new technologies would vastly increase powers of capitalist control and domination while diminishing individuality, freedom and democracy. Yet he also envisaged more optimistic possibilities, arguing that if 'only automation is deliberately used to promote the welfare of the human race it could help to banish poverty relatively quickly from the face of the earth. And this could be done on a scale that has hitherto been regarded as a mere Utopian dream' (*A*, p. 249). Interestingly, Pollock also perceived that such a utopian use of automation was not possible under market capitalism: 'It is, however, easy to show that this aim can never be achieved if we leave the direction of these new powers entirely to private enterprise and to the workings of a "free" market as envisaged by the classical economists' (ibid.). Instead of trusting 'free enterprise' to provide new jobs and reduce technological unemployment, Pollock concluded that: 'What must be done is to take a long-term view and to plan for the future with the aid of new machines and new techniques. And the object of economic planning must be to integrate automation with a free and democratic society. Success in such planning would mean that the second industrial revolution could help to establish a social system based upon reason' (p. 253).

Pollock thus analyzes the introduction of automation in the framework of the earlier Institute theory of the dialectic of technology, rationalization and domination, and he envisages at least the possibility of using technology and automation as instruments of liberation. Pollock's analysis of how automation would serve to increase the domination and oppression of workers was dramatically confirmed in Raya Dunayevskaya's book *Marxism and Freedom* (published in 1958) and in other studies of automation published by her *News and Letters* associates.[14] Dunayevskaya summarized the ways in which automation was being introduced in the capitalist economy, and analyzed how organized labor was unable to develop a coherent strategy toward automation, thus forcing rank-and-file workers to go on wild-cat strikes against speed-ups, loss of jobs, and other forms of oppression which automation produced. Dunayevskaya and her colleagues offered ample documentation of how automation was increasing the oppression of the working class and how workers in turn were battling automation.

In a 16 August 1960 letter to Herbert Marcuse, when he was working on *One-Dimensional Man*, Dunayevskaya summarized recent literature on automation and the positions of the *News and Letters* group toward it. Marcuse answered in a letter of 24 August 1960:

Dear R.D. [Raya Dunayevskaya]

It was wonderful to get from you such quick and good help. I read at once the issue of NEWS AND LETTERS. Don't misunderstand me: I agree with practically everything that is said there, and yet, somehow, there is something essentially wrong here. (1) What is attacked is NOT automation, but pre-automation, semi-automation, non-automation. Automation as the explosive achievement of advanced industrial society is the practically complete *elimination* of precisely that mode of labor which is depicted in these articles. And this genuine automation is held back by the capitalists as well as by the workers – with very good reasons (on the part of the capitalists: decline in the rate of profit; need for sweeping government controls, etc.; on the part of the workers: technological unemployment). (2) It follows that arrested, restricted automation saves the capitalist system, while consummated automation would inevitably explode it: Marx, *Grundrisse der Kritik der politischen Oekonomie*, pp. 592–593. (3) re Angela T. [who had written a stirring denunciation of the effects of automation on workers which Dunayevskaya sent to Marcuse]: you should really tell her about all that humanization of labor, its connection with life, etc. – that this is possible only *through* complete automation, because such humanization is correctly relegated by Marx to the realm of freedom beyond the realm of necessity, i.e., beyond the entire realm of socially necessary labor in the material production. Total *de*-humanization of the latter is the prerequisite.[15]

Building on Pollock's, Dunayevskaya's and other analyses of automation, Marcuse argued in *One-Dimensional Man* that automation was serving to integrate the working class into the capitalist organization of labor, and he conceptualized automation and technology as strengthening the capitalist apparatus of domination and power. Yet, developing automation to its fullest, Marcuse argued, elaborating the position sketched in his letter to Dunayevskaya, could serve to end the reign of alienated labor:

Automation, once it became *the* process of material production, would revolutionize the whole society. The reification of human labor power, driven to perfection, would shatter the reified form by cutting the chain that ties the individual to the machinery – the mechanism through which his own labor enslaves him. Complete automation in the realm of necessity would open the dimension of free time as the one in which man's private *and* societal existence would constitute itself. This would be the historical transcendence towards a new civilization.[16]

Thus Marcuse visualized the possibility that automation could end the reign of alienated labor and make possible an entirely new type of society organized around leisure and the development of human potentialities, and not around work and profit, thus providing concrete substance to Marx's vision of a 'realm of freedom' beyond the realm of necessity. With the exception of Marcuse, few Critical Theorists took up the issue of automation, new technologies and the possibilities of using computerization and the new high-tech instruments for human emancipation or postulated the need to break with capitalist technologies and to produce new, emancipatory technologies. Despite the critiques of technical civilization in *Dialectic of Enlightenment* and *One-Dimensional Man* and Pollock's studies of automation, later Critical Theorists have tended not to trace the development of new technologies and their impact on society.

Information, Deindustrialization and Class

Critical Theory's failure to follow the introduction and development of new technologies is somewhat curious, for it was this tradition that for several decades focused on the impact of science and technology on all realms of social life and which thus provided some of the most advanced theorizing of these phenomena. Consequently it was within other social theories and traditions that the trajectory of automation and the new technologies was traced and their impact on social life and organization examined. One tradition includes Daniel Bell and other theorists of 'post-industrial society' who argue that the industrial era is over and that a new social order is emerging in which knowledge and information will replace industrial commodity production as the 'axial principle' of social organization. Whereas industrial society is defined by 'fabricating', or manufacturing, Bell sees the post-industrial society as characterized by '*processing* in which telecommunications and computers are strategic for the exchange of information and knowledge.... If capital and labor are the major structural features of industrial society, information and knowledge are those of the post-industrial society.... A post-industrial society is characterized not by a labor theory of value but by a knowledge theory of value. It is the codification of knowledge that becomes directive of innovation.'[17]

Against Bell, I would argue that the production of knowledge and information takes place within the framework of corporate capitalism, and that while knowledge and information play significantly more central roles within techno-capitalism, they are still subject to processes of commodification, exchange, profitability and control by capital and should therefore be conceptualized within the framework of a theory of contemporary techno-capitalism. Indeed, techno-capitalism is defined as a phase of capitalist development that incorporates knowledge, information, computerization and automation into the production process precisely in order to enhance capitalist profitability, power and social control as a response to falling rates of profit, drives to realize new sources of profitability and strategies to replace highly paid, well-organized workers by more compliant machines.

In response to squeezes on profitability and productivity during the 1980s, computerization and automation of the labor process accelerated, and home computers became a fundamental constituent of everyday life, with wide-ranging implications. Yet computers are not autonomous technological forces, and so far their introduction and use have been, for the most part, subject to the imperatives of techno-capitalism. Studies of the history of computers, for instance, have revealed that IBM and other early producers first created the machines primarily for corporate and governmental use. IBM resisted 'open architecture' designs (which make it possible to insert and even create one's own programs) and the marketing of home computers which would provide access to ordinary individuals of data-bank information services and powerful word-processing tools.[18] And to the present, information, programming and computers themselves are still controlled primarily by market imperatives and corporate domination.

Indeed, using categories from Critical Theory, one could argue that the 1980s saw an increased commodification of information, knowledge, education, entertainment and so on, in which domains that were previously relatively free from commodity exchange relationships became subject to capitalist profit and control – as when computer information services replace libraries as sources of information or education is commodified into computer programs which students have to purchase or when pay-TV replaced 'free' TV. In this context, information, knowledge, entertainment and so forth become *techno-commodities* which embody new forms of technology that are subject to the laws of exchange value. Thus, rather than transforming contemporary society into a post-capitalist society, I would argue that techno-capitalism *increases* the power and hegemony of capital over social and individual life (though, as I shall argue below, it also creates new crises for capital and new possibilities for a post-capitalist social transformation).

Furthermore, new technologies and information have been subjected to increased control by the military-industrial complex.[19] The corporations and the state, and especially the military sector, have dominated research-and-development resources over the past two or three decades; and they continue to control new information technologies and to create and use them in the interests of increasing corporate and military domination of the society as a whole. From this perspective, it appears completely wrong to claim that information and knowledge are autonomous organizing principles of a new type of society, for their current production and control primarily serve to strengthen the dominant institutions of techno-capitalism and its military-industrial research complex.

While I reject the claims of Daniel Bell and other theorists of the post-industrial society, or information society, that we have now entered a new post-capitalist stage of history, these theorists provide research material, concepts and analyses essential for a theory of techno-capitalism. Bell and others have documented the growing importance of knowledge and information in social life, as well as the transformations of labor, class composition and social organization. By the mid-1950s, white-collar workers in the clerical, technical and professional strata outnumbered blue-collar workers, while a service sector eventually came to replace the industrial-manufacturing and agricultural sectors as the dominant economic sector in the United States and other capitalist societies.[20] During the 1960s and 1970s, white-collar and service sectors grew, while the industrial and agricultural sectors continued to decrease, often dramatically. Most important for our argument here, however, was the accelerating growth of automation, computerization, information and robotization during the 1970s and the 1980s. As Luke and White argue (within a framework influenced by Critical Theory):

By the late 1960s, the primary information sector of the economy – computer manufacturing, telecommunications, mass media, advertising, publishing, accounting, education, research, and development as well as risk management in finance, banking, and insurance – produced 25.1 percent of the national income [in the U.S.]. The secondary information sector – work performed by information workers in government and goods-producing and service-producing firms for internal consumption – produced 21.1 percent of the national income. Already by the late 1960s, prior to widespread computerization of the 1970s, informational activities produced 46 percent of the U.S. national income and earned 53 percent of total national wages. By the mid-1970s the primary information sector's overall share of national income production alone rose from 25 percent to 30 percent, and all information workers in both sectors surpassed noninformation workers in numbers.[21]

This transformation of the economy dramatically transformed class composition, by transferring individuals from industrial and agricultural production to service and knowledge industries. Within the industrial sector, new technologies, computerization and automation replaced many industrial jobs and severely affected the industrial working class, which suffered the brunt of these changes. Barry Bluestone and Bennett Harrison describe the socio-economic transformations as 'deindustrialization', and document the destruction of community and the suffering which these processes imposed on the working class, while David Gordon, Richard Edwards, and Michael Reich describe the types of fragmentation and segmentation of the working class in the United States over the last two decades.[22] Bluestone and Harrison describe in detail the continued deindustrialization process in which multinational corporations close down plants and factories in the United States and either move their capital into other areas or open new plants in the Third World, where they have lower labor costs, less unionization to contend with and less government regulation. The result is a dramatic decline in relatively well-paid, unionized industrial labor and a growing proletarization of the industrial working class, accompanied by deterioration of community and social life.

Gordons, Edwards and Reich describe the segmentation of the working class as an attempt by corporate capital to restructure the working class in the United States in response to high wages and a highly unionized work force, economic pressures from the still unresolved 1970s world economic crisis, and declining profit and productivity resulting from these and other factors. They – and Critical Theorists – have not yet, however, studied systematically the impact of automation and robotization on the working class or the problems of technological unemployment. Some theorists, however, are documenting the decline of industrial labor, the declining standards of living for the middle class and the growth of a large underclass in techno-capitalism.[23] Computerization, streamlining and costcutting have driven many corporations to fire executives, managers, engineers and other 'professionals', as well as industrial laborers. A shrinking labor market in the corporate and managerial sector has forced many of these previously well-off employees to seek lower pay and less secure employment. For Critical Theory, this raises the question of whether deindustrialization involves a reversal of the trends of the consumer society, and whether individuals will accept a reduction of consumption when they have been led to believe that it is their right and privilege to expect increased consumption as a reward for both their labor and their loyalty to a capitalist society which has precious little else to offer as legitimation other than increased consumption.[24]

From the classical Critical Theory standpoint, the processes of deindustrialization can be conceptualized as the production of new forms of socio-economic rationalization and domination. Here Habermas's notion of the 'colonization of the lifeworld' might also be of use. Yet, technological unemployment and the restructuring of labor and class may have even more momentous consequences for critical social theory and politics, and may require renewed attention to theories of crisis and alternative models of social organization. André Gorz notes that American economists like Peter Drucker project 30 to 50 percent unemployment rates by the end of the century, and Gorz believes that such estimates are conservative unless dramatic changes in the organization of labor – and social organization more generally – take place.[25] For Marxism, it means as well that the classical force of revolution, the industrial proletariat, is rapidly disappearing; and while the new, fragmented, de-skilled, and precariously employed working class is arguably being 'proletarianized', it is not (yet?) organized in any unions, parties or groups that would threaten capitalism in any significant way.[26]

Consequently, it appears that the development of techno-capitalism will involve growing class division, stratification, and potential class conflict and antagonisms. Yet it is not clear what form these struggles will take (see Chapter 8 for some speculation). Nor is it clear how or if techno-capitalism will be able to solve the problem of growing technological unemployment or to manage growing class stratification and antagonism. Interestingly, some corporate planners and ideologues are urging new concepts of 'small is beautiful', the 'conserver society', 'simple living' and downwardly mobile consumption as a replacement for the upward mobility, high consumption and rising expectations characteristic of life in post-World War II capitalist societies.[27]

In this context, attacks on consumption central to the classical Critical Theory may further social domination within the new phase of capitalist development by helping to convince people that they would be better off with less high-level consumption, and that therefore they should readjust their expectations and demands (while the elites of techno-capitalism at the same time dramatically increase *their* consumption). Yet it is by no means certain that people *will* accept lower levels of consumption; thus it is likely that increased burdens of providing welfare, crisis management and re-pression will fall upon the capitalist state. In any case, in view of the structural changes within techno-capitalism and the possibility of inten-sified crises, I would propose that Critical Theory today return to the sorts of studies carried out by Pollock and Marcuse concerning the impact of new technologies like automation – and now computerization, robotization and so forth – on class, social structure and politics in contemporary capitalist societies. A theory of techno-capitalism would combine analysis of new technologies with investigations of the dialectical interrelationships between technology and economy and of the impact of new technologies on eco-nomics, politics, society, culture and everyday life. Such investigations could chart the ways in which new technologies are being used as instru-ments of domination while at the same time containing possibilities for emancipation. Such investigations must also inquire into the role of the state within contemporary capitalist societies, with a view to ascertaining its functions, its crisis tendencies and its limitations, which point to possibil-ities for political intervention and change.

7.2 The Capitalist State

Within the tradition of Critical Theory, Offe and Habermas have been exploring the ramifications of growing pressures on the capitalist state to provide crisis management which will produce economic policies that will enhance capitalist accumulation, as well as legitimation for the capitalist system as a whole.[28] In a series of books and articles over the last two decades, Offe has produced aspects of a theory of the capitalist state and new crisis tendencies in contemporary capitalism which are continuous in some ways with the earlier phase of Critical Theory. In particular, Offe criticizes the accounts in liberal, pluralist theories of the state, as well as in conservative, functionalist and Marxian instrumentalist theories, for their failure to explain adequately the ways in which the capitalist state secures the interests of the capitalist class as a whole in capital accumulation and political legitimation, which together secure class domination. In this way Offe follows the implicit orthodox Marxism of the earlier generation of Critical Theorists by interpreting the state as an integral part of the capitalist mode of production. Yet he breaks with the earlier tradition by arguing that both traditional establishment and radical theories of the state cover over the new conflicts and crises within the capitalist state which he is concerned to describe.[29]

Although he rarely cites Institute texts, Offe begins from the standpoint central to 1930s Critical Theory that distinguished contemporary state capitalism from the earlier phase of market capitalism.[30] For Offe, the capitalist market itself provided legitimation for the emerging bourgeois order, through claims that a 'free' capitalist economic order would guarantee a maximum of economic and political freedom, as well as prosperity for the masses of citizens. Constant economic and political crisis, however, rendered it impossible to continue with a strictly laissez-faire political-economic order and ideology in which the state left the market to follow its own laws and imperatives. Threats to capital accumulation and to the political hegemony of the bourgeoisie forced the state to play an increasingly central role in crisis management and in preserving the capitalist order through state policies.

During the new phase of state capitalism, the state therefore assumed fundamental roles in crisis management and in preserving the existing political-economic order.[31] In 'organized' capitalism (to use Hilferding's term), the state assumes new responsibilities in managing both the economy and the political order. Offe claims that state intervention in the economy and crisis management lead to a growing politicization of the capitalist order: 'In an era of comprehensive state intervention, one can no longer reasonably speak of "spheres free of state interference" that constitute the "material base" of the "political superstructure"; an all-pervasive state regulation of social and economic processes is certainly a better description of today's order.'[32]

Offe elaborates this position by distinguishing between 'allocative' and 'productive' state policies.[33] Under liberal/market capitalism, allocative functions were predominant. Resources already controlled by the state were allocated to insure capitalist accumulation; examples would include the use of the military to protect capitalist interests, allocation of state expenditures to build roads or canals that would aid commerce and direct loans or tariff favors to business. Under what Offe calls 'late capitalism', 'productive policies' describe new state programs which help produce conditions which aid and enhance capitalist accumulation and which preserve the capitalist system of production. Examples would include growing state expenditure to higher education; health, housing and welfare measures; governmental training programs and investment in scientific and technological research and development.[34] Together, allocative and productive state policies provide both crisis management and crisis avoidance strategies which strive 'to restore accumulation or to avoid or eliminate perceived threats to accumulation'.[35]

Offe thus challenges contemporary theories of the capitalist state and examines the new ways in which the state is politicizing the economic and social order while assuming new forms of political power and authority. The result in his works is a highly contradictory, ambiguous capitalist state which serves primarily to aid in the accumulation of capital, to manage crises produced by an anarchic capitalist market and to regulate society in the interests of maintaining and reproducing the capitalist system. Yet the growing power of the state provides it with increasing autonomy, and makes it subject to demands from a wide range of interest groups, while putting new strains and burdens on it which produce new forms of instability and crisis in 'late capitalism'. Out of these contradictions and tensions emerges 'the welfare state', which in Offe's theorization is a contradictory amalgam that both serves the interests of capital and yet threatens the logic of capital by providing services, benefits and goods which often transcend and work against the logic of commodification.[36]

Offe provides one of the most convincing neo-Marxian theories of the state because he demonstrates in detail that the welfare state and other state forms under contemporary capitalism are forms of a *capitalist* state. Further, he also documents the ways in which the capitalist economy creates crises of management for the state, while analyzing its failures in crisis management. Like other Critical Theorists, however, Offe fails to analyze the ways in which social struggles and movements have forced the welfare state to grant reforms, though he points to some ways in which the welfare state sometimes serves the interests of the public against capital.

Some of Offe's most interesting analyses concern the contradictory imperatives that govern the capitalist state. On one hand, the capitalist state follows the logic of commodification by expanding goods and services, which are produced as commodities subject to capitalist profitability and exchange value. Yet, certain health and welfare benefits, he claims, further *de-commodification* – that is, the provision of goods and services that break with the logic of capital, and thus expand a socialized public sector while enhancing individual rights and abilities to make claims on this sector. This expansion of the welfare state in turn increases pressures on it, which then require growing state expenditures and thus contribute to the 'fiscal crisis of the state'.[37]

Yet the welfare state also attempts to depoliticize demands on it, to reduce its clients to objects of administration and to expand technocratic domination of society by a bureaucratic administrative elite. In Offe's words:

The welfare state is developing step-by-step, reluctantly and involuntarily. It is not kept in motion by the 'pull' of a conscious political will, but rather by the 'push' of emergent risks, dangers, or bottlenecks, and newly created insecurities or potential conflicts which demand immediate measures that avoid the socially destabilizing problem of the moment. The logic of the welfare state is not the realization of some intrinsically valuable human goal but rather the prevention of a potentially disastrous social problem. Therefore, welfare states everywhere demonstrate that the tendency of being transformed is less a matter of politics than a matter of technocratic calculus.[38]

Offe, Habermas and their colleagues have documented the growing technification of politics in the 1960s and 1970s and the emergence of a *technocracy* which serves as an instrument of crisis management in the service of capital. By the 1970s, both Offe and Habermas concluded that the capitalist welfare state and its technocracy produced new conflicts and contradictions that were potentially explosive. The structural problem for the capitalist state is that it must augment both capitalist accumulation *and* legitimation in attempting to preserve the capitalist system as a whole. In order to carry out its legitimation functions, it must masquerade as being above class or specific group interests by providing a neutral steering mechanism. Thus the capitalist state '*must at the same time practise its class character and keep it concealed*'. Consequently, 'the state can only *function* as a capitalist state by appealing to symbols and sources of support that *conceal* its nature as a capitalist state; the *existence* of a capitalist state presupposes the systematic *denial* of its nature as a *capitalist* state.'[39]

Yet contradictions emerge when the state produces policies which blatantly serve the interests of the capitalist class alone and when its reality (as a *capitalist* state) blatantly contradicts its appearance (to be a *democratic* political order). New conflict zones also emerge when groups take the state at its word and make demands on it that might contradict the logic and interests of capital – for less work, higher wages, more health and welfare benefits and so on. The results of state crisis management are extremely contradictory. On one hand, the state sector is able to assist capital in the many ways already mentioned and to further stabilize the system by helping to manage organized labor and its own growing labor force. To some extent, however, the capitalist state mediates between capital and labor while ensuring higher wages for certain sectors of labor which it at least tentatively is able to incorporate into its system.[40] On the other hand, the state's attempts to aid accumulation and legitimation become increasingly costly, putting new pressures on the economy and giving rise to new conflicts and tensions.

Capitalism thus faces the dilemma that the growing complexity of the system requires ever more sophisticated and comprehensive crisis management, which in turn strengthens the state vis-à-vis particular capitalist interests. This in turn provides a realm of growing autonomy that might be used against capitalist interests or, for certain sectors of capital, as the Reagan years demonstrate with their economic and military procurement scandals, that might greatly weaken the long-term economic viability and legitimacy of the capitalist system as a whole. Furthermore, the growing conflicts and contradictions managed by the capitalist state on the one hand increase tendencies toward growing organization and on the other hand produce a more *Disorganized Capitalism*, the title of a recent collection of Offe's essays.[41]

Offe attempts to chart the way in which new developments in the capitalist economy and state function to provide strategies of crisis management that in turn produce new conflicts and crisis tendencies. Both Offe and Habermas thus attempt to restore the theory of *crisis* to Critical Theory, and point to new crisis tendencies and new zones and possibilities for political intervention. I shall explore this theme in the next section, and will conclude this discussion by pointing to Offe's complex relationship to the previous generation of Critical Theorists.

While Offe expands and develops some of the central concepts of the earlier stage of Critical Theory, he departs in significant ways as well.[42] Although he tends to downplay his connection with the earlier generation and rarely quotes earlier Institute thinkers, he follows the earlier tradition of Critical Theory in charting the transition from the earlier phase of liberal/market capitalism to the new phase of contemporary capitalism, and in tracing ways in which the logic of capital comes to dominate more and more sectors of social life. In particular, like his Institute predecessors, Offe shows how commodification, exchange, reification and manipulation penetrate the domain of the state while entering other areas of social and everyday life through state activity. Furthermore, he uses terms like 'the universalization of the commodity form', 'authoritarian total administration', 'the end of the individual' and other phrases that unmistakably point to his Institute predecessors. Yet Offe also talks of 'de-commodification' and is concerned to chart the ways in which state policies go against the logic of capital, create a relatively autonomous public realm and produce new contradictions and conflicts that give rise to new crises and possibilities for political intervention.[43] Thus, while much of the earlier Institute work focused on capitalist modes of hegemony and stabilization, Offe is concerned as well to disclose destabilizing tendencies and thus spaces and possibilities for political intervention and struggle.

Yet Offe severs the connections between philosophy and the sciences often maintained by his Institute predecessors, and is more affirmative toward establishment social science, using distinctions like 'allocative' and 'productive' state functions current in mainstream political science. He tends to reject – as does Habermas – the radical critique of science and technology advanced in *Dialectic of Enlightenment* and some works by Marcuse, and tends to follow more gradualist Social Democratic reform politics, eschewing the revolutionary perspectives sometimes advanced by earlier Critical Theorists. He also tends to focus his inquiries on more empirical, regional studies and to avoid the more global, supradisciplinary perspectives created by his Institute predecessors.

In general, Offe is strongest and most useful (in empirical analysis and in theorizing crisis tendencies, that is) where many of his Critical Theory predecessors were weakest. On the one hand, Offe carries out patient, detailed empirical analysis and conceptual elaboration of the capitalist state which compensate for the neglect of empirical analysis of the state by many first generation theorists. He also counters tendencies to develop theories of a 'one-dimensional', 'totally administered society' by analyzing the contradictions and conflicts emerging in contemporary capitalist societies. Offe thus reconnects Critical Theory with a tradition of political economy that charts the complex relations between economy and state without, however, falling into either economic or political reductionism. On the other hand, he severs his analyses of the capitalist state from broader attempts to develop a theory of society, and tends to neglect or downplay the social, cultural and psychological mediations that were the primary focus of his predecessors.

Consequently, in contemporary attempts to develop a Critical Theory of society, it seems appropriate to call for a synthesis between the kind of patient, detailed, empirical research and analysis in political economy found in Offe and the broader, more comprehensive and more multidimensional and radical efforts of his predecessors. Some of Harbermas's work can be viewed in part as an attempt to continue the tradition of developing a totalizing Critical Theory of society while carrying out more detailed empirical analysis of some of the sectors of social, political and economic life than was found in most of the other post-1950s works of at least the first generation of Critical Theorists. For Habermas has continued analysis of the trends toward rationalization, domination and reification in contemporary capitalist societies begun earlier by Adorno, Horkheimer and Marcuse in their theories of the administered society. To continue the totalizing tradition of social theory of the first generation, Habermas adds elements from systems theory and other contemporary social theories which provide new substance and material for Critical Theory.[44]

In addition, Habermas has been concerned to maintain the critical standpoint of the first generation by searching for a normative dimension and justification for social critique and new ways to preserve or resurrect the relation between theory and practice which he sees as central to the tradition.[45] Furthermore, his critique of the notion of social action in the systems theories of the Parsonians and the Luhmannians, contrasted with his own theory of communicative action, does not fall prey to objectivistic or functional reason, but rather provides critical perspectives on both the current organization of society and some of the dominant legitimating ideologies and modes of thought.[46] Most important for our exercise in this chapter, however, are his attempts to resurrect and develop crisis theory which in effect provides new possibilities for social intervention and transformation which were precluded by the analyses of some of his predecessors within the tradition of Critical Theory.

7.3   Toward a New Crisis Theory: Habermas and Offe

Classical Marxism depended on a theory of capitalist crisis for its theory of revolution. Marx frequently argued that capitalist crisis and collapse were inevitable, and orthodox Marxists attempted to develop a crisis theory which would describe the mechanisms of capitalist crisis that would make possible the transition to socialism.[47] Lenin called 'imperialism the highest stage of capitalism', implying that it was the final stage, which would give way to world-wide socialist revolution; and orthodox Marxists as well as Habermas, Offe and others, continue to use concepts like 'late capitalism', which imply that capitalism is in its dotage, is about to pass away, is in its final days.[48] Against this position, the earlier Critical Theorists – Pollock, Horkheimer, Adorno, Marcuse and others – developed a theory of state capitalism and an analysis of the mechanisms by means of which contemporary capitalism attempted to avoid crisis and stabilize the existing mode of production (see Chapter 3).

While there are serious problems in linking a theory of radical social change with apocalyptic theories of capitalist collapse, a Critical Theory of social transformation should attempt, nonetheless, to specify which crisis tendencies within techno-capitalism provide progressive possibilities for social transformation. In this section, we shall see what crisis tendencies are presented by Habermas and Offe, two of the most influential members of the second generation of the Frankfurt School. In the concluding chapter, I shall discuss some other openings for moving beyond techno-capitalism and some possible political responses and strategies.

In *Legitimation Crisis*, Habermas provided a sketch of some of the crisis tendencies within contemporary capitalism. The book was a direct response to the model of the totally administered society developed by Pollock, Horkheimer and Adorno, and Marcuse in *One-Dimensional Man*, which implied that contemporary capitalism had overcome its dangers of crisis and had eliminated threatening forms of opposition.[49] Against this model, Habermas attempted to show that contemporary capitalist societies continued to be sites of crisis, contestation and potential transformation, and that there were still possibilities for radical politics and structural transformation. Building on Marx's theory of system crisis, Habermas analyzed some of the ways in which crises occur in complex capitalist societies 'through structurally inherent system-imperatives that are incompatible and cannot be hierarchically integrated' (*LC*, p. 2).

For Habermas, crises primarily concern fundamental social contradictions that cannot be resolved in a system controlled by capitalist interests and 'unresolved steering problems' (*LC*, pp. 4–30). Habermas distinguishes between the stages of 'liberal capitalism' and 'late capitalism', and between 'system crises', the sort of economic and political crises endemic to liberal capitalism, and 'social crises', which he believes are particularly symptomatic of 'late capitalism'. Habermas believes that crises of social integration are experienced as a threat to the identity of an individual and society, and constitute vulnerabilities to continued social reproduction, and thus openings for structural transformation in a post-capitalist direction.

Consistent once again with earlier Institute positions, Habermas claims that the sort of class conflict central to previous Marxian theories of crisis and revolution is now being managed by various 'steering mechanisms':

In the decades since World War II the most advanced capitalist countries have succeeded (the May 1968 events in Paris notwithstanding) in keeping class conflict latent in its decisive areas; in extending the business cycle and transforming periodic phases of capital devaluation into a permanent inflationary crisis with milder business fluctuations; and in broadly filtering the dysfunctional secondary effects of the adverted economic crisis and scattering them over quasi-groups (such as consumers, schoolchildren and their parents, transportation users, the sick, the elderly, etc.) or over natural groups with little organization. In this way the social identity of classes breaks down and class consciousness is fragmented. The class compromise that has become part of the structure of advanced capitalism makes (almost) everyone at the same time both a participant and a victim. Of course, with the clearly (and increasingly) unequal distribution of wealth and power, it is important to distinguish between those belonging more to one than the other category. (*LC*, pp. 38–9)

Habermas goes distinctly beyond earlier versions of Critical Theory, however, in his claim that in addition to the economic crises analyzed by classical and contemporary Marxism, *new* sorts of crises are emerging, which he specifies as legitimation crises, rationality crises and motivation crises. Crises for Habermas take place in what he sees as the three sub-systems of contemporary capitalism: the economic, political and socio-cultural systems. Since late capitalism is characterized by an extension of the state into other domains, the ideology of free market exchange is displaced by ideologies of state management and technocratic steering ideologies, which in turn are subject to criticism and contestation when crises appear in either the state or the economy.

In *Legitimation Crisis* Habermas provides a sketch of the central features of a wide range of contemporary crisis tendencies. Economic crises and rationality crises tend to be system crises based on contradictory imperatives and unresolved steering problems within the political-economic system, while legitimation crises and motivation crises tend to be crises of social integration concerning the integration of the individual within the social system. Economic crises emerge through the classical contradictions of the capitalist economy, though Habermas suggests that in view of the merger of the economy and the state in late capitalism, economic crises give way to or are 'displaced' by, rationality crises which concern failures of the state to steer the economic system (*LC*, pp. 50ff.). Following Offe and others,[50] Habermas sketches some of the ways in which the growing role of the state in the economy and all regions of social life puts new pressures on the political sphere and produces new potentialities for crisis when an overburdened state cannot deliver the goods (pp. 63ff.).

Habermas's concepts of the legitimation and motivation crises are among his most original – though problematical – concepts. He argues that for the economic and political sector to function properly, individuals must be adequately motivated to act (that is, to study, work, consume, socially conform and so forth) in ways consistent with the system's imperatives and values, and that the system itself must be perceived as legitimate if it is to provide these motivations. Thus Habermas suggests that the cultural sphere plays an especially important role in late capitalism in social reproduction, and that the system must provide legitimation and motivation in order to continue functioning. Precisely here, however, the system is vulnerable. Economic crises and rationality crises, Habermas claims, instigate legitimation crises that may produce 'a questioning, rich in practical consequences, of the norms that still underlie administrative action' (*LC*, p. 69). That is, whenever the system fails in the economic and political spheres, individuals may come to question the system's imperatives, practices, institutions, norms and so on, thereby calling into question at least some aspects of the capitalist system and instigating a demand for social transformation. Likewise, if legitimation of the system as a whole fails, then the system faces motivation crises in which individuals lose the motivation to do what the system requires them to do.

Habermas gives a detailed picture of the current cultural-ideological constellation which suggests that traditional values and religion, bourgeois ideologies of possessive individualism and achievement, as well as contemporary art and culture, are all failing to provide the amount of legitimation and motivation which the system needs to function (*LC*, pp. 68–92). He thus sketches a picture of a cultural-ideological crisis which may threaten the continued reproduction of the capitalist system.

Since the early 1970s, when Habermas carried out his analysis, attempts have been made to provide legitimation and motivation through increased consumerism, a highly aggressive ideological culture industry, rebirth of religion and traditional ideologies, and efforts to refurbish bourgeois ideologies of possessive individualism and achievement.[51] Yet it is not certain how successful these efforts at ideological re-legitimation are, or to what extent a system capable of 'delivering the goods' really needs legitimation. Thus it is still an open question as to how serious legitimation crises are and will be for the continued existence of techno-capitalism.[52]

In any case, Habermas shifted the focus of his crisis theory in his 1981 magnum opus *Theory of Communicative Action*.[53] In this book, he describes various types of colonization of the 'life-world' by the 'system' and analyzes the crisis potential when the imperatives of the system intrude upon norms, practices and institutions of everyday life. For Habermas, the 'life-world' – a term taken over from Husserl's phenomenology – centers on 'communicative action'. Its three components, culture, society and personality, are correlated by Habermas with modes of reaching understanding through communicative action.[54] The 'system' is constituted by subsystems of the capitalist economic system and state bureaucracies governed through the 'media of money and power'.[55] In this framework, crises result when subsystems of the life-world are invaded by the imperatives of the system, as when money and power erode culture, social relations or personality development and such things as the loss of meaning, alienation and anomie, or psychopathologies result. Following Parsons and systems theory, Habermas sees the domains of life-world and system – as well as the subsystems within them – as interrelated and looped together in feedback processes such that a disturbance in one realm affects other realms. Thus, if the economy does not produce requisite value in an economic crisis, or if the state produces a deficit of rationality or steering abilities within a rationality crisis, withdrawal of motivation will follow in the occupation system, accompanied by withdrawal of legitimation affecting the system as a whole.

Habermas's crisis theory thus increases in both complexity and abstractness, utilizing an ideal-type model of potential crises facing a capitalist society derived in large part from systems theory. Yet, like earlier Institute work, it is particularly weak on political economy, and the notion of an economic crisis is undertheorized. As Held points out, Habermas assumes the nation state as the unit of his ideal-type analysis, and thus excludes consideration of the world economic system and the ways in which the interconnection of national economies in a global economic system might produce new economic crisis tendencies.[56] In addition, Habermas's model of political or rationality crises omits discussion of specific state forms, political parties and struggles, and relationships between economic and political sectors.[57] Finally, it may be the case that crises of social integration and the life-world – that is, motivation and legitimation crises – may be more manageable and less threatening than system crises – that is, of the economy and state – which might be much more destructive in the long run. If this is the case, then Habermas's emphasis on legitimation crises may be misplaced.

On the other hand, Habermas's concept of a multidimensional crisis theory, which attempts to explicate the various levels and types of capitalist crisis, seems preferable to analyses which focus merely on economic crisis. Yet, like all theories, Habermas's is influenced by the specific conditions of his own history. To a certain extent, his social theory, like the earlier theory of Adorno, Horkheimer and Marcuse, was deeply influenced by the stabilization of capitalism from the 1940s through the 1960s and by the increasing decline in importance of the labor movements as a factor of political change. His turn to a crisis theory in the 1970s is in response to both the militance of 1960s social movements and the economic crisis of the early 1970s; yet he never really attributes much of a role to social movements or struggles as factors of social change, and tends to engage in rather abstract theoretical analysis of crisis tendencies, rather than more concrete historical analysis. Against such an ideal-type model for crisis theory, I would argue that more concrete empirical and historical analysis is needed to elucidate the specific crisis tendencies which emerge and become threatening in various societies at various historical junctures, combined with more global analysis of the world economy and how it affects specific national economies.

Yet, whatever the limitations of Habermas's notion of the legitimation crisis, his reintroduction of crisis to Critical Theory is an important contribution, as are his analyses of specific crisis tendencies which may open up new spaces for social transformation. In particular, the welfare state in most capitalist countries is especially vulnerable to rationality crises and economic crises. The state is overtly blamed for its failures, and economic crises force decline of state expenditures and make it more difficult to raise revenues and to govern. Yet it is not clear that these sorts of crises will elicit revolutionary upheaval or the collapse of capitalism. In the context of complex, multidimensional systemic crises, Offe proposes that we abandon both the notion of a final crisis – that is, that a system-ending apocalypse is on the horizon – and the assumption that the system has produced techniques and strategies to manage the system indefinitely, and adopt instead a notion of 'the crisis of crisis management'.[58] In particular, Offe proposes viewing the capitalist state not primarily as a provider of social services or manager of the economy and polity, but as an especially vulnerable locus of crisis management that is rife with conflicting goals, interests, demands, vulnerabilities and struggles.

This model calls for analysis of crisis tendencies within the capitalist state. On Offe's account, rising demands on the state by various groups lead to growing expenditures, which in turn produce fiscal crises and dissatisfaction with high levels of taxation. Lack of adequate coordination and management, Offe believes, produces an excess of failures and unplanned outcomes, which undermine the rationality and legitimacy of the system. Offe thus suggests, without really explicating or defending the concept, that contemporary capitalism should be seen as a system of *disorganized capitalism*, rather than as the organized capitalism described by Hilferding and accepted as the model of contemporary capitalism by the earlier generation of the Frankfurt School. He writes:

One of the models which seeks to explain (and, in some cases, normatively justify this type of mediation) is that of 'organized capitalism.' This model was first introduced by Rudolf Hilferding in 1910, developed by him and other German-speaking democratic-socialist theorists in the 1920s, and finally debated as a potentially useful theoretical concept by modern historians and political scientists. In this model, the competitive market interaction between individual economic actors is seen to be in the process of being superseded by formally organized collectivities of economic action (corporate firms, cartels) and interest representation (trade unions, business associations). To speak of 'disorganized capitalism' is not to propose an elaborate and coherent counter-model against that of 'organized capitalism.' Rather, my aim is to propose a heuristic perspective that is guided by the following questions: Do the procedures, patterns of organization, and institutional mechanisms that supposedly mediate and maintain a dynamic balance between social power and political authority (i.e. seek to coherently *organize* the socio-political systems of contemporary welfare state capitalism) actually *fail* to perform this function? If so, what are the symptoms, consequences and potential remedies of such failures of the process of mediation?[59]

Although Offe does not systematically develop the concept of disorganized capitalism, he describes some of the disorganizing tendencies that have emerged in contemporary capitalist societies in recent decades due to the end of the postwar settlement between capital and labor, the decline of Keynesianism, recognition of the limits to growth and the erosion of the work ethic. In disorganized capitalism, growing groups of individuals are excluded from labor markets (namely, ethnic minorities, emigrants, the aged, sectors of the underclass), and are thus not integrated into contemporary capitalism, with the result that 'the crisis of crisis management' is intensifying.

Offe's notions of the 'crisis of crisis management' and of disorganized capitalism put in question previous Institute perspectives on contemporary capitalism which presupposed that capitalism had achieved a crisis-free condition. He and Habermas present models of the state as a zone of conflict and of society as a contested terrain and battleground between conflicting interests and social forces that is rife with conflicts and contradictions. In contrast to the earlier Frankfurt School analyses of technological rationality and claims concerning 'organized capitalism' and 'the totally administered society', the second generation of Critical Theorists has thus provided a model of a disorganized capitalism governed by a strange dialectic of irrationality and rationality, of organization and disorganization.[60] These analyses put in question the thesis of the growing technological rationality of contemporary capitalist societies presupposed by the earlier generation of the Frankfurt School by pointing to trends toward irrationality and disorganization within contemporary capitalism. From this perspective, Habermas, Offe, Lash and Urry, and others appear to offer more useful conceptual frameworks for analyzing the dynamics of contemporary capitalist societies than the old Institute theories of technological rationality, one-dimensional society and a crisis-proof system.

The concept of disorganized capitalism connects social theory with crisis theory and with issues of political strategy and social transformation, while avoiding some of the more questionable aspects of classical Marxian crisis theory. For a certain Marxian orthodoxy, usually avoided by Critical Theory, relies on a theory of capitalist collapse as the lever of the transition to socialism. The twentieth century has shown that some of the most intense crises and greatest threats to capitalism have led to fascism rather than socialism, or were eventually overcome within the framework of the existing capitalist organization of production; thus it seems politically dubious to link a theory of social transformation to a theory of capitalist collapse. Indeed, the history of capitalism's ability to react to crisis with crisis management and to come up with new survival strategies in response to the most severe crises puts in question the rationality of waiting for capitalism to collapse before revolutionary struggle is begun.

On the other hand, I would argue that the theory of 'one-dimensional society' or notions of an 'organized' or 'state' capitalism – which postulate a situation that presupposes that capitalism has overcome its fundamental contradictions and can now manage or administer away its fundamental problems and conflicts indefinitely – are deeply flawed, and fail to provide adequate analytical perspectives to conceptualize the crisis tendencies of techno-capitalism. As I have argued in this chapter, contemporary capitalist societies should be seen as a peculiar combination of streamlined rationality and intense irrationality, of organization and disorganization, of crisis tendencies and efforts at crisis management. Likewise, from the standpoint of the classical Marxian theory of crisis, capitalist societies should be seen as both highly antagonistic and unstable *and* as capable of overcoming or stabilizing many of their contradictions.

The analysis of disorganized capitalism and of the various crisis tendencies in techno-capitalism thus points to openings for repoliticization of Critical Theory in the present age. It points to major shifts in contemporary capitalist societies since the 1960s and helps to explain some of the changes within these societies as a result of permanent legitimation crisis, the lack of a dominant ideology and growing disorganization. The lack of a dominant ideology can help explain why a society can veer rapidly to either the Right (as with Britain and the United States in the Thatcher and Reagan years) or the Left (as in France and southern European countries).[61] And the persistence of a whole series of crisis tendencies and of growing disorganization suggests that more dramatic political changes and transformations – from the Left or the Right – may be possible in future years. Since the evolution of capitalist – and now Communist – societies seems especially open at this point, it will depend to a large extent on forthcoming political struggles and movements which direction contemporary societies will take.

In the next chapter I will continue discussion of the crisis tendencies in techno-capitalism and will suggest some ways in which Critical Theory can be politicized in order to make it more relevant to contemporary challenges to radical social theory and politics. First, however, I shall discuss the various political positions taken by Critical Theorists from the 1960s to the present, and will note some of their limitations and some ways in which these limitations can be overcome.

8

Theory and Practice: The Politics of Critical Theory

The relationship between theory and practice was always a central focus of classical Marxism, and deeply influenced many versions of Critical Theory.[1] In the 1930s, its synthesis of philosophy, the sciences and politics was to serve, in Horkheimer's words, as a theoretical arm of political struggle: 'The Critical Theorist's vocation is the struggle to which his thought belongs. Thought is not something independent, to be separated from this struggle.'[2] For Marcuse, Critical Theory was linked with the project of human emancipation, and Habermas distinguished Critical Theory from traditional theory and science by virtue of its emancipatory interest; not by accident was one of his first major books entitled *Theory and Practice*.[3] Yet, despite the theoretical emphasis on practice, politics and emancipation, Critical Theory, with few exceptions, has suffered a political deficit. While the Critical Theorists produced detailed and comprehensive works in philosophy, social theory and cultural critique, their concrete political analyses and contributions are rather meager in view of the original concept of the theory which has been preserved in various forms through the decades but never fully realized. On the other hand, a thorough examination of the various Critical Theorists' political writings and interventions shows more significant political theorizing and engagement than has been noted in most studies. In this chapter, I shall examine some of the attempts to politicize or depoliticize Critical Theory from the 1960s to the present (8.1), and will then present a case for the need to repoliticize Critical Theory today (8.2), while attempting to link it once again to socialist politics and the most advanced new social movements (8.3). I shall conclude with some remarks indicating why I think that Critical Theory continues to be relevant today to the tasks of radical social theory and politics (8.4).

8.1 Critical Theory and Radical Politics

In the 1960s, the fragile theoretical and political unity among the major representatives of Critical Theory was shattered. With the eruption of New Left politics, Critical Theorists took extremely varied positions toward the 1960s radical movements.[4] These movements sometimes drew theoretical sustenance from Critical Theory, and sought support from its chief representatives. Marcuse generally defended the most radical wing of the student movement, while Habermas criticized some of what he considered its excesses, even as he defended many of its goals and positions. Horkheimer sharply attacked student radicals, and while Adorno sometimes supported their causes, he also distanced himself from the German New Left, and even called in the police to break up what he (wrongly) thought was a sit-in demonstration in the Institute for Social Research in Frankfurt.[5] Since I have treated Marcuse's political writings and adventures with the New Left in detail elsewhere,[6] I shall focus here on Habermas's political writings and interventions and contrast Habermas's position with the growing distance from the radical politics of the 1960s by Adorno and Horkheimer.

Some of Habermas's first work with the Institute concerned studies of the political opinions and potential of students. In a study of *Student und Politik* (published in 1961), Habermas and two empirically oriented members of the Institute carried out 'a sociological investigation of the political consciousness of Frankfurt students'.[7] The study was similar to the Institute's earlier *Gruppenexperiment* which had attempted to discern the democratic and anti-democratic potential in wide sectors of German society after World War II through survey analysis and in-depth interviews.[8] Just as earlier Institute studies of the German working class and post-World War II German citizens disclosed a high degree of political apathy and authoritarian-conservative dispositions, so the surveys of German students disclosed an extremely low percentage (4 per cent) of 'genuinely democratic' students, contrasted with 6 per cent rigid authoritarians; similarly only 9 per cent exhibited what the authors considered a 'definite democratic potential', while 16 per cent exhibited a 'definite authoritarian potential'.[9] And within the more apathetic and contradictory attitudes and tendencies of the majority, a larger number tended toward authoritarian than democratic orientations.

Habermas wrote the introduction to the study – 'On the Concept of Political Participation' – which provided the conception of genuinely democratic political participation that was used as a norm to measure student attitudes, views and behavior. As he was later to do in his studies of 'the public sphere', Habermas sketched out various conceptions of democracy, ranging from Greek democracy to the various forms of bourgeois democracy to current notions of democracy in welfare state capitalism. In particular, he contrasted the participatory democracy of the Greeks and radical democratic movements with the representative, parliamentary bourgeois democracy of the earlier stage of capitalism and the newer attempts at reducing citizen participation in the welfare state. Habermas defended the earlier 'radical sense of democracy' in which the people themselves would be sovereign in both the political and the economic realms against current forms of parliamentary democracy.

In his study Habermas defended principles of popular sovereignty, principles of formal law, constitutionally guaranteed rights and civil liberties as part of the progressive heritage of bourgeois society. His strategy was to use the earlier model of bourgeois democracy to criticize its later degeneration and decline, and thus to develop a normative concept of democracy which he could use as a standard for an 'immanent critique' of existing welfare state democracy. He believed that both Marx and the earlier Frankfurt School had underestimated the principles of universal law, rights and sovereignty, and that a re-democratization of radical social theory was thus an important task.

Student und Politik was published in 1961, and during the same period student radicals in the United States developed conceptions of participatory democracy, including emphasis on economic democracy.[10] Henceforth, Habermas himself would be concerned in various ways and contexts to develop theories of democratization and political participation. Indeed, from the beginning of his career to the present, Habermas's work has been distinguished by its emphasis on radical democracy, and this political foundation is an important and often overlooked subtext of many of his works.[11]

Habermas's focus on democratization was linked with emphasis on political participation as the core of a democratic society and as an essential element in individual self-development. His study *The Public Sphere* (1962) contrasted various forms of an active, participatory bourgeois public sphere in the heroic era of liberal democracy with the more privatized forms of spectator politics in a bureaucratic industrial society in which the media and elites controlled the public sphere.[12] The bourgeois public sphere, which began appearing around 1700 in Habermas's view, was to mediate between the private concerns of individuals in their familial, economic, and social life and the demands and concerns of the state. The public sphere consisted of organs of information and political debate, such as newspapers and journals, and institutions of political discussion, such as parliaments, political clubs and public spaces where socio-political discussion took place.

The principles of the public sphere were open discussion of all issues of public concern, in which discursive argumentation was employed to ascertain 'general interests' and the public good. The public sphere thus presupposed freedoms of speech and assembly and the right to freely participate in political debate and decision making. After the bourgeois revolutions, Habermas suggested, the bourgeois public sphere was institutionalized in democratic constitutional orders which guaranteed a wide range of political rights and which established a judicial system that was to mediate claims between various individuals or groups or between individuals and groups and the state.

In the bourgeois public sphere, public opinion was formed by political debate and consensus, while in the debased public sphere of late capitalism, public opinion is administered by political, economic and media elites which manage public opinion as part of systems management and social control. Thus, while in an earlier stage of bourgeois development, public opinion was formed in open political debate concerning matters of common concern which attempted to forge a consensus in regard to general interests; in the contemporary stage of capitalism, public opinion is formed by dominant elites and thus represents for the most part their particular private interests. No longer is rational consensus among individuals and groups in the interests of articulation of common interests the norm. Instead, struggle among groups to advance their own interests characterizes the scene of contemporary politics.

Habermas concludes with tentative proposals for 'a rational reorganiz- ation of social and political power under the mutual control of rival organ- izations committed to the public sphere in their internal structure as well as in their relations with the state and each other', although he did not really sketch out the features of a post-bourgeois public sphere.[13] Still, Horkheimer found Habermas's works to be too Left Wing, and refused to publish *Student und Politik* in the Institute monograph series, and then later rejected *The Public Sphere* as à habilitation dissertation, despite Adorno's support of Habermas's work.[14] Horkheimer seems to have become increasingly conservative, and thus rejected the work of the Institute's most promising student, forcing him to seek employment elsewhere. Habermas had no trouble, however, getting his works published and receiving academic positions; in 1961 he became a *Privatdozent* in Marburg, and in 1962 received a professorship in Heidelberg. In 1964, strongly supported by Adorno, Habermas returned to Frankfurt to take over Horkheimer's chair in philosophy and sociology; thus Adorno was ultimately able to bestow the crown of legitimate succession on the person whom he thought was the most deserving and capable Critical Theorist.[15]

Meanwhile, Horkheimer and Adorno became more distanced than ever from both radical social theory and politics. A collective volume, *Sociologica II*, published in 1962, contained essays by Horkheimer and Adorno, both of whom seemed increasingly skeptical about the very possibility of develop- ing a social theory of the present age (a skepticism that would appear later in the decade in France among those identified with post-structuralism and postmodernism).[16] In an introduction to the volume, Horkheimer claimed that the 'objective [social] situation' contradicted the possibility of a synthetic, totalizing social theory, and that the fragmentary observations contained in the articles in the collection were grounded 'in the factual situation of society' and not in the 'weaknesses' of the authors.[17] Horkheimer also claims that the essays renounced analysis of contextual connections and mediations because of the difficulties of perceiving and analyzing the fundamental social processes of the present age.

Adorno in turn wrote that the growing irrationality, fragmentation and complexity of contemporary societies – which he interpreted as a function of the extension of the hegemony of capital into ever more realms of society and life – made it increasingly difficult to conceptualize the dynamics and processes of the whole:

The tendency toward concentration, which seemingly has diminished the market mechanisms of supply and demand; imperialistic expansion, which has prolonged the life of the market economy by pushing it beyond its own realm; state interventionism in the sector of economic planning, which has penetrated the realm of market laws – all of this has made extremely problematical the attempt to construe society as a harmonious (*einstimmiges*) system, despite the total socialization of society. The growing irrationality of society itself, as manifested today in threats of catastrophe and society's obvious potential for self-destruction (*Selbstausrottung*), become incompatible (*unvereinbar*) with rational theory. Social theory can hardly characterize society any more with a word that it no longer speaks itself.[18]

This seeming renunciation of social theory was especially surprising in Adorno, who had written in the positivism debate shortly before that 'The renunciation of a Critical Theory of Society by sociology is an act of resignation: they do not dare to conceptualize the totality because they despair of changing it'.[19] In fact, Adorno wavered throughout the 1950s and 1960s between attempting to characterize the contours of the existing society and forsaking social theory for philosophy and cultural criticism. Yet, in a penetrating essay entitled 'Society', Adorno sketched out a neo-Marxian conception of society, arguing that the fundamental social processes of capitalism continued to rule social life and remained the object of critique.[20] Adorno here uses Hegelian-Marxian categories of totality, mediation and contradiction to describe the ways in which society comes to dominate the individual:

Above and beyond all specific forms of social differentiation, the abstraction implicit in the market system represents the domination of the general over the particular, of society over its captive membership. It is not at all a socially neutral phenomenon, as the logistics of reduction, of uniformity of work time, might suggest. Behind the reduction of men to agents and bearers of exchange values lies

the domination of men over men. This remains the basic fact, in spite of the difficulties with which from time to time many of the categories of political science are
confronted. (pp. 148-9)

In Adorno's conceptualization, society is organized around wage labor,
exchange relations, profit and accumulation, and class struggle. Thus he
tended to hold to the neo-Marxian conception of society developed earlier
by the Institute, though in *Negative Dialectics* and most of his later work
Adorno neglected social theory in favor of philosophical theory and critique.
Near the end of his life, in one of his last essays, 'Resignation', Adorno
defended the renunciation of practical politics by certain Critical Theorists
like himself, while defending the activity of thought and writing.[21] In
particular, Adorno argued that unthinking affirmation of practice over
theory simply reproduced the utilitarian/pragmatic aspects of existing
societies, and that only critical thought can understand the obstacles to
social change and thus make possible the transformation desired by those
activists who defame theory. Adorno attacked the 'pseudo-activity' of a
mindless activism which is based on a notion of 'pseudo-reality' (a phrase
coined by Habermas to designate an illusory belief that reality conforms, or
can be made to conform, to the demands of the revolutionary ideology) and
which falls prey to sectarian illusions.

While Adorno's critique of sectarianism and activism that renounces
theory is convincing, as is his defense of the importance of theory, he did
not really apply his theoretical skills to analyzing the current political situation; nor did he participate in the political movements of the day, as did
Marcuse and, to a lesser extent, Habermas. Generally, Adorno failed to
analyze the specific contradictions and antagonisms that were generating
the struggles in the 1960s against administration and domination. He did
not develop his social theory much in the 1960s either, usually repeating his
earlier notions of commodification, rationalization, culture industries and
so on without adding much new substance or new concepts to the old
theories. In fact, Adorno was entering his last years of life and productivity,
and was deeply concerned with finishing his major works in philosophy and
aesthetics.

In *Negative Dialectics* (1966), Adorno transcoded the dialectics between
philosophy, social theory and politics which had characterized earlier
versions of Critical Theory into philosophical critique and negation.[22] His
'non-identity' theory rejected concepts of mediation and determinate
negation, and transformed dialectics from a critical method of analyzing
history and society in the interests of socio-political transformation into
critique of philosophy. While he continued to defend radical thought and
critique, he tended to limit his 'negative dialectics' to destruction of
philosophical positions, and rarely engaged in concrete social analysis

and criticism, while distancing himself from the turbulent politics of the day.

Horkheimer, too, increasingly turned away from social theory and politics to philosophical and theological speculation.[23] A quasi-mystical yearning for 'the completely Other' (*das ganz Anderen*) moved to the center of his thought, which increasingly came to focus on theology. In interviews and articles he also took increasingly conservative political positions, as evidenced by his attitude toward Habermas and the New Left, whose politics he severely criticized. During this period, Habermas and others noted the anxiety which Horkheimer exhibited toward his early writings, and the ever greater distance he took from his earlier positions – such as the renunciation of critical social theory in the *Sociologica II* essay. In addition, Horkheimer had failed to produce anything of much interest or value for years, and it appears that his political regression was matched by theoretical collapse.

It would be a mistake, however, to discount the impact of the works of Horkheimer and Adorno and the earlier generation of the Institute on 1960s radical politics in Germany and elsewhere. While Horkheimer and Adorno did not participate directly in the struggles of the 1960s and usually distanced themselves from student radicals, their works had radicalized many young students, and they helped create an environment in which radical theory and politics could thrive. Indeed, I studied in Tübingen myself in 1969–71, and purchased copies of the key works of Critical Theory – along with copies of Lukács and Korsch – at student tables in the university and local radical bookstores. I also participated in a Critical Theory study group which was attempting to use the concepts and theories developed by Adorno, Horkheimer and Marcuse as a framework for radical politics. And many others of my generation in Europe and the United States were also radicalized through study of the works of Critical Theorists.

Wiggershaus points to the irony that, at the moment when Horkheimer was distancing himself most explicitly from student activism, his prestige, along with the influence of his earlier works, was growing in radical circles.[24] Marcuse's impact on the German New Left is well documented, and his visits to Berlin and Frankfurt in the 1960s are part of the mythology of the era.[25] Habermas was also involved in 1960s radical politics, and participated in the major political demonstrations and conferences of the day, while writing many articles analyzing, interpreting and often criticizing the student movement in West Germany.[26] Yet Marcuse alone among the first generation identified with and defended the radical movements of the day. Marcuse's motto of the 'great refusal' became one of the slogans of the movement, and he tirelessly defended, wrote for and lectured to the new radicals.

The affinities between Critical Theory and the student movement appeared as well in the works of Rudi Dutschke, Oskar Negt, Hans-Jürgen Krahl and many others who formed the second generation of Critical Theorists. For example, Johannes Agnoli, a former student of the Frankfurt School, wrote with Peter Bruckner *Die Transformation der Demokratie*, which followed the Institute analysis of trends toward increased totalitarianism in contemporary capitalist societies. Agnoli and Bruckner claimed that Western capitalist democracies had developed new control mechanisms to contain social change and to manage social conflict. Their analysis of the mechanisms of social integration and sharp critique of contemporary capitalism were clearly influenced by Critical Theory.[27]

'Social peace' in West Germany, the United States and elsewhere was interrupted, however, by frequent student protest, which included spectacular demonstrations against United States intervention in Vietnam. Students and others influenced by Critical Theory were active in both Germany and the United States in the anti-war movement,[28] and helped extend protest against imperialism to protest against exploitation, social injustice and conservative education in the universities. In addition, many people of the New Left influenced by Critical Theory resisted trends toward Marxist-Leninist sectarianism when radical activism subsided in the 1970s, and many former radicals turned to orthodox Marxian forms of political organization. In an article 'Don't Organize by Interests, but Organize by Needs', Oskar Negt called for new political organization and strategies which would address people's needs for education, housing, community, sexual gratification and so forth and that would thus produce a new politics of everyday life in opposition to the sectarian politics of the Old Left. Negt criticized bureaucratic and authoritarian tendencies on the Left, and urged the New Left to follow democratic and participatory modes of organization that had been defended for years by Habermas and others associated with the Institute for Social Research.[29]

8.2   Techno-Capitalism, Crisis and Social Transformation

Habermas emerges as the most prominent representative of Critical Theory during the 1970s and 1980s. Moving from Frankfurt to become director of the Max Planck Institute for Study of the Scientific and Technical World in 1971, he followed the earlier Institute practice of combining social theory with philosophical and cultural critique. By the early 1970s, however, he was beginning to take a 'linguistic turn', and while he continued to conceive of Critical Theory as a mode of social theory and critique with radical political intentions, most of his work in the 1970s and the 1980s focused on philosophical themes, and transformed Critical Theory into communications theory.[30] Thus, although Habermas returned to Frankfurt in the early 1980s to again assume theoretical leadership of the Institute for Social Research, he continued the practice of subordinating social theory and radical politics – evident as well in the post-1940s works of the first generation – to philosophy. Consequently, with the exception of Marcuse, the efforts of the first generation of Critical Theorists to develop a Critical Theory of society connected with the radical politics of the day had simply ceased. Although Marcuse, Habermas, Offe and others associated with the tradition attempted to develop Critical Theory in relation to the social, cultural and political changes of the period, no one developed a new comprehensive synthesis comparable to the projects of the 1930s and 1940s.

Although they do not present their analyses in precisely these terms, Habermas and Offe offer a theoretical foundation for a Social Democratic reform strategy within contemporary capitalism.[31] According to their analyses, crises of contemporary capitalist society and the state result from conflicts between capitalist imperatives for the maximization of profit at all costs and systemic needs for rational steering and management, democracy and legitimacy. Crises in state management and the economy produce legitimation crises which create the openings for readiness to support social transformation toward a more rational society that they covertly identify with socialism (see 7.3). Yet there are many crisis tendencies and possibilities for more radical social transformation which Habermas and Offe do not consider in their analyses. Critical Theory today should therefore inquire into the new crisis tendencies emerging from the dynamics of techno-capitalism. As Marx argued, accelerating automation, for instance, is likely to increase unemployment dramatically, which will conceivably promote serious economic and political crises.[32] Technological unemployment may overburden welfare state resources, and thus become a highly volatile crisis tendency in the technological society of the future. Growing unemployment would require increased welfare measures, to an extent perhaps impossible under capitalism; this would increase pressures toward implementing more socialist state planning, income redistribution, a guaranteed social wage and so forth. Likewise, the need to re-educate people for the new technological jobs of the future will also require increased public expenditure on education, which in turn will require expansion of the public sphere at the expense of the private sphere. Further, health care provides another arena likely to provoke intense future crises as cancer and AIDS epidemics overburden an already inadequate health-care system. In all these cases, new health, education and welfare programs will be needed to deal with growing social crises, which in turn will put new pressures on the welfare state and require new attitudes toward taxation, government programs, socialism and so on.

So far, the development of techno-capitalism has been highly uneven. While some sectors and regions have become ultra-modern and highly affluent, other sectors and areas are decaying and are underdeveloped. Most cities in the United States, for instance, provide striking contrasts between ultra-modern, high-tech centers and decaying industrial areas and urban ghettoes. Furthermore, it is not clear whether future technological development will benefit the majority of the people or only the ruling elites and whether technical solutions will be found to the endemic crisis tendencies of capitalism. Consequently, while new technologies may increase unemployment, they also provide contradictory possibilities for the future. On the one hand, they provide new possibilities for capital realization and new forms of capitalist hegemony which may help stabilize capitalism indefinitely. On the other hand, they provide new possibilities for progressive social transformation and emancipation by eliciting the possibility of significant social restructuring. Thus, while new technologies may increase the power of corporate capital to control and run the entirety of the society in their interest, they also provide new weapons of struggle and transformation for those who wish to radically transform society.

Unfortunately Critical Theory has never developed adequate dialectical perspectives on science and technology. Horkheimer and Adorno in *Dialectic of Enlightenment* and many, although not all, of their later writings tended to equate science and technology with domination, and thus to ascribe a *negative* essence to technologies and science, which, in fact, can be used either to benefit and enhance or to dominate and destroy human life.[33] Habermas, by contrast, takes a more positive attitude toward science and technology, but by equating the two with instrumental action, he naturalizes existing science and technology (as reproducing an anthropologically grounded instrumental action) while ruling out the possibility of the sort of new technology imagined by Marcuse which would enhance human life and provide a synthesis of art and technique.[34] In addition, by essentializing technology, Habermas covers over the extent to which many existing technologies are the product of capitalist relations of production and thus have domination inscribed in their very structure and functions. From the perspective of the destructive aspects of some technologies like nuclear energy and weapons, the factory and assembly line, pollutants and destroyers of the environment and human life, as well as the potentiality of new liberating technologies, Habermas's failure to critique existing technologies more radically and to consider the possibilities of new technologies are real deficits in his theory. Likewise, his failure to speculate on how new technologies and new social movements might be used against capitalist relations of production and institutions should be remedied by contemporary Critical Theory.

Following the lines of classical Social Democracy, Habermas tends to assume that rational management and social organization, leavened by more democracy and public debate, will provide a more rational (post-capitalist?) society. Yet he does not consider the ways in which new technologies, new energy sources, new de-centralized institutions and new forms of organization might provide more radical and emancipatory alternatives to the present system of techno-capitalism. From this perspective, both new 'radical technologies' and new uses of existing technologies would need to be created to provide a structurally different organization of society and a new way of life.[35] For instance, automation and robotization could replace alienating labor, and make it possible to decrease the length of the working day dramatically and to increase the realm of freedom. New computer technologies and data banks could be used to make information democratically available to all individuals in society, and could establish communication networks linking individuals of similar interests together, while making possible new modes for the exchange of information and ideas. New video technologies make possible new modes of media production, and provide the possibility of more control of one's communications environment. Public access television could make possible more participatory media and the communication of radical subcultures and groups excluded from mainstream media, while satellite television makes possible nationwide – indeed world-wide – communication networks which would allow groups and individuals excluded from public communications the opportunity to broadcast a wide range of alternative views.[36]

Consequently, while new technologies like computers, cable and satellite television, and other means of knowledge and communication may be commodified to increase capitalist profit and power, they may also be 'decommodified' (to use Offe's term), and used against the system. That is, while these technologies may be used by capital as instruments of profit and social control, they may also be used by oppositional groups as instruments of social transformation to create spheres outside the control of capital (as with public computer and information centers, public access television, home computer networks, and the like). This will require new modes of political thinking and new political strategies, which will be sketched out in the next section.

Furthermore, and crucially, the new technologies make possible not only a new organization of labor, but also a new form of life which may lead beyond the stage of capitalism that for centuries has constituted a society primarily dedicated to production and labor. Fully automated production would dramatically eliminate – or least substantially diminish – living labor from socially necessary production, and might lead to a dramatically decreased work day and a great increase in leisure time. Divisions between manual and mental labor could be overcome, and machines doing most of the manual labor, as well as calculation and other forms of mental labor, would free individuals from 'alienated labor', and make possible new forms of creative labor, new linkages between labor and everyday life and a new realm of freedom and leisure. Such transformation would require a whole new set of values, institutions, social practices and ways of life in a society which is now primarily organized around production and consumption. No longer would production be the core of individual life, and such transformation would create the space for an entirely new way of living.

Critical Theory today should therefore attempt to analyze the emancipatory possibilities unleashed by techno-capitalism. In *Farewell to the Working Class* and *Paths to Paradise*, André Gorz documents the far-reaching transformations that increased automation will bring and proposes a dual systems theory of an organization of society in which labor and production would be greatly diminished in relation to leisure and free time.[37] In Gorz's projection, within a new 'politics of time', individuals would have to work a given number of hours during a projected lifetime in exchange for a guaranteed income. He claims that this seemingly utopian projection might be a necessary solution to massive technological unemployment, which will require fundamental rethinking of the very premises, organizational principles and nature of society and everyday life. And it would provide possibilities for a dramatically decreased work week, new forms of culture and leisure and new possibilities for human and social development.[38]

Offe likewise proposes breaking the connection between labor and wages and eliminating the centrality of the labor market in the organization of society. Instead, he proposes opening up the boundary between the labor market and 'other forms of useful activity and income claims'. This would entail the 'uncoupling' of labor and wages, so that there would be a 'citizenship right' to a basic income, independent of one's contributions to social security or retirement programs. This break with the primacy of labor markets would require dramatically new taxation policies and 'a consciously designed dual economy' with an enlarged public sector. The dual economy would aim 'to institutionally recognize, promote, secure and extend the limited sphere of informal, self-organized and independent labour and ... to subject it to the same criteria of social justice which claim validity in the formal employment sector of the society'.[39]

Thus both Gorz and Offe envisage the possibility of a radically new organization of society necessitated by the crises produced by the introduction of new technologies in the labor force. Now, to be sure, by the 1980s the introduction of automation and computerization primarily had the effect of bringing increased misery to the majority of the working population affected by automation, while bringing increased wealth and power to a privileged few. Automation of coal-mining in the late 1940s and 1950s produced massive suffering and the poverty area known as Appalachia, while automation of the automobile, steel, oil, chemical and other sectors of (highly unionized and relatively well-paid organized labor) big industry led to unemployment for the workers or for many of the workers who managed (for how long?) to hold on to jobs to accepting new jobs with lower pay, fewer benefits and less power. More generally, as Harry Braverman has argued, the de-skilling of labor through mechanization and automation has weakened the position of the working class vis-à-vis capital, and quality of work and life has deteriorated for many sectors of the working class.[40] So far automation and techno-capitalism have been a disaster for the working class; yet it is still an open question as to whether technological unemployment generated by new technologies and automation will generate new economic and political crises which will lead to far-reaching social transformation that will ultimately benefit everyone, or whether techno-dystopia is our fate.[41]

Yet, new crisis tendencies emerge in techno-capitalism as well. Analysts of the process of deindustrialization stress the new contradictions between capitalism and community in ways that provide graphic illustrations of Habermas's analysis of how the intrusion of the imperatives of capital into the life-world have a destructive impact on traditional forms of life.[42] In particular, Bluestone and Harrison demonstrate the ways in which an unregulated capitalism inevitably destroys community; they also provide convincing arguments for the need of public controls on corporate investment and better governmental regulation to prevent corporations from arbitrarily closing down factories and bringing about the destruction of communities.

Other critics have stressed growing contradictions between capitalism and democracy and the need to curtail unrestricted capitalist development in the interests of preserving traditions of democratic rights and freedoms. Analyses of the crisis of democracy connect with themes central to Habermas's version of Critical Theory, and call for renewed emphasis on developing a multidimensional crisis theory. Likewise, continued discussions of the contradictions between capitalism and individuality build on the earlier Institute analyses of 'the end of the individual'.[43] As techno-capitalism develops, it is likely that these and other crises will intensify, and therefore that both detailed analysis and political responses to contemporary conflicts and crises should be part of an agenda for Critical Theory today.

Indeed, the crisis tendencies of techno-capitalism could lead either to the necessity of building a new type of more progressive social organization or to an increasingly repressive class society organized in the interests of the few. In the United States during the Reagan–Bush era, the ruling classes have dramatically increased their share of the wealth,[44] while public squalor has increased proportionally, with scores of homeless individuals roaming the streets, unable to find either work or housing, and so far no federal programs have even attempted to deal with the problem. Health-care systems are breaking down, and the AIDS epidemic – which the Reagan administration did little to ameliorate either directly or by providing funds for research – threatens to dramatically increase these burdens in the future. Farm bankruptcies mushroomed, and the economy was over-burdened with skyrocketing federal debt and deficits. Bank failures pro-liferated, and Third World inability, or (justified) reluctance to pay off their astronomical debts threatened the entire international banking and monetary systems.

On the level of politics, the Reagan administration exhibited an unrivaled level of corruption, lawlessness and irrationality, which is likely to increase the rationality crises and legitimation crises that it attempted to surmount in its earlier years. On the level of everyday life, the threat of unemployment, a decline in the standard of living, rising suicide and divorce rates and increased drug and alcohol addiction testify to accelerat-ing motivation crises that may threaten the rationality and functionality of the system. Thus, whatever sort of political administrations appear in the coming decades, it is not clear how techno-capitalism will be able to provide jobs, income and a meaningful existence in an age of growing computer-ization and automation. It is probable, therefore, that the economic, rationality, legitimation and motivation crises which Habermas described will intensify, as will the prospects of a new class politics and intensified political struggle. So far, however, no radical challenge or compelling alter-native politics has emerged, and the dominant paradigms visible today within techno-capitalism range from techno-liberalism to techno-fascism, all of which operate within the premises and structures of the existing capitalist system.

To keep abreast of the great transformation now under way, with its great dangers and exciting possibilities, Critical Theory must carefully chart the trajectory of techno-capitalism and continue to theorize and criticize the transformations of the economy, political sphere, culture, society and everyday life brought about by the vicissitudes of the current configurations of capitalist society. Against postmodernists and ideologues of the post-industrial society who claim that we are already in a totally new historical stage, I would argue that we are in a transitional stage leading to either a new stage of capitalism or a post-capitalist society. During this transitional period, categories from classical Marxism, Critical Theory and other critical social theories are thus of at least some use in describing, criticizing and transforming the existing social order, but we must also be open to new theories and political strategies as well.

Consequently I would argue that contemporary forms of modernity are still forms of *capitalist* modernity, and are thus best conceptualized as forms of techno-capitalism. Yet the current form of techno-capitalism requires a neo-Marxism in which the state, culture and technology are conceptualized as relatively autonomous and fundamental social (and asocial) forces. Crucial aspects of this new Marxism are found in Critical Theory, which provides many indispensable starting points for theorizing the new social conditions of techno-capitalism. Thus, while against the fossilized Marxism of the Second and Third International, it made perfect sense to go back to Marx and advocate *Marx against Marxism*, the retrieval of genuine Marxism has already taken place in such thinkers as Lukács, Korsch and Gramsci and in Critical Theory. Consequently, there is no need to go further back. It is now time to go forward. But until we are beyond capitalist modernity, it is questionable to assert that we are beyond Marxism or that we are now in a post-Marxist condition.

Yet, against rigid Marxian blueprints concerning the inevitability of the collapse of capitalism and the transition to socialism, Critical Theory today must operate with notions of an open future that do not depend on any determinate socio-economic trajectory or pre-given political strategy and blueprint. On the other hand, Critical Theory needs to take much more determinate political positions and to contribute more systematically and resolutely to developing a radical politics if it wants to continue to be relevant to the struggles, movements and political challenges of the future. With this in mind, I shall now sketch some perspectives for a new politics informed by the theoretical perspectives of Critical Theory.

8.3   New Social Movements and Socialist Politics

In this section, I want to discuss the affinities between the most advanced theoretical positions within Critical Theory and the most progressive new social movements, in order to suggest ways in which Critical Theory can be repoliticized today. My argument is that the Institute's conception of the relationship between theory and politics developed in the 1930s is still useful today and provides a method for contemporary radical social theory, and that many positions within the tradition of Critical Theory have a remarkable affinity with many new political movements of the present. I therefore believe that Critical Theory has important contributions to make to radical politics today, and that its theoretical and political positions can in turn be refreshed, reinvigorated and strengthened by repoliticization.

Habermas has noted some connections between the most advanced social movements of the present age and the positions of Critical Theory.[45] Developing a position that he, Offe and others had defended earlier, Habermas argues that new conflicts no longer arise in areas of material reproduction, and are not primarily class conflicts. Previous conflicts between capital and labor, Habermas argues, are displaced to new realms and take new forms. In particular, 'the new conflicts arise in areas of cultural reproduction, social integration, and socialization. They are manifested in sub-institutional, extra-parliamentary forms of protest' (p. 33). These conflicts concern in part efforts 'to defend or reinstate endangered life styles', and thus concern *the grammar of forms of life*' (p. 33). By this, Habermas means that the new social movements represent a break from the old politics of parties and representational democracy, and revolve instead around problems of quality of life, individual self-realization, norms and values, participation and human rights. The movements are rooted primarily in the new middle class and the younger generation, and consist of 'a colorful mixture of groups on the periphery' (pp. 33–4). Most of the groups oppose unregulated economic growth and development. They include

the antinuclear and environmental movement; the peace movement ...; the citizens' action movement; the alternative movement (which comprises urban scenarios with squatters and the elderly, homosexuals, disabled people, etc.); the psychological scene with support groups and youth sects; religious fundamentalism; the tax protest movement; parent associations; school protest; resistance to 'modernist reforms'; and finally, the women's movement. (p. 34)

With the exception of the women's movement, which he interprets as an offensive movement seeking new rights and privileges, Habermas sees most of the other new social movements as defensive in character, seeking to protect the environment, cities, neighborhoods, traditional values and so on against what he calls 'the colonization of the life-world', by which capital, technology, the state and so forth attempt to dominate and control domains of everyday life previously immune from such penetration. These movements attack highly specific 'problem situations' concerned with the quality of life:

What sparks the protest is the tangible destruction of the urban environment, the destruction of the countryside by bad residential planning, industrialization and pollution, health impairments due to side effects of civilization-destruction, pharmaceutical practices, and so forth. These are developments that visibly attack the *organic foundations of the life-world* and make one drastically conscious of criteria of livability, of inflexible limits to the deprivation of sensual-aesthetic background needs. (p. 35)

In addition to compensating for the pain and deprivations of unfettered capitalist technological development, the new social movements contain further emancipatory potential, Habermas believes, by virtue of their furthering alternative practices and counter-institutions to the established institutions which are organized around the market and state and ruled by money and power (p. 36). The new social movements thus tend to instantiate forms of participatory democracy, which Habermas believes is necessary for genuine democratization and self-realization. The counter-institutions and alternative practices thus both block and limit capitalist and state control, while providing beginnings of a new society organized around community, democratic participation and self-realization.

Such a highly synoptic and generalized presentation of new social movements is bound to cover over differences between the movements, and from a United States perspective, it seems a mistake to include 'religious fundamentalism' within the new social movements. For, in the United States at least, most religious fundamentalist groups tend to the Right, are rarely democratic and often attack progressive forms of modernization while supporting some of the more reactionary and destructive forms of capitalist modernity (nuclear weapons, imperialist intervention and so on). Yet it is significant that Habermas has attempted to link Critical Theory with the new social movements, and has challenged others to relate Critical Theory to radical politics – a challenge taken up by Offe, Klaus Eder and others in the second and third generations.[46]

The growth of the Green movement and party in West Germany stimulated many of these efforts, as have the struggles of the peace movement in the 1980s. In an article 'A New Social Movement?' Eder provides a typology of social movements, and interprets the new social movements as responses to developments within capitalist modernity. He distinguishes between cultural movements which present anti-rationalist positions as responses to excessive societal rationalization (nineteenth-century romanticism and forms of the 1960s counterculture are his examples), and political movements which seek political power or institutional restructuring. The 'new social movements', he claims, contain neo-romantic and neo-populist forms, and often combine cultural and political tendencies (the ecology movement is his paradigm case).

In general, 'social movements' are prototypically 'modern' phenomena and involve responses to developments within modernity. For Eder, 'modernity entails that *cultural orientations can be challenged*'; thus social movements which contest dominant social forms and institutions play a role in constituting society itself (p. 10). His examples here are nationalist movements for political emancipation and the labor movements. A social movement, Eder claims, 'must have a self-image and a clear idea of who those are against whom it defends a way of life' (p. 11). Building on (social) action theory (developed by N. J. Smelser and Alain Touraine), Eder argues that new social movements are defined by 'a collective identity, an antagonistic relation to an opposed group, and a common field of action' (p. 16). In general, social movements 'move society by providing an alternative cultural model, and a moral order to institutionalize it' (ibid.). It is instructive to compare the new ecology movement with the trade union movement, Eder suggests, since the ecology movement wishes to overturn the productivist bias of the previous social order and to replace the model of unlimited growth and development of productivity with an ecological model based on limiting growth to enhance the quality of life. Eder thus sees new social movements pushing beyond modernity toward a post-industrial order, and interprets them as advancing new values and a new mode of life – goals stressed earlier by Marcuse and other Critical Theorists. Eder also suggests that the new social movements exhibit the virtues of autonomy and reflexivity against the heteronomy of capitalist and state rationalization – goals congruent, once again, with classical Critical Theory.

Different sectors of the Left have taken dramatically different positions vis-à-vis the new social movements, and have offered conflicting interpretations of their origins, nature and potential.[47] Some have celebrated the new movements as providing a progressive substitute for the working-class movement now dismissed as reactionary or obsolete. Others have dismissed the new social movements themselves as reactionary, either from an orthodox Marxian standpoint which insists on holding onto the working class as the revolutionary subject or from a neo-Adornoesque stance which criticizes their alleged impurities. In particular, many American followers of Critical Theory have eschewed participation and sympathy with these movements, and instead have engaged in a distanced critique of the alleged limitations and imperfections of the movements, using an Adornoesque ultra-radicalism to criticize the compromises, conservative elements and failures of the new social movements.[48]

For example, Paul Piccone claims that the post-1960s political movements practice 'artificial negativity' which, allegedly, only rationalizes and strengthens the existing order.[49] On this account, the 'totally administered society' has rationalized and homogenized the system to such a degree that it requires injections of 'artificial negativity' as an 'internal control mechanism' to keep the system from stagnating. All new social movements, therefore, simply spur the system to carry out necessary reforms which its bureaucratic inertia impede, or are themselves the (perhaps unwitting) agents of bureaucratically directed systemic reforms. 'Artificial negativity' is contrasted by Piccone with (a never really clarified or concretized) 'organic negativity' which would supposedly develop institutions, practices or free spaces outside and totally other than the administered system of neo-capitalism.

In opposition to either uncritical celebration of the movements or one-dimensional rejection, other theorists have attempted to provide more complex interpretations and to speculate on ways in which the new social movements could be synthesized with a new democratic, socialist politics. In an article on the new movements, Chantal Mouffe offers perspectives close to earlier Critical Theory positions.[50] She interprets the new movements as resistance to the commodification of life and the hegemony of capital in the restructuring of capitalist societies from the end of World War II to the present. This restructuring – and here the theory is congruent with Critical Theory – involved bureaucratic intervention by the state in ever more domains of the economy, society, culture and so on, combined with a homogenization of culture and everyday life with the triumph of the consumer society and culture industries. Consequently the new social movements manifest resistance to domination of society by capital and the state, and represent struggles against commodification, bureaucratization and homogenization.

On the positive side, the new social movements exhibit radicalized demands for democracy, equality and citizen participation during an era when the restructuring of capitalist hegemony involved efforts toward de-democratization and increased domination. Mouffe's interpretation of the offensive and positive demands of the new movements thus seems preferable to Habermas's interpretation of their mainly defensive character. In addition, she points to the contradictory potentials of the new movements, indicating how they can be steered to either the Left or the Right.

In general, theorists within the tradition of Critical Theory have not conceptualized adequately the importance of the struggles of the 1960s or the contradictory potential of the new social movements. Yet, as I have noted, some theorists within the tradition have attempted in various ways to repoliticize Critical Theory and to develop new political positions. Against Carl Boggs and others who argue that the new social movements require the development of a new *post-Marxist* theory and politics,[51] I shall argue in the following discussion that there is a remarkable affinity between the theoretical perspectives of Critical Theory and the new social movements and that a reconstructed and neo-Marxian Critical Theory can provide a viable framework for a new radical politics in the present era.

Toward a New Politics

To begin, some versions of Critical Theory have a natural affinity for the peace and environmental movements. Critical Theory's critical perspectives on the domination of nature and alternative values of peace, security, reconciliation and so on provide both a theoretical framework and a set of normative values which could help provide a theoretical foundation for a new politics. In addition, its dialectical perspectives allow the formulation of linkages, or mediations, between such things as nuclear weapons and energy and the imperatives of capitalism and imperialism, thus providing the systematic social critique lacking in many single-issue movements. Likewise, the (sometimes) dialectical positions within Critical Theory on technology, rationality, individuality and nature provide critical perspectives on these phenomena which could counterbalance tendencies toward technophobia, irrationalism, personalism, naturalism and so forth that some of the critics of new social movements cite and deplore. That is, while neo-romantic and technophobic positions simply denounce all technology, and sometimes modernity itself, as repressive and dominating, in contrast to technocratic ideologues who celebrate all technology and modernization as inherently progressive, a more differentiated view could sort out which technologies and development projects, what kind of growth and so on actually benefit human life and which benefit primarily capital and its agents. By providing such differentiated positions, Critical Theory could thus make potentially significant contributions to contemporary political movements.

In many versions of Critical Theory, however, 'social ecology' is under-developed, although this situation has been changing in recent years.[52] In addition to an environmentalist perspective, Critical Theory offers perspectives on cultural and sexual politics which are either akin to some of the more progressive tendencies in the new social movements or provide correctives to common deficiencies in various movements. Critical Theory has always been concerned with the aesthetic-erotic dimension of experience, and has defended pleasure, happiness, play and sensual grati-fication. Its emphasis on the body and its materialist focus on needs and potentialities thus lends itself to dialogue with the sort of sexual politics advanced by progressive feminism. Indeed, Critical Theory has always emphasized the importance of human sexuality for individual life, and has stressed the need for better human relations between and within the sexes. Critical Theorists have also pointed to the importance of the family as an instrument of socialization, and have criticized the ways in which the patriarchal family produced authoritarian personalities while oppressing women and children (see Chapters 3 and 4). While some (male) Critical Theorists often projected male attitudes and perceptions in their works, others like Marcuse had relatively progressive perspectives on sexual politics, and responded positively to the emergence of a new feminist move-ment in the 1960s.[53]

In any case, Critical Theory is, as I argued earlier (4.1), consistent with development of the sort of critique of patriarchy and demand for women's liberation advanced by feminism. So far, Critical Theory has not produc-tively developed feminist perspectives, though recent efforts have been made to link Critical Theory with feminism. Seyla Benhabib, for instance, ends a critique of 'the aporias of Critical Theory' with a call to develop an 'emancipatory politics in the present that would combine the perspective of radical democratic legitimacy in the organization of institutional life with that of a cultural-moral critique of patriarchy and the industrial exploitation of the nature within and without us'.[54]

Critical Theory's emphasis on the importance of culture and the emancipatory role of art might also contribute to a revitalized cultural politics. As I argued earlier, the particular fetish of 'high art' by Adorno and others and their contempt for all forms of popular art have traditionally rendered Critical Theory extraneous to projects of cultural revolution (5.3). Yet there is no reason why the present generation needs to repeat the peculiar aesthetic biases of the first generation of Critical Theorists, and there are indications that Critical Theory might yet develop more nuanced perspectives on contemporary culture and alternative cultural practices.[55]

Developing theories and politics of alternative cultural practices will require more attention to oppositional movements in film, television, the arts and other cultural arenas than has so far been evident within the tradition of Critical Theory. From these perspectives, Critical Theorists could then devise theories of subversive and alternative cultural practices similar to earlier projects carried out by Guy Debord and the situationists and a variety of other groups in many countries. For example, within the aestheticized environment of contemporary society, production of alternative billboards, wall-murals, graffiti and other modes of cultural expression could project images and messages counter to the productions of consumer capitalism.[56] Alternative film and video could produce subcultures of oppositional culture which, via public access and satellite television, could even enter mainstream culture. By taking culture seriously and politicizing its production and effects, Critical Theory provides a framework for future theoretical and practical work within cultural politics which could contribute to expansion of the domain of political struggle.

Since the media and information are playing increasingly central roles in the constitution of consciousness and experience under techno-capitalism, the repoliticization of Critical Theory requires more emphasis on the politics of information. This will include reflection on the use of information and media by radical political groups and movements and on ways of democratizing information and media so as to serve the interests of the entire society, while increasing the scope of political participation and democratic debate.[57] Such projects would counter the efforts at monopolization and control of the media and information by dominant social powers, and thus could be an increasingly important part of the politics of the future which will be increasingly mediated by information and media.

For example, community information centers could teach computer literacy to individuals, and make accessible data banks of information now inaccessible to those who cannot afford to pay for it or who do not possess computer information retrieval skills. Such projects could also involve community computer bulletin boards which would make available information and the exchange of ideas between those who had access to home computers and a modem to link them with the computer center and its data banks and bulletin boards. Critical Theory should be concerning itself with such information alternatives and with reflection on how progressives might intervene in the production of a future information society which would serve human needs rather than those of capital accumulation and bureaucratic power.

A repoliticized Critical Theory should also concern itself with consumer politics, the politics of education and peace research, and indeed, individuals influenced by Critical Theory have been producing impressive work in these areas.[58] Furthermore, the utopian tradition of Critical Theory helps nourish visions of an alternative organization of society and another way of life. As a response to the specter of technological unemployment, Critical Theory could outline a realm of freedom beyond socially necessary labor, and could project a new mode of social organization, centered on sociality, community, development of human potentialities, play and gratification, rather than the labor and productivity which have characterized capitalist modernity. This would truly be a break in history that might justify a discourse of 'postmodernity' (which now is mostly a rhetoric of novelty and change with many regressive features).

Reversing the productivist bias of modernity, Critical Theory could provide new values and new visions of life which could be the basis for a nonrepressive society – which would be the first in history to break with the continuum of oppression and domination which has defined human life so far. Already Marcuse has attacked what he called the 'performance principle', and sketched outlines for a nonrepressive civilization.[59] The utopian impetus of Critical Theory and its interest in emancipation render it relevant to the most radical demands for social restructuring and transformation, and Critical Theorists today should once again take up Marcuse's efforts to imagine the contours of a nonrepressive civilization. Such claims raise the question of the relationship between Critical Theory and socialism.

Critical Theory, Democracy and Socialism

As noted, Critical Theory's radical critique of capitalist modernity makes it possible for it to provide critical perspectives on the state and on what has been called the crisis of the welfare state, or the 'crisis of crisis management'. The analyses of Critical Theory make it clear that the state in capitalist countries is a capitalist state, and that in order to solve the fiscal crisis of the state, its deficits, rationality crises and so on, incursions must be made against the prerogatives of capital. Thus, a tradition of Critical Theory provides socialist perspectives on the state which make it clear that reforms alone will not solve the problems of contemporary society, and that without dramatically limiting the hegemony of capital over the state – and the rest of society – the state will not be able to provide the planning, programs, personnel, budget and so forth to solve fiscal and rationality crises and other related problems of techno-capitalism (see 7.2, 7.3 and 8.2).

On the other hand, in order to militate against the state becoming a repressive bureaucratic apparatus, efforts must be made to dramatically increase the boundaries and extent of democracy. Critical Theory lends itself to theorization of the connections between socialism and democracy, and in view of the consistent tradition of individualism within Critical Theory and its attendant critique of bureaucracy and domination, it naturally has strong affinities with the tradition of democratic socialism. While no Critical Theorist has yet proposed a fully developed conception of socialism, Marcuse was already calling for a 'new concept of socialism' in the 1960s, and there has been a recent proposal from within the tradition of Critical Theory calling for reflection on new de-centralized organizations of the economy which would be built on municipalization – that is, on municipal ownership of key industries – rather than on nationalization.[60] Yet the calls for radical democratization which ritualistically conclude all politically correct books of the Left today, often neglect the issues of a planned economy and the full development of technology, individual potentialities and what Marcuse called the 'pacification of existence' in *ODM*. Such measures would seem to necessitate a mixture of political democracy and allocation of planning and distribution responsibilities to a political class. So far, discussions of democratization within Critical Theory have for the most part focused on the conditions for unconstrained consensus and domination-free communication; but the earlier demand for a 'rational society' needs to be supplemented by emphasis on relationships between a planning and steering sector and those areas in which a more participatory democracy would be possible.

In addition, the issue of institutionalization and the development and preservation of democratic institutions and civil society needs to be taken up by Critical Theory today.[61] Moreover, following Marcuse's demands that socialism also contain a new way of life, Critical Theory today should take up the issue of socialist humanism and the humanization of society in ways sensitive to environmentalism and consistent with the perspectives of eco-socialism.[62] With these issues in view, one sees that Critical Theory has some definite contributions to make to the problem of combining democracy, ecology and socialism, for Critical Theorists like Marcuse have attempted to humanize the tradition of socialism, while others like Habermas have attempted to democratize it.

Yet many issues remain to be developed within a future repoliticized Critical Theory, such as developing theoretical and political linkages with anti-imperialist movements, consideration of the politics of race and ethnicity, and the politics of health. Sympathy for the oppressed and concern for human suffering require solidarity with oppressed peoples, much of whose oppression derives from the policies and practices of the imperialist superpowers. Here the emphasis on solidarity within some versions of Critical Theory provides linkages between various movements of oppressed people which might help overcome the one-sidedness of many of the new social movements.[63]

In many ways the new social movements highlight some of the blind spots of previous socialist politics in their varying Social Democratic, Communist and ultra-Leftist forms. For many traditional socialist projects have failed to address issues of gender, race, ethnicity or sexual politics. Many varieties of socialism have failed to address environmental concerns or to make peace and arms reduction an important priority. Much socialist politics has neglected culture, as well as the concerns of the individual and everyday life. On the other hand, reflections on some of the more progressive elements of the socialist heritage also show the limitations of the new social movements, which generally lack analysis of the political constraints under which they act. In many of these movements, there are few, if any, linkages between the specific interests articulated by the various movements and more general, or generalizable, interests. In particularistic social movements (any and all of which may fall prey to this problem), few linkages are made between the specific interests or programs advanced and what they have in common with other social movements. A new politics of the future, however, could mediate between a socialist politics and new social movement politics by articulating interests, values and goals held in common, while also articulating and respecting differences between various groups and agendas. This might require a temporary moratorium on attacks on each other by members of socialist and new social movements in favor of the exploration of common goals and ends. It could also involve the formation of new organizations – such as the Austin Peace and Justice Coalition which provides an umbrella organization that attempts to coordinate activities among progressive groups and provide local (or national) coalitions among them.

From this standpoint, the theoretical perspectives of Critical Theory could provide the conceptual means to promote dialogue between the demands and struggles of the most advanced contemporary movements. Such a dialogue might promote consensus around shared issues and concerns and respect for differences, in the interests of promoting a potentially more efficacious counter-movement and counterculture to mainstream political movements. While there has been concern in some quarters that Habermas's emphasis on consensus could lead to authoritarian manipulation and the repression of differences, I would counter that the emphasis on the preservation of individuality and particularity within Critical Theory, militates against repressive political centralization and authoritarian bureaucratic politics – as does its emphasis on democratization.

On the other hand, socialist emphasis on planning and dialectical perspectives on technology and rationalization could help overcome the often technophobic and irrationalist perspectives of some in the new social movements. Rather than simply limiting growth and development, a socialist perspective would call for planned growth in the interests of the majority of the people. Rather than seeking a return to nature or premodernity, socialism would plan for a better future, building on the accomplishments of the past and learning from past mistakes. The dialectical perspectives of a repoliticized Critical Theory could therefore help mediate between the perspectives of a new socialism and those of the new social movements. For these reasons I believe that Critical Theory has many contributions to make to radical politics today, and that a repoliticization of Critical Theory will invigorate, strengthen and radicalize the theory. Such discussions inevitably evoke criticism, however, from those who believe that radical social theory is properly grounded in working-class struggles, movements and organizations.

For traditional and some forms of contemporary Marxism, the proletariat is the privileged agent of revolution or social transformation, and thus – on this view – radical politics should concern itself primarily with the working class, especially the industrial working class, or proletariat, which allegedly has the power to bring the capitalist system to its knees and even to overthrow it. From the late 1930s to the present, Critical Theorists have been extremely skeptical concerning the role of the proletariat within various projects of revolutionary politics, and they were in the forefront of radical theorizing which attempted to develop theories of social transformation which did not depend on the proletariat as a revolutionary subject. Their skepticism concerning the exalted role of the proletariat within the classical Marxian theory of revolution and its pessimism concerning the possibility of a dramatic revolutionary upheaval within contemporary capitalist societies was grounded in a series of empirical studies and theoretical reflections that provided strong arguments for the need for a new politics and a rethinking of the problematic of political transformation toward a post-capitalist world in the most technically (and militarily) advanced capitalist societies.[64]

Yet it must be admitted that failures to carry out a thorough and differentiated class analysis and to investigate the political potentials of different class strata and groups have been among the major deficiencies of Critical Theory. Against those on the Left and the Right who claim that the concept of class is no longer of fundamental importance for social theory and politics,[65] it can be argued that in a curious way, the concept of class has become even more central for radical social theory in the era of technocapitalism. Consequently, it would appear that it is time for a *new class analysis* of the new stratifications and reorganization of the working class, rather than for an abandonment of class analysis and politics.

Against theories of the vanishing or diminishing of class contradictions in contemporary capitalism, recent studies have disclosed that class divisions and distinctions are growing.[66] In particular, the decline of the standard of living of the middle class and the growth of an underclass threaten the stability of contemporary techno-capitalism. Bluestone and Harrison argue, for example, that democratic capitalism requires a large middle strata as the foundation of a stable socio-economic order. Without a large buffer zone between the rich and the poor, the capitalist class and the underclass, a capitalist society is inevitably conflict-ridden and unstable. The dominant trends of social development in recent years, however, are class stratification between a shrinking upper class, a growing underclass and a compression of the middle classes downward such that class divisions and inequalities are increasing rather than diminishing.

The growth of an underclass and the deterioration of the situation of both the industrial working class and the middle class within techno-capitalism raise questions concerning whether a new proletarianization is taking place that may promote and make possible a new class politics. Although earlier Critical Theorists assumed a basic class division within contemporary capitalism, they never undertook any systematic examinations of class and class struggles. The result was a serious political deficit within classical Critical Theory and a failure to connect the theory with struggles actually going on. A new class politics thus involves analysis of the role of unions and organized labor within the social movements of the future, and this is surely one of the areas in which Critical Theory has been most underdeveloped. Such studies also involve more analysis of labor, production and the workplace, including analysis of new technologies. Such studies should return to the investigations of automation by Pollock and others, and should proceed to the present with analysis of the role of information and media, as I suggested in the chapter on techno-capitalism and at the beginning of the discussion in this chapter.

It would be a great mistake, however, to attempt to return to an older class politics at the cost of ignoring the new social movements. Rather, Critical Theory should investigate today the possibilities of a new class politics, the radicalization of the new social movements and the possibilities of fusing a class and cultural politics with the new social movements. None of these alone will be adequate to the demands which the crises of techno-capitalism will pose in the future, as we move into the 1990s. For example, the critique of nuclear weapons in the peace movement directly attacks the prerogatives of some of the most powerful corporations in the military-industrial complex and their militarist sponsors in the state apparatus.

These struggles have an immediate political and economic thrust, and could be linked with other efforts to radically alter the priorities of state budgets and the privileges of certain sectors of corporate capital and to advance struggles for economic conversion from a war to a peace economy.

Consequently, I am suggesting that Critical Theory today should attempt to provide systematic and comprehensive theoretical and political perspectives linked to the radical political movements and struggles of the present age. I shall conclude therefore with some reflections on the meta-theoretical structure of a Critical Theory needed to encompass these theoretical and political concerns.

8.4   For Supradisciplinary Radical Social Theory with a Practical Intent

A repoliticized Critical Theory should return to history and study the crises and struggles of the past decades. Such perspectives will suggest that techno-capitalism is a terrain of struggle between different social forces and tendencies. This sort of historical analysis – rather than abstract philosophical conceptualizations – will provide the grounding for a new Critical Theory, and will show that the values, norms and alternatives advocated by Critical Theory are rooted in existing social movements, tendencies and struggles. Repoliticizing Critical Theory thus involves historicizing it as well.

In this book I have charted the development of efforts to develop a Critical Theory of society by theorists associated with the Institute for Social Research. We have seen that Critical Theory provides a dialectical, totalizing social theory which describes the contours, dynamics and tendencies of the present age, as well as the possibilities for radical social transformation. I have argued that new socio-economic conditions, new configurations of culture and technology, and new social tendencies and developments require a constant updating and revising of Critical Theory and radical politics, and have attempted to make some contributions to clarifying these issues.

I wish to conclude with several brief indications of why I believe that Critical Theory today continues to be relevant to these tasks, and will summarize my positions concerning its limitations. First, I have suggested that Critical Theory provides a set of supradisciplinary inquiries into the many dimensions of social reality and their interconnections within a social system full of contradictions and antagonisms during specific historical eras. Critical Theory thus provides a comprehensive, multidimensional social theory which both builds on and surpasses the limitations of special-ized disciplines. Against empiricist and postmodernist critiques of totalizing social theory, I would argue that Critical Theory provides a much needed framework to carry out social inquiry and critique today, and that its multi-perspectival approach overcomes the one-sidedness of specific disciplines while providing the basis for a more comprehensive, many-sided, multi-dimensional social theory than other competing models.

The most compelling argument against totalizing theories is that a total-izing perspective gives a one-sided, reductive (Hegelian or Marxian or Weberian or whatever) perspective on contemporary social reality, and thus precludes more multidimensional approaches. Yet I have argued that Critical Theory is compatible with a multiperspectival approach which allows a multiplicity of perspectives (Marxian, Freudian, Weberian, feminist, post-structuralist and so on) to articulate a complex, multidimen-sional social reality.[67] In addition, its rejection of identity theory and belief in the nonidentity between concept and object rules out all dogmatic, reductionist approaches; while its respect for particularity and individuality militate against repressive totalizing narratives. Yet, with some exceptions, it refuses to fall prey to a nihilistic skepticism concerning the impossibility of conceptualizing contemporary social reality by projecting theoretical perspectives that at least attempt to chart the fundamental tendencies and developments within contemporary society.

Secondly, I have suggested that the specific thematic focuses of Critical Theory center on fundamental problems for social theory today. Earlier stages of Critical Theory focused on such novel and important themes as the merger of the economy and the state in state capitalism, the genesis and nature of fascism and the authoritarian personality, the integration of the working class, the culture industries and the consumer society, the insti-tutionalization of science and technology and many other issues central to critical social theory in the last several decades. In the last two chapters, I have argued that the theoretical framework, categories and methods of Critical Theory make it especially appropriate to addressing such issues as new technologies and their impact on social and class structure, politics and culture and the crises of techno-capitalism. Every era must develop its own radical social theory and politics, and I believe that the tradition of Critical Theory provides an excellent starting point for a new theory of today's techno-capitalism, its crisis tendencies and its potential for emancipatory social transformation. For Critical Theory is a theory of history, and its historical perspectives sensitize it to historical changes, developments and novelties.

Thirdly, in this chapter I have argued that Critical Theory provides an illuminating and useful social theory for radical politics today. Critical Theory is by definition bound up with social critique, and it should return to earlier demands for a unity of theory and practice. Moreover, its themes are relevant to many of the new social movements which have appeared in the last decades, and its systematic, global viewpoint might enable it to play a role in providing a more unified and democratic Left in the future.

Having briefly mentioned its contributions and virtues, I wish to conclude by pointing to some of its limitations and blind spots, and to some of the directions that Critical Theory today should take to overcome these limitations. Critical Theory has frequently been deficient in empirical and historical research, and has often failed to provide clear historical presentations of its theoretical positions. Future Critical Theory should therefore put more effort into empirical and historical research, and to more successfully integrating theoretical and empirical work than it has done in the past. Particularly in the last decade since Marcuse's death, Critical Theory has been overly theoretical and has exhibited both sociological and political deficiencies. This has been a result of the academization of Critical Theory and an excessive focus on its foundations and philosophical components at the expense of developing radical social theory and cultural critique connected to transformative politics.

It seems that as the crisis of philosophy deepens and more analyses of 'the end of philosophy' appear every year,[68] those desperate to save philosophy recycle Critical Theory and distill it in homeopathic doses in an attempt to keep alive the rapidly disintegrating corpus of modern philosophy. Yet another alternative presents itself. One way to reconstruct philosophy in the present age is to carry through new syntheses of philosophy, social theory and radical politics, as was attempted by Critical Theorists in different ways at different stages of development. Thus, rather than subsume social theory into philosophy, Critical Theory today might produce new syntheses of philosophy, social theory, cultural critique and radical politics. In any case, the dimension of substantive social theory has been neglected in recent years by Critical Theorists, and if it is to continue to be relevant to the theoretical and political concerns of the present age, Critical Theory today should provide a systematic and dialectical analysis of the economy, the state and the political realm and its linkages to culture, ideology and everyday life. This Critical Theory of contemporary society would analyze the mediations, connections and contradictions between and within these spheres. Such dialectical analysis involves both making connections and demonstrating the contradictions that provide the opening for political intervention. Traditionally, Critical Theory has been better at making connections than in demonstrating contradictions and openings for political struggle and transformation. The entire tradition of Critical Theory provides parts, or aspects, of a theory of society, and Critical Theory today should reassemble these parts and add new dimensions to provide a Critical Theory of the present age linked with radical politics.

On the other hand, Critical Theory should continue to pursue those tasks in which it has always excelled: cultural theory and ideology critique.

Although it is often argued that Critical Theory overemphasizes culture and the 'superstructures' at the expense of political economy and the 'base', I would argue that techno-capitalism today requires more and better analysis of culture and the superstructures precisely because of the increased importance of culture, technology, media, information, knowledge and ideology (which encompasses all of the above) in ever more domains of social life – indeed, they increasingly constitute the very base of society itself. Moreover, in a society that is increasingly ideological, ideology critique increases in importance and relevance for both social theory and radical politics.

Finally, Critical Theory has traditionally been bound up with the vicissitudes of capitalist modernity and Marxism, and has – in my interpretation at least – provided a series of attempts to reconstruct the Marxian theory to account for and attack new developments within the vicissitudes of capitalist modernity. In view of current postmodern claims that modernity is now over and post-Marxist claims that classical or even neo-Marxism is no longer relevant to the theoretical and political tasks of the present age, Critical Theory needs to address these critiques and to appraise which features of Marxism and modernity continue to be operative and which have been surpassed. This study is only a prolegomenon to such a project, and has proceeded through historical and analytical investigations of the tradition of Critical Theory with the aim of discovering and assembling aspects that could be used by radical social theory and politics today. I have also pointed to those aspects of Critical Theory which I believe to have been historically superseded and transcended. The task now is to proceed with the many theoretical and political tasks of the present age, with careful glances back at where we have been, systematic and critical analyses of where we are, and resolute struggles for a better future.

Notes

Chapter 1 Theory, Politics and History

1 On the history of the Institute for Social Research, which provided the institutional context within which Critical Theory was developed, see Martin Jay, *The Dialectical Imagination* (Boston: Little, Brown and Company, 1973); Helmut Dubiel, *Theory and Politics* (Cambridge, Mass.: MIT Press, 1985); and Rolf Wiggershaus, *Die Frankfurter Schule* (Munich: Hanser, 1986), hereafter *FS*. For the reasons cited in the text, in this study I shall privilege the term 'Critical Theory' rather than 'the Frankfurt School' to describe the Institute's work. Critical Theory will be capitalized to distinguish it from the common use of the term 'critical theory' in the English-speaking world to refer to critical literary or cultural theory. My focus on Critical Theory will force me to neglect the work of other important Institute members such as Karl Wittfogel, Henryk Grossmann, Franz Borkenau, Franz Neumann and Otto Kirchheimer, who were not part of Horkheimer's 'inner circle' and did not usually identify with the notion of Critical Theory.

2 On the features and history of the concept of modernity, see Jean Baudrillard, 'Modernity', *Canadian Journal of Political and Social Theory*, 11, no. 3 (1987), pp. 63–72, and Jürgen Habermas, *The Philosophical Discourse of Modernity* (Cambridge, Mass.: MIT Press, 1987).

3 Habermas, *Modernity*, pp. 4ff.

4 Karl Marx and Frederick Engels, *The Communist Manifesto*, in Marx and Engels, *Collected Works*, vol. 6 (New York: International Publishers, 1976), p. 487 (further page references in text). See the illuminating discussion of this text in relation to the dynamics of modernity in Marshall Berman, *All that is Solid Melts into Air* (New York: Simon and Schuster, 1982), pp. 88ff.

5 On modernity and postmodernity, see Jean-François Lyotard, *The Postmodern Condition* (Minneapolis: University of Minnesota Press, 1984); Fredric Jameson, 'Postmodernism – the Cultural Logic of Capital', *New Left Review*, 174 (1984), pp. 53–93; Arthur Kroker and David Cook, *The Postmodern Scene* (New York: St Martin's Press, 1986); and Jürgen Habermas, *Modernity*.

6   Rudolf Hilferding, *Finance Capital* (London: Routledge & Kegan Paul, 1981).
7   This interpretation of Critical Theory, focusing on Marcuse, informs my book *Herbert Marcuse and the Crisis of Marxism* (London and Berkeley: Macmillan and University of California Press, 1984).
8   David Held, *Introduction to Critical Theory* (Berkeley: University of California Press, 1980). Held stresses the differences between Marcuse, Horkheimer, Adorno, Habermas and others in his exposition. While I too will stress differences between various Critical Theorists and stages of Critical Theory, I will also be concerned to point out similarities and to define the Critical Theory project as a specific alternative to mainstream philosophy and social theory.
9   For Marxian critiques of Critical Theory, see Phil Slater, *Origin and Significance of the Frankfurt School* (London: Routledge & Kegan Paul, 1977); Zoltan Tar, *The Frankfurt School* (New York and London: John Wiley & Sons, 1977); and the issues of *Soviet Studies in Philosophy* on *The Social Philosophy of the Frankfurt School*, 23, no. 4 (Spring 1985) and 24, no. 4 (Spring 1986). For neo-conservative critiques, see Gunther Rohrmoser, *Das Elend der kritischen Theorie* (Freiburg: 1971), and George Friedman, *The Political Philosophy of the Frankfurt School* (Ithaca: Cornell University Press, 1981). On the philosophical roots and normative foundation of Critical Theory, see Seyla Benhabib, *Critique, Norm, and Utopia* (New York: Columbia University Press, 1986). For an overview of the first wave of books on Critical Theory, see Douglas Kellner and Rick Roderick, 'Recent Literature on Critical Theory', *New German Critique*, 23 (Spring–Summer 1981), pp. 141–77.
10 This periodization is similar to that presented by Tom Bottomore, *The Frankfurt School* (London and New York: Tavistock Publications, 1984).
11 Dubiel, *Theory and Politics*, distinguishes between: (1) an early 'materialism' phase distinguished by commitment to a materialist social theory defined by the unity of philosophy and science which characterized this position from 1930 to 1936; (2) a second phase when the Institute adopted the term 'Critical Theory' to characterize its enterprise and self-consciously developed a Critical Theory of society rooted in the Marxian critique of political economy; and (3) the work on the theory of 'dialectic of enlightenment' developed by Adorno and Horkheimer in the 1940s.
12 Leo Lowenthal, cited in Martin Ludtke, 'The Utopian Motif is Suspended: Conversation with Leo Lowenthal', *New German Critique*, 38 (Spring–Summer 1986), p. 109. On the project of developing a supradisciplinary social theory, see Dubiel, *Theory and Politics*, especially Part 2. In this book, however, I shall not use the term 'interdisciplinary' research as Dubiel does, because of its associations with liberal pluralism today in the United States, and will instead refer to Critical Theory as a supradisciplinary or multidisciplinary research project.
13 For further elaboration, see my 'Boundaries and Borderlines: Reflections on Jean Baudrillard and Critical Theory', *Current Perspectives in Social Theory*, vol. 9 (1989), pp. 5–22.
14 Against Critical Theory, certain 'postmodern' social theories like that espoused by Lyotard, *Postmodern Condition*, want to throw out 'grand narratives' and totalizing social theory in favor of microtheory and 'smaller narratives'. Since

I believe that some of Critical Theory's most interesting contributions are bound up with their grand narratives and macrotheories, I will argue later that it would be a mistake to reject this sort of social theory. On the limitations of postmodern social theory, see my 'Postmodernism as Social Theory: Some Challenges and Problems', *Theory, Culture & Society*, 5, nos 2–3 (June 1988).

15 On the context of the German revolution and the turmoil in Germany during the early Weimar Republic, see my *Karl Korsch: Revolutionary Theory* (Austin: University of Texas Press, 1977).

16 For biographical material on the involvement of Institute members in World War I and the German revolution and their turn to Marxism, see Jay, *Dialectical Imagination*; Kellner, *Herbert Marcuse*; and Wiggershaus, *FS*.

17 The sources in n. 16 also document the influence of the Russian revolution on the Institute's 'inner circle'.

18 Georg Lukács, *History and Class Consciousness* (Cambridge, Mass.: MIT Press, 1971), and Karl Korsch, *Marxism and Philosophy* (New York: Monthly Review Press, 1971). For a good overview of Korsch, Lukács and Western Marxism as the origins of Critical Theory, see Jay, *Marxism and Totality* (Berkeley: University of California Press, 1984).

19 See Korsch, *Marxism*, and my discussion in *Karl Korsch*.

20 For the 'Western Marxist' critique of orthodox Marxism, see Maurice Merleau-Ponty, *Adventures of the Dialectic* (Evanston: Northwestern University Press, 1973), and Russell Jacoby, *Dialectic of Defeat* (Cambridge: Cambridge University Press, 1981).

21 On the 'philosophy of praxis,' see Merleu-Ponty, *Adventures*.

22 Interestingly, in the early days of the Institute Horkheimer planned to write a book on 'Die Krise des Marxismus'. This project is cited by Wiggershaus, though he does not provide details of what Horkheimer had in mind (*FS*, p. 50).

23 On Felix Weil and the founding of the Institute for Social Research, see Jay, *Marxism*, pp. 5ff., and Wiggershaus, *FS*, pp. 19ff.

24 For Grunberg's inaugural address, see 'Festrede gehalten zur Einweihung des Instituts für Sozialforschung an der Universität Frankfurt a. M. am 22 Juni 1924', in *Frankfurter Universitätsreden 1924*; reprinted in Max Horkheimer and Carl Grunberg, *Anfänge der Kritischen Theorie* (Frankfurt: Bauers Nachdruck Verlag, 1972), pp. 1–16. On Grunberg, see Jay, *Dialectic Imagination*, pp. 9ff., and Wiggershaus, *FS*, pp. 33ff.

25 On the political affiliations of Institute members, see Jay, *Dialectical Imagination*, pp. 4ff., and *FS*, pp. 45ff. Debate continues as to whether Felix Weil, Horkheimer, Pollock and others belonged to the Communist Party. All three denied it in later years, and no convincing evidence exists to document that they were indeed party members. Likewise, despite frequent allegations that the Soviet Union helped fund the Institute, no convincing proof exists to document the claim, although a close relationship developed between the Institute and the Marx-Engels Institute in Moscow.

26 *FS*, p. 46.

27 On Horkheimer's central role within the Institute, see Jay, *Dialectical Imagination*, pp. 24ff. and *passim*; Dubiel, *Theory and Politics*, *passim*; and *FS*, pp. 49ff. On Horkheimer's life and thought, see Helmut Gumnior and Rudolf Ringhuth,

Horkheimer (Hamburg: Rowohlt, 1973), and the collection of essays *Max Horkheimer heute: Werk und Wirkung*, edited by Alfred Schmidt and Norbert Altwicker (Frankfurt: Fisher, 1986), which contains a full bibliography. No biography or major critical study devoted to Horkheimer exists in English.

28 Heinrich Regius (pseudonym for Max Horkheimer), *Dammerung* (Zurich: Verlag Oprecht & Helbling, 1934); selections translated by Michael Shaw in Horkheimer, *Dawn and Decline. Notes 1926–1931 and 1950–1969* (New York: Seabury, 1978). I shall cite the pagination of *Dawn and Decline* (hereafter *D&D*) in parentheses within the text, though I sometimes alter the translations.

29 The concern for human suffering appears to have been a chief determinant of Horkheimer's radicalization, and remains a motif that runs through his entire work. For early passages which disclose an extreme sensitivity to suffering, especially of the working class, see Gumnior and Ringhuth, *Horkheimer*, pp. 7ff., and his early novels, stories, notebooks and plays collected in *Aus der Pubertät* (Munich: Kosel, 1974).

30 There have been significant differences among interpreters and critics as to whether the Institute's distance from the politics of the day was a benefit or a liability, and the extent to which its members were active in politics. Dubiel, *Theory and Politics*, documents their various positions as regards fascism, communism and the political issues of the day, but focuses on their interdisciplinary research apparatus. Jay, *Dialectical Imagination*, stresses the benefits to their theoretical work of distance from immediate political engagement; while Slater, *Origin and Significance*, and conventional Marxists criticize their distance from organized politics, and Wiggershaus, *FS*, stresses the extent to which Horkheimer avoided taking explicit political positions on the issues of the day, especially during the exile period.

31 Horkheimer, 'Die gegenwärtige Lage der Sozialphilosophie und die Aufgaben eines Instituts für Sozialforschung', in *Anfänge*, pp. 17–31: also in Horkheimer, *Sozialphilosophische Studien* (Frankfurt: Fisher, 1972), and I shall translate and cite pagination to this edition. The first English translation will appear in *Politics, Culture and Society: A Critical Theory Reader*, edited by Stephen Eric Bronner and Douglas Kellner (New York: Methuen, 1989).

32 Original publication details for these books are given in *FS*, p. 739.

33 The text was translated as Erich Fromm, *The Working Class in Weimar Germany* (Cambridge, Mass.: Harvard University Press, 1984), and page references to the text will be cited from the English edition.

34 Ibid. Fromm's split with the Institute is a matter of controversy, and has never been systematically investigated. His later distance from the Institute and the growing hostility between him and its members have led to a downplaying and distortion of his contributions to Critical Theory. See Wolfgang Bonss's introduction to Fromm, *The Working Class*, pp. 2ff.; Jay, *Dialectical Imagination*, pp. 101ff.; and *FS*, pp. 298ff. and *passim*, for some details.

35 To many observers the Institute appeared as a highly orthodox center of Marxism. An American visitor wrote to Max Eastman complaining of spending 'hours of exasperating argument in a Marxist Institute with a younger generation settling down to an orthodox religion and the worship of an iconographical literature, not to mention blackboards full of mathematical juggling

with blocks of 1000 k and 400 w of Marx's divisions of capital's functions, and the like' (cited in Jay, *Dialectical Imagination*, p. 12). See the more positive recollections cited in *FS*, which recall that the emphasis on Marxism was highly exciting and liberating in the conservative atmosphere of German intellectual life.

36 Compare Grunberg, 'Festrede', with Horkheimer, 'Lage'.

Chapter 2   From Supradisciplinary Materialism to Critical Theory

1 Dubiel, *Theory and Politics*, p. 17.

2 On the Institute critique of the sciences and positivism, see Albrecht Wellmer, *Critical Theory of Society* (New York: Seabury, 1974). On its critique of the dominant philosophical currents of the day, see Jay, *Dialectical Imagination*, and Hauke Brunkhorst, 'Dialektischer Positivismus des Glucks', *Zeitschrift für Philosophische Forschung*, 39, no. 8 (1985), pp. 353–81.

3 Horkheimer, 'Materialism and Metaphysics', in *Critical Theory* (hereafter *CT*) (New York: Herder and Herder, 1972), p. 34. For English-speaking students beginning the study of Critical Theory, I would propose that, after reading the translation of Horkheimer's *Dammerung* in *Dawn and Decline*, they read the essays of Horkheimer translated in *Critical Theory* and then Marcuse's 1930s essays in *Negations* (hereafter *N*) (Boston: Beacon Press, 1968) for the key texts of the first phase of Critical Theory.

4 Horkheimer, 'A New Concept of Ideology?', originally published as 'Ein neuer Ideologiebegriff?' in *Grunbergs Archiv*, 15, no. 1 (1930); page references in the text refer to the original German publication. Thanks to Gerd Schroeter for providing me with his forthcoming translation which I drew upon.

5 For a polemical discussion of the various critiques of Mannheim by the Institute for Social Research, see the exchange between Martin Jay and James Schmidt in *Telos*, 21 (Fall 1974), pp. 168–79, and *Telos*, 22 (Winter 1974–5), pp. 106–17. It might be noted here that Lukács was a strong influence on both Mannheim, who might be read in this context as a Right Wing Lukácsian, and the Institute, which might be interpreted as carrying forward a Left (early) Lukácsianism.

6 See Wilhelm Dilthey, *Pattern and Meaning in History* (New York: Harper and Row, 1962).

7 Interestingly, Mannheim cut the more metaphysical passages that were the target of Horkheimer's polemic from his later English translation. Compare Karl Mannheim, *Ideologie und Utopie* (Bonn: F. Cohen, 1929), with *Ideology and Utopia* (New York: Harcourt, Brace & World, 1936).

8 On the concept of ideology and ideology critique, see Marx and Engels, *The German Ideology*, in *Collected Works*, vol. 5 (New York: International Publishers, 1975), as well as my 'Ideology, Marxism, and Advanced Capitalism', *Socialist Review*, 42 (Nov.–Dec. 1978), pp. 37–65, and John Thompson, *Studies in the Theory of Ideology* (Berkeley: University of California Press, 1984).

9 See Jay, *Dialectical Imagination*, for a fine discussion of the Institute's ideology critiques of *Lebensphilosophie*, existentialism, pragmatism, positivism, etc. I do

not agree with Jay, however, that Critical Theory was developed essentially in dialogue with other positions (p. 41), and in this book I am stressing the project of developing a supradisciplinary social theory as the fundamental defining feature of Critical Theory.

10 On the *Zeitschrift* as the platform for the Institute's common social theory, see Jay, *Dialectical Imagination*, pp. 26ff.; Alfred Schmidt, 'Die *Zeitschrift für Sozialforschung*. Geschichte und gegenwartige Bedeutung', in *Zur Idea der kritischen Theorie* (Munich: Hanser, 1974); and Habermas, 'The Frankfurt School in New York', in *Foundations of the Frankfurt School of Social Research*, edited by Judith Marcus and Zoltan Tar (New Brunswick, NJ.: Transaction Books, 1984), pp. 55–66.

11 *FS*, p. 136.

12 Horkheimer, 'Bemerkungen über Wissenschaft und Krise', *Zeitschrift für Sozialforschung*, 1, nos. 1–2, pp. 1–7; translated in *CT*; and Friedrich Pollock, 'Die gegenwartige Lage des Kapitalismus und die Aussichten einer planwirtschaftlichen Neuordnung', *Zeitschrift*, 1, nos. 1–2, pp. 8–27. Erich Fromm, 'Über Methode und Aufgabe einer analytischen Sozialpsychologie', *Zeitschrift*, 1, nos. 1–2, pp. 28–54; T. W. Adorno, 'Zur gesellschaftlichen Lage der Musik', *Zeitschrift*, 1, nos. 1–2, pp. 103–24; and Lowenthal, 'Zur gesellschaftlichen Lage der Literatur', *Zeitschrift*, 1, nos. 1–2, pp. 85–102.

13 Horkheimer, 'Vorwort', *Zeitschrift*, 1, p. 1; (further page references in text).

14 I reject Brunkhorst's claim in 'Dialektischer Positivismus', that Horkheimer at the time was 'anti-philosophy' (p. 357), or that he performed 'a *sublation (Aufhebung)* of philosophy into science' (p. 379). Instead, I am arguing that *all* phases of Critical Theory are characterized by a synthesis, a dialectical mediation, of science and philosophy, although the relationship is portrayed differently at different stages – an issue to which I shall return later.

15 Throughout his career, Horkheimer would present different, usually aphoristic, notions of philosophy and science and their relationships. Compare, e.g., *CT*, pp. 34ff., 182ff. and 188ff. Consequently, his concepts of philosophy, science and their relationships are constantly shifting.

16 Horkheimer, 'Materialism and Morality', *Telos*, 69 (Fall 1986), pp. 85–118 (further page references in text). See also Herbert Schnadelbach, 'Max Horkheimer and the Moral Philosophy of German Idealism', *Telos*, 66 (Winter 1985–6), pp. 81–104, for a useful contextualization of Horkheimer's ethics in relation to the ethical theory of German idealism. Schnadelbach, however, does not emphasize the importance of the relationships in Horkheimer between compassion and suffering, and ethics and politics, that I am focusing on. On Horkheimer's commitment to a eudaemonistic ethics, see 'Materialism and Morality', pp. 93ff., and Gerard Raulet, 'Remarks on Horkheimer's Pessimism', *Telos*, 42 (Winter 1979–80), which stresses the influence of Schopenhauer's ethics on Horkheimer.

17 Schnadelbach, 'Horkheimer', p. 92. Schnadelbach cites a passage from *Dialectic of Enlightenment* (hereafter *DoE*) in which Horkheimer and Adorno argue that compassion represents a 'naturalized mediation' of 'the sensuous consciousness of the identity of general and particular', and thus is a reasonable basis for ethics, because 'this form of mediation was the only one "that was left

after the formalization of reason" ' (p. 92). For Horkheimer's attempt to provide a materialist reinterpretation of Kant's categorical imperative, see 'Materialism and Morality', pp. 95ff.

18   On this theme, see also Horkheimer, 'Egotism and the Freedom Movement', *Telos*, 54 (Winter 1982-3), pp. 10-60.

19   On the project of developing a synthesis of Marx and Freud, see Jay, *Dialectical Imagination*, pp. 86ff.; Russell Jacoby, *Social Amnesia* (Boston: Beacon Press, 1975); and esp. the anthology *Marxismus, Psychoanalyse, Sex-Pol*, 2 vols. (Frankfurt: Fisher, 1970), which highlights the role of Siegfried Bernfeld, Wilhelm Reich and the Critical Theorists as early adherents of the attempt to develop a Freudo-Marxism, a project later taken up by French theorists such as Lyotard, Deleuze, Guattari, etc.

20   See the essays by Fromm in his book *The Crisis of Psychoanalysis* (hereafter *CoP*) (New York: Fawcett, 1970), pp. 109-88. Fromm's important role during the earlier stages of the development of Critical Theory has been underestimated by most interpreters. His contributions deserve to be studied in much more detail than has previously been the case.

21   Fromm, 'The Method and Function of an Analytic Social Psychology', in *CoP*, pp. 137-62.

22   Fromm, 'Psychoanalytic Characterology and Its Relevance for Social Psychology', in *CoP*, pp. 163-88.

23   Fromm, *Man for Himself* (New York: Holt, Rinehart & Winston, 1947), and *idem, The Sane Society* (New York: Holt, Rinehart & Winston, 1955).

24   Fromm, 'The Theory of Mother Right and its Relevance for Social Psychology', in *CoP*, pp. 109-36.

25   See Nancy Chodorow, *The Reproduction of Mothering* (Berkeley: University of California Press, 1978).

26   See Fromm, Horkheimer et al., *Autorität und Familie* (Paris: Alcan, 1936).

27   Horkheimer, 'Authority and Family', in *CT*.

28   Fromm continued to develop these themes in his later work. See Rainer Funk, *The Courage to Be Human* (New York: Continuum, 1982).

29   Dubiel, *Theory and Politics*, p. 42.

30   Marcuse, 'Philosophy and Critical Theory', in *N*, pp. 144-5.

31   Horkheimer, 'Traditional and Critical Theory', in *CT*, pp. 188-252. On the supradisciplinary research program outlined in this article, see Dubiel, *Theory and Politics*, pp. 119ff.

32   For elaborations of this position, see Alfred Söhn-Rethel, *Intellectual and Manual Labor* (London: Macmillan, 1978), and Robert Young, 'Science as Social Relations', *Radical Science Journal*, 5 (1977), pp. 65-131.

33   On varying uses of the concept of 'totality', see Jay, *Marxism and Totality*. New French Theory tends to draw semantic and theoretico-political connections between 'totality' and 'totalitarian', and to reject totalizing modes of thought as inherently repressive, reductionist and totalitarian. See, e.g., Lyotard, *Postmodern Condition*, and Mark Poster, *Foucault, Marxism & History* (Cambridge: Polity Press, 1984). Such broadside polemics erase differences between varying concepts and uses of totality, however, and cover over the multiplicity of modes of totalizing theories.

34 Horkheimer, *Autorität und Familie*, pp. 899 and 903.
35 Horkheimer, 'Postscript', in *CT*, pp. 244–53.
36 On the primacy of production in Marxism, see Marx, *Grundrisse* (Harmondsworth: Penguin Books, 1973), and *idem, Capital* (New York: International Publishers, 1967).
37 Dubiel, *Theory and Politics*, p. 53.

Chapter 3   Economy, State, Society

1 Andrew Arato, Introduction to *The Essential Frankfurt School Reader* (hereafter *FSR*) (New York: Seabury, 1982). Perry Anderson and Goran Thorburn have both argued that the Frankfurt School replaced political economy with philosophy and neglected empirical and historical analysis. See Anderson, *Western Marxism* (London: New Left Books, 1974), and Thorburn, 'The Frankfurt School', in *The Western Marxism Reader* (London: New Left Books, 1976). This position is also argued in Bottomore, *Frankfurt School*, and is contested both by Dubiel, *Theory and Politics*, who stresses the role of social science and research in Critical Theory, and by Arato and Eike Gebhardt in *FSR* (further page references in text).
2 The best Lukács scholarship – that of Arato and Breines, Feenberg, Lowi, Jay, and others – has pointed to Lukács's affinity with Critical Theory, and the best scholarship into the Institute for Social Research has also stressed the importance of Lukács.
3 Lukács, 'Reification and the Consciousness of the Proletariat', in *Class Consciousness*.
4 Lukács, *Class Consciousness*. See my study of the trajectory from Weber to Lukács to Critical Theory, 'Critical Theory, Max Weber, and the Dialectics of Domination', in *The Weber-Marx Dialogue*, edited by Robert J. Antonio and Ronald M. Glassman (Lawrence: University of Kansas Press, 1985), pp. 89–116.
5 On Critical Theory's attempts to redeem the particular and its attacks on totalizing thought which abstracts from and neglects particulars, see the study of Adorno and Benjamin in Susan Buck-Morss, *The Origins of Negative Dialectics* (New York: Free Press, 1977).
6 Lukács, *Class Consciousness*, p. 88.
7 See ibid. and Kellner, 'Critical Theory and Weber'.
8 On the Institute's presentation of the Marxist theory of capitalist crisis and collapse, see Grossmann, *Das Akkumulations- und Zusammenbruchsgesetz des kapitalistischen Systems* (Leipzig: Institut für Sozialforschung, 1929), and Pollock, 'Bemerkungen zur Wirtschaftskrise', *Zeitschrift*, 2 (1933), pp. 321–54 (hereafter cited in text as Pollock 1933). For commentary on these theories and comparison with other Marxian theory of crisis, see Giacomo Marramao, 'Political Economy and Critical Theory', *Telos*, 24 (Summer 1975), pp. 56–80, and Russell Jacoby, 'The Politics of the Crisis Theory', *Telos*, 23 (Spring 1975), pp. 3–52.
9 Pollock, 'Die gegenwartige Lage des Kapitalismus und die Aussichten einer

planwirtschaftlichen Neuordung', in *Zeitschrift*, 1 (1932), pp. 8–27 (cited hereafter in the text as Pollock 1932); Kurt Baumann, 'Autarkie und Planwirtschaft', *Zeitschrift*, 2 (1933), pp. 79–103; Kurt Mandelbaum, 'Neue Literatur zur Planwirtschaft', *Zeitschrift*, 4 (1935), pp. 81ff.; Gerhard Meyer, 'Krisenpolitik und Planwirtschaft', *Zeitschrift*, 4 (1935), pp. 398ff.; and Erich Baumann, 'Keynes Revision der liberalistischen Nationalokonomie', *Zeitschrift*, 5, no. 1 (1936), pp. 384–403. On Pollock, see Jay, *Dialectical Imagination*, pp. 5ff.; *FS*, pp. 76ff.; and the articles by Brick and Postone cited in n. 5 below.

10 His report was published as Pollock, *Die planwirtschaftlichen Versuche in der Sowjetunion 1917–1927* (Leipzig: Institut für Sozialforschung, 1929).

11 Pollock 1932.

12 Grossmann, *Zusammenbruchsgesetz*.

13 Pollock 1933, *Zeitschrift*, and *idem*, 'State Capitalism', *Studies in Philosophy and Social Science*, 9 (1941), pp. 200–25; reprinted in *FSR*, from which I shall cite page numbers in text.

14 Yet, in n. 32 (*FSR*, p. 176), Pollock doubts 'whether our model of state capitalism fits the Soviet Union in its present phase'. In general the Institute did not publicly criticize the Soviet Union during the 1930s; nor did it critically discuss the construction of socialism in that country or participate in the debates over the nature of the system being developed. For Institute references to the Soviet Union during this period, see Dubiel, *Theory and Politics*. A left-Trotskyist tendency, however, utilized the term 'state capitalism' to describe the form of political economy in the USSR; see Raya Dunayevskaya, 'Russia as State-Capitalist Society', *News & Letters* pamphlet (1973; reprint of 1940s articles), and her later development of the theory in *Marxism and Freedom* (New York: Columbia University Press, 1988; orig. 1958). See also C. L. R. James, *State Capitalism and World Revolution* (Chicago: Charles Kerr, 1986; orig. 1950).

15 See Barbara Brick and Moishe Postone, 'Friedrich Pollock and the "Primacy of the Political": A Critical Examination', *International Journal of Politics*, 6, no. 3 (Fall 1976), pp. 3–28, and *idem*, 'Critical Pessimism and the Limits of Traditional Marxism', *Theory and Society*, 11, no. 5 (Sept. 1982), pp. 617–58.

16 Franz Neumann, *Behemoth* (New York: Oxford University Press, 1942 and 1944) (hereafter *B*).

17 See the later discussion in Chapters 7 and 8 of the relationship between politics and economics in the capitalist state in Offe's and Habermas's work, where I cite contemporary literature and debates on this topic.

18 Brick and Postone, 'Friedrich Pollock', p. 16. Such a framework also makes it impossible to criticize the construction of socialism in supposedly socialist societies which, like the Soviet Union, might have institutionalized something like a socialist mode of distribution, but without eliminating alienated labor, social hierarchy and domination in the workplace or community.

19 Horkheimer, 'The End of Reason', *Zeitschrift*, 9 (1941), pp. 366–88; reprinted in *FSR*, from which I shall cite page numbers in the text.

20 Marcuse, 'Some Social Implications of Modern Technology', *Zeitschrift*, 9 (1941), pp. 414ff.; reprinted in *FSR*, from which I shall cite in the text.

21 See my *Herbert Marcuse*, p. 96, and Marcuse, 'The Struggle against Liberalism in the Totalitarian View of the State', in *N*.

22 Horkheimer, 'Die Juden und Europa', *Zeitschrift*, 6 (1939), pp. 115–37, translated by Mark Ritter, in Bronner and Kellner, *Politics, Culture, and Society*.

23 See Pollock, 'Is National Socialism a New Order?' in *Zeitschrift*, 9 (1941), pp. 440–55, and Neumann, *Behemoth*. For the debates between Pollock and Neumann over the interpretations of fascism and the concepts of state capitalism and the primacy of the political, see the articles by Brick and Postone cited in n. 15; Alfons Söllner, *Geschichte und Herrschaft* (Frankfurt: Suhrkamp, 1979), pp. 139ff.; *idem* and Dubiel, Introduction to their collection of Institute essays on fascism, *Wirtschaft, Recht, und Staat im Nationalsozialismus* (Frankfurt: Europäische Verlagsanstalt, 1981), pp. 11ff.; and *FS*, pp. 214ff. My position in this debate is that it is a mistake to dogmatically posit either 'the primacy of the economic' or 'the primacy of the political', and that a more dialectical analysis of the interaction between economic and political factors in the constitution of fascism provides a less problematic approach. Careful reading of the key essays in the debate shows, as I shall attempt to demonstrate below, that, except for some one-sided claims by Pollock concerning the primacy of the political, most of the Institute analyses of fascism are characterized by dialectical analysis of the interconnection of political and economic factors in the constitution of the new syntheses of the state and the economy visible by the 1930s.

24 Pollock 1933, pp. 321ff.

25 For the reception of *Behemoth*, see Söllner, *Geschichte*, pp. 139ff.

26 See ibid. and the article by A. R. L. Gurland, 'Technological Trends and Economic Structure under National Socialism', *Zeitschrift*, 9 (1941), pp. 226ff. which tends to support Neumann's analysis of the continued capitalistic nature of the Nazi economy.

27 Kirchheimer, 'Changes in the Structure of Political Compromise', *Zeitschrift*, 9 (1941), pp. 264ff.; reprinted in *FSR*, from which I shall cite in the text.

28 Marcuse, 'Some Social Implications of Modern Technology'.

29 Horkheimer, 'Preface', *Zeitschrift*, 9 (1941), pp. 195ff. (further page references in text).

30 The article was originally published in 1942 in a private collection of essays to commemorate the death of Walter Benjamin, and was not publically distributed. It is reprinted in *FSR*, from which I shall cite in the text.

31 The Institute resolved to publicly refrain from criticism of the Soviet Union because it feared that such criticism would only strengthen anti-communism and weaken the Left; some Institute members were far more sympathetic than others. See Jay, *Dialectical Imagination*; Dubiel, *Theory and Politics*; and *FS* for discussion. The first systematic discussion and critique of the Soviet Union by an Institute member was Marcuse's *Soviet Marxism*; see my Introduction to the 1985 Columbia University Press reprint.

32 'Workers' Councils' (*Arbeitersräte*) were the institutional form of workers' self-management, modeled on the Russian 'Soviets', which emerged as the preferred institution for the construction of socialism with certain segments of the Left. See my discussion in *Karl Korsch*.

33 *FS*, pp. 314ff., documents the general rejection of Pollock's concept of state capitalism within the Institute, and suggests that Horkheimer urged the publication of the essay partly because he agreed with much of it and partly

because he wanted his good friend Pollock to play a more active theoretical role in Institute debates, so loyally stood by him despite some misgivings concerning the concept. I shall argue here that the notion of state capitalism is one of the Institute's more questionable conceptions, and that it contains aspects of the Institute's later pessimism concerning the impossibility of radical social transformation and social progress in contemporary capitalist societies.

34   Adorno to Horkheimer, in *FS*, pp. 316–17.

35   See also ibid., pp. 319ff.

36   See ibid., p. 319.

37   One of the few references to the New Deal and the 'democratic capitalist' state form in the United States from the Institute's inner circle is found in Horkheimer's Preface to a 1941 issue of *Zeitschrift*, where he writes:

> For more than eight years the government of this country has attempted to overcome the difficulties of the prevailing economy by incorporating into it the elements of planning, in the industrial as well as the agricultural sector. The alarming predicament of agriculture in Germany under the Weimar Republic was an important factor in the rise of fascism. In this the government of the United States has recognized the danger and has attempted to bring agriculture under its control. The same holds true for other sectors of economic life. . . . The unprecedented governmental power necessarily associated with state capitalism is now in the hands of a democratic and humanitarian administration. It will be the goal of fascist groups within and without to wrest it away, and it is not too much to expect that the coming years will be marked by such attempts. (pp. 198–9)

38   In programmatic statements Horkheimer frequently refers to the general theory of society that informs the Institute's analyses and is currently being produced. For example, in the Introduction to *Studies on Authority and the Family*, he writes that 'the range of questions treated by the studies will attain their true meaning only in a comprehensive theory of social life – in which these questions are embedded'. Or, 'The term *social research* does not propose to draw in new borders on the map of the sciences. Research in the most diverse areas and at the most diverse levels of abstraction . . . is united by the goal of furthering the theory of contemporary society as a whole' (both cited in Dubiel, *Theory and Politics*, pp. 165 and 179). Yet I would argue that the Institute never really produced this general theory, of which only fragments actually appeared.

39   See ibid. Wiggershaus is much more skeptical concerning the degree to which the Institute ever intended to genuinely merge theory with revolutionary politics. Yet his book and other studies of the Critical Theorists indicate that several Institute members were politically active in the Weimar Republic, while others – including Horkheimer – were hardly ever actively engaged in actual political movements and struggles.

40   Horkheimer, p. 198.

41   Jay, *Dialectical Imagination*, p. 31.

42   Tar, *The Frankfurt School*, pp. 181–9. See also Tar's discussion in his Introduction to *Foundations of the Frankfurt School of Social Research*, pp. 3ff., where he stresses once again the fundamentality of the Institute's Jewish roots.

43   George Friedman, *Political Philosophy*, pp. 92–102 and *passim*.

44   On the Institute's institutional alliance with Columbia University while in

exile, see Jay, *Dialectical Imagination*, pp. 39ff., 114ff. and *passim*, and Wiggers-haus, *Geschichte*, pp. 166ff. and *passim*. Columbia University's generosity was attacked in an article by Lewis Feuer, who saw its hospitality in terms of liberals being duped by Marxist radicals. See Feuer, 'The Frankfurt Marxists and the Columbia Liberals', *Survey* (Summer 1980), pp. 156–76. Feuer's distortions are criticized in a sharp reply by Jay, 'Misrepresentations of the Frankfurt School: A Reply to Lewis Feuer', *Survey* (Summer 1982), pp. 131–70.

45   On the difficulties faced by the German exile community, see Henry Pachter, 'On Being an Exile', in *Weimar Etudes* (New York: Columbia University Press, 1982), pp. 311–61, and Anthony Heilbut, *Exiles in Paradise* (Boston: Beacon Press, 1983).

46   Adorno, *Minima Moralia* (hereafter *MM*) (London: New Left Books), p. 18.

Chapter 4   From *Dialectic of Enlightenment* to *The Authoritarian Personality*

1   Although Herder and Herder and Seabury are to be praised for translating and publishing *DoE*, the translation is uneven, and the text should probably be retranslated. For useful readings of the text, see Jay, *Dialectical Imagination*; Dubiel, *Theory and Politics*; Wiggershaus, *FS*.

2   One of the major themes of Wiggershaus's *Die Frankfurter Schule* is the long-term plan of the Institute to write a definitive book on dialectics. His study documents how the plan was conceived in the early 1930s, continued into the 1940s and was finally pursued by Adorno and Horkheimer in the project that became *DoE*. Wiggershaus shows how various key Institute members, as well as outsiders like Karl Korsch, were involved in the project at one stage or another, and suggests that one of Horkheimer's motivations in effectively dissolving the Institute in the early 1940s was his desire to, at last, with Adorno, write the envisaged book on dialectics. See *FS*, pp. 338ff. and *passim*.

3   On Adorno, see Buck-Morss, *Negative Dialectics*; Gillian Rose, *The Melancholy Science* (London: Macmillan, 1978); and Jay, *Adorno* (Cambridge, Mass.: Harvard University Press, 1984). For an insightful analysis of the collaboration between Adorno and Horkheimer, see Habermas, 'Bemerkungen zur Entwick-lungsgeschichte des Horkheimerschen Werkes', in *Max Horkheimer heute*, pp. 163–79.

4   On the method of juxtaposition and illumination which Adorno may have gleaned from Walter Benjamin, see Buck-Morss, *Negative Dialectics*. She suggests that there were two dominant models for Critical Theory in the 1930s, that of Benjamin and Adorno, which utilized philosophy, cultural inter-pretation and a method of illumination and juxtaposition to reveal social truth, and that of Horkheimer and Marcuse, who maintained the Institute position that a synthesis of philosophy and the social sciences presented the model of critical social theory. In the 1940s, Adorno did some work in the social sciences (see 4.4 below), while Horkheimer came to share more positions with Adorno,

thus making it more difficult to specify contrasting methodological models within Critical Theory.

5   In a letter to Lowenthal, written in 1942, Horkheimer wrote: 'Enlightenment here is identical with bourgeois thought, nay, thought in general, since there is no other thought properly speaking than in cities' (cited in Jay, *Dialectical Imagination*, p. 258). This passage suggests that Horkheimer saw a profound connection between bourgeois thought and society and 'enlightenment'. Walter Benjamin also saw the historical specificity of the Institute work in terms of a critique of bourgeois thought when he wrote, 'The workers of the Institute for Social Research converge in a critique of bourgeois consciousness. This critique takes place not from without, but as self-criticism' (cited in Jay, *Dialectical Imagination*, p. 292).

6   For interpretations of this position that are somewhat clearer and easier to follow, see Horkheimer, *The Eclipse of Reason* (New York: Oxford University Press, 1947; repub. 1972); Herbert Marcuse, *One-Dimensional Man* (Boston: Beacon Press, 1964), hereafter *ODM*; and William Leiss, *The Domination of Nature* (Boston: Beacon Press, 1975). I shall discuss Horkheimer's presentation below in 4.2 and have already discussed Marcuse's in my *Herbert Marcuse*.

7   Both Adorno and Horkheimer wavered between more radical breaks with Enlightenment rationality and attempts to defend a form of critical reason against current forms of irrationalism. Habermas and the second generation of Critical Theorists tended to reject the more radical critiques of Enlightenment, however, and to defend versions of critical reason or communicative rationality. See Habermas, *Modernity*.

8   The connection between mimesis and happiness was a theme of Walter Benjamin's which is also present in Marcuse. See Buck-Morss, *Negative Dialectics*, on Benjamin and Adorno, and Jay's study of Marcuse in *The Concept of Totality*, pp. 220ff.

9   On some connections between Critical Theory and feminism, see Jessica Benjamin, 'The End of Internalization: Adorno's Social Psychology', *Telos*, 32 (Summer 1977), pp. 42–64, and *idem*, 'Authority and the Family Revisited: Or, a World Without Fathers?' *New German Critique*, 13 (Winter 1978), pp. 35–58.

10 Patricia Mills, *Women, Nature and Psyche* (New Haven: Yale University Press, 1987).

11 On the ways in which mind/body and subject/object dichotomies are rooted in the fundamental categories of Western metaphysics, Critical Theory, feminism and Jacques Derrida are in agreement, though the theme of reconciliation with nature is usually dropped and often opposed by deconstructionists.

12 A recent anthology of feminist thought contains many similarities with Critical Theory; see *Rocking the Ship of State. Toward a Feminist Peace Politics*, edited by Adrienne Harris and Ynestra King (Boulder, Colo.: Westview Press, 1989).

13 From the beginning, Habermas and his followers were more sympathetic to science and technology than the earlier generation of Critical Theorists. For further discussion of the debates on science and technology within Critical Theory, see Wellmer, *Critical Theory*, and Fred Alford, *Science and the Revenge of*

Nature (Gainesville: University of Florida Press, 1985).

14 On the relationship between Marxism and science, see the articles in *Radical Science*, 13 (1983).

15 On the more positive views of science in Horkheimer's work from 1930 to 1937, see the discussion in 2.1 and 2.3, as well as Dubiel, *Theory and Politics*, and Brunkhorst, 'Dialektischer Positivismus'. The Institute took very different positions on science and the relationship between philosophy and science in critical social theory at different stages of its development. Yet I disagree with Brunkhorst, who claims that in the earliest stage Horkheimer and his circle were 'anti-philosophy'; for there was always a strong philosophical component in their theory, though by the 1940s it had clearly become superordinate, and their critique of the sciences and science itself was radicalized.

16 Lukács, *Class Consciousness*, pp. 103ff. (further page references in text).

17 See Gareth Stedman Jones, 'The Marxism of the Early Lukács', in *Western Marxism: A Critical Reader* (London: New Left Books, 1977).

18 Friedrich Nietzsche, *On the Genealogy of Morals* (New York: Vintage, 1967). On Nietzsche and Critical Theory, see James Miller, 'Some Implications of Nietzsche's Thought for Marxism', *Telos*, 37 (Fall 1978), pp. 22–41; Peter Putz, 'Nietzsche and Critical Theory', *Telos*, 50 (Winter 1981–2), pp. 103–14; and Nancy S. Love, 'Marx, Nietzsche and Critical Theory', *New German Critique*, 41 (Spring–Summer 1987), pp. 71–94. These studies fail to note the critique of Nietzsche as a theorist of the will to power which Adorno and Horkheimer interpret as part of the dialectic of Enlightenment.

19 See Marx, *Capital*.

20 On modernity in Benjamin, see Buck-Morss, *Negative Dialectics*.

21 On Wittfogel, see Ulmen, *The Science of Society*.

22 Habermas, *Theory of Communicative Action*, vols. 1 and 2 (Boston: Beacon Press, 1981 and 1987), and *idem*, *Modernity*.

23 This point is emphasized by Paul Connerton, *The Tragedy of Enlightenment*. For further discussion of the German sociological tradition and its theories of modernity, see David Frisby, *Fragments of Modernity* (Cambridge: Polity Press, 1985).

24 Hereafter *EoR*. Horkheimer also presents his more optimistic theory of the role of philosophy in social enlightenment in such articles as 'The Social Function of Philosophy', in *CT*, pp. 253–72.

25 Adorno was a much more relentless critic of bourgeois humanism than Horkheimer, who seemed to believe that humanism contained some critical potential in a completely inhuman society. See Jay, 'The Frankfurt School's Critique of Marxist Humanism', *Social Research*, 39, no. 2 (Summer 1972), and Jay, *Adorno*.

26 See Jay, *Adorno*.

27 Adorno, *Minima Moralia*, and *idem*, 'Reflexionen zur Klassentheorie', in *Soziologische Schriften*, vol. 1 (Frankfurt: Suhrkamp, 1972), pp. 373–91 (further page references in text).

28 See Wiggershaus, *FS*, pp. 427ff.

29 Ibid., pp. 429ff.

30   See ibid., p. 430.

31   See ibid., p. 431.

32   Ibid., p. 432.

33   See Kellner, *Herbert Marcuse.*

34   Wiggershaus points out that with Neumann, Kirchheimer and Marcuse in Washington and Fromm, Wittfogel and Grossmann distanced from the Institute in various ways, the 'inner circle' henceforth consisted of Adorno, Horkheimer and Pollock, with Lowenthal as a 'veilseitig verwendbarer mitverschworener Helfer' (*FS*, p. 426).

35   Ibid., pp. 446–7.

36   See ibid., pp. 434ff.

37   Quoted in ibid., p. 435.

38   Consequently, even at his most radical, Adorno never went as far in rejecting Marxian categories as many post-structuralist French theorists. Compare Baudrillard, *The Mirror of Production* (St Louis, Mo.: Telos Press, 1973), and the discussion in my *Jean Baudrillard: From Marxism to Postmodernism and Beyond* (Cambridge: Polity Press, forthcoming).

39   *FS*, p. 439.

40   See ibid., pp. 437ff.

41   Habermas, 'The Inimitable *Zeitschrift für Sozialforschung*', *Telos*, 45 (Fall 1980), p. 116.

42   *FS*, pp. 446ff. and *passim.*

43   Jay reports that 'Horkheimer's lecturing virtuosity – Everett Hughes, who was a visiting professor in Frankfurt during those years, remembers him as the finest German speaker he had ever heard – and his personal warmth in seminars quickly won him a sizable student following' (*Dialectical Imagination*, p. 282). Wiggershaus also documents Horkheimer's skill as a lecturer, as well as his successful integration into the German educational system and society upon his return to Germany (*FS*, pp. 479ff.). It appears that Horkheimer was too successful, however, and that his success contributed to his abandonment of his previous radical perspectives in both social theory and politics.

44   Jay, *Dialectical Imagination*, pp. 220ff., and *FS*, pp. 390ff.

45   Jay, *Dialectical Imagination*, p. 221.

46   Max Horkheimer and Samuel Flowerman, foreword to Adorno et al., *The Authoritarian Personality* (hereafter *AP*) (New York: Norton, 1950).

47   Jay, *Dialectical Imagination*, pp. 238ff., and *FS*, pp. 456ff.

48   Edward Shils, 'Authoritarianism: "Right" and "Left" ', in *Studies in the Scope and Method of* 'The Authoritarian Personality', edited by Richard Christie and Marie Jahoda (Glencoe, Ill.: The Free Press, 1954).

49   Adorno, 'Freudian Theory and the Pattern of Fascist Propaganda', in *FSR.*

50   Jay, *Dialectical Imagination*, pp. 281ff., and *FS*, pp. 479ff.

51   See Adorno et al., *The Positivism Dispute in German Sociology* (London: Heinemann, 1976).

Chapter 5   From 'Authentic Art' to the Culture Industries

1   Adorno, 'Cultural Criticism and Society', in *Prisms* (hereafter *P*) p. 30. Adorno was influenced by the view held by his friend and mentor Siegfried Kracauer that social reality was articulated within works of art which required hermeneutical deciphering. See Kracauer, 'The Mass Ornament', in *New German Critique*, 5 (Spring 1975), pp. 67–76; collected in *Politics, Culture and Society*.

2   See the translations in Adorno, 'On the Social Situation of Music', in *Telos*, 35 (Spring 1978), p. 130, and Lowenthal, 'On Sociology of Literature', in *Literature and Mass Culture* (New Brunswick, N.J.: Transaction Books, 1984) (page references to the latter cited in the text).

3   See, e.g., Adorno, 'On the Social Situation of Music'; *idem*, 'On the Fetish Character of Music and the Regression of Hearing', in *FSR*; and *idem*, 'On Popular Music', *Studies in Philosophy and Social Science*, 9, no. 1 (1941).

4   Walter Benjamin, 'The Work of Art in the Age of Mechanical Reproduction', in *Illuminations* (New York: Schocken, 1969). On Adorno's and Benjamin's shared aesthetic interests and debates, see Buck-Morss, *Negative Dialectics*.

5   Adorno, 'Jazz. Perennial Fashion', in *P*.

6   On the relationship between Lazarsfeld, Adorno and the Institute, see the memoirs of Paul Lazarsfeld, 'An Episode in the History of Social Research: A Memoir', and Adorno, 'Scientific Experiences of a European Scholar in America', both in *The European Migration*, edited by Donald Fleming and Bernard Bailyn (Cambridge, Mass.: 1969), and David E. Morrison, 'Kultur and Culture: The Case of Theodor W. Adorno and Paul F. Lazarsfeld', *Social Research*, 45, no. 2 (Summer 1978), pp. 331–55. Lazarsfeld published over fifty books and many articles that helped to found the new discipline of communications research.

7   Marcuse, 'On Affirmative Culture', in *N*. For further discussion, see my analysis in *Herbert Marcuse*.

8   Lowenthal, 'Popular Culture in Perspective', in *Literature, Popular Culture, and Society* (hereafter cited in the text as *LPCS*) (Englewood Cliffs, N.J.: Prentice-Hall, 1961), p. 4.

9   Adorno, 'commitment', in *Aesthetics and Politics* (London: New Left Books, 1977), pp. 180, 191. The notion of authentic-art-as-negation runs throughout Adorno's writings on art, which generally formulate the notion in paradoxical terms:

> Art records negatively just that possibility of happiness which the only partially positive anticipation of happiness ruinously confronts today. All 'light' and pleasant art has become illusory and mendacious. What makes its appearance esthetically in the pleasure categories can no longer give pleasure, and the promise of happiness, once the definition of art, can no longer be found except where the mask has been torn from the countenance of false happiness. (*FSR*, p. 274)

10   Although Adorno began the Institute critique of mass culture in his analyses of the standardization, pseudo-individuality and manipulative effects of popular music (see the sources cited in n. 2, 3 and 5), Horkheimer spoke of the 'entertainment industry' in several 1930s articles, and analyzed the differences

between 'authentic art' and 'mass culture' in 'Art and Mass Culture', now in *CT*. Lowenthal, who had earlier carried out a study of popular magazine biographies in Germany, analyzed images of success in American magazines, noting a shift from 'heroes of production' to 'heroes of consumption', in which the 'stars' of the culture industry played a major role (in *LPCS*). A 1941 issue, in English, of *Studies in Philosophy and Social Science* (vol. 9, no. 1) was devoted to mass communications, and advanced the notion of 'critical research' which combined 'theoretical thinking with empirical analysis'. Thus the famous study of the 'culture industry' in *DoE* built on earlier work, and highlighted a theme that had become central to Critical Theory.

11   See William Dieterle, 'Hollywood and the European Crisis', in *Studies*, 9, no. 1, pp. 96ff.

12   See Adorno, 'The Culture Industry Revisited', *New German Critique*, 6 (Fall 1975), pp. 11; reprinted in *Politics, Culture, and Society*.

13   Lukács, *Class Consciousness*; Bertolt Brecht, *Gesammelte Schriften*, vol. 18 (Frankfurt: 1967), translated as 'Radio as a Means of Communication', in *Screen*, 20, nos 3–4 (Winter 1979–80), pp. 24–8; and Benjamin, *Illuminations*. On the other hand, the culture industry theory can also be seen as an application to artifacts of mass communications and culture of Lukács's theory of the commodity fetishism and the reification of culture and consciousness in capitalist society, which is then turned against Lukács's political theory by claiming that these phenomena prevent the development of class consciousness, upon which Lukács's theory of revolution depends.

14   On Gramsci's theory of hegemony, see Antonio Gramsci, *Prison Notebooks* (New York: International Publishers, 1971), and Carl Boggs, *The Two Revolutions* (Boston: South End Press, 1984).

15   This is a key theme of *DoE* and *One-Dimensional Man*.

16   See the discussion of the impact of fascism and emigration on Critical Theory in Chapter 3.

17   On the culture industries and the black list, see Victor Navasky, *Naming Names* (New York: Viking, 1980).

18   Adorno, 'How to Look at Television', *The Quarterly of Film, Radio, and Television*, 7 (Spring 1954); republished as 'Television and the Patterns of Mass Culture', in *Mass Culture*, edited by Bernard Rosenberg and David Manning White (Glencoe, Ill.: The Free Press, 1957). Interestingly, Horkheimer and Adorno also anticipated in the early 1940s that television would become the most powerful part of the culture industry:

> Television aims at a synthesis of radio and film, and is held up only because the interested parties have not yet reached agreement, but its consequences will be quite enormous and promise to intensify the impoverishment of aesthetic matter so drastically, that by tomorrow the thinly veiled identity of all industrial culture products can come triumphantly out into the open, derisively fulfilling the Wagnerian dream of the *Gesamtkunstwerk* – the fusion of all the arts in one work. (*DoE*, p. 124)

They foresaw a condition in which television would be the apotheosis of the commercialization of culture to such an extent that the movies would be perceived as a cultural form relatively uncluttered with commercial messages.

'If technology had its way – the film would be delivered to people's homes as happens with the radio. It is moving towards the commercial system. Television points the way to a development which might easily enough force the Warner Brothers into what would certainly be the unwelcome position of serious musicians and cultural conservatives' (*DoE*, p. 161).

19 See the sources in n. 6. For a further discussion of the relation between the Institute and Lazarsfeld and the impact of Critical Theory on media theory and research in the United States, see my 'Critical Theory, Mass Communications and Popular Culture', *Telos*, 62 (Winter 1984–5), pp. 196–206. For a provocative critique of Lazarsfeld's paradigm, see Gitlin, 'Media Sociology: The Dominant Paradigm', *Theory and Society*, 6, no. 2 (1978), pp. 205–53. Although Gitlin presents an excellent critique of Lazarsfeld's paradigm, especially as set forth in *Personal Influence*, he tends to neglect the critical elements of Lazarsfeld's work, and also fails to point out that an alternative critical paradigm was present alongside Lazarsfeld's in the work of the Institute. Many essays in the *Journal of Communication, Ferment in the Field*, 33, no. 3 (Summer 1983), contain appraisals of Lazarsfeld's influence on communications research in the United States, though none of these studies systematically demonstrates how Critical Theory influenced theories of communications, culture and social theory.

20 C. Wright Mills *White Collar* (Boston: Beacon Press, 1951), p. 333 (further page references in text).

21 Mills, *The Power Elite* (Boston: Beacon Press, 1956).

22 Mills, 'IBM plus Reality plus Humanism = Sociology', in *Power, Politics, and People* (Boston: Beacon Press, 1963), p. 572.

23 Fromm, *Escape from Freedom* (New York: Holt, Rinehart & Winston, 1941), p. 128 (further page references in text). This underrated book helped introduce Critical Theory to an American audience, and influenced many American social and cultural theorists who wrote on popular culture, such as Dwight Macdonald, who reviewed it in *Common Sense*, 11 (Jan. 1942), p. 29.

24 Fromm, *The Sane Society* (New York: Holt, Rinehart & Winston, 1955) (hereafter *SS*), and Marcuse, *Eros and Civilization* (Boston: Beacon Press, 1955) (further page references in text). Fromm's book provides an accessible version of Critical Theory for an American audience, and is surprisingly similar to Marcuse's developing social theory and analysis of mass culture. Indeed, despite the bitter public arguments that they had over psychoanalysis in the mid-1950s, Fromm claims that Marcuse asked him if he could write a review of *One-Dimensional Man* for *The New York Times* 'as being almost the only one who would understand him' (Fromm, letter to Martin Jay, 14 May 1971, p. 10). A letter from Marcuse to Fromm confirms that Marcuse hoped that Fromm would write such a review (8 Dec. 1963). I am grateful to Martin Jay, Rainer Funk and John Rickert for providing me with these letters.

25 Marcuse, *One-Dimensional Man*. On Marcuse's impact on critical social theory and the New Left, see my book *Herbert Marcuse*.

26 Habermas, *Strukturwandel der Öffentlichkeit* (Munich: Luchterhand, 1962). I shall discuss Habermas's theory of the public sphere in 8.1.

27 Riesman dedicated his book *Abundance for What? and Other Essays* (Garden City,

N.Y.: Doubleday, 1964) to Fromm, and has frequently acknowledged Fromm's influence on his work. On Adorno's perception of the unacknowledged impact of Critical Theory on Riesman's work, Jay writes: 'An attempt in 1955 to get him to contribute to a book on David Riesman's *The Lonely Crowd* produced a negative response because he considered Riesman a popularizer of his and Horkheimer's work' (based on a letter from Adorno to Lowenthal, 22 Sept. 1955, cited in 'The Frankfurt School in Exile', *Perspectives in American History*, 6 (1972), p. 368). Alvin W. Gouldner notes the influence of the Institute on his work in *The Dialectic of Ideology and Technology* (New York: Seabury, 1976), p. 22.

28 George Gerbner and Larry Gross, 'Living with Television', *Journal of Communication*, 26, no. 2 (Spring 1976). In the original 1954 publication of his article on television, Adorno thanks Gerbner for his help on the research, and Gerbner later indicated Adorno's influence on his work; see *Behavior Today* (8 Jan. 1979), p. 3.

29 In addition to articles in *Ferment in the Field* which argue that Critical Theory does not provide the only model for critical communications research, Kurt Lang has argued that there are several earlier attempts, often by German theorists and emigrants, to provide more historical and empirical critical communications research (see Lang, 'The Critical Functions of Empirical Communications Research: Observations on German-American Influences', in *Media, Culture and Society*, 1 (1979), pp. 83–96). Although Lang is correct to call attention to the tradition of empirical critical communications research that pre-dated the Institute's work and to point out that empirical and historical work is not necessarily incompatible with the sort of theoretical analysis and critique developed by the Institute, he fails to sort out the differences between the tradition of empirical critical communications research and the more theoretical Institute work, and thus does not really appraise either the contributions or the limitations of the culture industry model developed by the Institute. More empiricist and political economy-minded Marxian critiques of the Frankfurt School within the field of communications theory tend to be generally dismissive, and often cover over the Institute's contributions to critical communications theory; see the articles collected in 'Beyond the Frankfurt School', *Media, Culture and Society*, 5 (1983).

30 Many recent books on the so-called mass culture debate feature chapters on the Institute intervention. See, e.g., Alan Swingewood, *The Myth of Mass Culture* (London: Macmillan, 1977), and Patrick Brantlinger, *Bread and Circuses: Theories of Mass Culture as Social Decay* (Ithaca: Cornell University Press, 1983).

31 Rosenberg and White, in *Mass Culture*, pp. 3–21.

32 Lowenthal, 'Historical Perspectives of Popular Culture', in *Mass Culture*; also in *LPCS*. See also the special issue of *Telos* devoted to Lowenthal: *Telos*, 45 (Fall 1980).

33 Shils, 'Daydreams and Nightmares: Reflections on the Criticism of Mass Culture', *Sewanee Review*, 45, no. 4 (Autumn 1957) (further page references in text).

34 Adorno, in Jay, *Dialectical Imagination*, p. 318.

35 Many studies which were influenced by or similar to the Institute critique of popular culture appeared in the 1970s, such as Robert Jewett and John

Lawrence, *The American Monomyth* (Garden City, N.Y.: Doubleday, 1977); Michael Real, *Mass-Mediated Culture* (Englewood Cliffs, N.J.: Prentice-Hall, 1977); and many articles published in journals like *Tabloid, Discourse, Social Text*, etc.

36 See Hans Magnus Enzensberger, 'Constituents toward a Theory of the Media', in *The Consciousness Industry* (New York: Seabury, 1974); Swingewood, *Myth of Mass Culture*; and Diane Waldman, 'Critical Theory and Film', *New German Critique*, 12 (Fall 1977).

37 See Jameson, 'Reification and Utopia in Mass Culture', *Social Text*, 1 (Winter 1979), pp. 130–48.

38 See Peter Biskind, *Seeing is Believing: How I Stopped Worrying and Came to Love the Fifties* (New York: Pantheon, 1983), and Douglas Kellner and Michael Ryan, *Camera Politica: Politics and Ideology in Contemporary Hollywood Cinema* (Bloomington: Indiana University Press, 1988).

39 I will cite some qualifications below which are seized upon by Adorno's defenders to pose alternative readings of Adorno's denunciation of the culture industry. Alternative readings are always possible, and are sometimes fruitful, but the overwhelming force of Adorno's writing on mass culture is negative, and, I believe, provides obstacles to more incisive radical approaches to mass-mediated culture.

40 See Adorno, 'Transparencies on Film', *New German Critique*, nos 24–5 (Fall–Winter 1981–2), pp. 199–206 (further page references in text). In the same issue (pp. 186–98), Miriam Hansen attempts to indicate how Adorno might be used to contribute to a more positive reading of film.

41 Adorno, 'Freizeit', *Stickwörte* (Frankfurt: Suhrkamp, 1969); cited in Andreas Huysen, 'Introduction to Adorno', *New German Critique*, 6 (Fall 1975), p. 10.

42 See Biskind, *Seeing is Believing*, and Kellner and Ryan, *Camera Politica*.

43 Enzensberger, 'Constituents'; Kellner, 'TV, Ideology, and Emancipatory Popular Culture', *Socialist Review*, 45 (Nov.–Dec. 1979); and Kellner, 'Public Access Television: Alternative Views', in *Making Waves, Radical Science*, 16 (London: 1975). For Brecht's radio theory and Benjamin's analysis of the radicalizing potential of film, see the material cited in n. 4. Brecht's radio plays are found in *Gesammelte Schriften*, vol. 2; and Benjamin's are collected in *Gesammelte Schriften*, vol. 4, part 2, and *Werkausgabe*, vol. 11 (Frankfurt: 1980).

44 Most Adorno critics have noted his almost paranoiac fear of co-optation, and Peter Burger makes a salient argument that fear of regression motivated Adorno's aesthetic theory, in 'The Decline of the Modern Age', *Telos*, 62 (Winter 1984–5), pp. 117–30.

45 On Adorno's aesthetic theory, see Buck-Morss, *Negative Dialectics*; Richard Wolin's review of Adorno's *Aesthetic Theory* in *Telos*, 41 (Fall 1979); and the forthcoming study by Lambert Zuidervaart, *Adorno's Aesthetic Theory: A Philosophical Critique*.

Chapter 6   From the Consumer Society to Postmodernism

1   See Real, *Mass-Mediated Culture*. On postmodernism, see Jameson, 'Post-modernism, or the Cultural Logic of Late Capitalism', *New Left Review*, 146 (July–Aug. 1984), pp. 53–93; Lyotard, *Postmodern Condition*; Kroker and Cook, *Postmodern Scene*; and Kellner, 'Postmodernism as Social Theory'.

2   See Stuart Ewen, *Captains of Consciousness* (New York: McGraw-Hill, 1976), for the birth of the consumer society, and Marty Jezer, *Life in the Dark Ages* (Boston: South End Press, 1982), for discussion of the rise of the consumer society after World War II.

3   Adorno, 'On the Fetish Character of Music', in *FSR*, p. 280.

4   Adorno's article 'Veblen's Attack on Culture' was published in the Institute journal in 1941, and was collected in *P*, pp. 73–94.

5   Adorno, 'Aldous Huxley and Utopia', in *P*, pp. 95–118.

6   Lowenthal, 'The Triumph of Mass Idols', in *LPCS*, pp. 109–40.

7   Fromm, *Escape from Freedom*, and *idem*, *Man for Himself*.

8   Fromm, *The Sane Society*, pp. 131ff. (hereafter *SS*). This book is similar in many ways to Marcuse's *One-Dimensional Man*, and a comparative analysis of Fromm's and Marcuse's texts from this period remains to be carried out. For a beginning which proposes a rereading of Fromm's relationship to Critical Theory, see John Rickert, 'The Fromm-Marcuse Debate Revisited', *Theory and Society*, 15 (1986), pp. 351–400. Space limitations prevent me here from carrying out a more thorough discussion of the debates within the Institute concerning psychoanalysis and its varied applications to social theory, cultural critique and politics – topics explored by Rickert, 'Fromm-Marcuse Debate'; Jacoby, *Social Amnesia*; and others.

9   On Fromm's continuing commitment to socialism, see *FS*, pp. 303ff. and *passim*. Fromm often criticized Marcuse and other Institute members for failing to make concrete proposals and to involve themselves in actual struggles and movements, though in light of Marcuse's 1960s involvement this criticism is somewhat strained. See Fromm's polemic against Marcuse in 'The Crisis of Psychoanalysis', in *CoP*; reprinted in *Politics, Society, and Culture*.

10 See *ODM* and my discussion in *Herbert Marcuse* of Marcuse's critique of the consumer society upon which I am drawing here.

11 *ODM*, p. 2, discussed in Kellner, *Herbert Marcuse*, pp. 241ff.

12 On Marcuse's influence on the New Left, see Kellner, *Herbert Marcuse*, pp. 276ff. New Left critiques of the consumer society influenced by Marcuse include Ewen, *Captains of Consciousness*; William Leiss, *The Limits to Satisfaction* (Toronto: Toronto University Press, 1976); and Stuart Ewen and Elizabeth Ewen, *Channels of Desire* (New York: McGraw-Hill, 1982). In a series of articles written in the late 1970s and early 1980s, Leiss tended to be critical of Marcuse, and to turn to more empirical and historical research into the consumer society that often breaks with Marcusian perspectives. See Leiss et al., *Social Communication in Advertising* (New York: Methuen, 1986).

13 For French critiques of the consumer society, see the discussions of Debord, Lefebrve, and Baudrillard in Kellner, *Jean Baudrillard*.

14 Ewen and Ewen, 'Americanization and Consumption', *Telos*, 37 (Fall 1978), pp. 42–51. See their elaboration of this position in *idem*, *Channels of Desire*.

15 Ewen and Ewen, 'Americanization', p. 49.

16 For an early critique of the anti-consumption ethos of the New Left, see Ellen Willis, 'Consumerism and Women', *Socialist Revolution*, 1, no. 3 (May–June 1970), pp. 76–82, and the article by Enzensberger in ch. 5, n. 36, which indicates the anti-consumption position of the Left in Germany. Both mention the Frankfurt School critique of the consumer society as an important component in propagating the anti-consumption bias of the Left.

17 Enzensberger, 'Constituents', p. 110.

18 Marx, *Economic and Philosophical Manuscripts of 1844*, in Marx and Engels, *Collected Works*, vol. 3 (New York: International Publishers, 1975), p. 322.

19 *ODM*. This argument draws on my 'Critical Theory, Commodities and the Consumer Society', *Theory, Culture and Society*, 1, no. 3 (1983), pp. 66–84, which contains a fuller development of the position indicated here.

20 See, e.g., *SS*, pp. 131ff., and Lowenthal, 'Triumph', pp. 109ff.

21 On oppositional consumer practices, see Michel de Certeau, *The Invention of Everyday Life* (Berkeley: University of California Press, 1984); and for an appraisal of the possibilities of critical consumer behavior, see Peter Grahame, 'Criticalness, Pragmatics, and Everyday Life: Consumer Literacy as Critical Practice', in *Critical Theory and Public Life*, edited by John Forester; and Claus Offe, 'Alternative Strategies in Consumer Policy', in *Contradictions of the Welfare State*, edited by John Keane (London: Hutchinson, 1984), pp. 220–38. On the theory of self-valorization, see Antonio Negri, *Marx Beyond Marx* (South Hadley, Mass.: Bergin and Garvey, 1984). These notions are more fully discussed in my *Jean Baudrillard*.

22 See the speculations on the abolition of work in André Gorz, *Farewell to the Working Class* (Boston: South End Press, 1978), and *idem*, *Paths to Paradise* (Boston: South End Press, 1980), which I shall discuss in Chapters 7 and 8.

23 See Habermas, *Strukturwandel der Öffentlichkeit*, and *idem*, *Theory of Communicative Action*.

24 See Barry Commoner, *The Closing Circle* (New York: Bantam, 1971).

25 On documentations of this argument, see ibid., and Commoner, *The Poverty of Power* (New York: Knopf, 1976).

26 Zygmunt Bauman, 'Industrialism, Consumerism, and Power', *Theory, Culture and Society*, 1, no. 3 (1983), pp. 32–43.

27 Jezer, *The Dark Ages*, pp. 135ff. I expand on this argument in my 'The Great American Dream Machine: The Ideological Functions of Popular Culture in the United States', in *Democracy Upside-Down*, edited by Fred Exoo (New York: Praeger, 1987).

28 For documentation and a further critique of advertising, see my 'Great American Dream Machine'. Many valuable non-Marxist critiques of advertising exist which can be used by Critical Theorists to condemn advertising and the consumer society. Jules Henry, for instance, has produced a moral and epistemological critique of advertising in an underrated, neglected book, *Culture Against Man* (New York: Vintage, 1963), published just before *One-*

Dimensional Man. Henry argues in a brilliant essay entitled 'Advertising as a Philosophical System' that American advertising contains a 'new kind of truth': *'pecuniary pseudo-truth* – which may be defined as a false statement made as if it were true, but not intended to be believed. No proof is offered for a pecuniary pseudo-truth, and no one looks for it. Its proof is that it sells merchandise; if it does not, it is false.' Henry analyzes in detail advertising's 'para-poetic hyperbole', 'pecuniary logic' and the underlying 'pecuniary philosophy'. Through a detailed examination of American advertising, Henry condemns the system in its totality, sharply criticizing the consumer society's theories of human nature, logic, epistemology and concept of truth.

29 See Marcuse, *Counterrevolution and Revolt* (Boston: Beacon Press, 1972), pp. 18ff.

30 See Andrew Werneck, 'Sign and Commodity: Aspects of the Cultural Dynamic of Advanced Capitalism', *Canadian Journal of Political and Social Theory*, 8, nos 1–2 (Winter–Spring 1984), pp. 17–34, and my discussion in *Jean Baudrillard*.

31 For discussion of the debates over postmodernism, see Jameson, 'Postmodernism'; *idem*, 'The Politics of Theory', *New German Critique*, 33 (Fall 1984), pp. 53–66; Huyssen, 'Mapping the Postmodern', *New German Critique*, 33 (Fall 1984), pp. 5–52; and Kellner, 'Postmodernism as Social Theory'.

32 For critiques of modern philosophy and arguments for what is now seen as a 'postmodern turn', see Jacques Derrida, *Of Grammatology* (Baltimore: Johns Hopkins University Press, 1976), and Richard Rorty, *Philosophy and the Mirror of Nature* (Princeton: Princeton University Press, 1979).

33 Lyotard, *Postmodern Condition*; Baudrillard, *Simulations* (New York: Semiotext, 1983); *idem, In the Shadow of the Silent Majorities* (New York: Semiotext, 1983); Jameson, 'Postmodernism', and Kroker and Cook, *Postmodern Scene*.

34 Habermas, 'Modernity versus Postmodernity', *New German Critique*, 22 (Winter 1981), pp. 3–14.

35 Habermas, *Modernity*.

36 Habermas, 'Modernity', pp. 3ff. (further page references in text).

37 See the articles in Kenneth Baynes, James Bohman and Thomas McCarthy, eds, *After Philosophy. End or Transformation?* (Cambridge, Mass.: MIT Press, 1987), and Michael Ryan, *Culture and Politics* (London: Macmillan, 1988).

38 Habermas, 'Modern and Postmodern Architecture', in *Critical Theory and Public Life*.

39 Wellmer, 'Truth, Semblance and Reconciliation: Adorno's Aesthetic Redemption of Modernity', *Telos*, 62 (Winter 1984–5), pp. 89–116 (further page references in text).

40 Russell Berman, 'Modern Art and Desublimation', *Telos*, 62 (Winter 1984–5), pp. 31–58; and Richard Wolin, 'Modernism versus Postmodernism', *Telos*, 62 (Winter 1984–5), pp. 9–30 (page references to their articles will be placed henceforth within the text).

41 Such neo-Adornoesque ultra-negativism in the realm of cultural critique is

paralleled in the United States by ultra-negativism in the realm of politics; see the discussion in 8.2.

42 In a 1983 conference on the avant-garde at the University of Houston, neither Berman nor Wolin, when pressed on the issue, could provide any examples of 'authentic art' beyond the Schönberg-Kafka-Beckett triumvirate deified by Adorno. In 'Modern Art and Desublimation', however, Berman calls for a neo-classicist 'reauraticization' (pp. 56–7) of art, which counters Adorno's own critique of neo-classicist aesthetic tendencies.

43 See Wellmer, 'On the Dialectic of Modernism and Postmodernism', *Praxis International*, 4, no. 4 (Jan. 1985), pp. 337–62 (further page references in text); Axel Honneth, 'An Aversion Against the Universal: A Commentary on Lyotard's *Postmodern Condition*', *Theory, Culture & Society*, 2, no. 3 (1985), pp. 147–57; and Seyla Benhabib, 'Epistemologies of Postmodernism', *New German Critique*, 33 (Fall 1984), pp. 103–26.

44 Honneth, 'An Aversion', and Benhabib, 'Epistemologies', take on Lyotard, with Honneth attacking Lyotard's aversion to the universal and stressing the importance of universality for critical social theory and politics, and Benhabib stressing the importance of having a normative standpoint from which to criticize other positions.

45 Habermas, 'Consciousness-Raising or Redemptive Criticism', *New German Critique*, 17 (1979), pp. 30–59. Habermas certainly does not employ 'redemptive criticism' in his *Auseinandersetzung* with New French Theory, engaging instead in ideology critique.

46 See my *Jean Baudrillard*.

47 Curiously, the 'post-history' arguments by contemporary French thinkers reproduce earlier criticisms that Critical Theorists were denying the possibility of significant historical change in their theories of self-reproducing 'one-dimensional' or 'totally administered' societies and that Critical Theory was thus similar to conservative German social theories which were also maintaining the 'end of history'. See the discussion in Connerton, *Tragedy of Enlightenment*, pp. 122ff. and my *Jean Baudrillard*.

48 Jameson, 'Postmodernism', pp. 53ff.

49 Ibid., pp. 77ff., and Ernest Mandel, *Late Capitalism* (London: New Left Books, 1974).

50 Jameson, 'Cognitive Mapping', in *Marxism and the Interpretation of Culture*, edited by Cary Nelson and Lawrence Grossberg (Urbana and Chicago: University of Illinois Press, 1988).

51 Jameson, *The Political Unconscious* (Ithaca: Cornell University Press, 1981).

52 Ibid., p. 353. For further discussion of Jameson's work, see my 'Jameson, Marxism and Postmodernism', in Kellner, ed., *Jameson/Postmodernism/Critique* (Washington D.C.: Maisonneuve, 1989).

Chapter 7   Techno-Capitalism

1 Habermas, *Legitimation Crisis* (hereafter *LC*) (Boston: Beacon, 1975), p. 17.

2 This is the classical Marxian position which has been defended and elabor-

ated in the contemporary era by Mandel, *Late Capitalism*; Harry Cleaver, *Reading Capitalism Politically* (Austin: University of Texas Press, 1977); James O'Connor, *Accumulation Crisis* (Oxford: Basil Blackwell, 1984); and Negri, *Marx Against Marxism*. In this chapter, I shall indicate how Critical Theorists of the second generation, like Offe and Habermas, argue for the continuing primacy of the imperatives of capitalist accumulation as a mode of social organization; and I will argue throughout this and the next chapter against those who claim that we have now passed over into a new post-capitalist society.

3 See Norbert Wiener, *The Human Uses of Human Beings* (New York: Houghton Mifflin, 1954), and Pollock, *Automation* (Oxford: Basil Blackwell, 1957). For claims concerning the transition to a post-industrial or post-modern society, see Daniel Bell, *The Coming of Post-industrial Society* (New York: Basic Books, 1973); Jean Baudrillard, *Simulations*; and Lyotard, *Postmodern Condition*.

4 Mandel, *Late Capitalism*, pp. 184ff. (further page references in text).

5 Harry Braverman, *Monopoly Capital and Labor* (New York: Monthly Review Press, 1974).

6 On post-World War II affluence and the sharp drop in corporate profits in the 1967 and 1973–4 world-wide economic recession and ensuing corporate offensive, see Lester Thurow, *The Zero-Sum Society* (New York: Basic Books, 1980), and Thomas Ferguson and Joel Rogers, *Right Turn* (New York: Hill and Wang, 1986).

7 On changes of class composition, see Stanley Aronowitz, *False Promises* (New York: 1973); Braverman, *Monopoly Capital and Labor*; and David M. Gordon, Richard Edwards and Michael Reich, *Segmented Work, Divided Workers* (New York: Cambridge University Press, 1982).

8 Hilferding, *Finance Capital*, and Paul Baran and Paul Sweezy, *Monopoly Capital* (London: Penguin Books, 1968).

9 On transnational capitalism, see Mandel, *Late Capitalism*; Richard Barnett and Ronald E. Muller, *Global Reach* (New York: Simon and Schuster, 1974); and Fölker Fröbel, Jürgen Heinrichs and Otto Kreye, *The New International Division of Labor* (New York: 1980). See also Gordon, 'The Global Economy: New Edifice or Crumbling Foundations', *New Left Review*, 168 (Mar.–Apr. 1988), pp. 24–65, who argues against exaggerating the impact of the new 'international division of labor' or the power of transnational corporations.

10 On the forms of techno-culture, see Wolfgang Fritz Haug, *Critique of Commodity Aesthetics* (Cambridge and Minneapolis: Polity and University of Minnesota Press, 1986); Herbert Schiller, *Who Knows? Information in the Age of the Fortune 500* (New Jersey: Ablex, 1984); *idem, Information and the Crisis Economy* (New Jersey: Ablex, 1985); Tony Solomonides and Les Levidow, eds, *Compulsive Technology* (London: Free Association Books, 1985); and the studies by Bell and Baudrillard cited in n. 3.

11 Many orthodox Marxist theories tend to fall prey to economic determinism, while most theories of the post-industrial or postmodern society tend to succumb to technological determinism. For critiques of economic determinism within orthodox Marxism, see Jacoby, *Dialectic of Defeat*, and O'Connor,

Accumulation Crisis. For critiques of technological determinism in theories of postmodernism, see my 'Postmodernism as Social Theory'.

12 On the concept of a 'post-industrial society', see Bell, *Coming.* On the allegedly fundamental role of a 'mode of information' in contemporary capitalist societies, see Poster, *Foucault, Marxism,* and *idem, Mode of Information* (Cambridge: Polity, forthcoming).

13 Pollock, *Automation* (henceforth *A,* with page references cited in text).

14 See Dunayevskaya, *Marxism and Freedom;* Charles Denby, *Workers Battle Automation* (Detroit: News and Letters, 1960); *The Coal Miners' General Strike of 1949–50 and the Birth of Marxist-Humanism in the U.S.* (Chicago: News and Letters Publication, 1984); and the newspaper *News and Letters.*

15 The Marcuse–Dunayevskaya correspondence is included in the microfiche collection of Dunayevskaya's works, and is available through inter-library loan and for purchase through the Chicago *News and Letters* group. I am grateful to Dunayevskaya and her associates for making this material available to me before it was ready for microfiche distribution, and I drew on it for my 1984 book on Marcuse.

16 See *ODM,* pp. 36–7, and the discussion in Kellner, *Herbert Marcuse.* I might note that Marcuse later revised this position, and envisaged automation as making possible incursion of the realm of freedom *within* socially necessary labor, thus eventually coming to accept Dunayevskaya's position; for details, see Kellner, *Herbert Marcuse,* pp. 326ff.). In *ODM,* by contrast, Marcuse argued that overcoming domination would require development of *new* technologies which would break with the logic of capitalist technology and production (pp. 227ff.). Pursuing these aporias to a higher dialectical level, one could argue that both new technologies and a new organization of labor and society are necessary to the project of liberation, which is, after all, the only really interesting project for both individuals and the species.

17 Bell, *Coming,* pp. xii–xiv.

18 Ferguson and Rogers, *Right Turn.*

19 See Steven Levy, *Hackers* (New York: Anchor Press/Doubleday, 1984).

20 On the control of knowledge, research and information by the military-industrial complex, see Herbert Schiller, *Mass Communications and American Empire* (Boston: Beacon Press, 1969); Seymour Melman, *Pentagon Capitalism* (New York: McGraw-Hill, 1970); and Vincent Mosco, *Computers, Communication, and the Information Society* (Toronto: Gallamono, forthcoming).

21 Timothy W. Luke and Stephen K. White, 'Critical Theory, the Informational Revolution, and an Ecological Path to Modernity', in *Critical Theory and Public Life,* p. 33. This collection of essays indicates some of the directions which should be taken if Critical Theory is to continue to be relevant to radical social theory and politics today.

22 Barry Bluestone and Bennett Harrison, *The Deindustrialization of America* (New York: Basic Books, 1982); and Gordon, Edwards and Reich, *Segmented Work.*

23 On new configurations of class and decline of the middle class, see Paul Blumberg, *Inequality in an Age of Decline* (Oxford: Oxford University Press, 1980); Frances Fox Piven and Richard Cloward, *The New Class War* (New

York: Pantheon, 1982); Robert Kuttner, 'The Declining Middle', *Atlantic* (July 1983), pp. 55–65; and Thomas Edsall, *The New Politics of Inequality* (New York: Norton, 1984).

24 See Chapter 6 below and Mandel, *Late Capitalism*, pp. 377ff.

25 Gorz, *Paths*, p. 31.

26 Gorz, *Farewell*. Frankfurt School theorists were arguably the first within the Marxist tradition to draw consequences for the theory of revolution from the structural integration of the working class into contemporary capitalism (see Chapters 4 and 8 below).

27 See Luke and White, 'Critical Theory', pp. 47ff.

28 See esp. Offe, *Contradictions of the Welfare State*; *idem*, *Disorganized Capitalism* (Cambridge: Polity, 1985); and Habermas, *LC*. The best introduction to Offe's work is Keane, 'The Legacy of Political Economy: Thinking With and Against Claus Offe', *Canadian Journal of Political and Social Theory*, 2, no. 3 (Fall 1978), pp. 49–92, and *idem*, Introduction to Offe's *Contradictions*, pp. 11–34.

29 Offe, 'Political Authority and Class Structures – An Analysis of Late Capitalist Societies', *International Journal of Sociology*, 2, no. 1 (Spring 1972), pp. 73–81, and *idem*, 'Structural Problems of the Capitalist State', in K. V. Beyme, ed., *German Political Studies*, 1 (1974), pp. 31–6.

30 See esp. Offe, 'Political Authority'; *idem*, 'Structural Problems'; and Keane, 'Legacy', pp. 50ff. Habermas utilizes a similar framework in *LC*, though he criticizes Offe at several places in the text.

31 Offe, *Contradictions*.

32 Offe, 'Political Authority', p. 78; see also p. 98 and Offe, 'The Theory of the Capitalist State and the Problem of Policy Formation', in *Stress and Contradiction in Modern Capitalism*, edited by L. N. Lindberg et al. (Lexington, Mass.: 1975), p. 125.

33 Offe, 'Capitalist State', pp. 127–34.

34 Ibid.

35 Ibid., p. 132.

36 See the essays in Offe, *Contradictions*; and *idem*, *Disorganized Capitalism*.

37 Offe, 'Political Authority', pp. 103–5. See also O'Connor, *The Fiscal Crisis of the State* (New York: St Martin's Press, 1973).

38 Offe, 'Advanced Capitalism and the Welfare State', *Politics and Society* (Summer 1972), p. 485.

39 Offe, 'Structural Problems', p. 47; see also Offe, 'Capitalist State', p. 127.

40 Offe, 'Political Authority', pp. 95–6, 101–2. Offe elaborates here the earlier individual arguments concerning the integration of labor in contemporary capitalist societies and the need for new theories of class and social transformation.

41 See Offe, *Disorganized Capitalism*, and Scott Lash and John Urry, *The End of Organized Capitalism* (Cambridge: Polity Press, 1987), who use the same concept of 'disorganized capitalism' to describe the current structure(lessness) and crises of the capitalist system. These arguments concerning the contradictory complex of organization and disorganization in capitalism put in question the orthodox Institute position concerning growing technological rationality in capitalist societies.

42 For Offe's own presentation of his relationship with the earlier generation of
    the Frankfurt School, see the interview in Offe, *Contradictions*, pp. 252ff. –
    though I believe that the relationship is more complex and interesting than
    Offe's own comments indicate.

43 On Offe's theory of decommodification, see the Introduction by John Keane
    and the essays in Offe, *Contradictions*, esp. pp. 262ff.

44 *LC* and Habermas, *Theory of Communicative Action*. Although Habermas has
    been criticized for bringing systems theory into his version of Critical Theory,
    in fact, such notions, properly reconstructed, are compatible with earlier
    notions of apparatus and domination used by the first generation of Critical
    Theorists. In addition, in both the texts cited, Habermas criticized orthodox
    systems theory, and in his post-1980s works he provides his own version.

45 On Habermas and Critical Theory, see Thomas McCarthy, *The Critical Theory
    of Jürgen Habermas* (Cambridge, Mass.: MIT Press, 1978); Rick Roderick,
    Habermas and the Foundations of Critical Theory (New York: St Martin's Press,
    1986); and Benhabib, *Critique, Norm, and Utopia*. I shall not inquire here into
    the various attempts by Habermas and his followers to provide a normative
    foundation for Critical Theory, and will instead focus on Habermas's 'sub-
    stantive' positions on contemporary capitalism and its crisis tendencies.

46 Habermas, *Theory of Communicative Action*.

47 On the Marxian theory of crisis and collapse, see the literature cited in
    ch. 3, n. 8.

48 Lenin, *Imperialism, the Highest Stage of Capitalism* (Peking: Foreign Languages
    Press, 1970), and Mandel, *Late Capitalism*. Both Habermas and Offe use the
    concept of 'late capitalism'. This concept seems both imprecise (how late is it?)
    and to embody a degree of wish-fulfillment (that capital is about to pass away).
    In addition, the two-stage theory of liberal versus late capitalism covers over
    some of the features of the new capitalist societies which have emerged since the
    1950s. For these and other reasons, I prefer a concept like 'techo-capitalism'.

49 Compare *LC* with Pollock, 'State Capitalism', *DoE* and *ODM*.

50 Offe, *Contradictions*, and *idem, Disorganized Capitalism*.

51 This has been the agenda of the New Right; see the discussions in Peter
    Steinfels, *The Neo-Conservatives* (New York: Simon and Schuster, 1979), and
    Alan Crawford, *Thunder on the Right* (New York: Pantheon, 1980).

52 Many of Habermas's followers believe that his concept of a 'legitimation crisis'
    is of crucial importance in analyzing contemporary capitalist societies, while his
    critics doubt its analytic and political value. See the discussion in David Held,
    'Crisis Tendencies, Legitimation and the State', in *Habermas, Critical Debates*,
    edited by John B. Thompson and David Held (London: Macmillan, 1982).

53 Habermas, *Theory of Communicative Action*, and *idem*, 'A Response to my
    Critics', in *Habermas. Critical Debates*.

54 Habermas, *Theory of Communicative Action*, and *idem*, 'Response', pp. 278ff.

55 Habermas, *Theory of Communicative Action*, pp. 358ff. and *passim*, and *idem*,
    'Response'.

56 Held, 'Crisis Tendencies', p. 194.

57 Ibid. Habermas believes that he has answered Held's objections with his new
    analysis of system/life-world (see 'Response', p. 281); but I would argue that

he simply displaces the problems with his early ideal-type crisis theory model onto a higher level of abstraction.

58 Offe, *Contradictions*, pp. 35ff.

59 Offe, *Disorganized Capitalism*, pp. 5–6.

60 This perspective is similar to that of Mandel, who argues in *Late Capitalism* that:

> In reality, however, late capitalism is not a completely organized society at all. It is merely a hybrid and bastardized *combination* of organization and anarchy. . . . The notion of capitalist rationality developed by Lukács, following Weber [and taken over by the Frankfurt School] is in fact a *contradictory combination of partial rationality and overall irrationality*. For the pressure toward exact calculation and quantification of economic processes, generated by the universalization of commodity production, comes up against the insuperable barrier of capitalist private ownership, competition and the resultant *impossibility of exactly determining the socially necessary quantities of labour* actually contained in the commodities produced. (p. 508)

See also Lash and Urry, *End of Organized Capitalism*.

61 Recent studies have put in question whether there is a 'dominant ideology' in contemporary capitalist societies or whether such a shared ideology is even necessary. See Nicholas Abercrombie, Stephen Hill and Bryan S. Turner, *The Dominant Ideology Thesis* (London: George Allen and Unwin, 1980).

Chapter 8   Theory and Practice

1 Dubiel, *Theory and Politics*.

2 Horkheimer, 'Traditional and Critical Theory', in *CT*, p. 245.

3 See Kellner, *Herbert Marcuse*; Habermas, *Theory and Practice* (Boston: Beacon Press, 1973); and *idem*, *Human and Human Interests* (Boston: Beacon Press, 1971).

4 Wiggershaus provides the best account (*FS*, pp. 501ff.), though there is much interesting material in Claus Grossner, *Verfall der Philosophie* (Hamburg: Wegner, 1971).

5 *FS*, pp. 702ff.

6 Kellner, *Herbert Marcuse*, pp. 276ff.

7 Habermas et al., *Student und Politik* (Berlin: Neuwied, 1961).

8 Pollock, ed., *Gruppenexperiment* (Frankfurt: Institut für Sozialforschung, 1955).

9 Habermas et al., *Student und Politik*, p. 234.

10 On the organization Students for a Democratic Society, see Kirkpatrick Sale, *SDS* (New York: Vintage, 1974); James Miller, *SDS* (New York: Simon and Schuster, 1986); and Todd Gitlin, *The Sixties. Years of Hope, Days of Rage* (New York: Doubleday, 1987).

11 On Habermas's politics, see *FS*; Grossner, *Verfall*; and John Keane, *Public Life and Late Capitalism* (Cambridge: Cambridge University Press, 1984).

12 Habermas, *Struckturwandel der Öffentlichkeit*. A précis was published as 'The Public Sphere', *New German Critique*, 3 (Fall 1974), pp. 49–55. For an excellent discussion of the various interpretations and critiques of the book, see Peter Hohendahl, 'Critical Theory, Public Sphere and Culture: Habermas and his Critics', *New German Critique*, 16 (Winter 1979), pp. 89–118.

13 Habermas, 'Public Sphere', p. 55.

14 See *FS*, p. 615ff.

15 Ibid., p. 628.

16 Horkheimer and Adorno, eds, *Sociologica II* (Frankfurt: Institut für Sozialforschung, 1962).

17 Horkheimer, cited in *FS*, p. 626.

18 Adorno, cited in ibid., p. 627.

19 Adorno, cited in ibid.

20 Adorno, 'Society', *Salmagundi*, nos 10–11 (Fall 1969–Winter 1970), pp. 144–53; reprinted in *Politics, Culture and Society*. (Further page references from *Salmagundi* in text.)

21 Adorno, 'Resignation', *Telos*, 35 (Spring 1978), pp. 166–9.

22 Adorno, *Negative Dialectics* (London: Routledge & Kegan Paul, 1973). I cannot fully discuss here the ramifications of Adorno's later philosophy for Critical Theory, though I shall take up this issue in future studies of Critical Theory and postmodernism.

23 Horkheimer, *Die Sehnsucht nach dem ganz Anderen* (Hamburg: Furche, 1970), and *idem*, 'Zur Zukunft der "Kritishchen Theorie" ', in Grossner, *Verfall*, pp. 262–77.

24 *FS*, pp. 692–3, and Horst Mewes, 'The Gèrman New Left', *New German Critique*, 1 (Winter 1973), pp. 28ff. A fuller history of the German New Left and the Frankfurt School remains to be written.

25 'Professoren als Staats-Regenten?', interview with Marcuse in *Der Spiegel* (21 Aug. 1967), pp. 112–18, discussed in *FS*, pp. 691ff.

26 For a collection of Habermas's political essays of the period, see *Protestbewegung und Hochschulreform* (Frankfurt: Suhrkamp, 1969), some of which are collected in *Towards a Rational Society* (Boston: Beacon Press, 1970).

27 Johannes Agnoli and Peter Bruckner, *Die Transformation der Demokratie* (Berlin: Voltaire, 1967).

28 See Oskar Negt, *Politik als Protest* (Frankfurt: Agit-buch, 1971). On the influence of Marcuse and Critical Theory on the European and American New Left, see Habermas, ed., *Antwörten auf Herbert Marcuse* (Frankfurt: Suhrkamp, 1968), and Paul Breines, ed., *Critical Interruptions* (New York: Herder and Herder, 1972).

29 See also Oskar Negt, 'Don't Go by Numbers, Organize According to Interests: Current Questions of Organization', *New German Critique*, 1 (Winter 1974), pp. 42–51. See Negt's later works with Alexander Kluge, a German film-maker who was also influenced by Adorno, *Öffentlichkeit und Erfahrung* (Frankfurt: Suhrkamp, 1972) and *Geschichte und Eigensinn* (Frankfurt: Suhrkamp, 1981).

30 On Habermas's 'linguistic turn', see Wellmer, 'Communications and Emancipation: Reflections on the Linguistic Turn in Critical Theory', in *On Critical Theory*, and Peter U. Hohendahl, 'Habermas' critique of the Frankfurt School', *New German Critique*, 35 (Spring–Summer 1985), pp. 3–26.

31 No one has adequately carried out an analysis of the specifically Social Democratic version of Critical Theory developed by Habermas, his colleagues and students. Yet Habermas's interviews make clear his allegiance to Social Democracy, and I would argue that his theoretical writings are also consistent with the traditions of reformist democratic socialism. For specific commitments to socialism, see 'Interview with Jürgen Habermas', *New German Critique*, 18

(Fall 1979), pp. 44–73, and 'Conservativism and Capitalist Crisis', *New Left Review*, 115 (May–June 1979), esp. pp. 81–3, collected with other interviews in *Habermas. Autonomy and Solidarity*, edited by Peter Dews (London: New Left Books, 1986).

32 Marx, *Capital*. Few neo-Marxist analyses of the labor process and the changed conditions of labor, with the exception of Gorz, seriously consider the implications of automation and technical unemployment; nor do they articulate a strategy for labor and for social restructuring consistent with the potentialities of new technologies.

33 On the generally negative presentations of science and technology in *DoE* and *ODM*, see Kellner, *Herbert Marcuse*, and Alford, *Science and Nature*.

34 Habermas, 'Technology and Science as Ideology', in *Toward a Rational Society*, and my critique in *Herbert Marcuse*, pp. 330ff.

35 My remarks here draw on Murray Bookchin, *Post-Scarcity Anarchism* (San Francisco: Ramparts Press, 1971), the discussion of new technologies in *Radical Technology*, edited by Peter Harper et al. (New York: Pantheon, 1976), and the two books discussed below by Gorz, who, despite some limitations, has the most advanced theoretical and political perspectives on these issues in a framework which I find consistent with the tradition of Critical Theory.

36 I shall elaborate on these possibilities in *Television, Politics, and Society* (Boulder, Colo.: Westview Press, forthcoming).

37 Gorz, *Farewell*, and *idem*, *Paths*.

38 A full discussion and critique of Gorz's positions would take us beyond the boundaries of the present book, although I would note that the all too sharp dichotomy between the 'realm of necessity' – that is, socially necessary labor – and the 'realm of freedom' – that is, autonomous activity outside the realm of labor – precludes the possibility of more autonomy and self-realization *within* labor, and thus de-emphasizes the importance of new work relations and organization.

39 Offe, *Disorganized Capitalism*, pp. 65ff.

40 On automation and Appalachia, see *The Coal Miner's General Strike*. On the de-skilling of labor, see Braverman, *Monopoly Capital and Labor*.

41 For cultural representations of a techno-fascist future, see many of the dystopic and political conspiracy movies of the 1970s discussed in Kellner and Ryan, *Camera Politica*; 1980s films like *Video-drome*, *Brazil* and *1984*; and the TV series *Max Headroom*.

42 See Bluestone and Harrison, *Deindustrialization*, and Habermas, *Theory of Communicative Action*.

43 On contradictions between capitalism and democracy, see Alan Wolfe, *The Limits of Legitimacy* (New York: 1972); Joshua Cohen and Joel Rogers, *On Democracy* (New York: Penguin Books, 1983); Samuel Bowles and Herbert Gintis, *Democracy and Capitalism* (New York: Basic Books, 1986); and Ernesto Laclau and Chantal Mouffee, *Hegemony and Socialist Strategy* (London: New Left Books, 1985). For discussion of the continued crisis of the individual in contemporary capitalism, see Joel Whitebrook, 'Saving the Subject', *Telos*, 50 (Winter 1981–2), pp. 79–102. In general, whereas the first generation of Critical Theorists did not develop adequate perspectives on democracy or stress

its centrality for radical social theory, this is not the case with the second and third generations, which have presented consistently democratic perspectives.

44 As Ferguson and Rogers argue:

> The combination of social-spending cuts, other budget initiatives, and the massively regressive tax bill produced a huge upward distribution of American income. Over the 1983–1985 period the policies reduced the incomes of households making less than $20,000 a year by $20 billion, while increasing the incomes of households making more than $80,000 by $35 billion. For those at the very bottom of the income pyramid, making under $10,000 per year, the policies produced an average loss of $1,100 over 1983–85. For those at the top, making more than $200,000 a year, the average gain was $60,000. By the end of Reagan's first term, U.S. income distribution was more unequal than at any time since 1947, the year the Census Bureau first began collecting data on the subject. In 1983, the top 40% of the population received a larger share of income than at any time since 1947. (*Right Turn*, p. 130)

45 Habermas, 'New Social Movements', *Telos*, 49 (Fall 1981), pp. 33–7 (further page references to this version in text).

46 See Offe, *Disorganized Capitalism*; *idem*, ' "Reaching for the Brake": The Greens in Germany', *New Political Science*, 11 (Spring 1983), pp. 45–52; and Klaus Eder, 'A New Social Movement', *Telos*, 52 (Summer 1982), pp. 5–20 (further page references to this article will be in the text). I have found no systematic discussion of the profound similarities between certain versions of Critical Theory and perspectives in the Green movement, apart from John Ely's 'Marxism and Green Politics in West Germany', *Thesis Eleven*, 13 (1986), pp. 22–38. Although Ely does not systematically develop this theme, it appears that the critique of orthodox Marxism developed by major Green theorists is extremely similar to that developed by Critical Theory, as are many of its positive perspectives.

47 For positive evaluations of the emancipatory potentials of new social movements combined with aggressive critiques of traditional Marxism, see Isaac Balbus, *Marxism and Domination* (Princeton: Princeton University Press, 1982); Carl Boggs, *Social Movements and Political Power* (Philadelphia: Temple University Press, 1986); Alain Touraine, *L'Après socialisme* (Paris: Grasset, 1980); *idem, La voix et la o'eil* (Paris: 198); and Mouffe, 'Hegemony and New Political Subjects: Toward a New Concept of Democracy', in *Marxism and the Interpretation of Culture*, pp. 89–104, and Laclau and Mouffe, *Hegemony*.

48 In the early 1980s the journal *Telos* ran a series of articles on the new social movements which elicited intense polemics. The debates included Russell Berman's attacks on the German peace movement in 'Opposition to Rearmament and West German Culture', *Telos*, 51 (Spring 1982), pp. 141–7, and *Telos* 52 and 57. Other symptomatic *Telos* attacks on the new social movements include Orville Lee III, 'Metacritique of Non-Criticism', *Telos*, 52 (Summer 1982), pp. 108–13, and Jeffrey Herf, 'Western Strategy and Public Discussion: The "Double Decision" Makes Sense', *Telos*, 52 (Summer 1982), pp. 114–28. These positions were attacked by other *Telos* contributors over the next several issues.

49 On 'artificial negativity', see Paul Piccone, 'The Crisis of One-Dimensionality', and Timothy Luke, 'The Age of Artificial Negativity', both in *Telos* 35

(Spring 1978). Piccone 'intervened' in the debates over the new social movements – frequently using his pen-name Moishes Gonzales – in *Telos* 53. In *Telos* 69, he (as Sr Gonzales) wonders why 'the pseudo-Marxist, pseudo-Left despises capitalism so much', and provides an 'argument' that capitalist 'market mechanisms do a better job than bureaucratic procedures or political conpromises [sic]' (p. 160), thus completing a cycle from ultra-Left critic to apologist for market capitalism.

50 Mouffe, 'Hegemony and New Political Subjects'.

51 Carl Boggs, *Social Movements*.

52 The proposal for Critical Theory to develop a social ecology is found in Murray Bookchin, 'Finding the Subject: Notes on Whitebrook and Habermas Ltd.', *Telos* 52 (Summer 1982), pp. 78–98. Since Bookchin's polemic against the lack of ecological perspectives in Critical Theory, several works combining Critical Theory with ecology have appeared, including Alford, *Science and Nature*, and Luke and White, 'Ecological Modernity'. One might also cite earlier works such as Leiss, *The Domination of Nature*, and Marcuse, 'Ecology and Revolution. A Symposium', *Liberation*, 17, no. 6 (1972), pp. 10–12. In fact, many texts of Adorno, Horkheimer, Benjamin, Wittfogel, Marcuse and other Critical Theorists make the relation between humans and nature central to their work, and thus contain proto-ecological perspectives. They also anticipate what has become known as 'eco-socialism'. On this trend, see Wolfgang Rudig, 'Eco-Socialism: Left Environmentalism', *New Political Science*, 14 (Winter 1985–6), pp. 3–38.

53 For a feminist appreciation and critique of Critical Theory, see Mills, *Woman, Nature and Psyche*. For Marcuse's attempt to merge Critical Theory and feminism, see Marcuse, 'Marxism and Feminism', *Women's Studies*, 2, no. 3 (1974), pp. 279–88. For a sharp feminist critique of Habermas, see Nancy Fraser, 'What's Critical about Critical Theory? the Case of Habermas and Gender', *New German Critique*, 35 (Spring–Summer 1985), pp. 97–132.

54 Benhabib, 'Modernity and the Aporias of Critical Theory', *Telos*, 49 (Fall 1981), p. 59. This position is developed in her *Critique, Norm, and Utopia*. See also Mills, *Woman, Nature and Psyche*.

55 For discussion of the emancipatory potential of certain children's games and other oppositional cultural forms, see Aronowitz, *False Promises*. Wellmer proposes consideration of the emancipatory potential of rock music in 'Reconciliation', and I look at the emancipatory potential of television in 'TV, Ideology, and Emancipatory Popular Culture', and the progressive potentials in film (with Michael Ryan) in *Camera Politica*.

56 For some reflections on 'billboards of the future', see Ewen and Ewen, *Channels of Desire*. Alternative image cultures are promoted in such journals as *Jump Cut, Cineaste, Screen* and *Left Curve* and books like *Cultures in Contention*, edited by Douglas Kahn and Diane Neumaier (Seattle: Real Comet Press, 1986), as well as others published by Real Comet Press.

57 For some speculation on the information society and information and media politics from a Critical Theory perspective, see Luke and White, 'Ecological Path', and Kellner, *Television, Politics, and Society*.

58 For discussion of consumption and consumer politics from the Critical Theory

perspective, see Leiss, *The Limits to Satisfaction*; Kellner, 'Commodities' and Grahame, 'Criticalness, Pragmatics, and Everyday Life: Consumer Literacy as Critical Practice', in Forester, *Critical Theory*, edited by J. Forester. For perspectives on education from a standpoint influenced by Critical Theory, see Stanley Aronowitz and Henry Giroux, *Education under Siege* (South Hadley, Mass.: Bergin and Garvey, 1983); and Dieter Misgeld, 'Education and Cultural Invasion', in *Critical Theory*, edited by J. Forester, pp. 77–120.

59 Marcuse, *Eros and Civilization*, and *idem*, *An Essay on Liberation* (Boston: Beacon Press, 1969).

60 Marcuse, *An Essay on Liberation*, discussed in Kellner, *Herbert Marcuse*, and Luke and White, 'Ecological Modernity'.

61 For some contemporary perspectives on a new concept of socialism, see Stephen Eric Bronner, *Socialism Unbound: Studies in Theory and Practice* (New York: Methuen, 1989).

62 On eco-socialism, see Rudig, 'Eco-Socialism'. On the need to preserve and develop a public sphere, or civil society, see Jean Cohen, 'Between Crisis-Management and Social Movements', *Telos*, 52 (Summer 1982), pp. 21–40. This position is elaborated in her book *Class and Civil Society* (Amherst: University of Massachusetts Press, 1982).

63 On the importance of the value of solidarity for Critical Theory, see Marcuse, *An Essay on Liberation*, and Habermas, *Autonomy and Solidarity*. Laclau and Mouffe, *Hegemony*, have argued that stressing the importance of solidarity helps overcome the one-sidedness of some of the new social movements which have tended to be oriented to single issues.

64 See 2.2, 4.3 and 4.4 for discussion of earlier Institute studies of the working class. See 8.1 and n. 7 and 8 above for later Institute studies of the political potential of the working class.

65 For attacks on the continuing relevance of class, see many of the contributions in the symposium *On Class*, in *Telos*, 28 (Summer 1976).

66 On the decline of the middle class and increases in poverty in the United States during the 1980s, see Blumberg, *Inequality*; Pliven and Coward, *New Class War*; Edsall, *New Politics*; and Kuttner, 'Declining Middle'.

67 I elucidate this concept of a multiperspectival social theory more fully in my book *Jean Baudrillard*.

68 See Rorty, *Philosophy and the Mirror of Nature*; Richard Bernstein, *Philosophical Profiles: Essays in a Pragmatic Mode* (Cambridge: Polity Press, 1985); and the articles in Baynes et al., *The End of Philosophy*.

Index